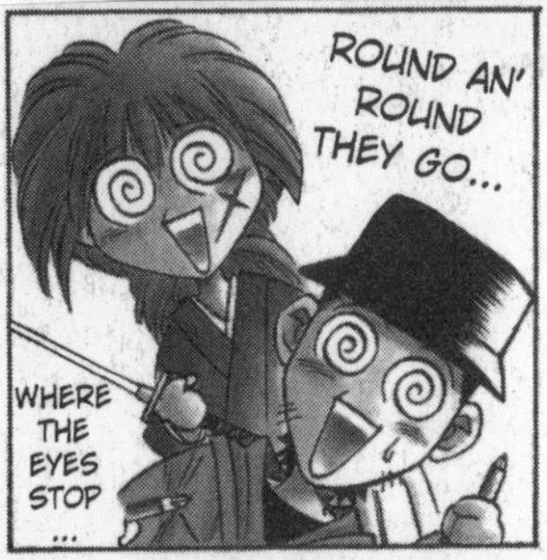
ROUND AN' ROUND THEY GO...
WHERE THE EYES STOP ...

和月伸宏

NOBUHIRO WATSUKI

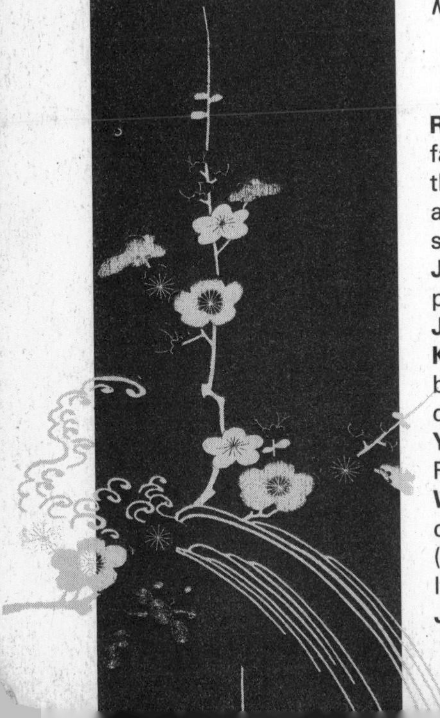

## WATSUKI IS STILL A LIAR.

IN THE INTERESTS OF FULL DISCLOSURE, THE KANJI FOR "RUROUNI" ISN'T READ "RUROUNI" AT ALL—YOU SURE WON'T FIND IT IN ANY DICTIONARY! ONCE AGAIN, WATSUKI HAS BEEN PULLING YOUR LEG. (IF YOU'RE ONE OF THOSE PEOPLE TAKEN IN BY THE LITTLE RUSE, SORRY!)

THAT ASIDE, IT'S BEEN SO CRAZY-BUSY LATELY THAT I FEEL EXACTLY LIKE THE LITTLE SKETCH UP THERE. I HAVEN'T EVEN HAD TIME TO DO A NEW, ORIGINAL ILLUSTRATION FOR THIS GRAPHIC NOVEL. IT DOESN'T LOOK LIKE I'LL HAVE TIME TO DO IT FOR VOLUME 3, EITHER, BUT I WILL FOR VOLUME 4—PROMISE! CROSS MY HEART!!

**Rurouni Kenshin**, which has found fans not only in Japan but around the world, first made its appearance in 1992, as an original short story in Japan's **Weekly Shonen Jump Special**. Later rewritten and published as a regular, continuing **Jump** series in 1994, **Rurouni Kenshin** ended serialization in 1999 but continued in popularity, as evidenced by the 2000 publication of **Yahiko no Sakabatô** ("Yahiko's Reversed-Edge Sword") in Japan's **Weekly Shonen Jump**. His most current work, **Busô Renkin** ("Armored Alchemist"), began publication this June, also in Japan's **Jump**.

**RUROUNI KENSHIN VOL. 2**
**The SHONEN JUMP Graphic Novel Edition**

STORY AND ART BY
NOBUHIRO WATSUKI

English Adaptation/Gerard Jones
Translation/Kenichiro Yagi
Touch-Up Art & Lettering/Steve Dutro
Cover, Graphics & Layout Design/Sean Lee
Editor/Avery Gotoh

Supervising Editor/William Flanagan/Kit Fox
Production Manager/Noboru Watanabe
Managing Editor/Annette Roman
Associate Managing Editor/Albert Totten
Editor in Chief/Hyoe Narita
Sr. Director of Licensing and Acquisitions/Rika Inouye
V.P. of Marketing/Liza Coppola
V.P. of Strategic Development/Yumi Hoashi
Publisher/Seiji Horibuchi

PARENTAL ADVISORY
**Rurouni Kenshin** may contain violence, language and alcohol or tobacco usage. It is rated "T+" for older teens.



Printed in Canada.

Published by VIZ, LLC
P.O. Box 77010 • San Francisco, CA 94107

SHONEN JUMP Graphic Novel Edition
10 9 8 7 6 5 4 3 2 1
First printing, November 2003

SHONEN JUMP GRAPHIC NOVEL

# Rurouni Kenshin™

## MEIJI SWORDSMAN ROMANTIC STORY

## Vol. 2: THE TWO HITOKIRI



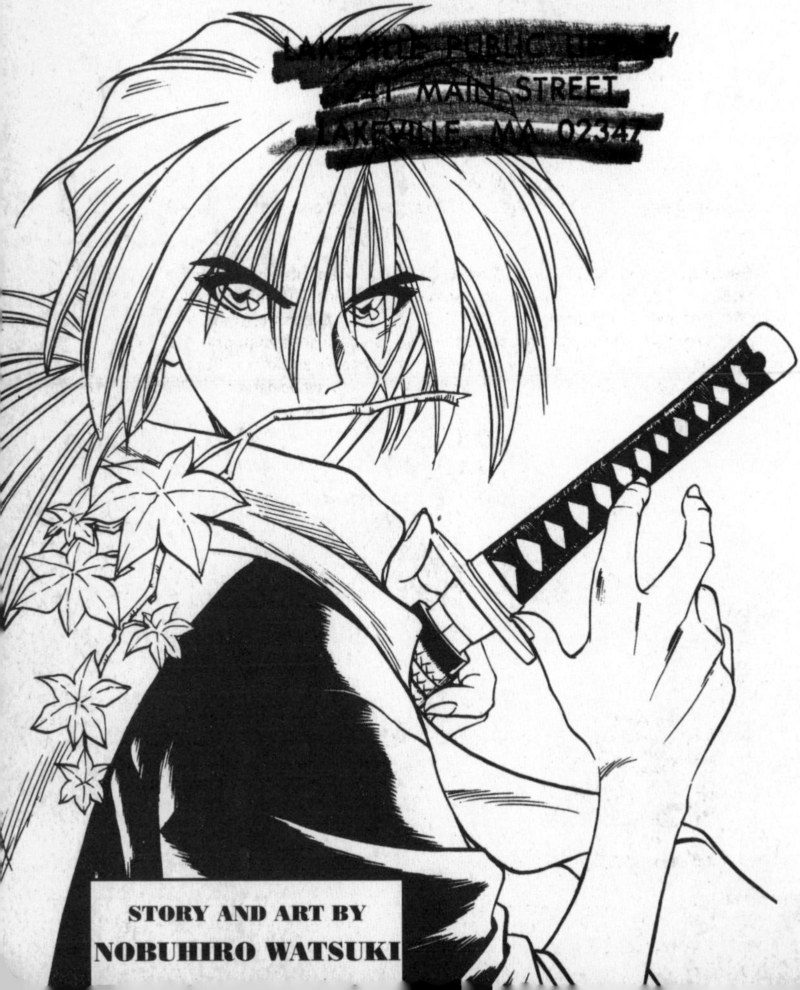

STORY AND ART BY

NOBUHIRO WATSUKI

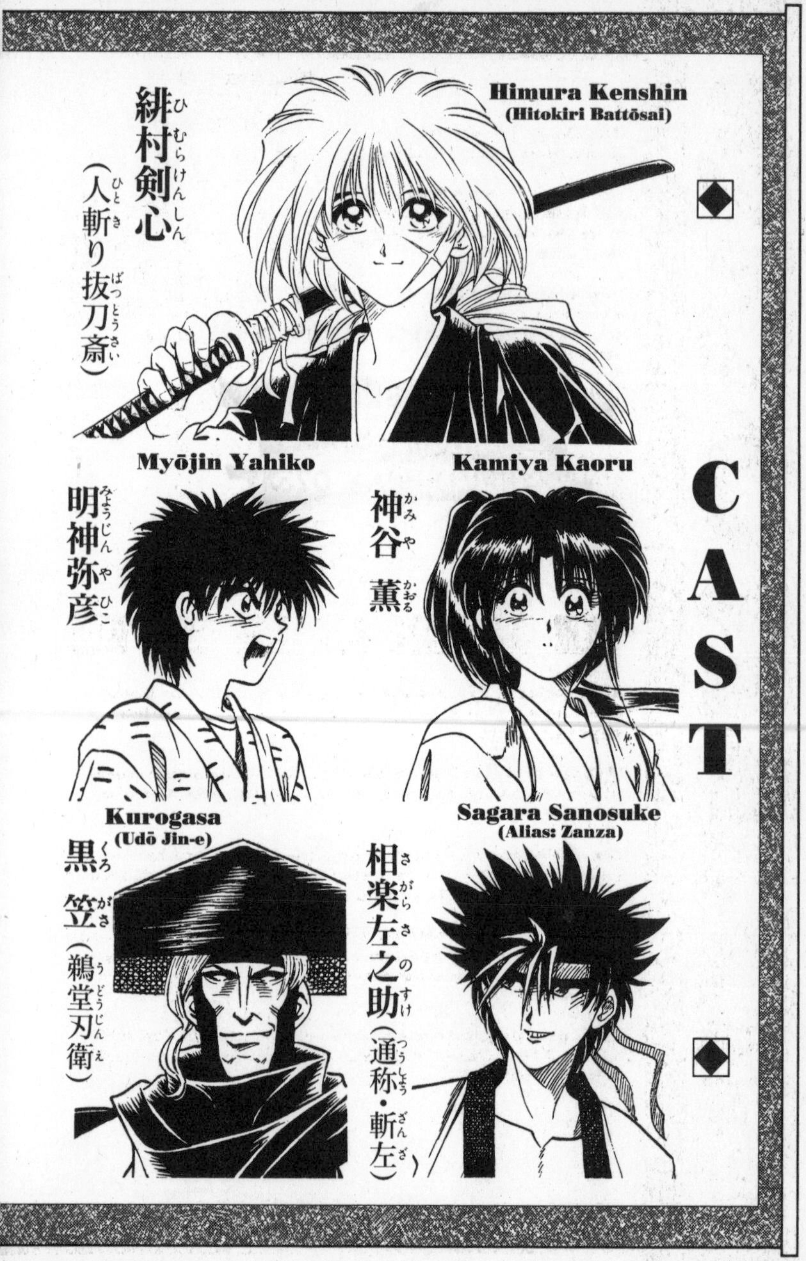
CAST
Himura Kenshin
(Hitokiri Battōsai)
緋村剣心
（人斬り抜刀斎）
Kamiya Kaoru
神谷薫
Myōjin Yahiko
明神弥彦
Sagara Sanosuke
(Alias: Zanza)
相楽左之助
（通称・斬左）
Kurogasa
(Udō Jin-e)
黒笠
（鵜堂刃衛）

# るろうに剣心

和月伸宏

**Himura Kihei**

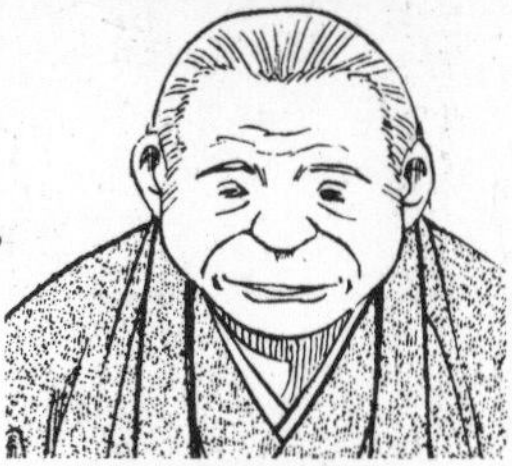

**Himura Gohei**

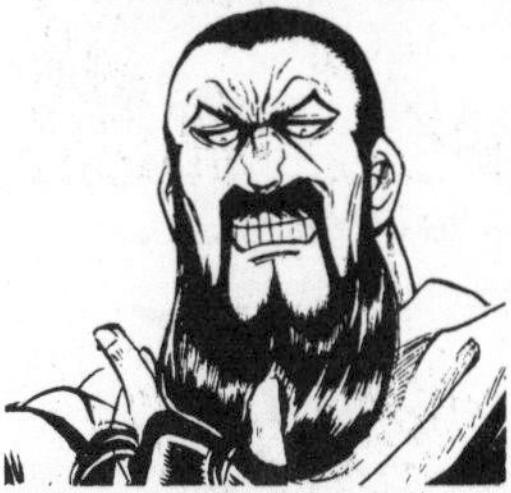

比留間喜兵衛・伍兵衛

**Once he was a *hitokiri*, an assassin, called *Battōsai*.**

**His name was legend among the *Ishin Shishi* or "patriot" warriors who launched the Meiji Era.**

**Now Himura Kenshin is a *rurouni*, a wanderer, who carries a reversed-edge *sakabatō* blade to prohibit himself from killing.**

**Having exposed the scheme of the Hiruma Brothers to steal the Kamiya school's property with a "fake Battōsai," Kenshin's decided to stay on at the dojo for a while.**

## T H U S F A R

**After losing all its students because of the hoax, the Kamiya dojo and its "*Kasshin-ryū*" sword style is taking its first steps toward revival.**

**Kenshin brings in Myōjin Yahiko, the son of an ex-samurai whom he rescued from the yakuza, to become its first new student.**

**But, still greedy for the property, the Hiruma Brothers escape from jail and hire Sagara Sanosuke, who fights the fights of others for a living, to get rid of the annoying Kenshin.**

**At first unwilling, Sanosuke takes the job when he learns who Kenshin *really* is—Sanosuke hates the so-called patriots and the chance to humble the greatest of them all is too tempting to pass by.**

**Ultimately Kenshin accepts Sanosuke's challenge, and while Kaoru, Yahiko, and the Hiruma Brothers watch, the deadly serious battle begins.**

# CONTENTS

**Rurouni Kenshin**
Meiji Swordsman Romantic Story
BOOK TWO: THE TWO HITOKIRI

**ACT 7**
**Mark of Evil**
7

**ACT 8**
**And Then, Another**
29

**ACT 9**
**Kurogasa**
49

**ACT 10**
**One Side of the Soul**
69

**ACT 11**
**The Ribbon That Binds**
89

**ACT 12**
**The Two Hitokiri**
109

**ACT 13**
**The Meaning of the Name**
129

**ACT 14**
**End Beneath the Moon**
149

**ACT 15**
**Beauty on the Run**
169

# Act 7—Mark of Evil

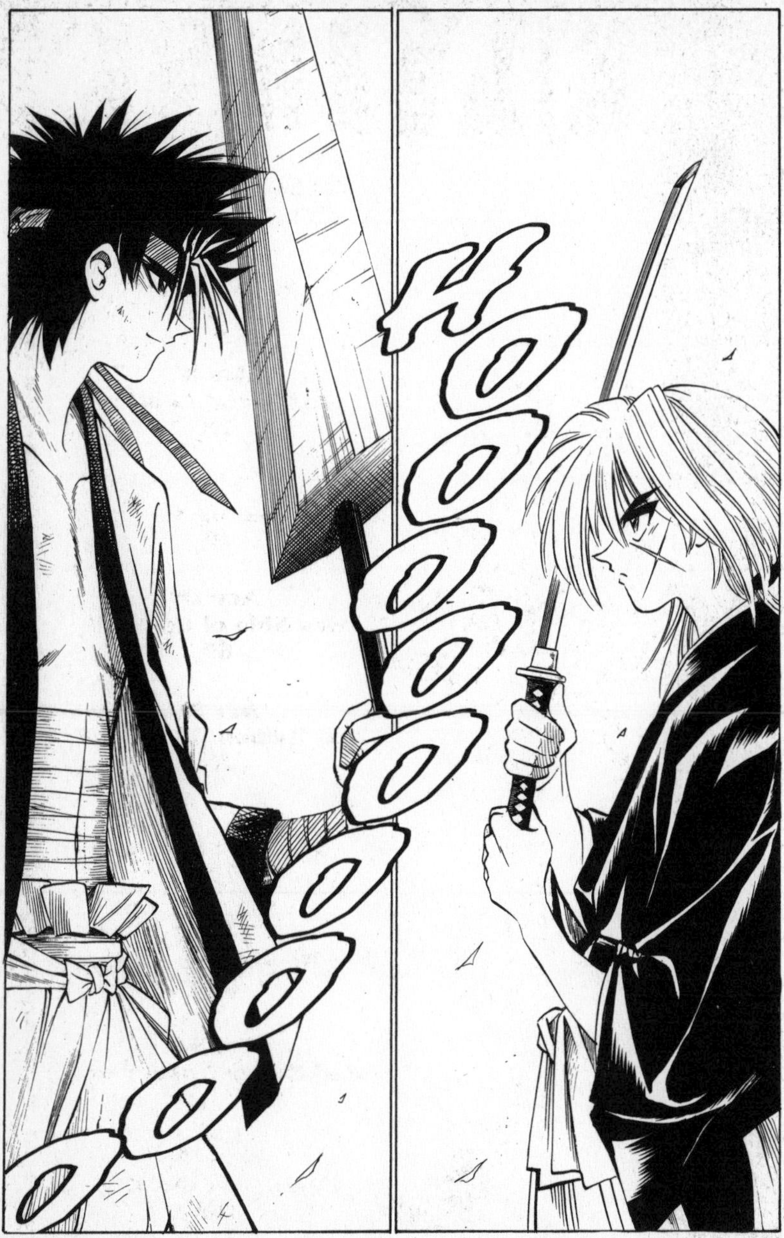
HOOOOOOOOO

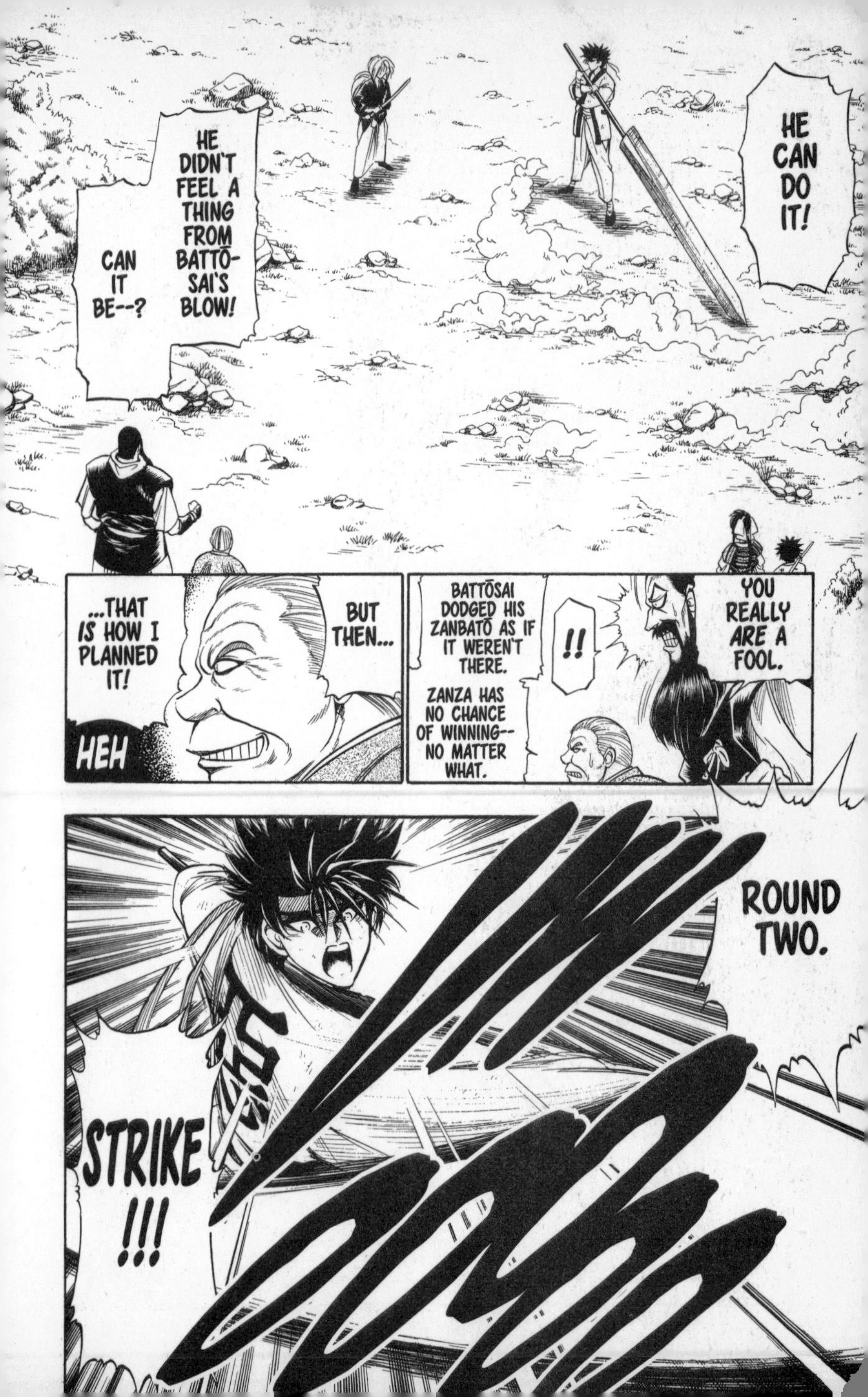
HE CAN DO IT!
HE DIDN'T FEEL A THING FROM BATTŌSAI'S BLOW!
CAN IT BE--?
YOU REALLY ARE A FOOL.
!!
BATTŌSAI DODGED HIS ZANBATŌ AS IF IT WEREN'T THERE.
ZANZA HAS NO CHANCE OF WINNING--NO MATTER WHAT.
BUT THEN...
...THAT IS HOW I PLANNED IT!
HEH
ROUND TWO.
STRIKE !!!

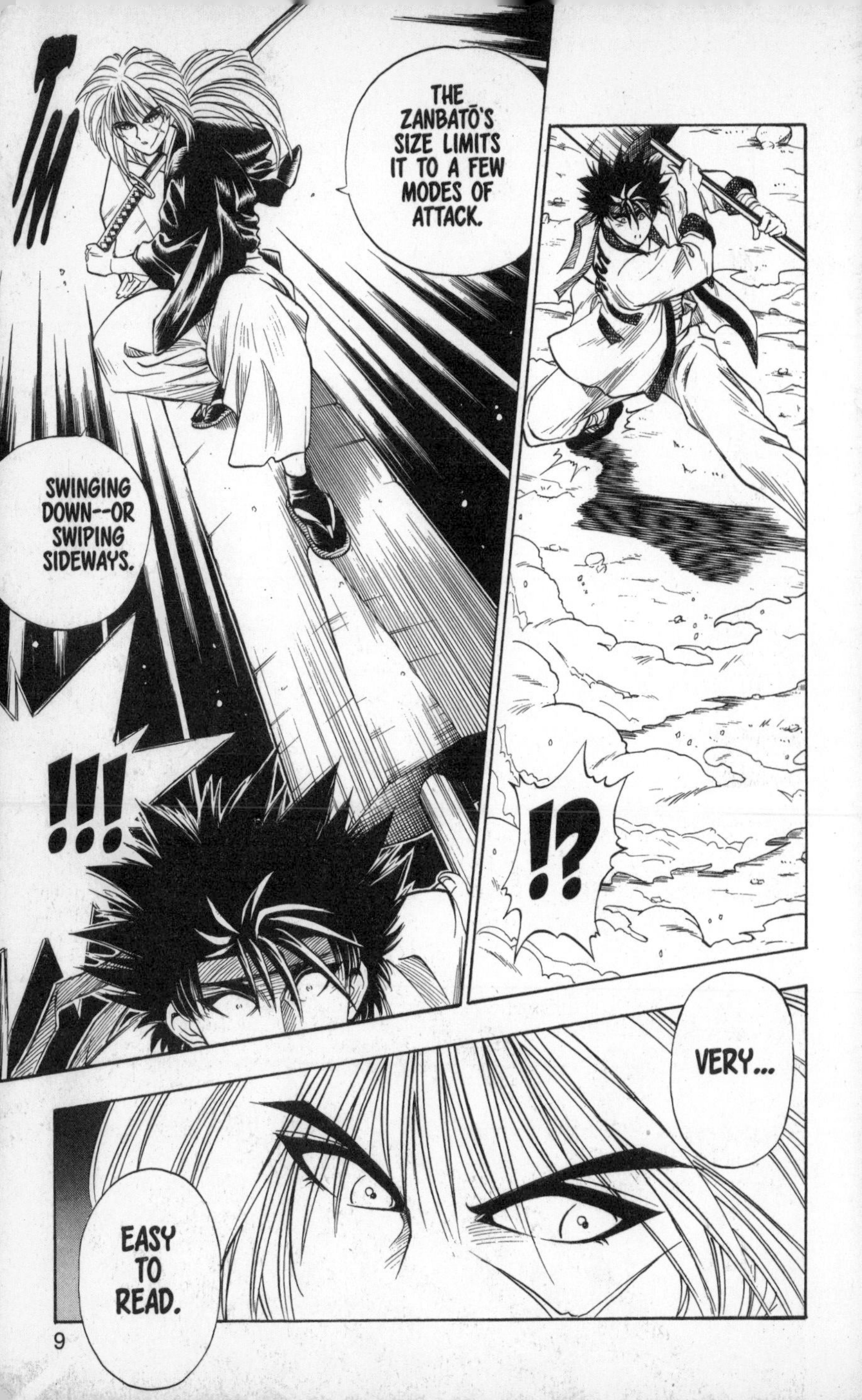
!?
THE ZANBATŌ'S SIZE LIMITS IT TO A FEW MODES OF ATTACK.
SWINGING DOWN--OR SWIPING SIDEWAYS.
!!!
VERY...
EASY TO READ.

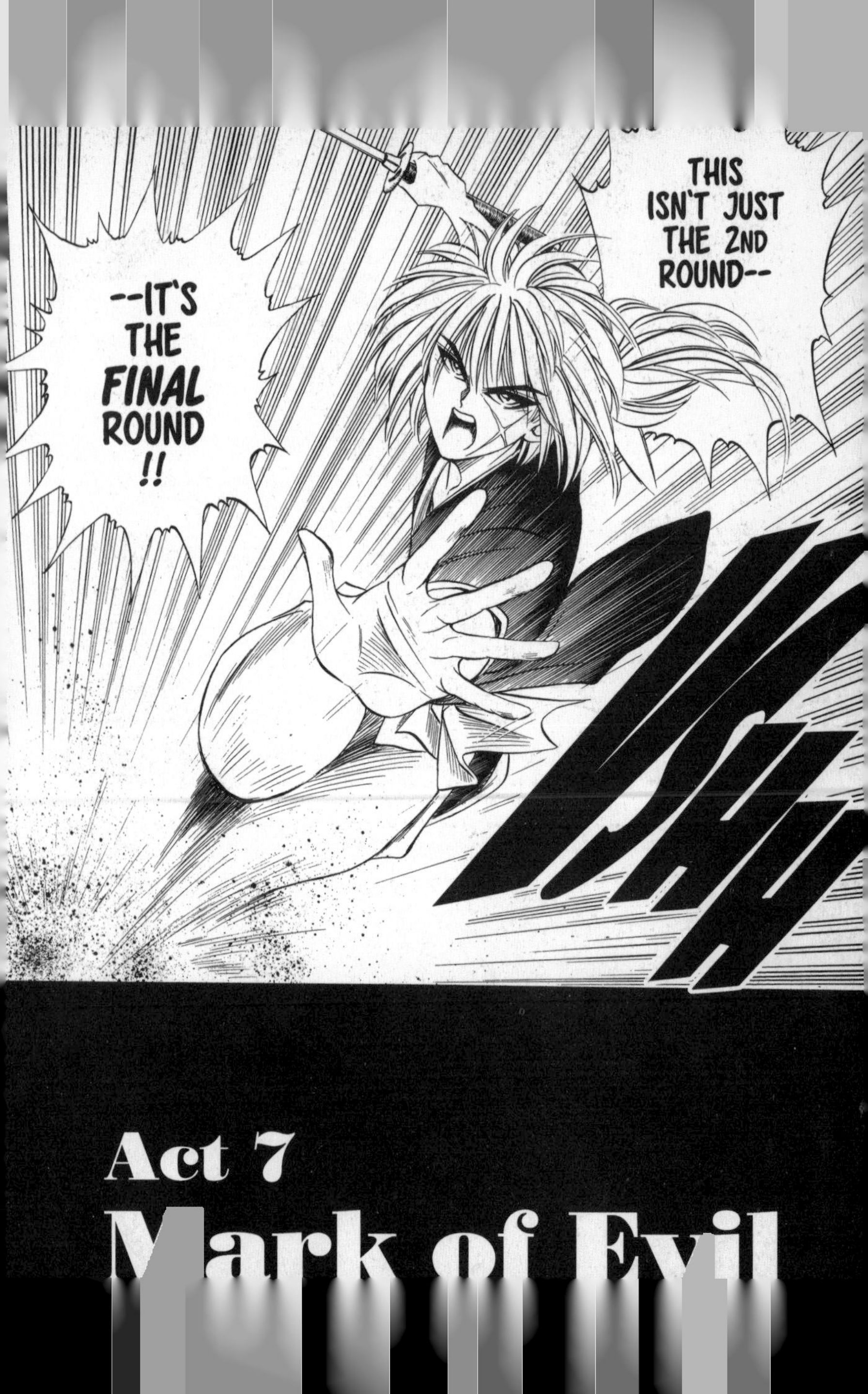
THIS ISN'T JUST THE 2ND ROUND--
--IT'S THE FINAL ROUND!!

# Act 7
# Mark of Evil

READ THIS WAY

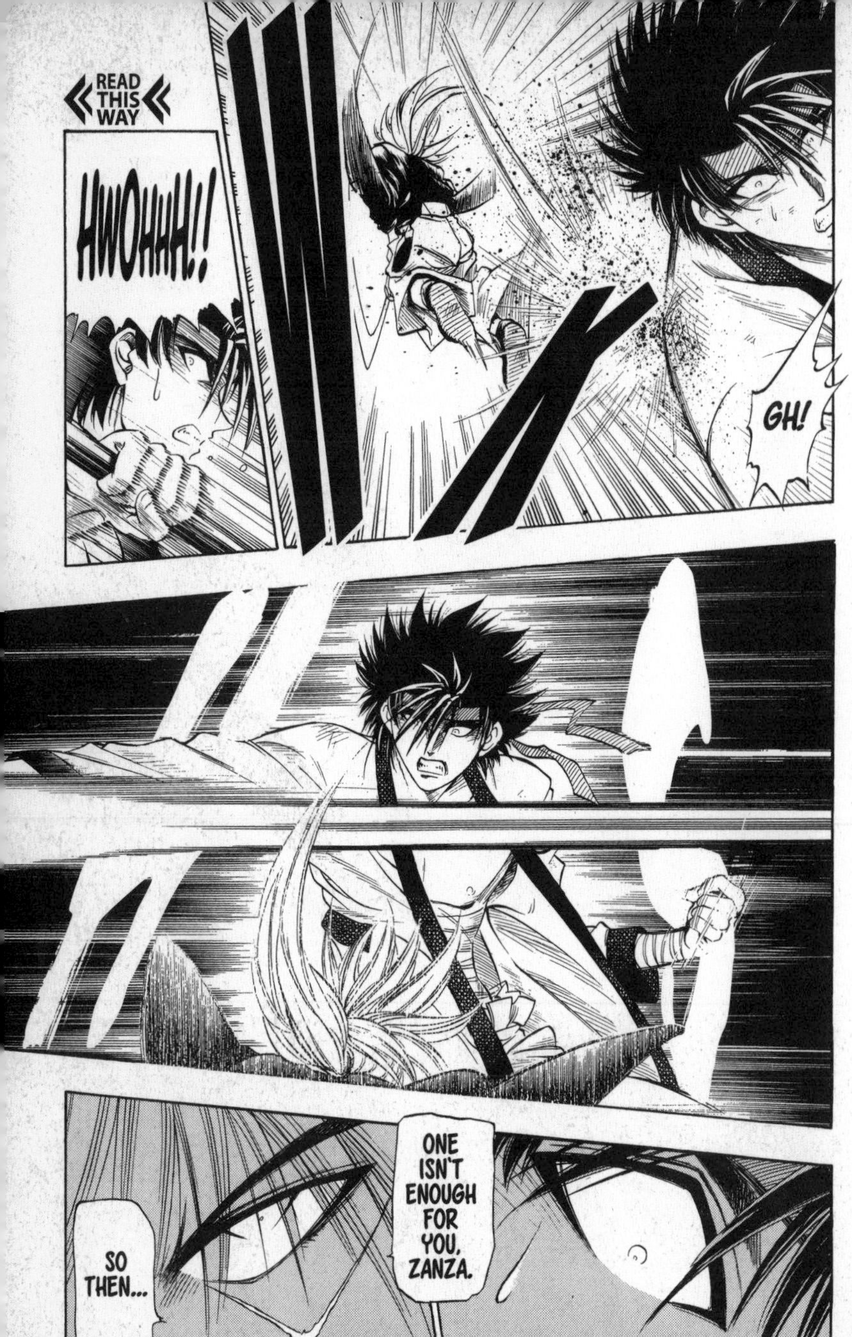
GH!
HWOHHH!!
ONE ISN'T ENOUGH FOR YOU, ZANZA.
SO THEN...

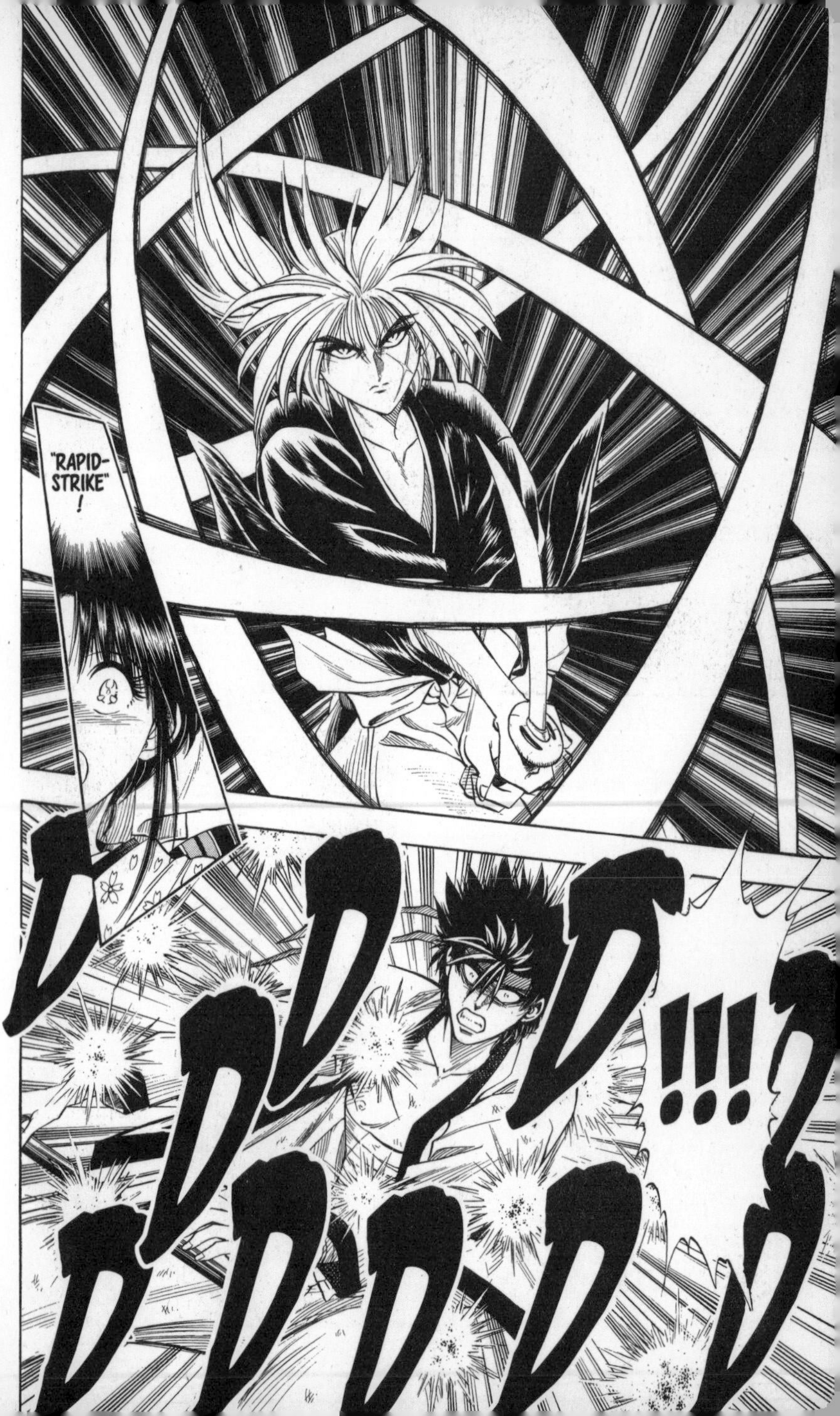
"RAPID-STRIKE"!

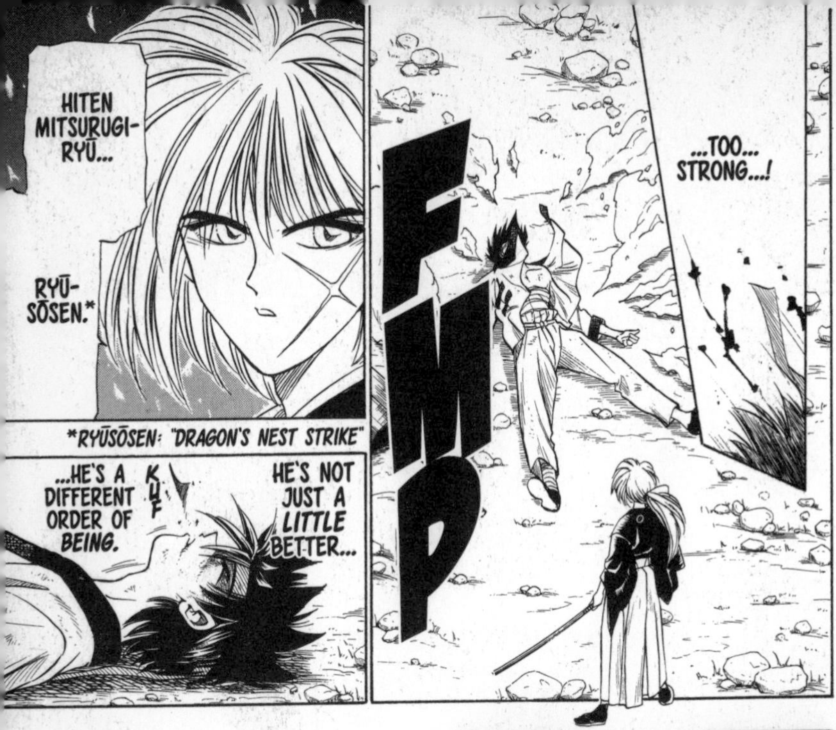
...TOO... STRONG...!
FWMP
HITEN MITSURUGI-RYŪ...
RYŪ-SŌSEN.*
HE'S NOT JUST A LITTLE BETTER...
KUF
...HE'S A DIFFERENT ORDER OF BEING.

*RYŪSŌSEN: "DRAGON'S NEST STRIKE"

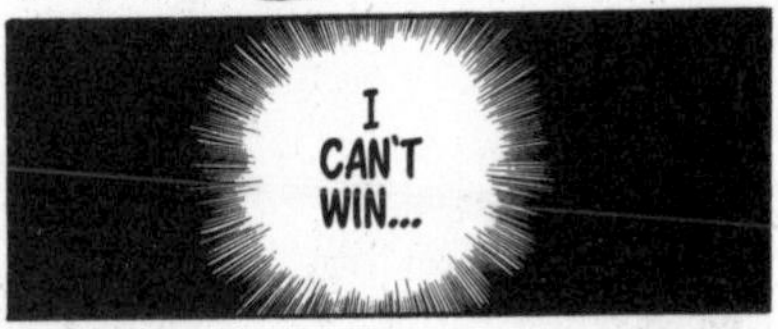
I CAN'T WIN...

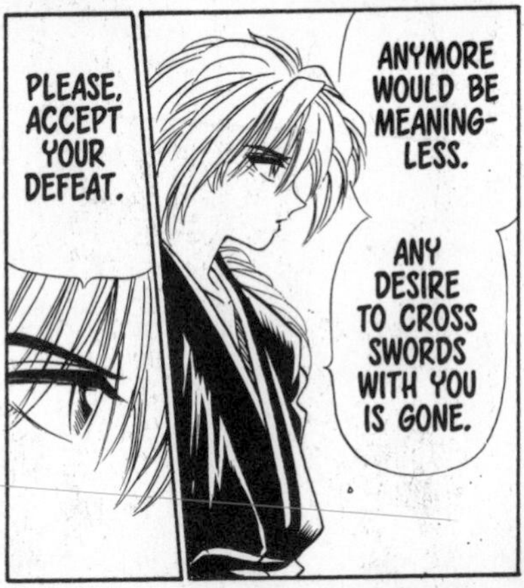
ANYMORE WOULD BE MEANING-LESS.
ANY DESIRE TO CROSS SWORDS WITH YOU IS GONE.
PLEASE, ACCEPT YOUR DEFEAT.

So-o-o. *Rurouni Kenshin* is to become a CD book! I bet you're all surprised...but none more so than me. It's only been half a year, and already Kenshin is crossing over to other media...thanks to your support. Thank you—really!—so much.

伸宏 和月

Watsuki

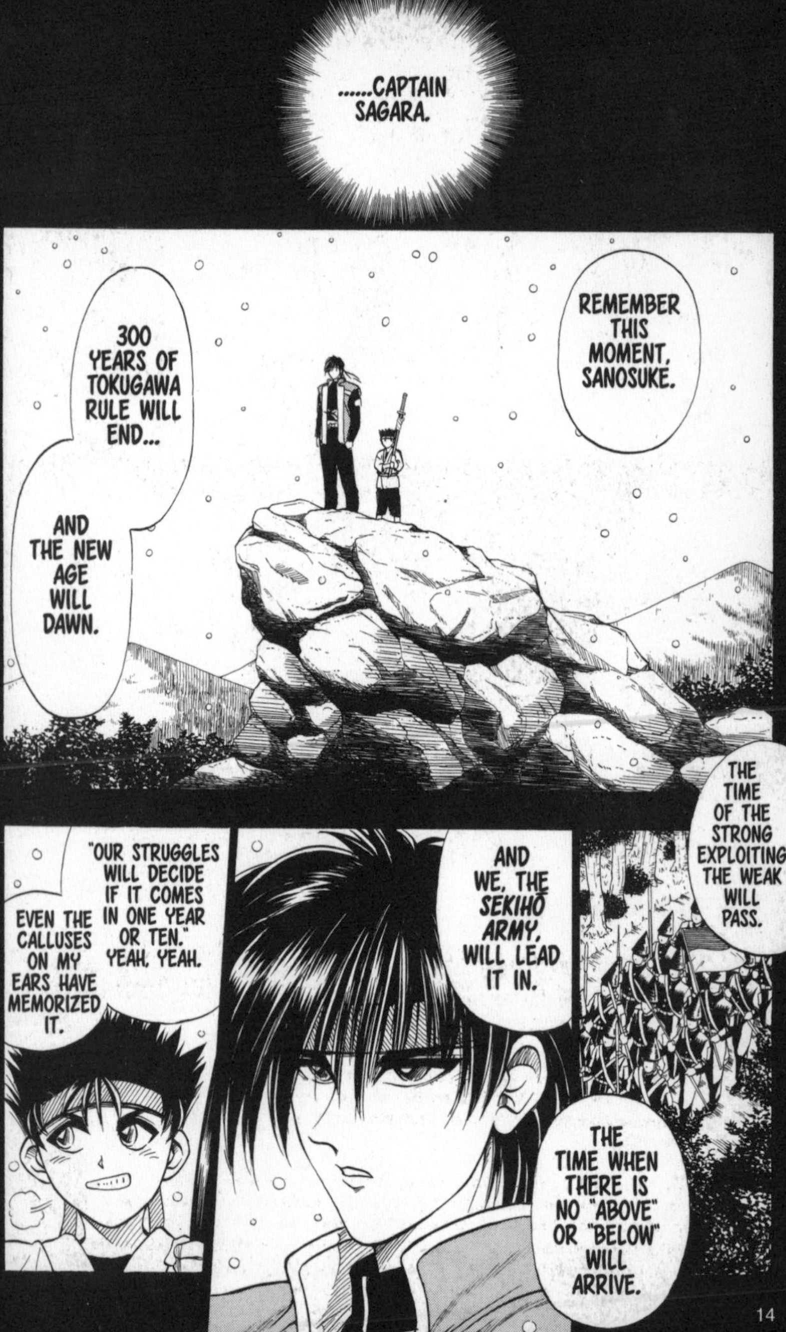
......CAPTAIN SAGARA.
REMEMBER THIS MOMENT, SANOSUKE.
300 YEARS OF TOKUGAWA RULE WILL END...
AND THE NEW AGE WILL DAWN.
THE TIME OF THE STRONG EXPLOITING THE WEAK WILL PASS.
AND WE, THE *SEKIHŌ ARMY*, WILL LEAD IT IN.
THE TIME WHEN THERE IS NO "ABOVE" OR "BELOW" WILL ARRIVE.
"OUR STRUGGLES WILL DECIDE IF IT COMES IN ONE YEAR OR TEN." YEAH, YEAH.
EVEN THE CALLUSES ON MY EARS HAVE MEMORIZED IT.

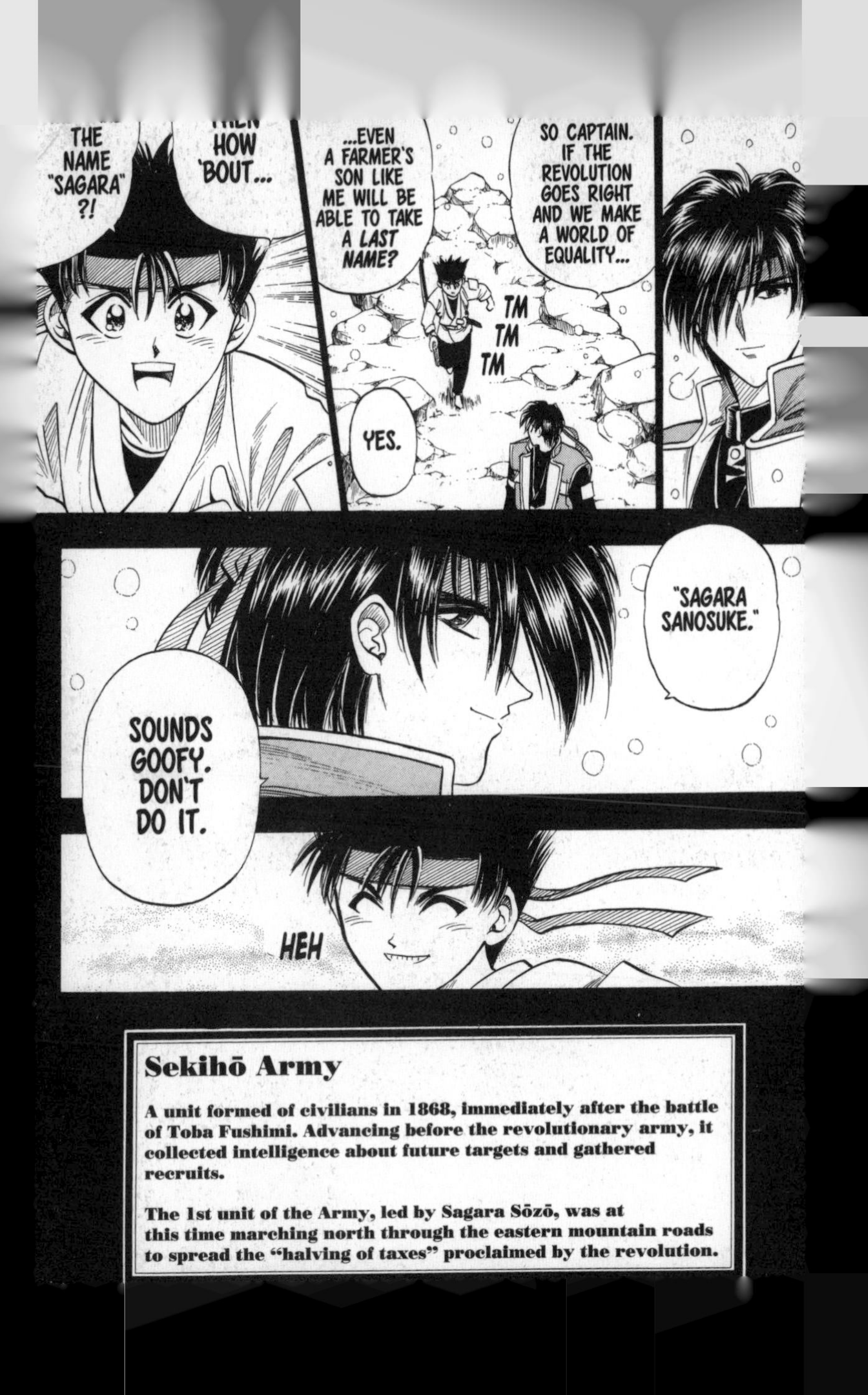
SO CAPTAIN. IF THE REVOLUTION GOES RIGHT AND WE MAKE A WORLD OF EQUALITY...
...EVEN A FARMER'S SON LIKE ME WILL BE ABLE TO TAKE A *LAST* NAME?
TM TM TM
YES.
HOW 'BOUT...
THE NAME "SAGARA"?!
"SAGARA SANOSUKE."
SOUNDS GOOFY. DON'T DO IT.
HEH

## Sekihō Army

**A unit formed of civilians in 1868, immediately after the battle of Toba Fushimi. Advancing before the revolutionary army, it collected intelligence about future targets and gathered recruits.**

**The 1st unit of the Army, led by Sagara Sōzō, was at this time marching north through the eastern mountain roads to spread the "halving of taxes" proclaimed by the revolution.**

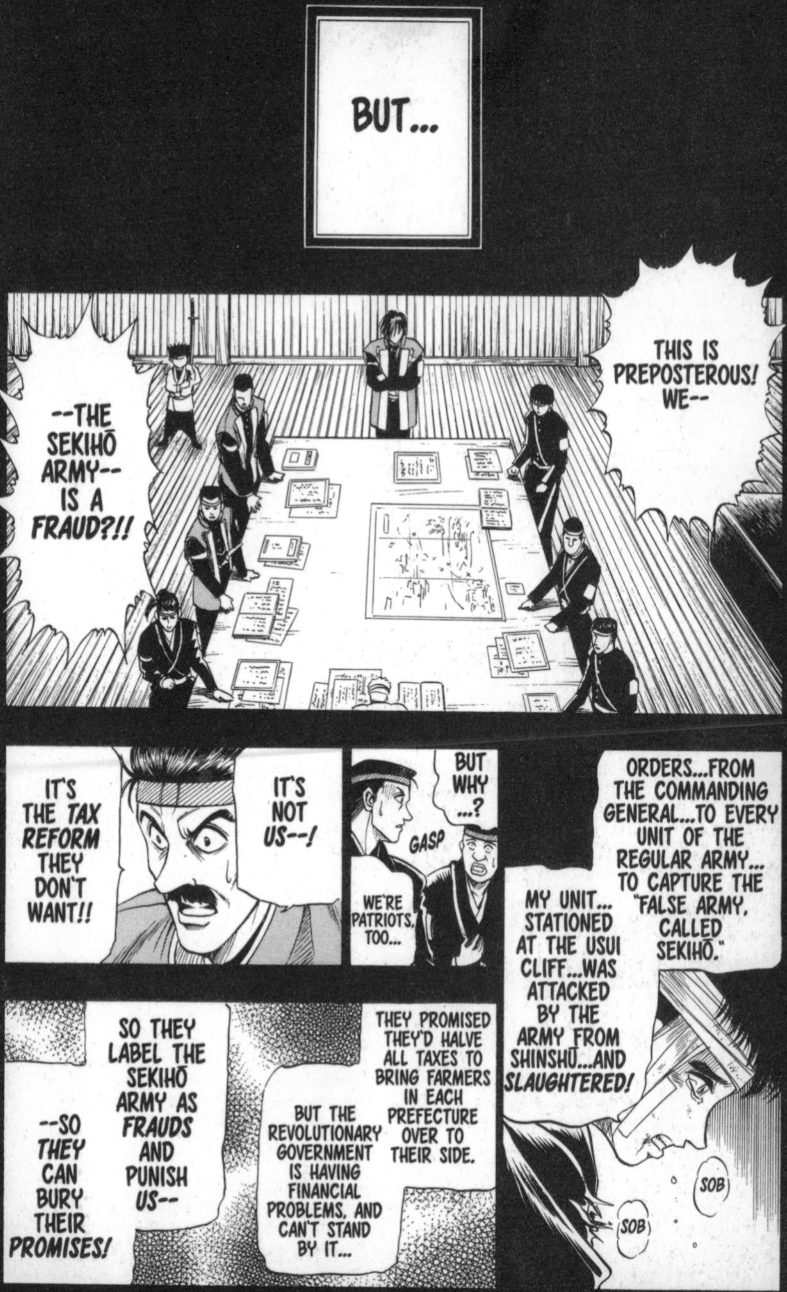
BUT...
THIS IS PREPOSTEROUS! WE--
--THE SEKIHŌ ARMY-- IS A *FRAUD?!!*
ORDERS...FROM THE COMMANDING GENERAL...TO EVERY UNIT OF THE REGULAR ARMY...TO CAPTURE THE "FALSE ARMY, CALLED SEKIHŌ."
MY UNIT...STATIONED AT THE USUI CLIFF...WAS ATTACKED BY THE ARMY FROM SHINSHŪ...AND *SLAUGHTERED!*
SOB
SOB
BUT WHY ...?
GASP
WE'RE PATRIOTS, TOO...
IT'S NOT *US*--!
IT'S THE *TAX REFORM* THEY DON'T WANT!!
THEY PROMISED THEY'D HALVE ALL TAXES TO BRING FARMERS IN EACH PREFECTURE OVER TO THEIR SIDE.
BUT THE REVOLUTIONARY GOVERNMENT IS HAVING FINANCIAL PROBLEMS, AND CAN'T STAND BY IT...
SO THEY LABEL THE SEKIHŌ ARMY AS *FRAUDS* AND PUNISH *US*--
--SO *THEY* CAN BURY THEIR *PROMISES!*

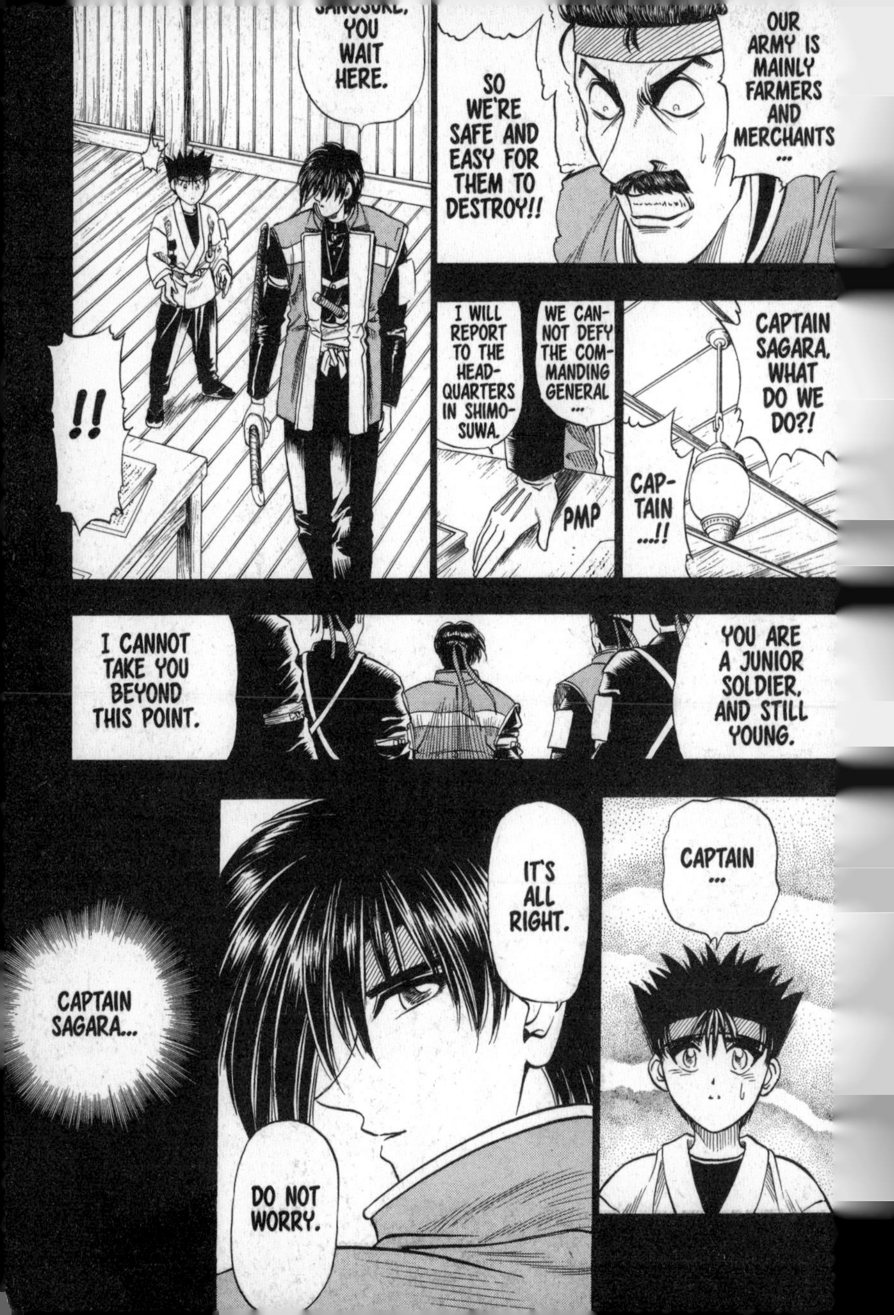
OUR ARMY IS MAINLY FARMERS AND MERCHANTS ...
SO WE'RE SAFE AND EASY FOR THEM TO DESTROY!!
CAPTAIN SAGARA, WHAT DO WE DO?!
CAP-TAIN ...!!
WE CAN-NOT DEFY THE COM-MANDING GENERAL ...
I WILL REPORT TO THE HEAD-QUARTERS IN SHIMO-SUWA.
PMP
YOU WAIT HERE.
!!
YOU ARE A JUNIOR SOLDIER, AND STILL YOUNG.
I CANNOT TAKE YOU BEYOND THIS POINT.
CAPTAIN ...
IT'S ALL RIGHT.
DO NOT WORRY.
CAPTAIN SAGARA...

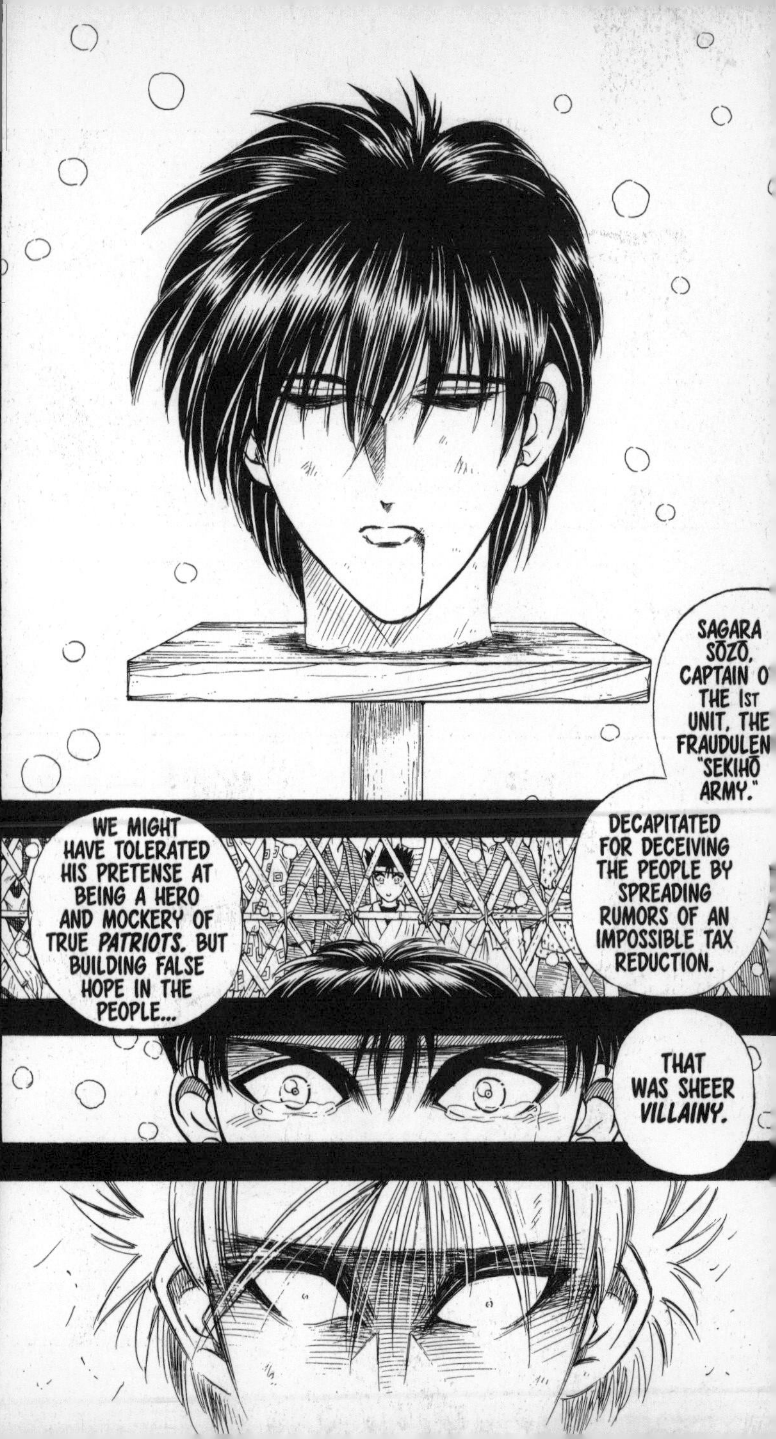
SAGARA SŌZŌ, CAPTAIN O THE 1ST UNIT, THE FRAUDULEN "SEKIHŌ ARMY."
DECAPITATED FOR DECEIVING THE PEOPLE BY SPREADING RUMORS OF AN IMPOSSIBLE TAX REDUCTION.
WE MIGHT HAVE TOLERATED HIS PRETENSE AT BEING A HERO AND MOCKERY OF TRUE *PATRIOTS.* BUT BUILDING FALSE HOPE IN THE PEOPLE...
THAT WAS SHEER *VILLAINY.*

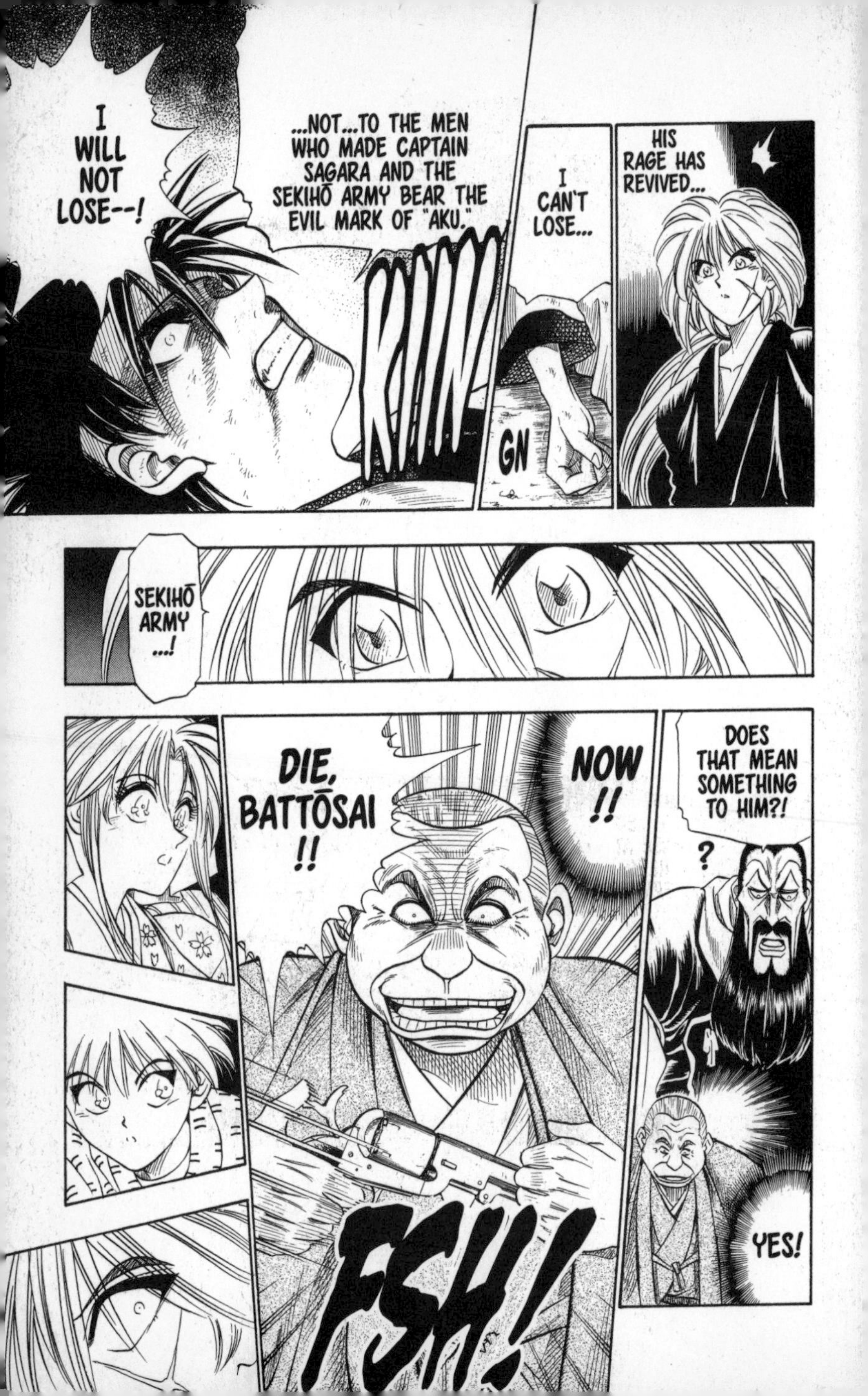
HIS RAGE HAS REVIVED...
I CAN'T LOSE...
GN
...NOT...TO THE MEN WHO MADE CAPTAIN SAGARA AND THE SEKIHŌ ARMY BEAR THE EVIL MARK OF "AKU."
I WILL NOT LOSE--!
SEKIHŌ ARMY ...!
DOES THAT MEAN SOMETHING TO HIM?!
?
YES!
NOW !!
DIE, BATTŌSAI !!
FSH!

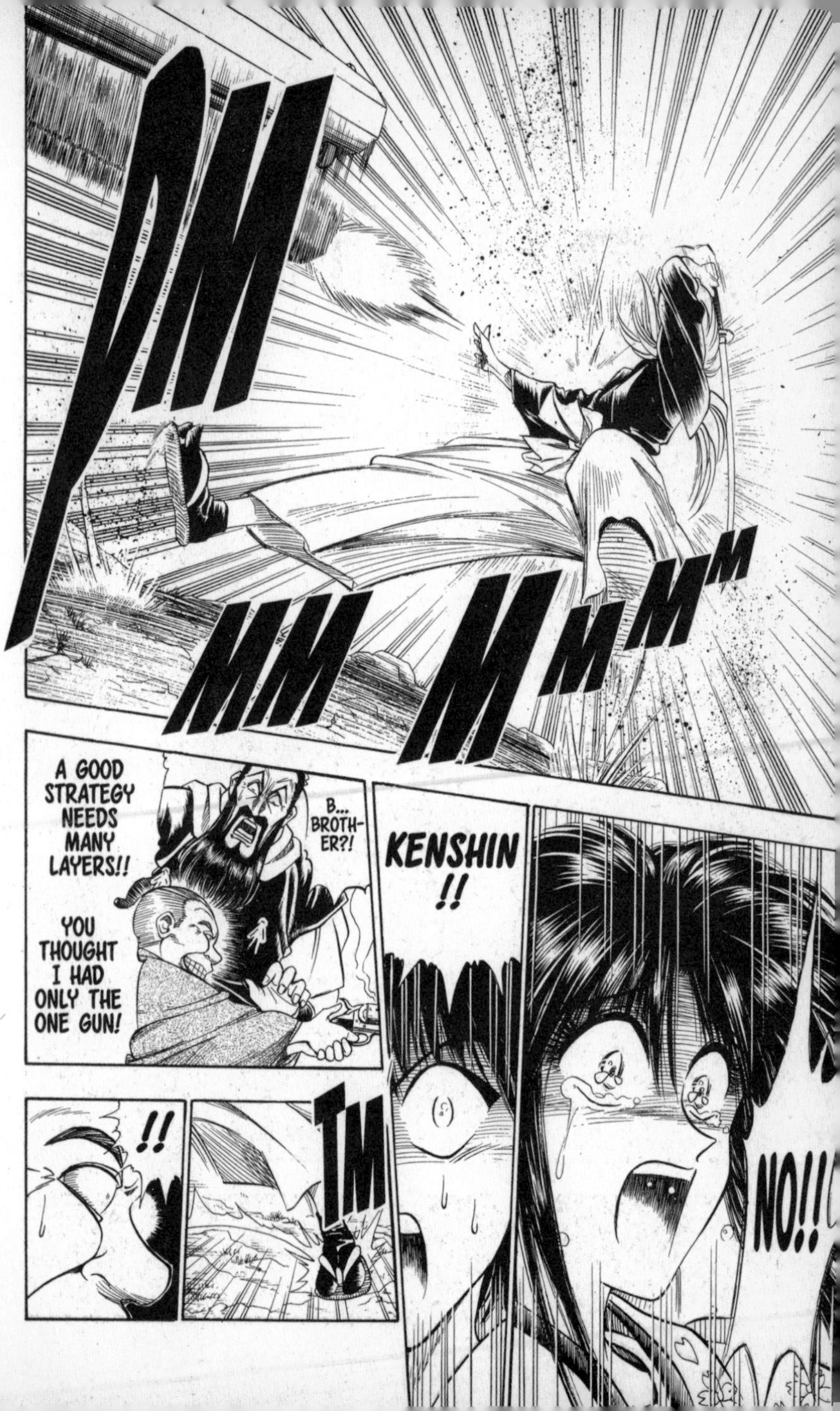

DMMMMMMMM
KENSHIN!!
NO!!
B... BROTHER?!
A GOOD STRATEGY NEEDS MANY LAYERS!!
YOU THOUGHT I HAD ONLY THE ONE GUN!
TM
!!

READ THIS WAY

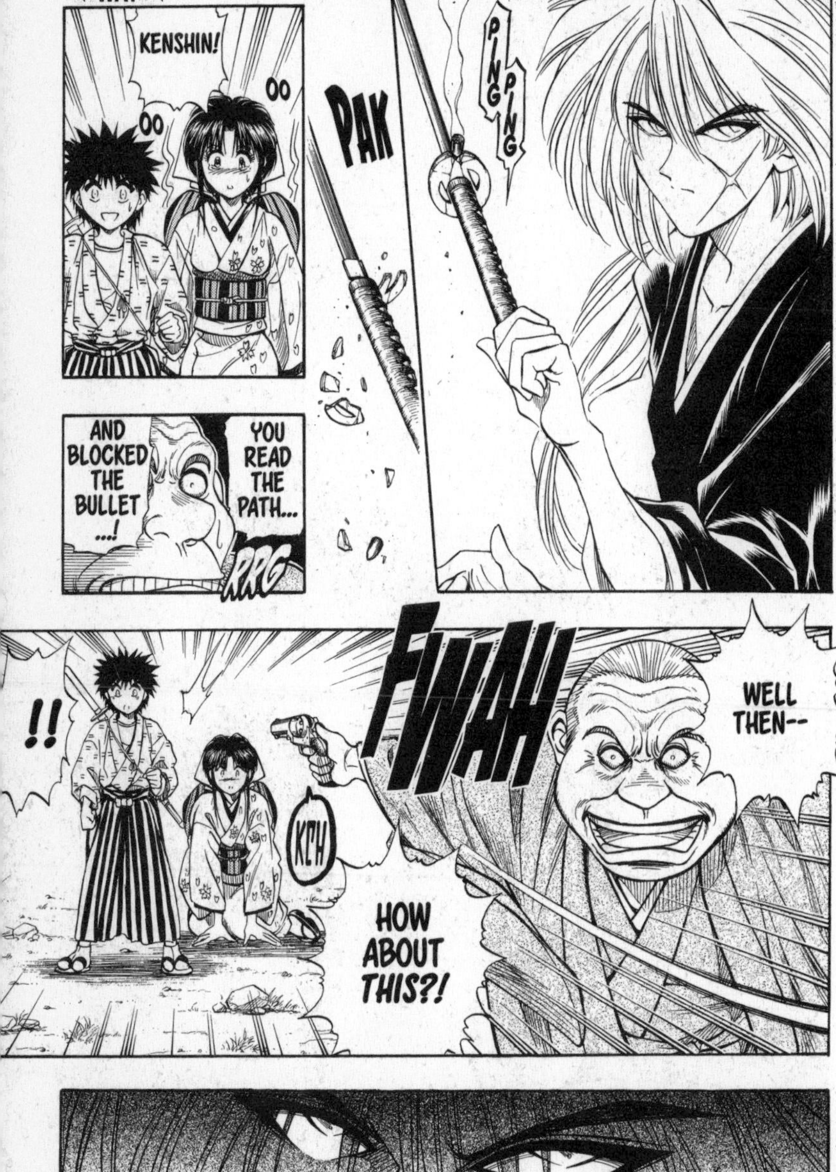
PAK
PING PING
KENSHIN!
OO
OO
YOU READ THE PATH...
AND BLOCKED THE BULLET ...!
RRG
WELL THEN--
FWAH
HOW ABOUT THIS?!
KCH
!!

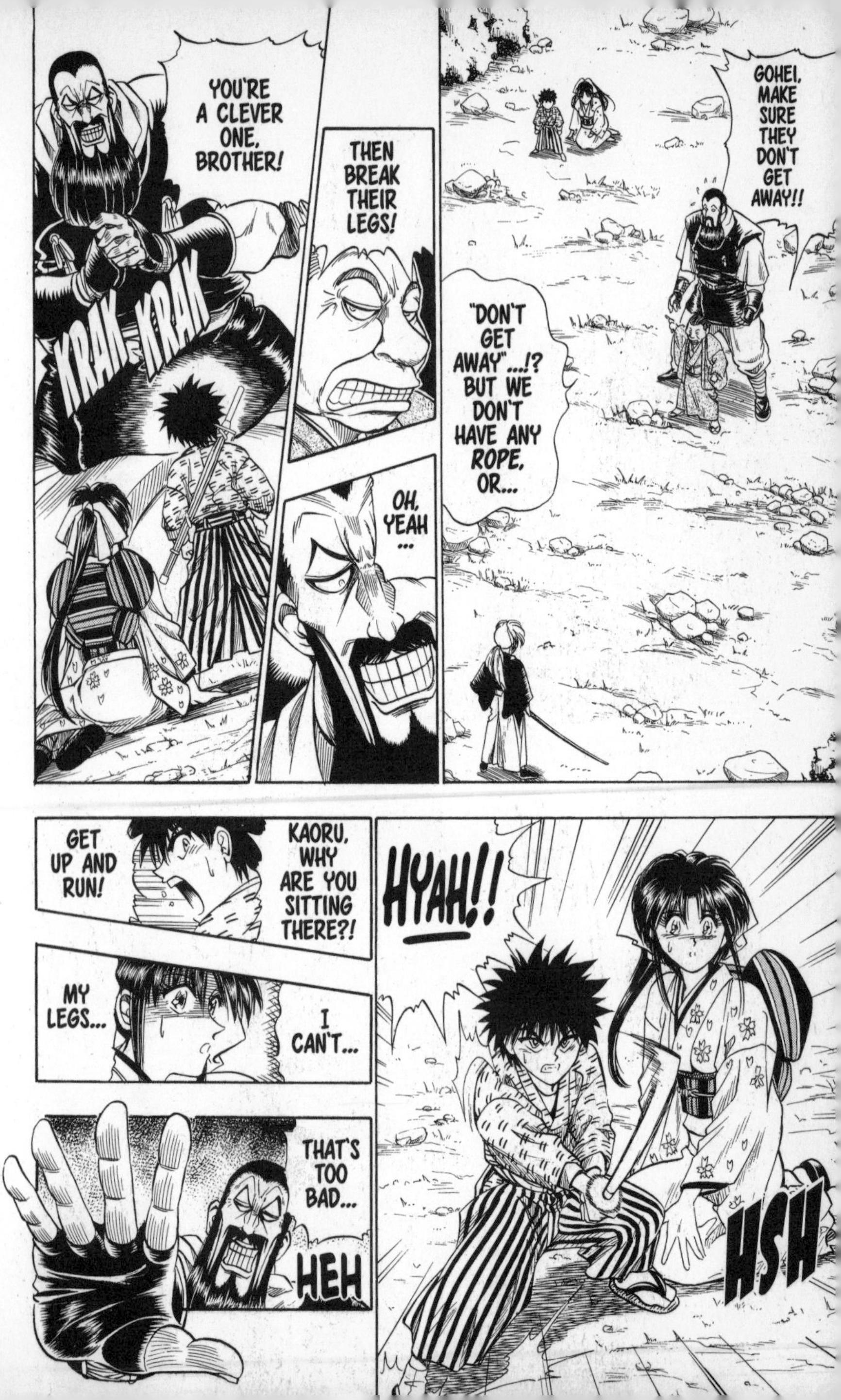
GOHEI, MAKE SURE THEY DON'T GET AWAY!!
"DON'T GET AWAY"...!? BUT WE DON'T HAVE ANY ROPE, OR...
THEN BREAK THEIR LEGS!
OH, YEAH ...
YOU'RE A CLEVER ONE, BROTHER!
KRAK KRAK
HYAH!!
HSH
KAORU, WHY ARE YOU SITTING THERE?!
GET UP AND RUN!
MY LEGS...
I CAN'T...
THAT'S TOO BAD...
HEH

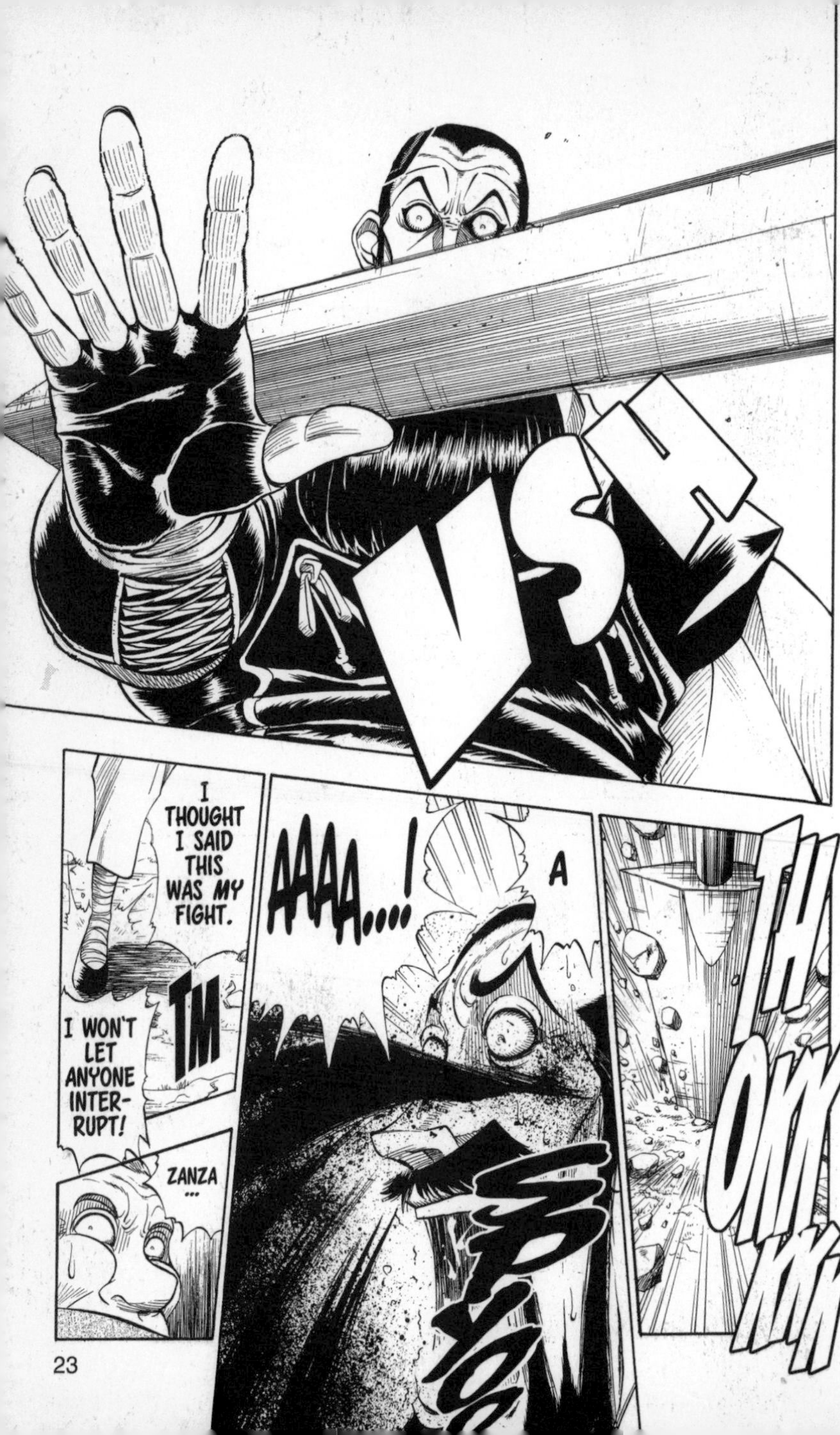
VSH
THONKKK
A
AAAA...!
I THOUGHT I SAID THIS WAS MY FIGHT.
TM
I WON'T LET ANYONE INTER-RUPT!
ZANZA...

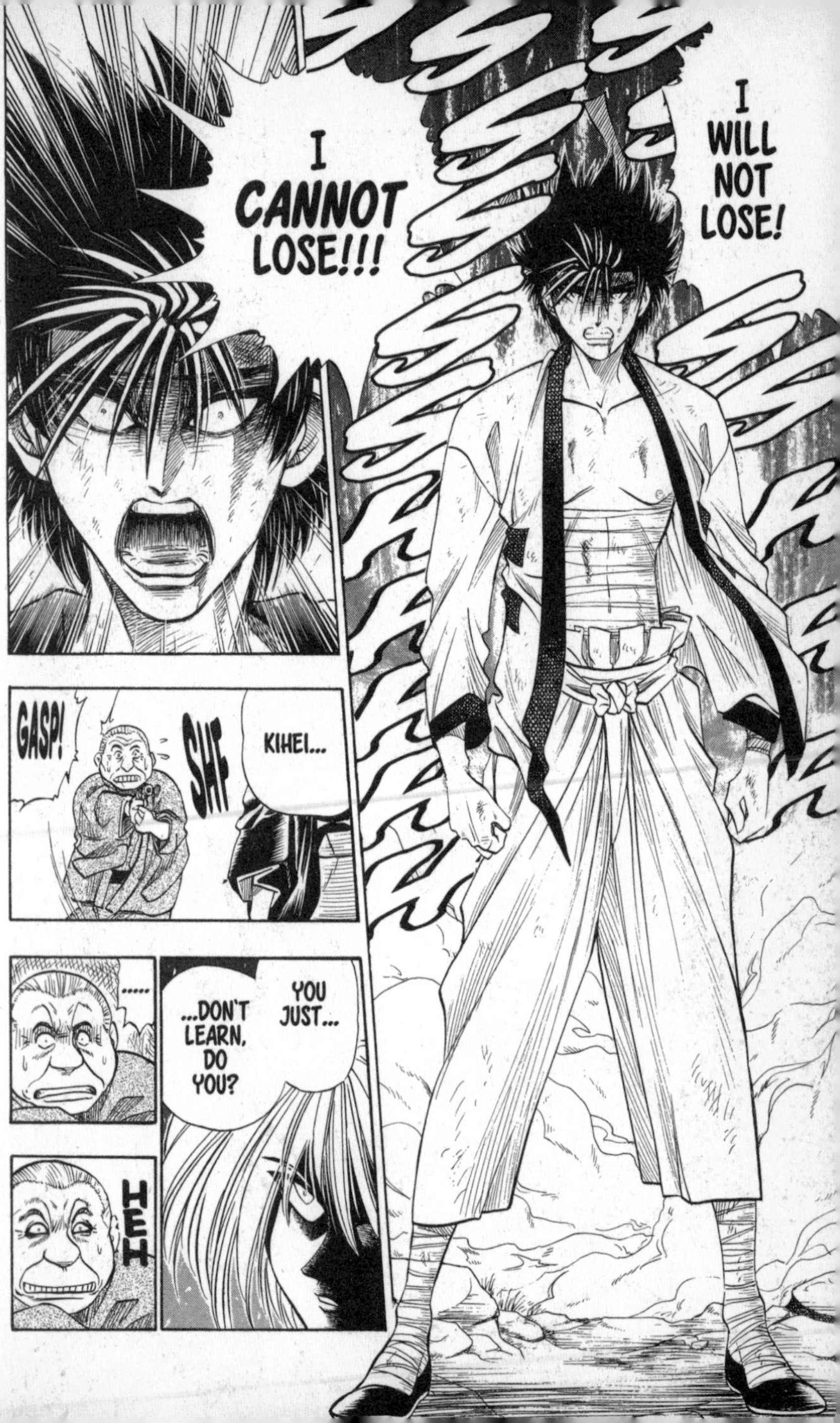
I WILL NOT LOSE!
I CANNOT LOSE!!!
KIHEI...
SHF
GASP!
YOU JUST...
...DON'T LEARN, DO YOU?
......
HEH

READ THIS WAY

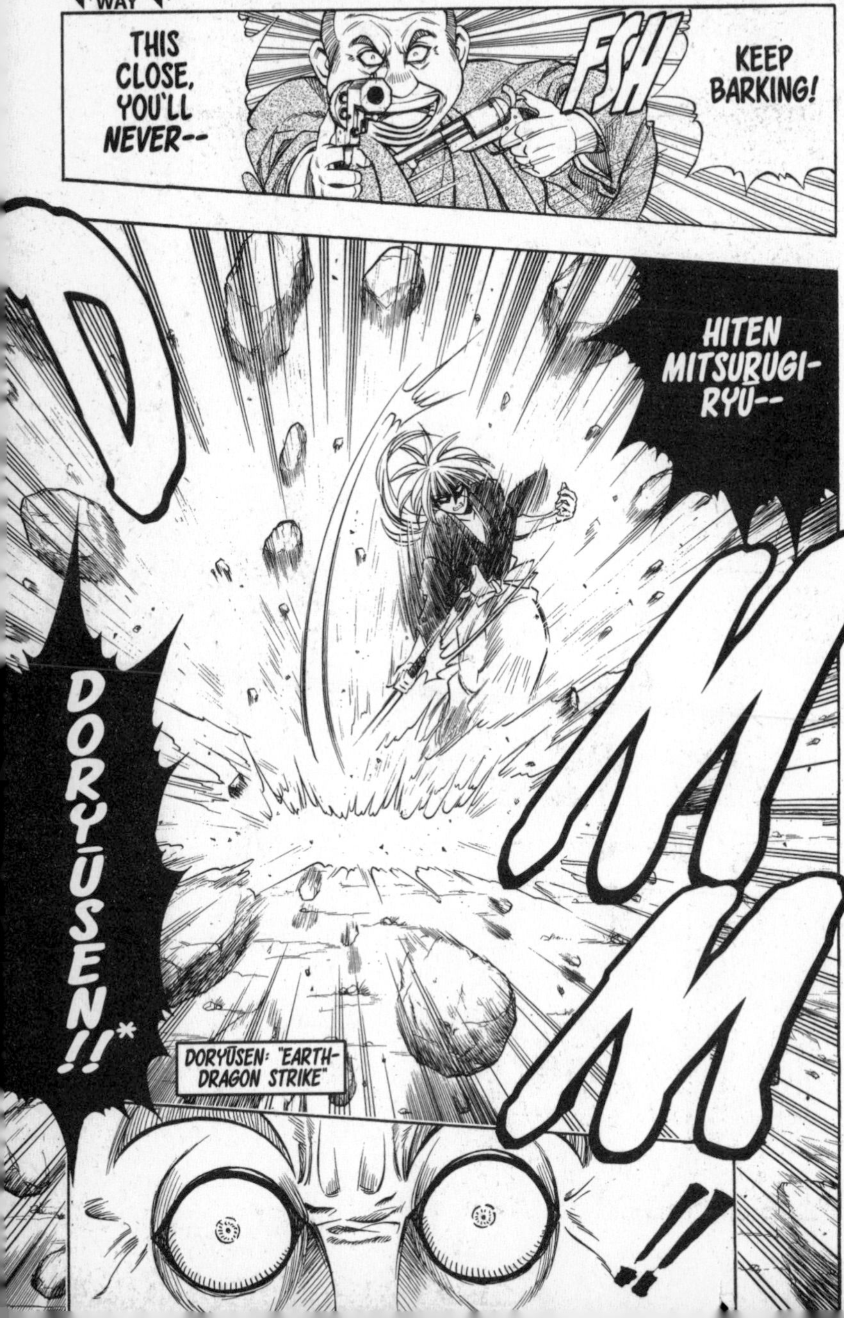
KEEP BARKING!
FSH
THIS CLOSE, YOU'LL NEVER--
HITEN MITSURUGI-RYŪ--
DMM
DORYŪSEN!!*
DORYŪSEN: "EARTH-DRAGON STRIKE"
!!

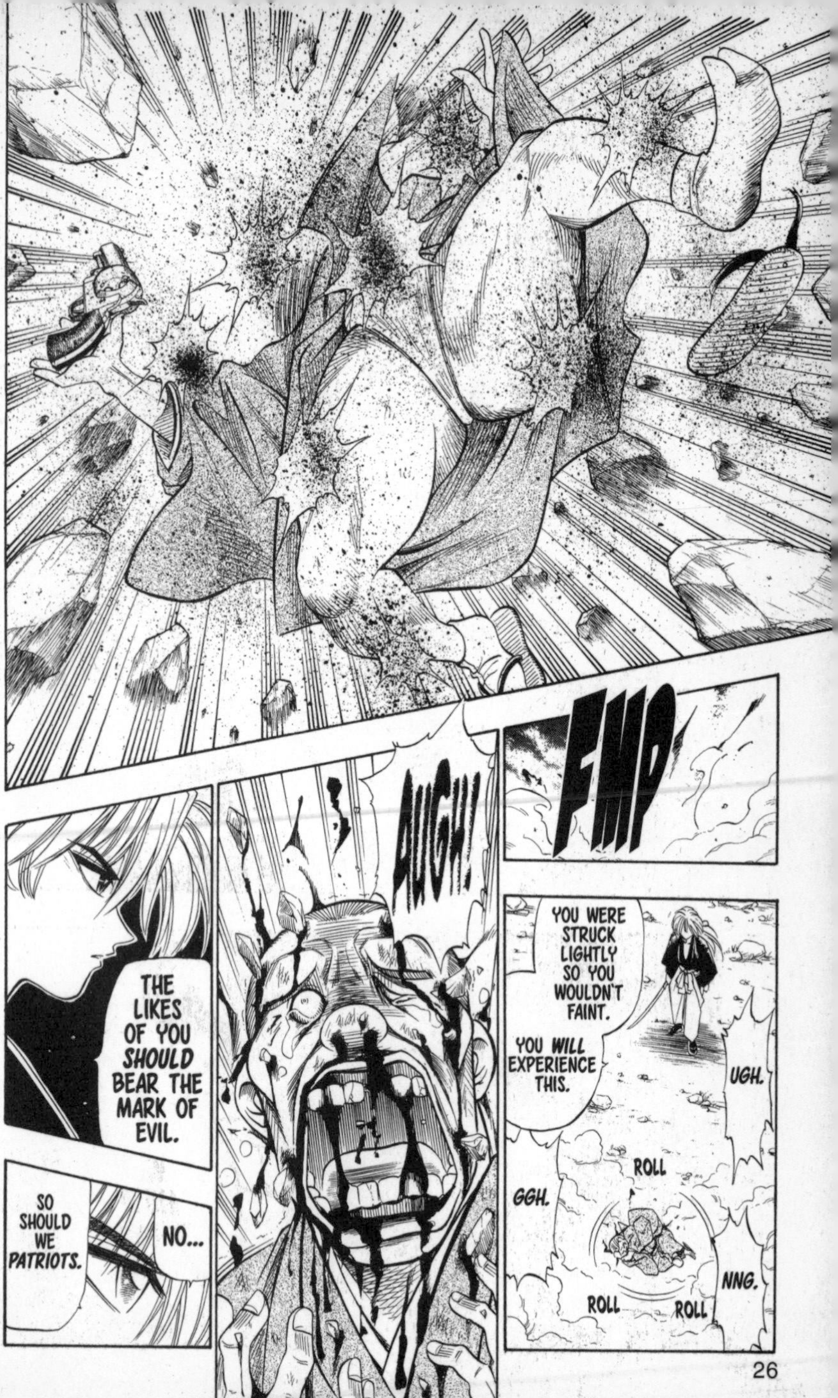
FMP
YOU WERE STRUCK LIGHTLY SO YOU WOULDN'T FAINT.
YOU *WILL* EXPERIENCE THIS.
UGH.
ROLL
GGH.
NNG.
ROLL
ROLL
AUGH!
THE LIKES OF YOU *SHOULD* BEAR THE MARK OF EVIL.
NO...
SO SHOULD WE *PATRIOTS*.

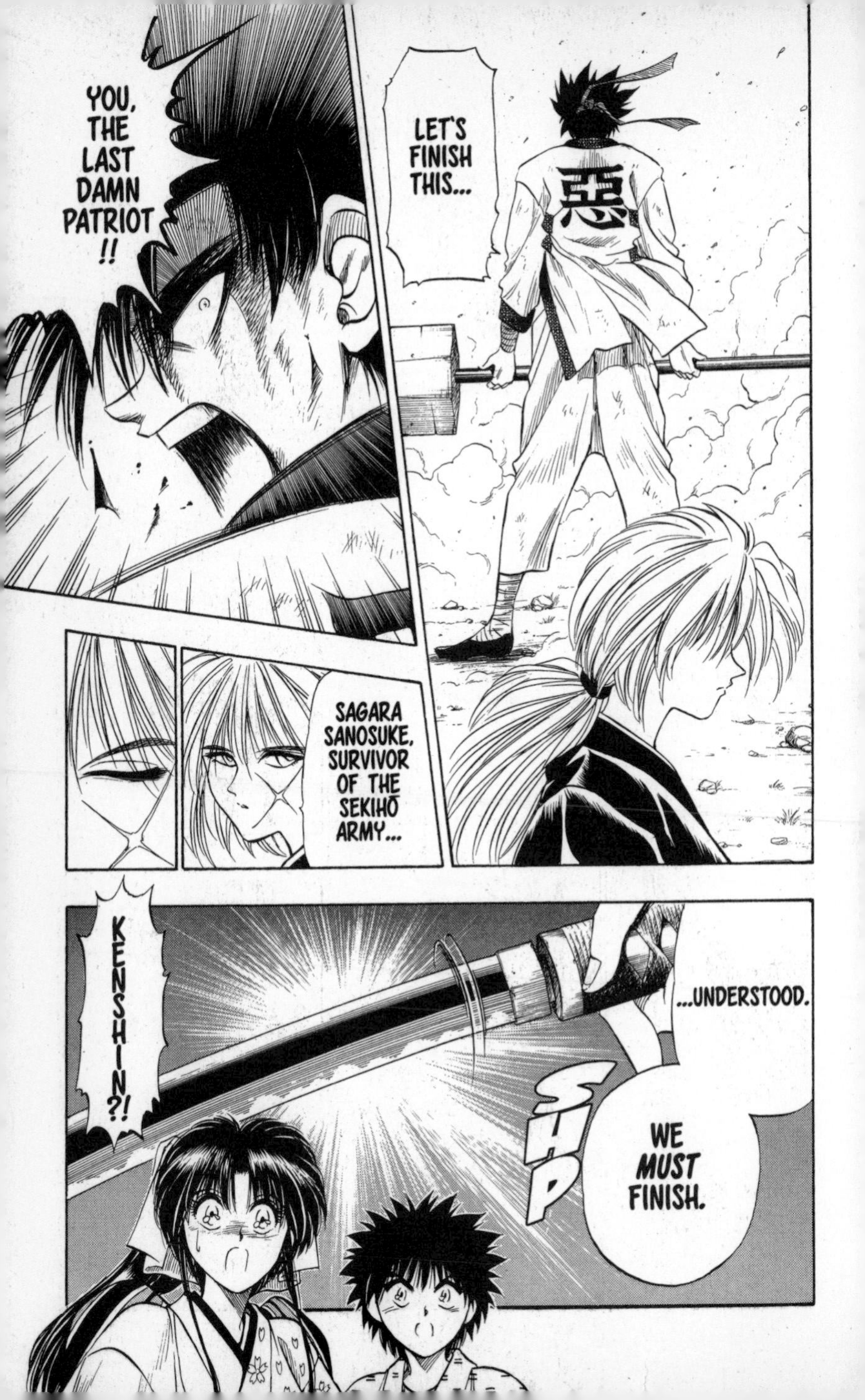
LET'S FINISH THIS...
YOU, THE LAST DAMN PATRIOT!!
SAGARA SANOSUKE, SURVIVOR OF THE SEKIHŌ ARMY...
...UNDERSTOOD.
WE MUST FINISH.
SHP
KENSHIN?!

## The Secret Life of Characters (5)

# —Sagara Sōzō—

**In that Sagara Sōzō is an actual historical personage, talking about his "motif" as a character seems beside the point. Ultimately, what ended up taking precedence was Watsuki's own mental image. Sagara Sōzō (real name: *Kojima Shirō*) seems to have been an extravagant man, samurai not by birth, but scion of a wealthy family. Leaving his wife and children behind, he joined the cause as a pro-Imperialist and, as in this story, was eventually turned upon by the Imperial Army and executed (beheaded) at 29 years of age. Since he appears here within the framework of Sanosuke's memories, he is of course somewhat glorified. But Sagara Sōzō did truly see equality for all as the final objective of the revolution. What would he have thought, had he lived, had he seen what passed for "equality" during the subsequent Age of Meiji...?**

**The real-life "Sekihō Army (*Sekihō-tai*) Incident" is in fact little-known, and I did debate whether or not to include it. In the end, because I felt it showed so clearly the truths and the lies of the Meiji Restoration, I couldn't just skip it. A friend told me then that another friend—a popular manga creator—had cautioned that I might be "getting in too deep." There's also the fact that, while doing this storyline, the popularity of the series (in Weekly Shonen Jump) fell to its lowest point since beginning publication. Still, Watsuki did feel at the time that, in order to explore the true story of the Meiji Restoration, leaving out the story of the Sekihō Army was not an option.**

**Design-wise (and as mentioned above), there's not much reason to discuss "motif." Back in the previous volume, in Act Two when I drew *Yamagata Aritomo*, I couldn't get my version of the character to resemble the surviving photos of him, and so I'd had to take a different route and use imagination as my guide. (I did search for photos or other images of the real Sagara Sōzō, but never could find them. What did he look like...?) Beautiful as he was—the sun, the moon, and the stars to Sanosuke—Sagara Sōzō becomes only more popular in the eyes (and hearts) of female readers.**

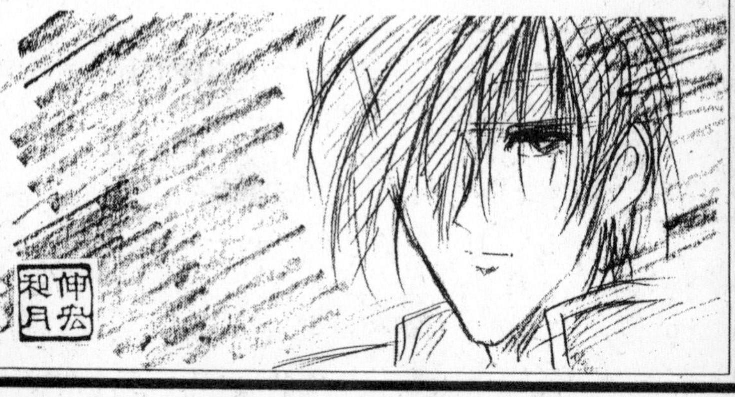
伸宏
和月

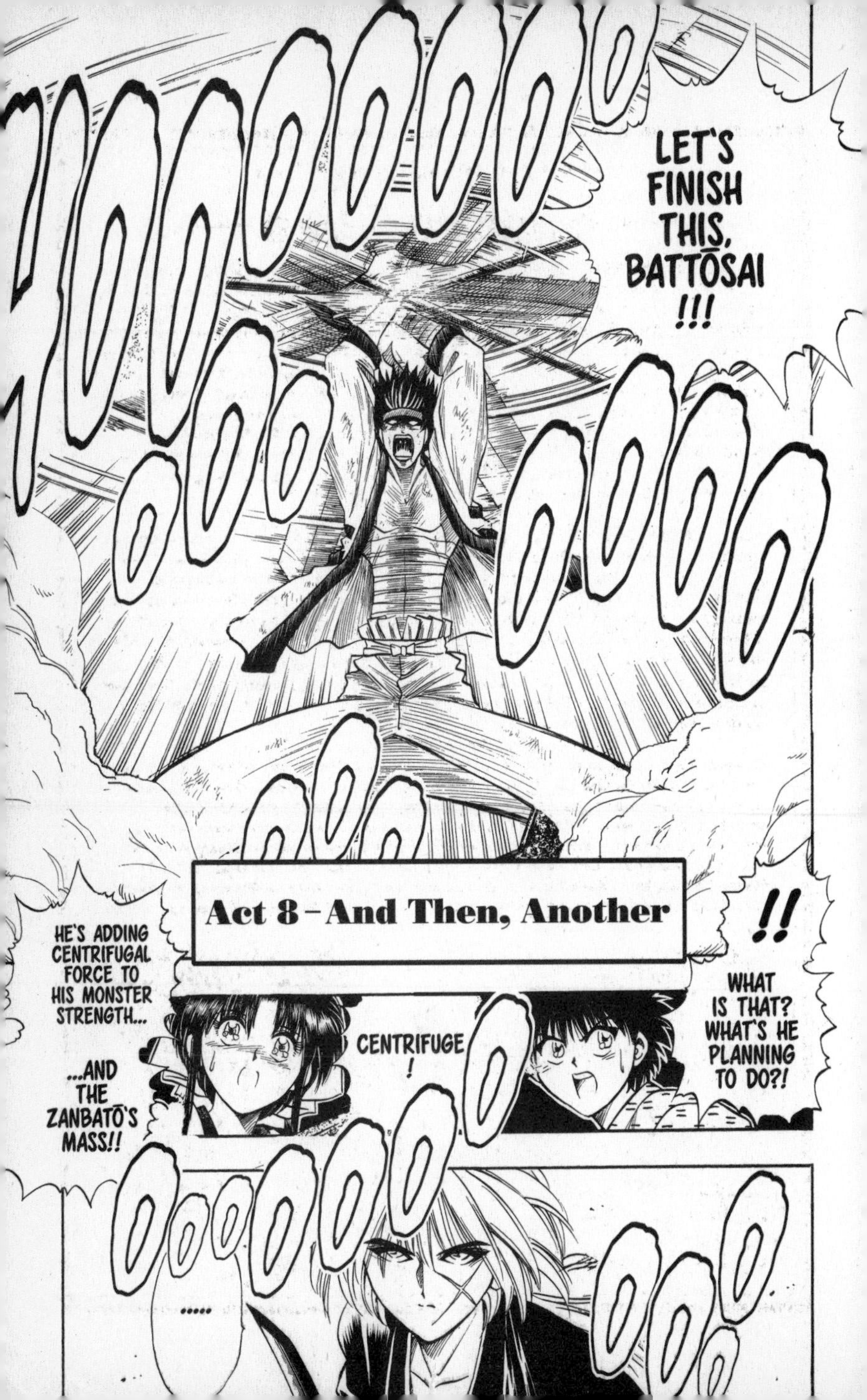
LET'S FINISH THIS, BATTŌSAI!!!
Act 8 – And Then, Another
!!
WHAT IS THAT? WHAT'S HE PLANNING TO DO?!
CENTRIFUGE!
HE'S ADDING CENTRIFUGAL FORCE TO HIS MONSTER STRENGTH...
...AND THE ZANBATŌ'S MASS!!
.....

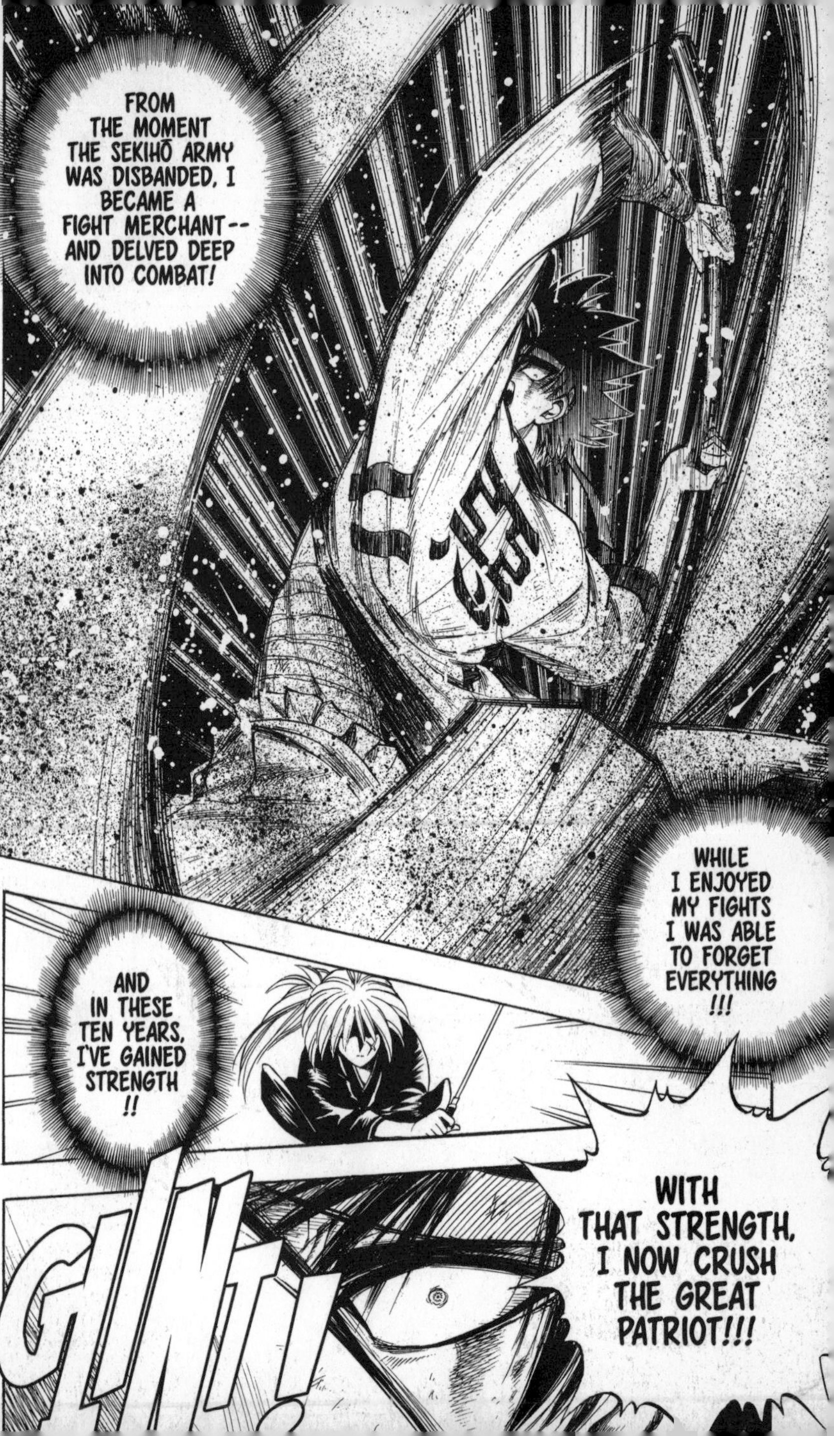
FROM THE MOMENT THE SEKIHŌ ARMY WAS DISBANDED, I BECAME A FIGHT MERCHANT-- AND DELVED DEEP INTO COMBAT!
WHILE I ENJOYED MY FIGHTS I WAS ABLE TO FORGET EVERYTHING !!!
AND IN THESE TEN YEARS, I'VE GAINED STRENGTH !!
WITH THAT STRENGTH, I NOW CRUSH THE GREAT PATRIOT!!!
GIN!!

READ THIS WAY

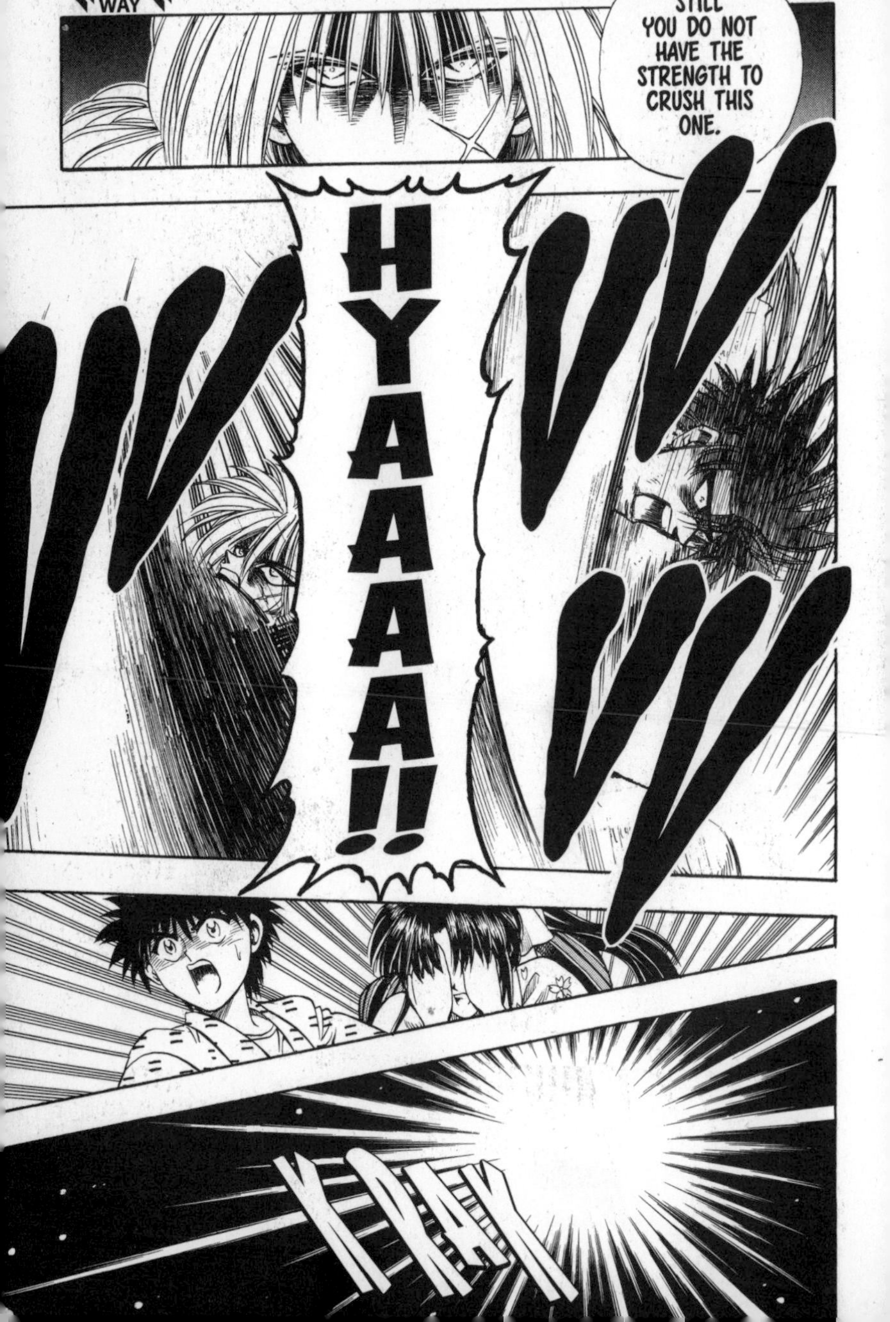
STILL YOU DO NOT HAVE THE STRENGTH TO CRUSH THIS ONE.
HYAAAA!!

# Act 8
# And Then, Another

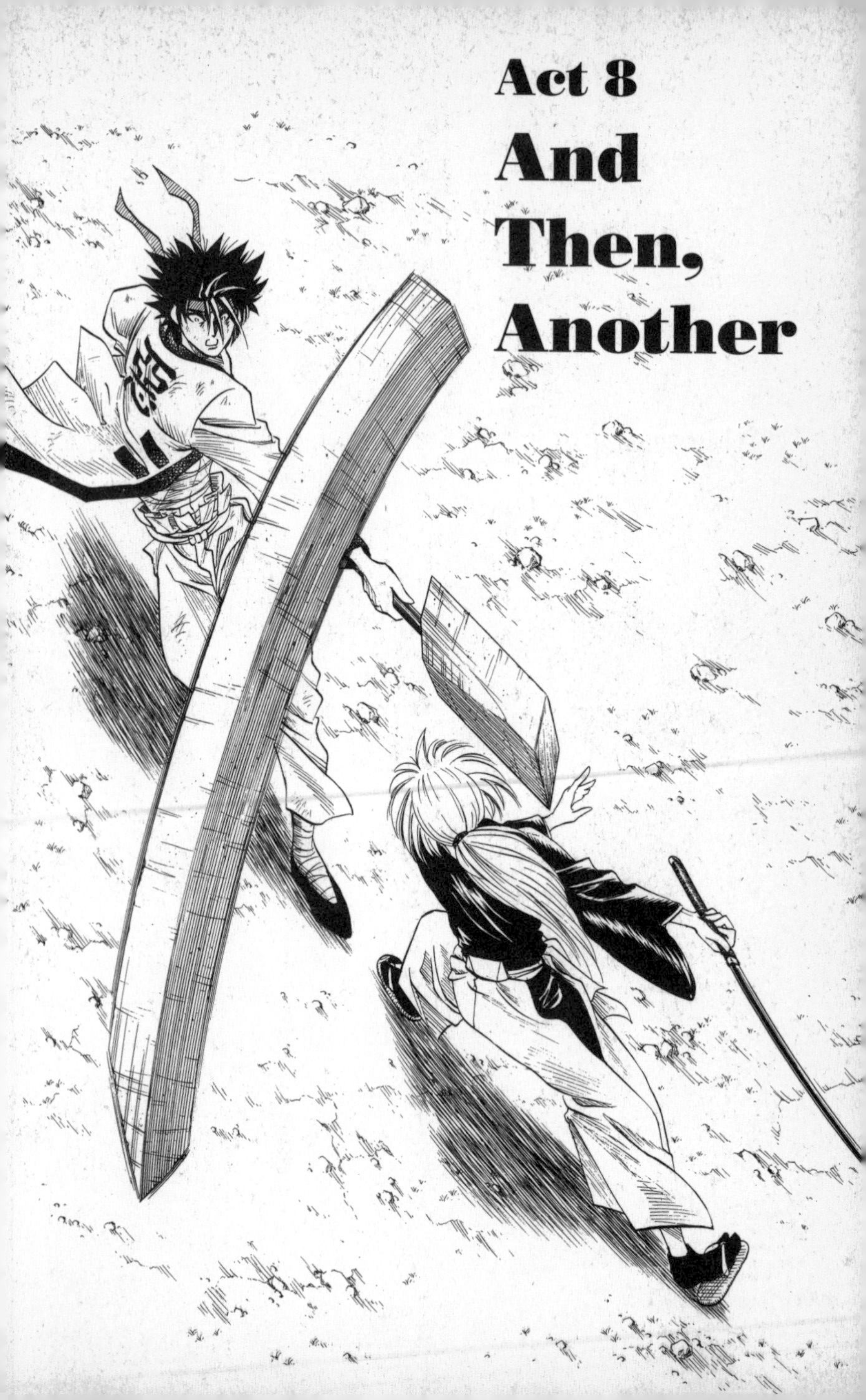

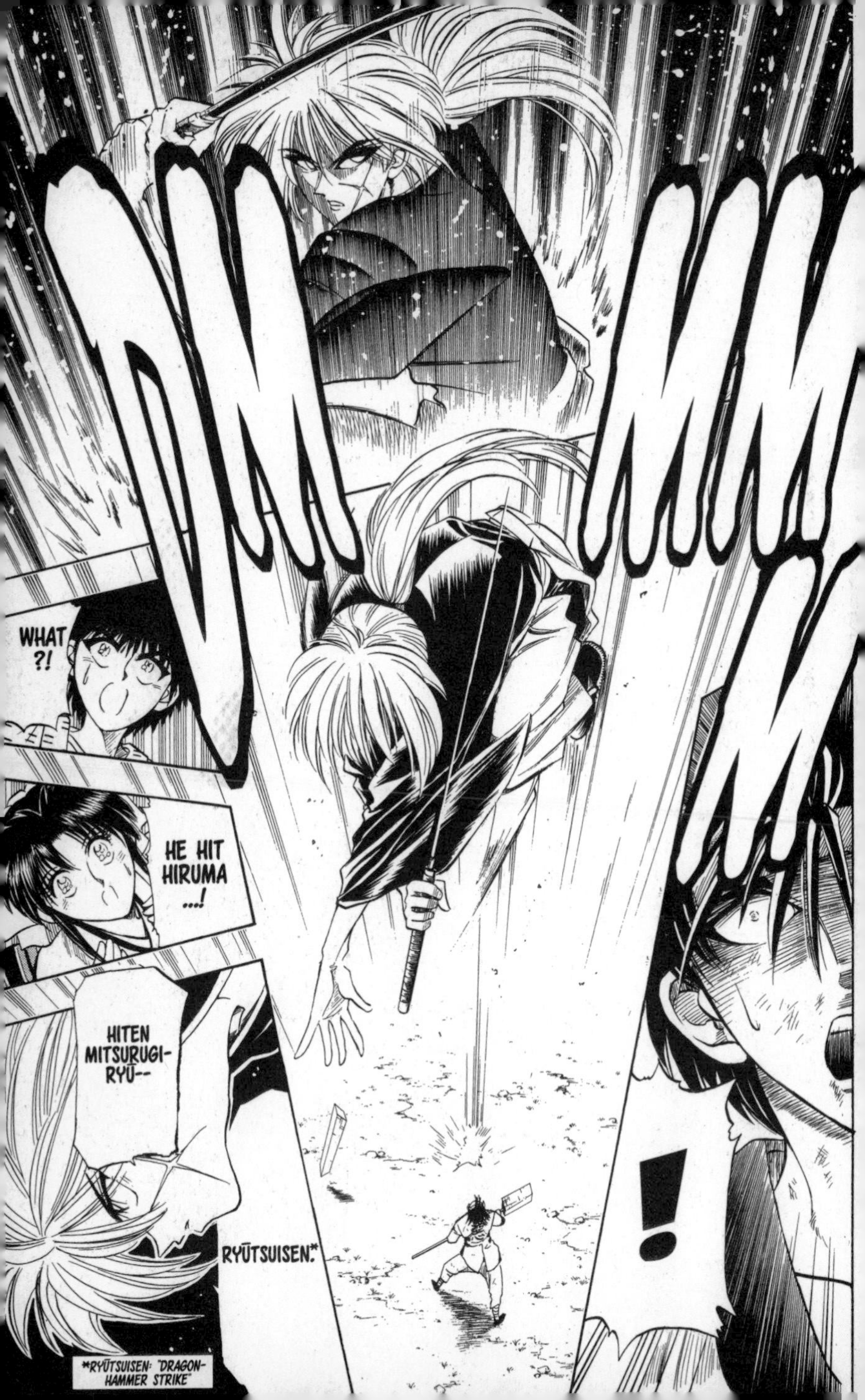
!
WHAT ?!
HE HIT HIRUMA ...!
HITEN MITSURUGI-RYŪ--
RYŪTSUISEN!*

*RYŪTSUISEN: "DRAGON-HAMMER STRIKE"

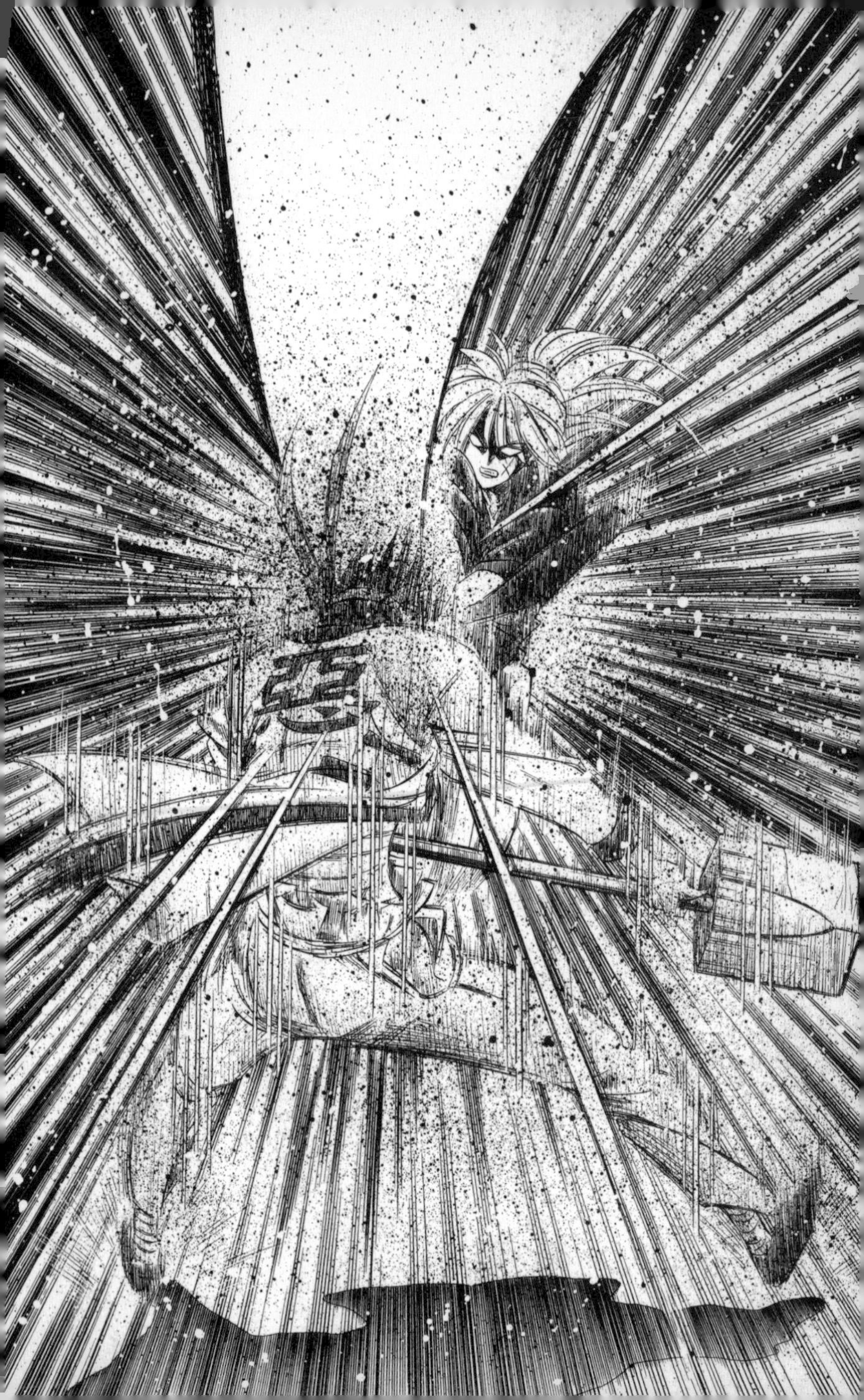

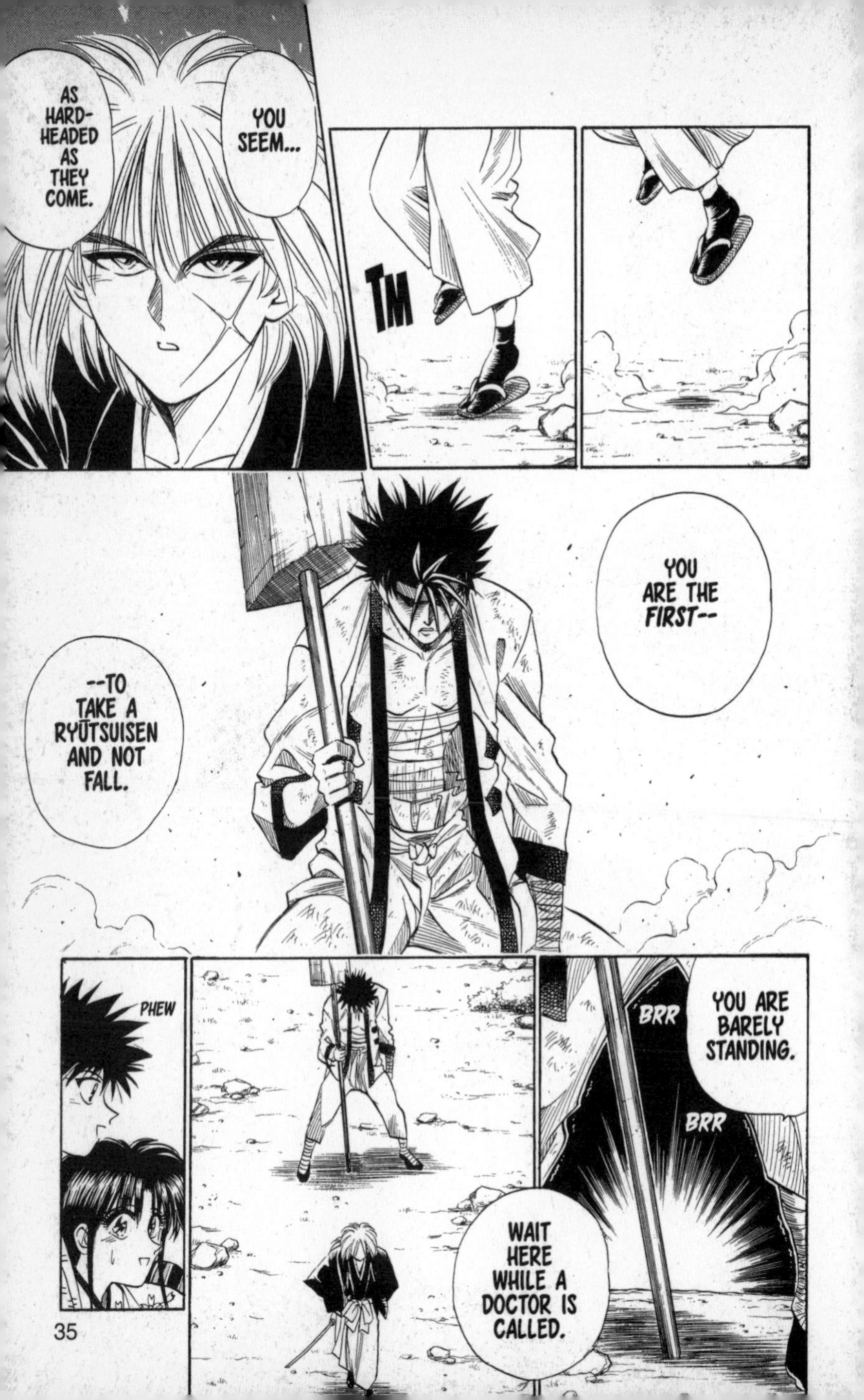
TM
YOU SEEM...
AS HARD-HEADED AS THEY COME.
YOU ARE THE FIRST--
--TO TAKE A RYŪTSUISEN AND NOT FALL.
BRR
YOU ARE BARELY STANDING.
BRR
WAIT HERE WHILE A DOCTOR IS CALLED.
PHEW

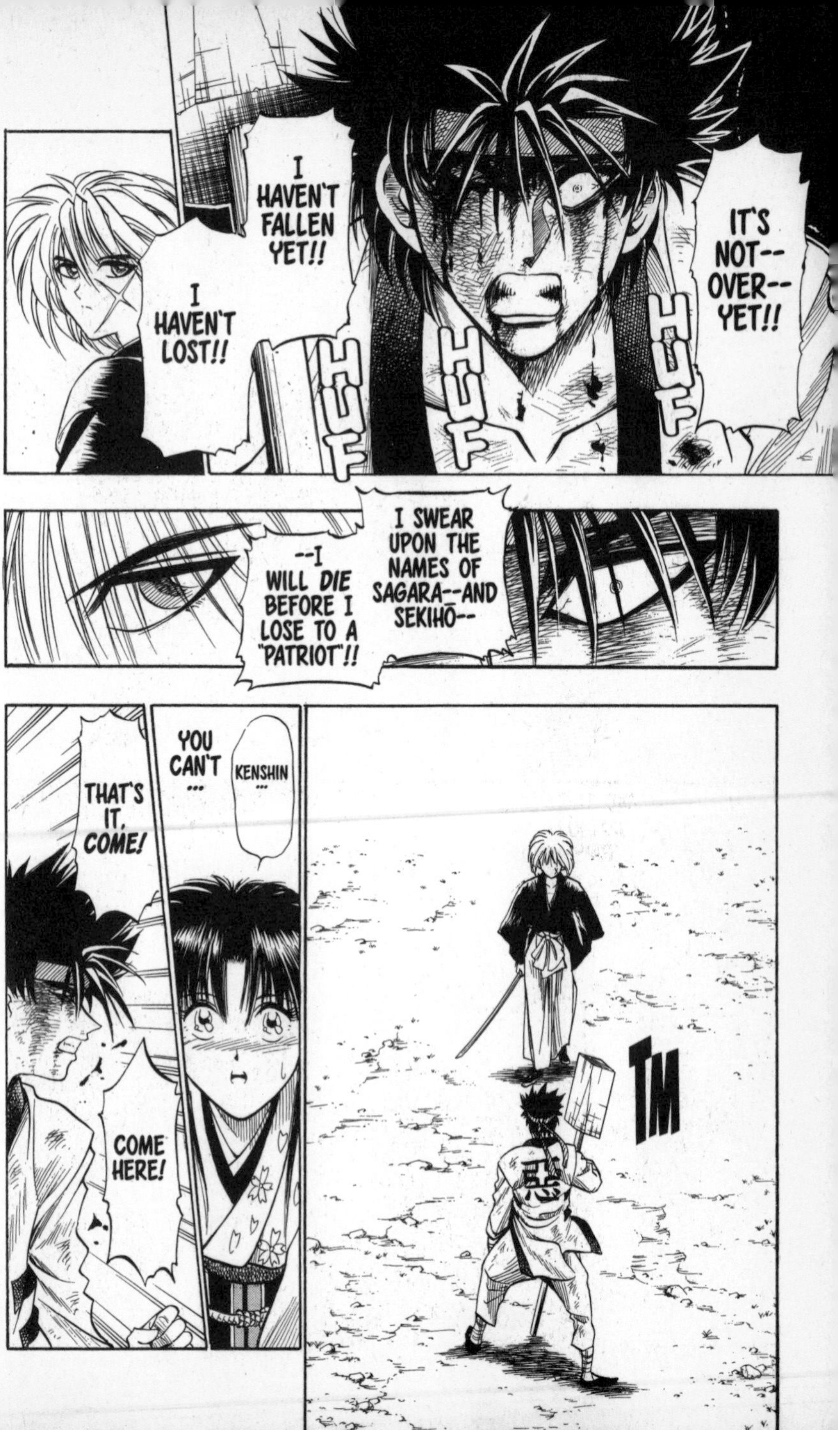
IT'S NOT-- OVER-- YET!!
HUF HUF HUF
I HAVEN'T FALLEN YET!!
I HAVEN'T LOST!!
I SWEAR UPON THE NAMES OF SAGARA--AND SEKIHŌ--
--I WILL *DIE* BEFORE I LOSE TO A "PATRIOT"!!
TM
KENSHIN ...
YOU CAN'T ...
THAT'S IT, *COME!*
COME HERE!

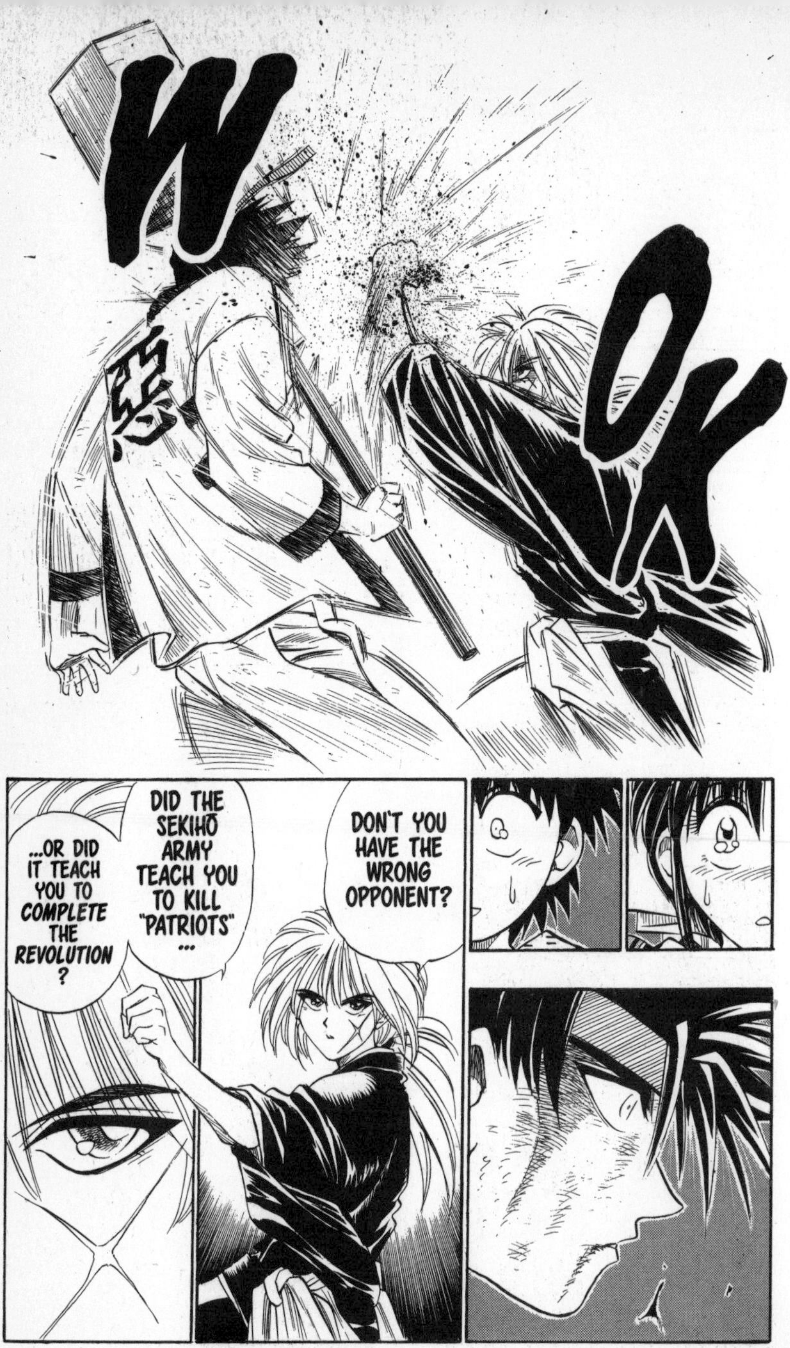
WOK
DON'T YOU HAVE THE WRONG OPPONENT?
DID THE SEKIHŌ ARMY TEACH YOU TO KILL "PATRIOTS"...
...OR DID IT TEACH YOU TO COMPLETE THE REVOLUTION?

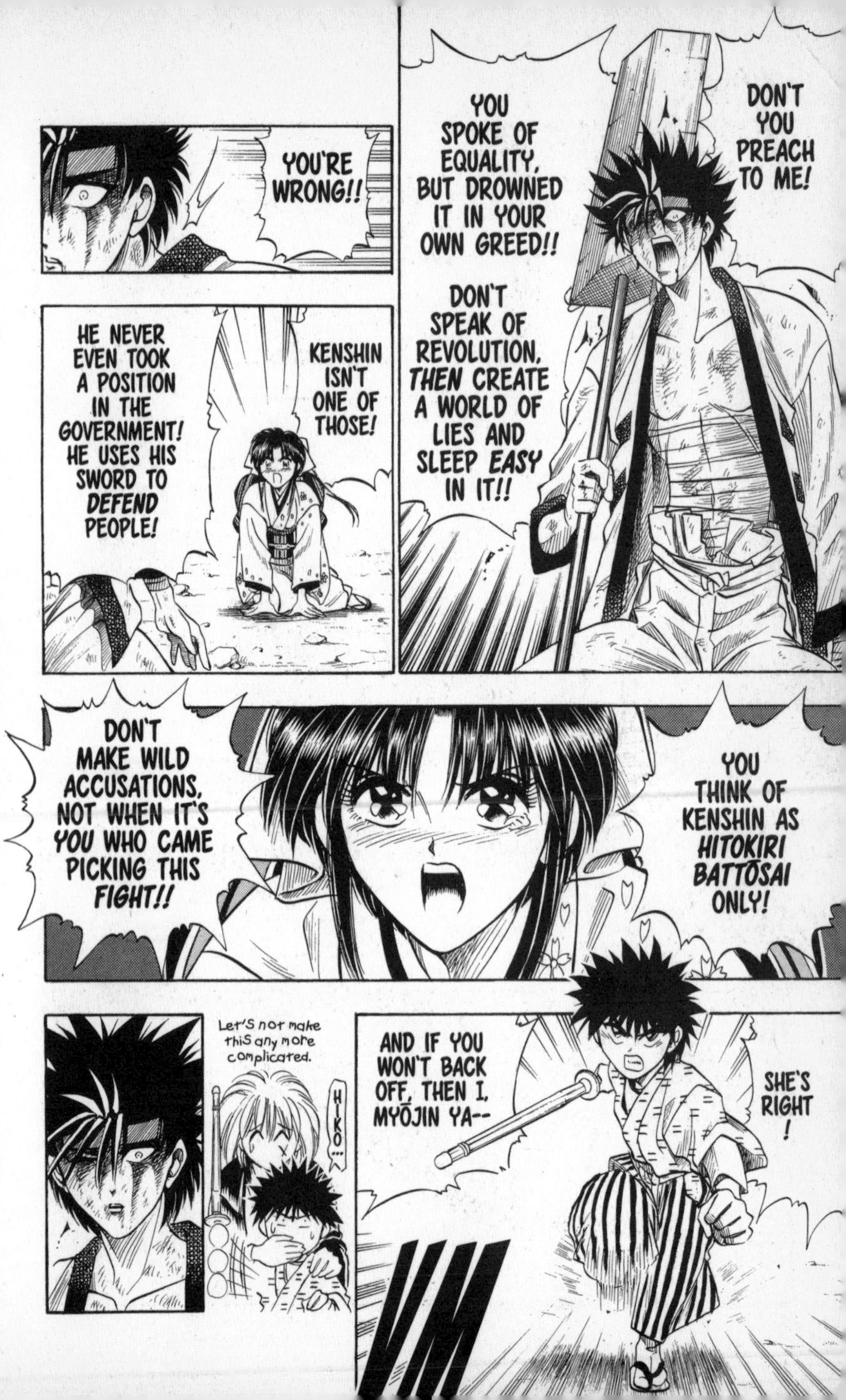
DON'T YOU PREACH TO ME!
YOU SPOKE OF EQUALITY, BUT DROWNED IT IN YOUR OWN GREED!!
DON'T SPEAK OF REVOLUTION, THEN CREATE A WORLD OF LIES AND SLEEP EASY IN IT!!
YOU'RE WRONG!!
KENSHIN ISN'T ONE OF THOSE!
HE NEVER EVEN TOOK A POSITION IN THE GOVERNMENT! HE USES HIS SWORD TO DEFEND PEOPLE!
YOU THINK OF KENSHIN AS HITOKIRI BATTŌSAI ONLY!
DON'T MAKE WILD ACCUSATIONS, NOT WHEN IT'S YOU WHO CAME PICKING THIS FIGHT!!
SHE'S RIGHT!
AND IF YOU WON'T BACK OFF, THEN I, MYŌJIN YA--
Let's not make this any more complicated.
HIKO...

READ THIS WAY

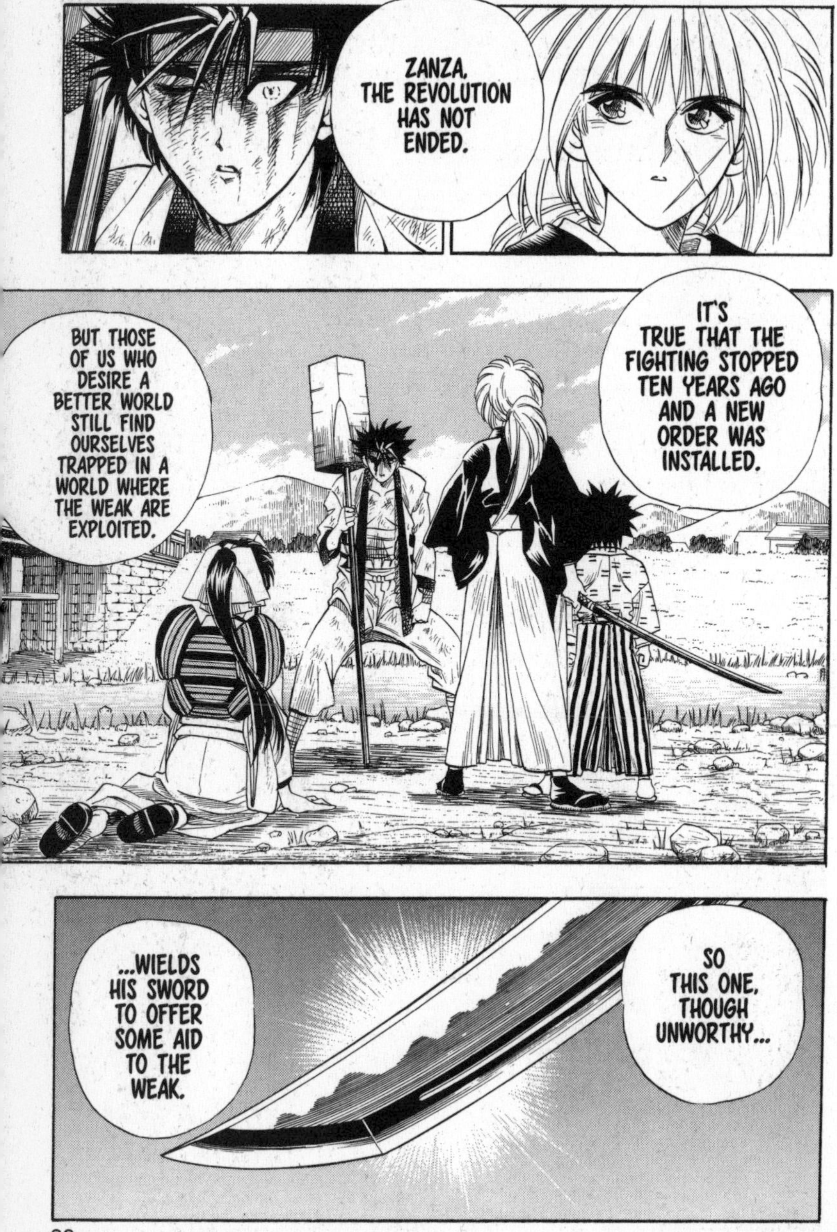
ZANZA, THE REVOLUTION HAS NOT ENDED.
IT'S TRUE THAT THE FIGHTING STOPPED TEN YEARS AGO AND A NEW ORDER WAS INSTALLED.
BUT THOSE OF US WHO DESIRE A BETTER WORLD STILL FIND OURSELVES TRAPPED IN A WORLD WHERE THE WEAK ARE EXPLOITED.
SO THIS ONE, THOUGH UNWORTHY...
...WIELDS HIS SWORD TO OFFER SOME AID TO THE WEAK.

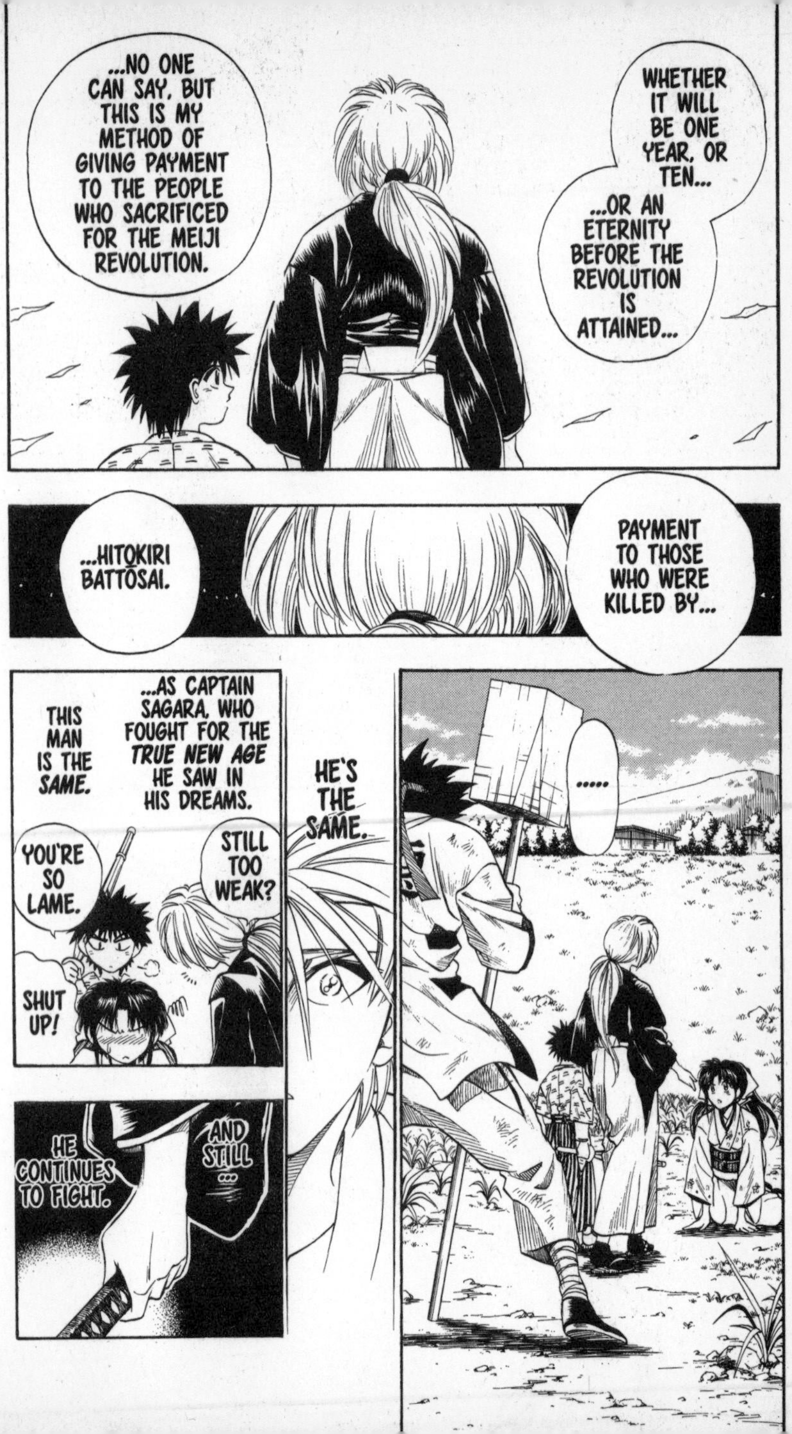
WHETHER IT WILL BE ONE YEAR, OR TEN...
...OR AN ETERNITY BEFORE THE REVOLUTION IS ATTAINED...
...NO ONE CAN SAY, BUT THIS IS MY METHOD OF GIVING PAYMENT TO THE PEOPLE WHO SACRIFICED FOR THE MEIJI REVOLUTION.
PAYMENT TO THOSE WHO WERE KILLED BY...
...HITOKIRI BATTOSAI.
.....
HE'S THE SAME.
...AS CAPTAIN SAGARA, WHO FOUGHT FOR THE *TRUE NEW AGE* HE SAW IN HIS DREAMS.
THIS MAN IS THE *SAME.*
STILL TOO WEAK?
YOU'RE SO LAME.
SHUT UP!
AND STILL...
HE CONTINUES TO FIGHT.

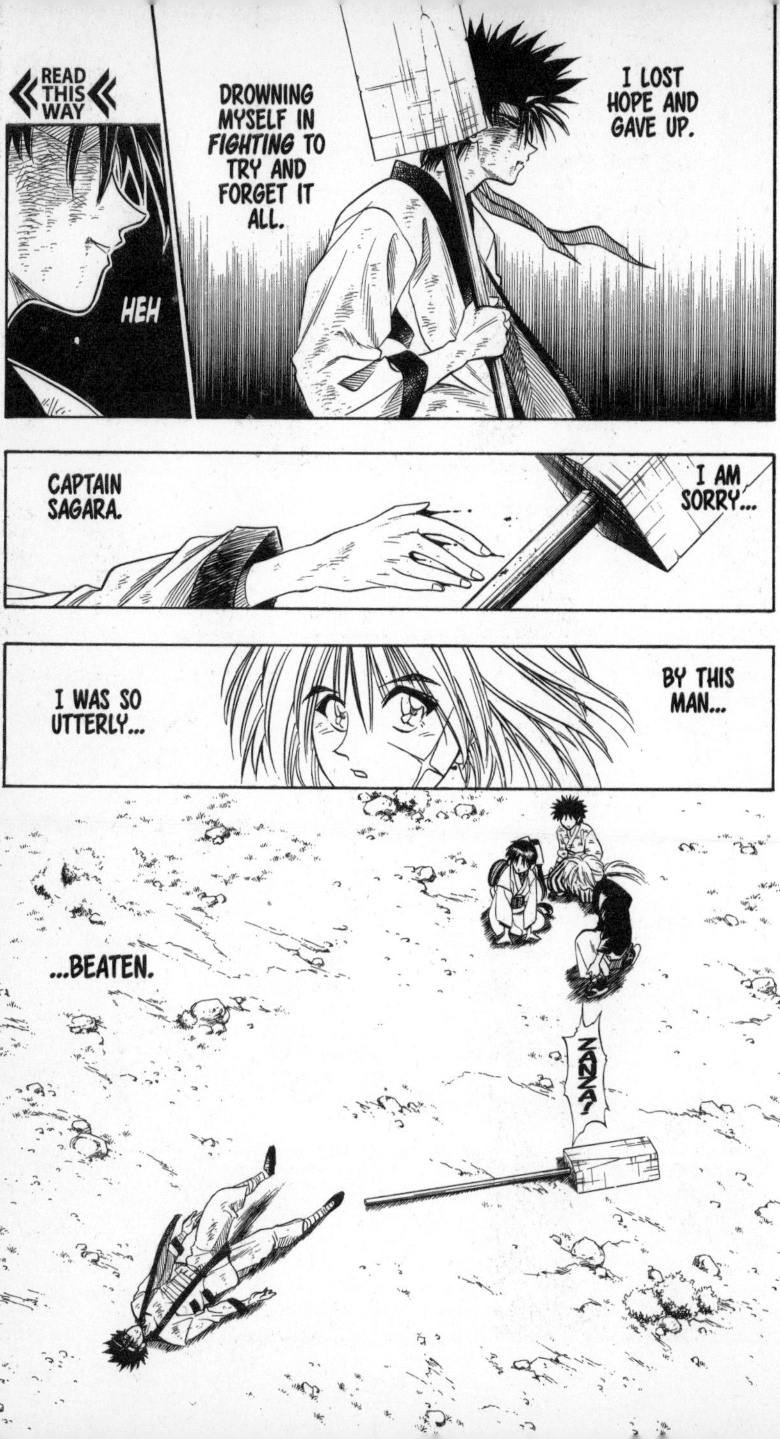
READ THIS WAY
I LOST HOPE AND GAVE UP.
DROWNING MYSELF IN FIGHTING TO TRY AND FORGET IT ALL.
HEH
I AM SORRY...
CAPTAIN SAGARA.
BY THIS MAN...
I WAS SO UTTERLY...
ZANZA!
...BEATEN.

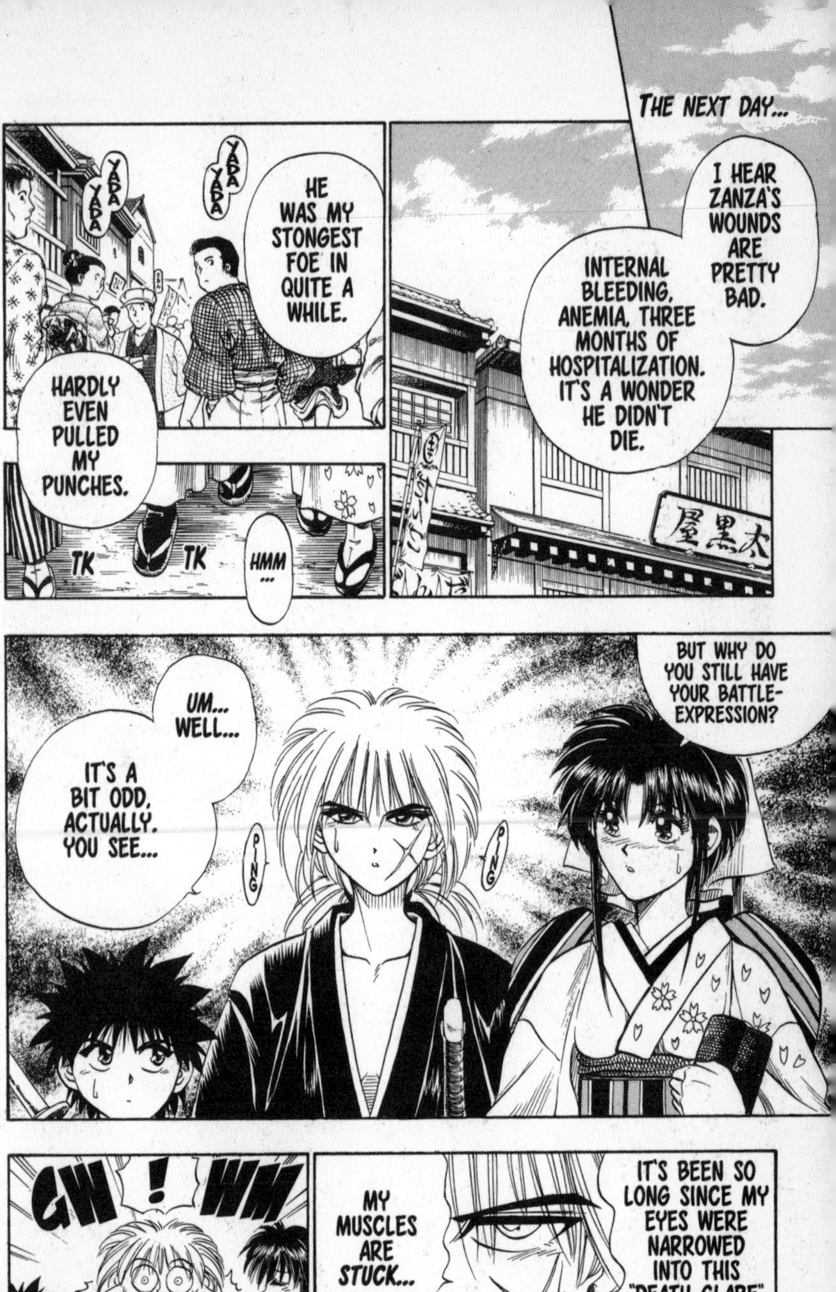
THE NEXT DAY...
I HEAR ZANZA'S WOUNDS ARE PRETTY BAD.
INTERNAL BLEEDING, ANEMIA, THREE MONTHS OF HOSPITALIZATION. IT'S A WONDER HE DIDN'T DIE.
YADA YADA
YADA YADA
HE WAS MY STONGEST FOE IN QUITE A WHILE.
HARDLY EVEN PULLED MY PUNCHES.
TK
TK
HMM...
BUT WHY DO YOU STILL HAVE YOUR BATTLE-EXPRESSION?
PING
PING
UM... WELL...
IT'S A BIT ODD, ACTUALLY. YOU SEE...
IT'S BEEN SO LONG SINCE MY EYES WERE NARROWED INTO THIS "DEATH GLARE" AND...WELL...
AHEM
MY MUSCLES ARE STUCK...
GN ! WM

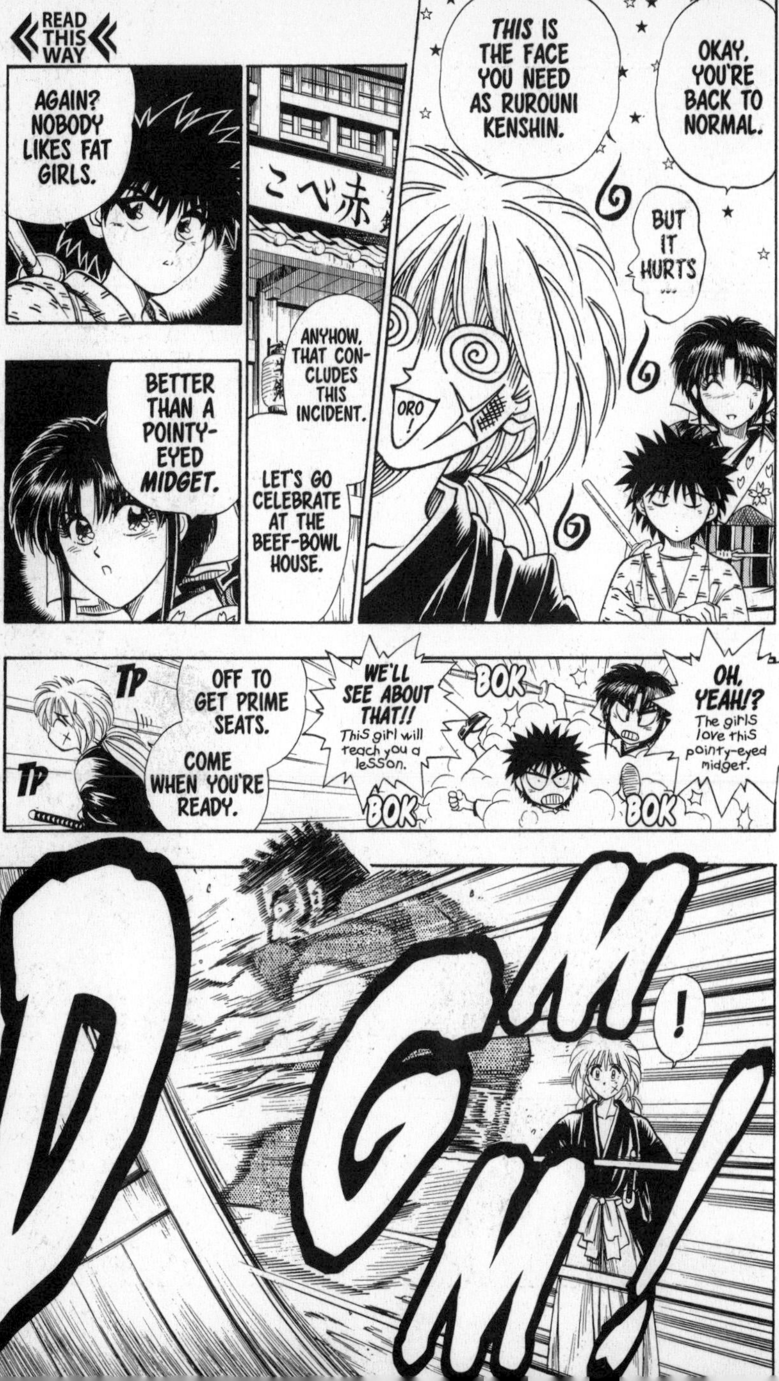
READ THIS WAY
OKAY, YOU'RE BACK TO NORMAL.
THIS IS THE FACE YOU NEED AS RUROUNI KENSHIN.
BUT IT HURTS...
ORO!
ANYHOW, THAT CONCLUDES THIS INCIDENT.
LET'S GO CELEBRATE AT THE BEEF-BOWL HOUSE.
AGAIN? NOBODY LIKES FAT GIRLS.
BETTER THAN A POINTY-EYED MIDGET.
OH, YEAH!? The girls love this pointy-eyed midget.
BOK
WE'LL SEE ABOUT THAT!! This girl will teach you a lesson.
BOK
BOK
OFF TO GET PRIME SEATS.
COME WHEN YOU'RE READY.
TP
TP
!

READ THIS WAY

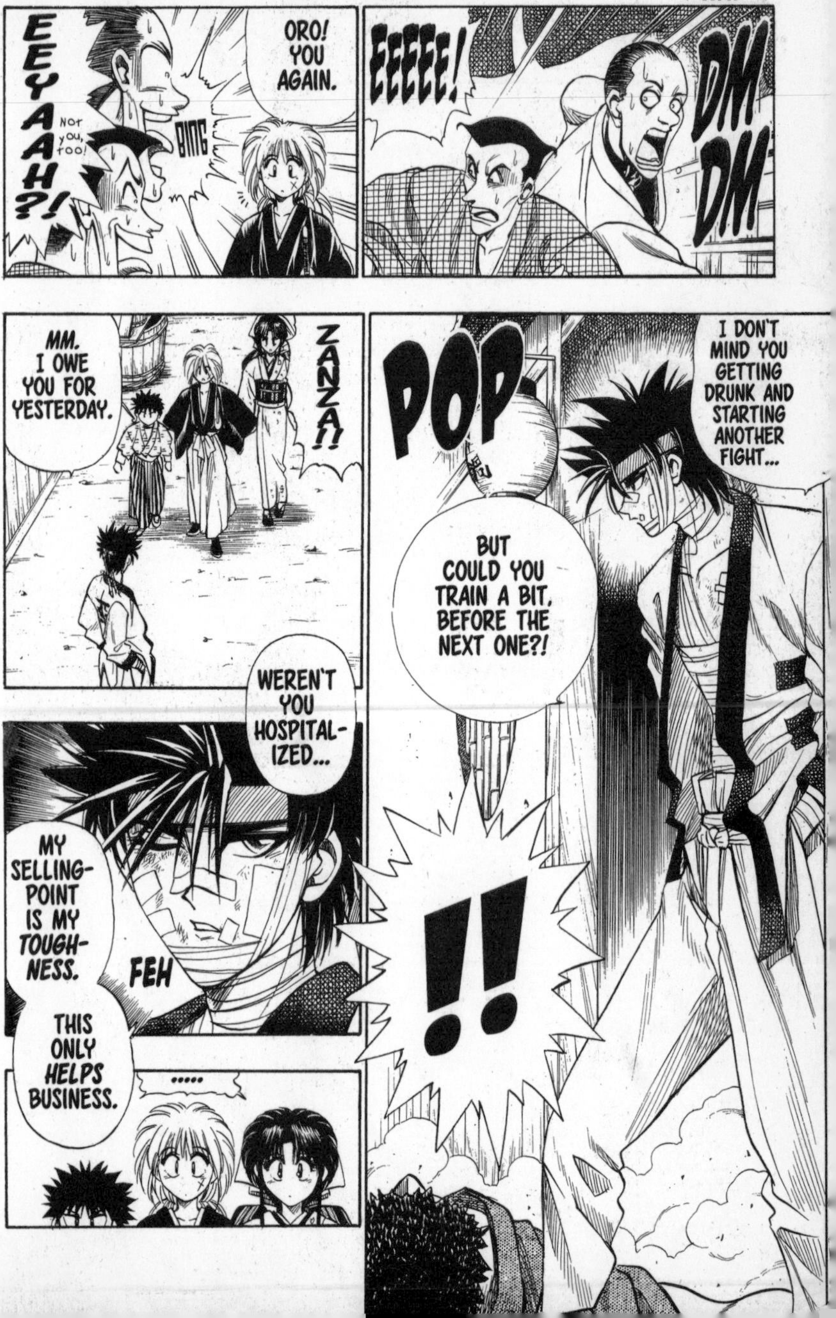
EEEEE!
DM DM
ORO! YOU AGAIN.
BING
EEYAAAH?!
Not you, too!
POP
I DON'T MIND YOU GETTING DRUNK AND STARTING ANOTHER FIGHT...
BUT COULD YOU TRAIN A BIT, BEFORE THE NEXT ONE?!
!!
ZANZA!!
MM. I OWE YOU FOR YESTERDAY.
WEREN'T YOU HOSPITAL-IZED...
MY SELLING-POINT IS MY TOUGH-NESS.
FEH
THIS ONLY HELPS BUSINESS.
.....

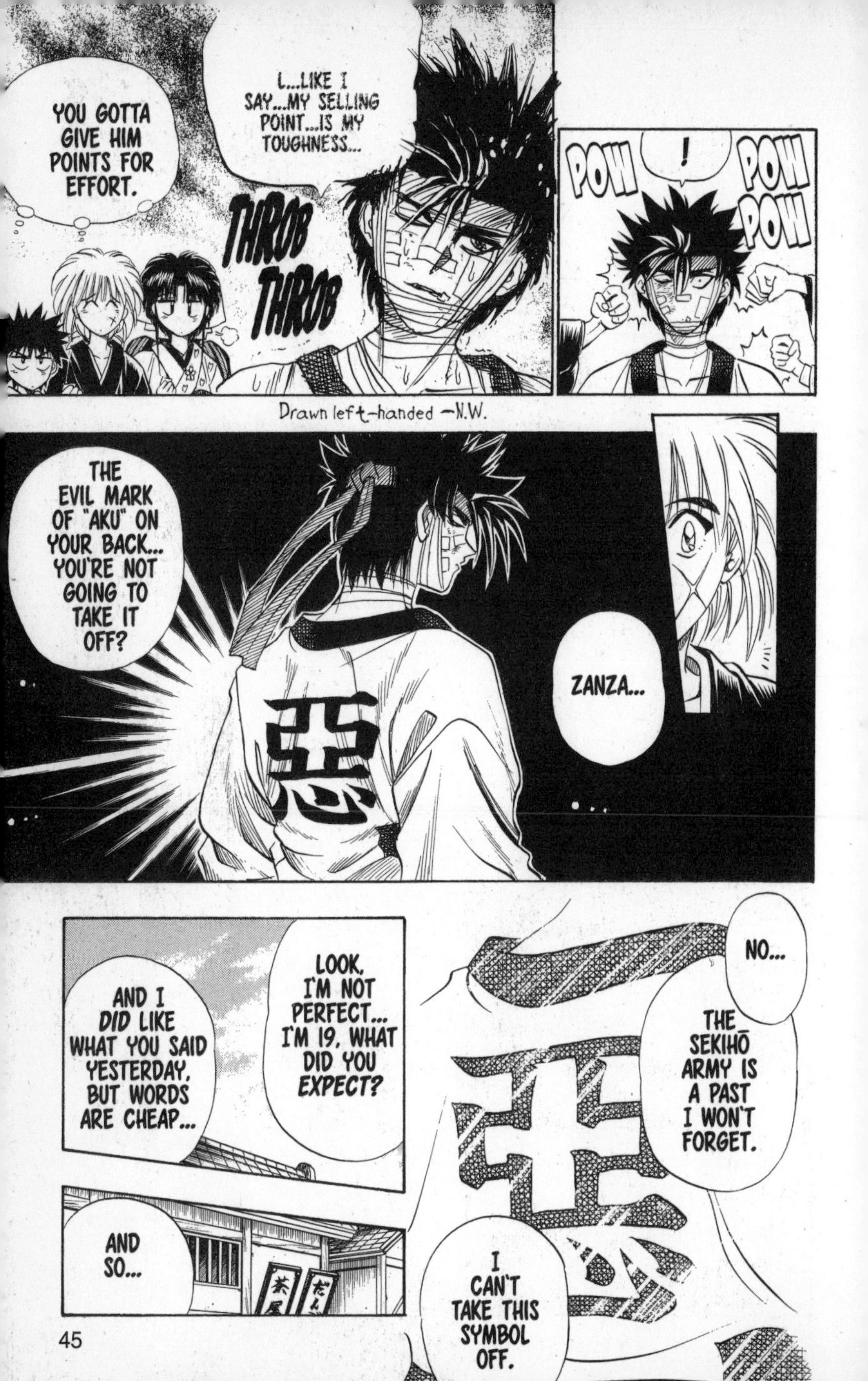
POW
!
POW POW
L...LIKE I SAY...MY SELLING POINT...IS MY TOUGHNESS...
THROB THROB
YOU GOTTA GIVE HIM POINTS FOR EFFORT.
Drawn left-handed —N.W.
ZANZA...
THE EVIL MARK OF "AKU" ON YOUR BACK... YOU'RE NOT GOING TO TAKE IT OFF?
NO...
THE SEKIHŌ ARMY IS A PAST I WON'T FORGET.
I CAN'T TAKE THIS SYMBOL OFF.
LOOK, I'M NOT PERFECT... I'M 19. WHAT DID YOU *EXPECT?*
AND I *DID* LIKE WHAT YOU SAID YESTERDAY, BUT WORDS ARE CHEAP...
AND SO...

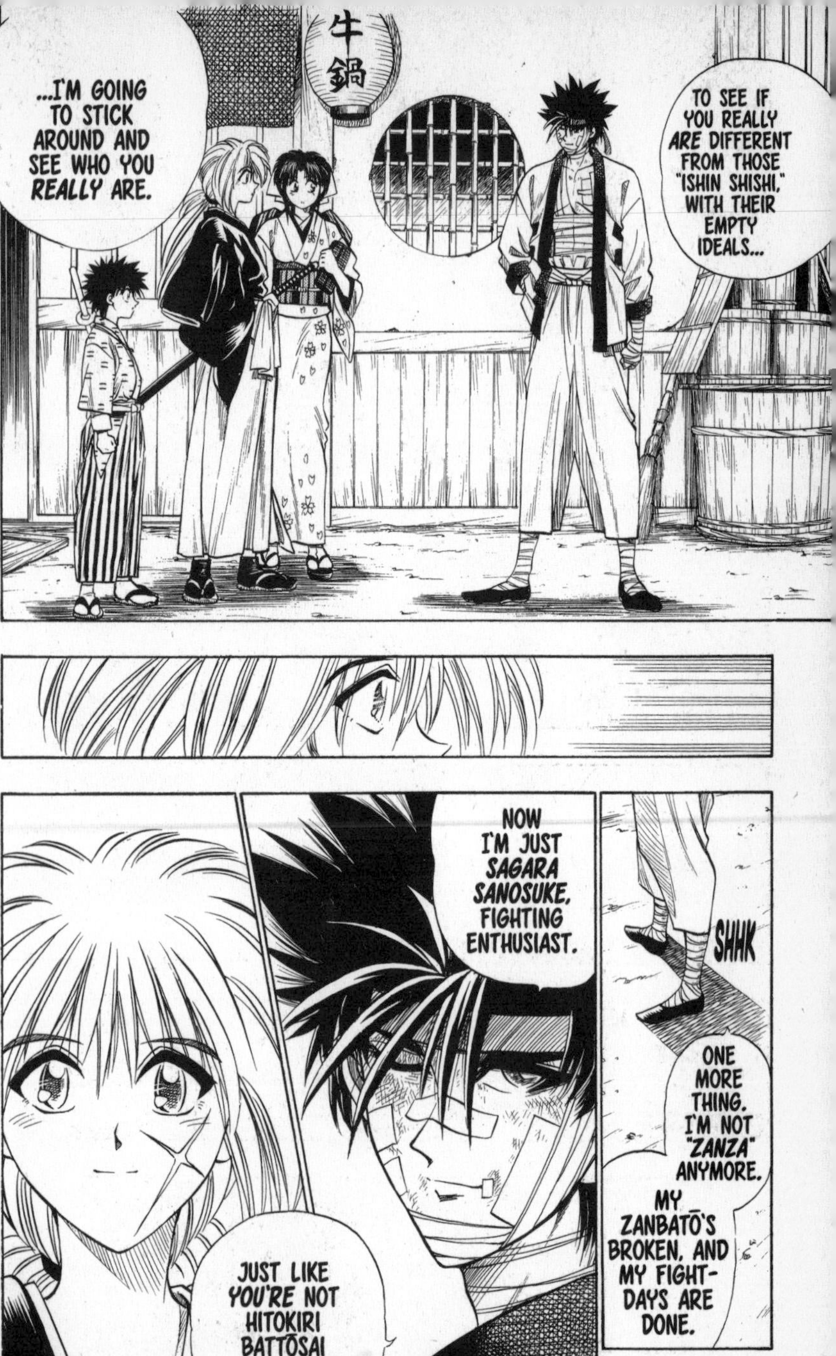
TO SEE IF YOU REALLY ARE DIFFERENT FROM THOSE "ISHIN SHISHI," WITH THEIR EMPTY IDEALS...
...I'M GOING TO STICK AROUND AND SEE WHO YOU REALLY ARE.
SHHK
ONE MORE THING. I'M NOT "ZANZA" ANYMORE.
MY ZANBATŌ'S BROKEN, AND MY FIGHT-DAYS ARE DONE.
NOW I'M JUST SAGARA SANOSUKE, FIGHTING ENTHUSIAST.
JUST LIKE YOU'RE NOT HITOKIRI BATTŌSAI ANYMORE.

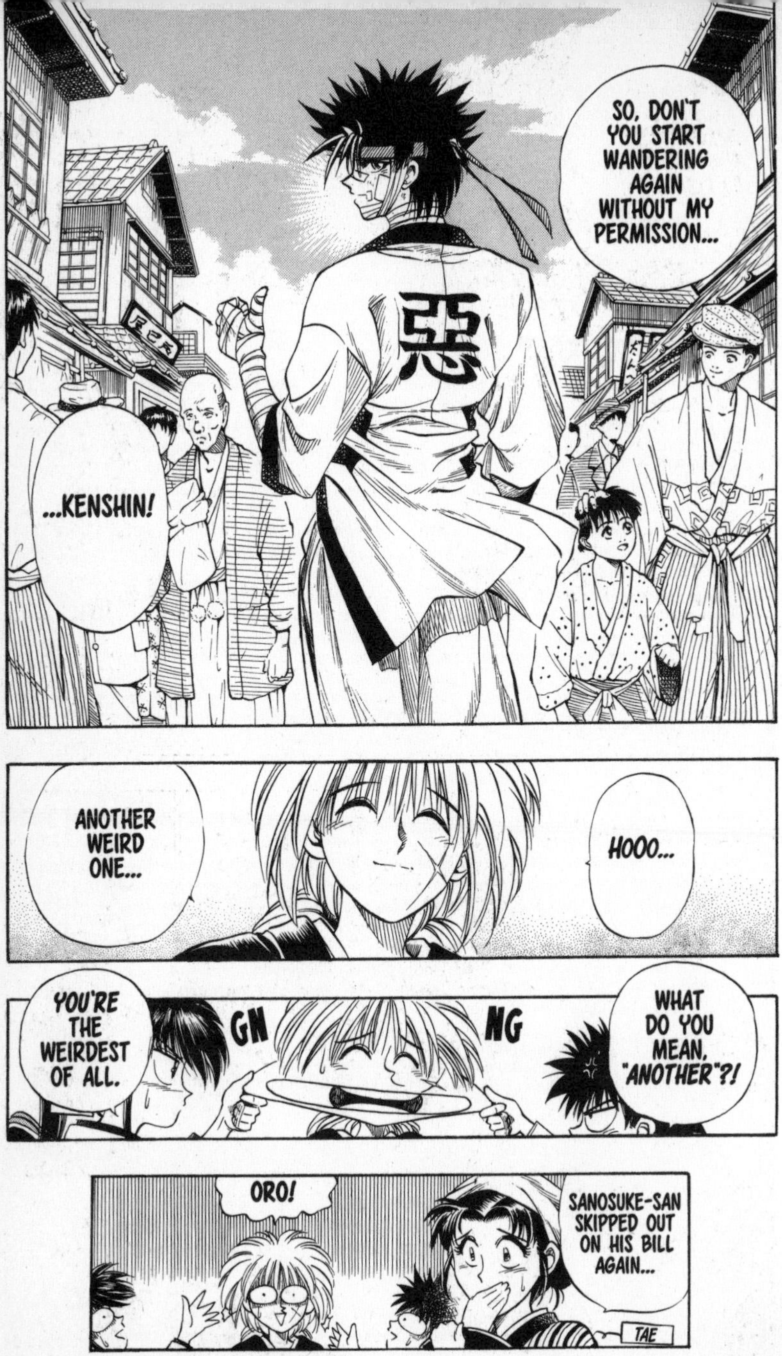
SO, DON'T YOU START WANDERING AGAIN WITHOUT MY PERMISSION...
...KENSHIN!
HOOO...
ANOTHER WEIRD ONE...
WHAT DO YOU MEAN, "ANOTHER"?!
GN NG
YOU'RE THE WEIRDEST OF ALL.
SANOSUKE-SAN SKIPPED OUT ON HIS BILL AGAIN...
TAE
ORO!

# The Secret Life of Characters (6)
## ── Sagara Sanosuke ──

If you're a Shinsengumi fan, you've probably figured
this one right away: Sanosuke's motif is Captain of the
Shinsengumi's 10th division, *Harada Sanosuke*.

Harada Sanosuke was among the top five best-looking guys in the
Shinsengumi...despite his depiction as "chubby" in (well-known
historical novelist) *Shiba Ryōtarō's "Moeyo Ken (Burn, O Sword)"*—
Watsuki's bible! A spear-wielder of great strength and forever fighting,
Harada Sanosuke was active in every decisive battle of the Shinsengumi.
Rough-mannered and short-tempered, he also had a softer side—due,
perhaps, to his humble beginnings. He was considerate of his comrades
and took special care with subordinates. Quick to pass judgment and
prone to seeing things in black and white, Harada Sanosuke can
probably be thought of as the kind of "big brother" character so
common in manga for young men. Accepted history states that he was
K.I.A. during the Ueno War, but legend has him crossing the continent
(to China) and becoming chief of his very own bandit army. To his
contemporaries, no doubt, he must have cut quite a dashing figure;
obviously, Watsuki liked him quite a bit as well, and wanted him for
*RuroKen*. Thus was born Sagara Sanosuke.

Sano's popularity has been climbing of late, and that's a good thing.
But as the *Rurouni Kenshin* character voted "Most Likely to Have
His First Name Mangled" (I see people writing the *kanji* for "Sanosuke"
with the *"Sa-"* wrong, the *"-no"* wrong, the *"-suke"* wrong...even, in
one case, writing it *"Sasuke"*?!), all I can say is, C'mon, people—he's not
a ninja! (Sad...so sad.)

*Visual Motif:* People are also always assuming he's based on such-and-
such a character from such-and-such a manga series (he's not, though
I'm a big fan of such-and-such series, myself). The model for Sano is
actually the main character "Lamp" from *"Mashin Bōken Tan
Lamp-Lamp (Arabian Genie Adventure Lamp-Lamp)"* by *Obata
Takeshi*, the *Hikaru No Go* artist. As for where *that* all started, that was
with me, doodling in sketchbooks during my days as an assistant, adding and
subtracting then eventually calling it Sano—with blessings from the original
artist, of course.

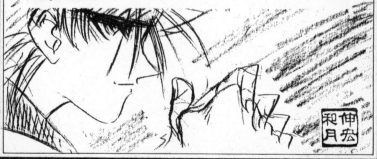

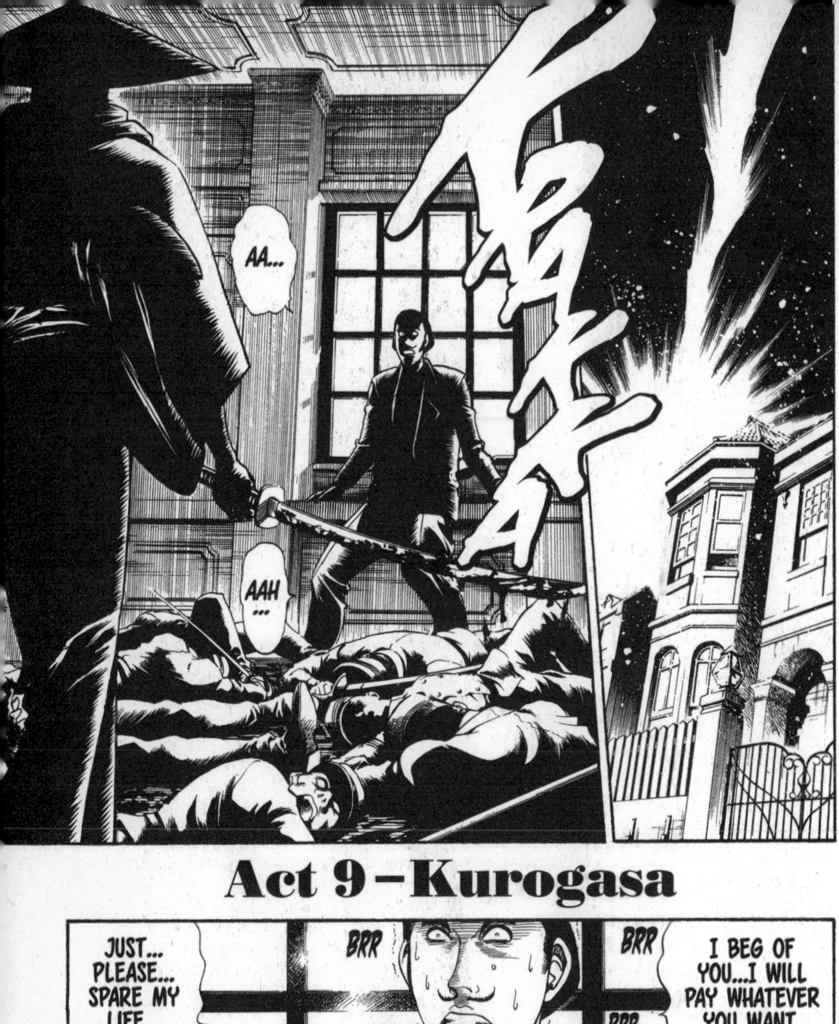
AA...
AAH ...

# Act 9 – Kurogasa

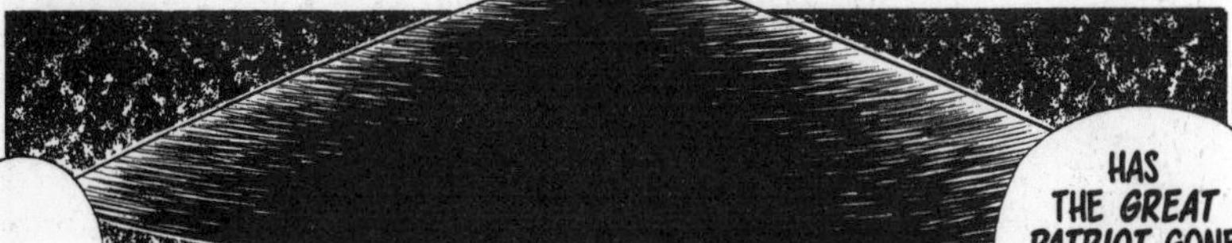
I BEG OF YOU...I WILL PAY WHATEVER YOU WANT.
BRR
BRR
BRR
BRR
JUST... PLEASE... SPARE MY LIFE...

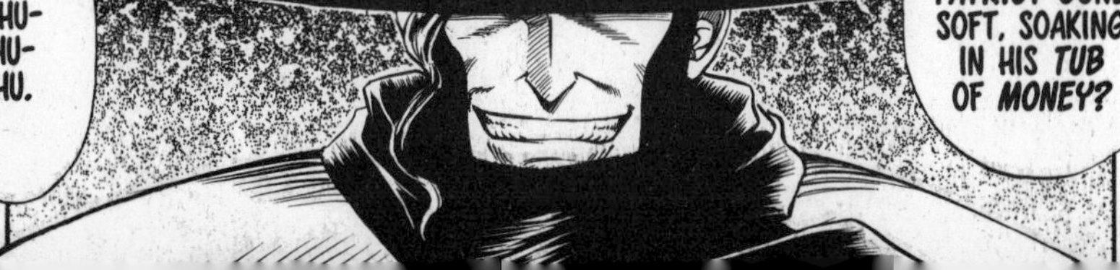
HAS THE GREAT PATRIOT GONE SOFT, SOAKING IN HIS TUB OF MONEY?
UHU-HU-HU.

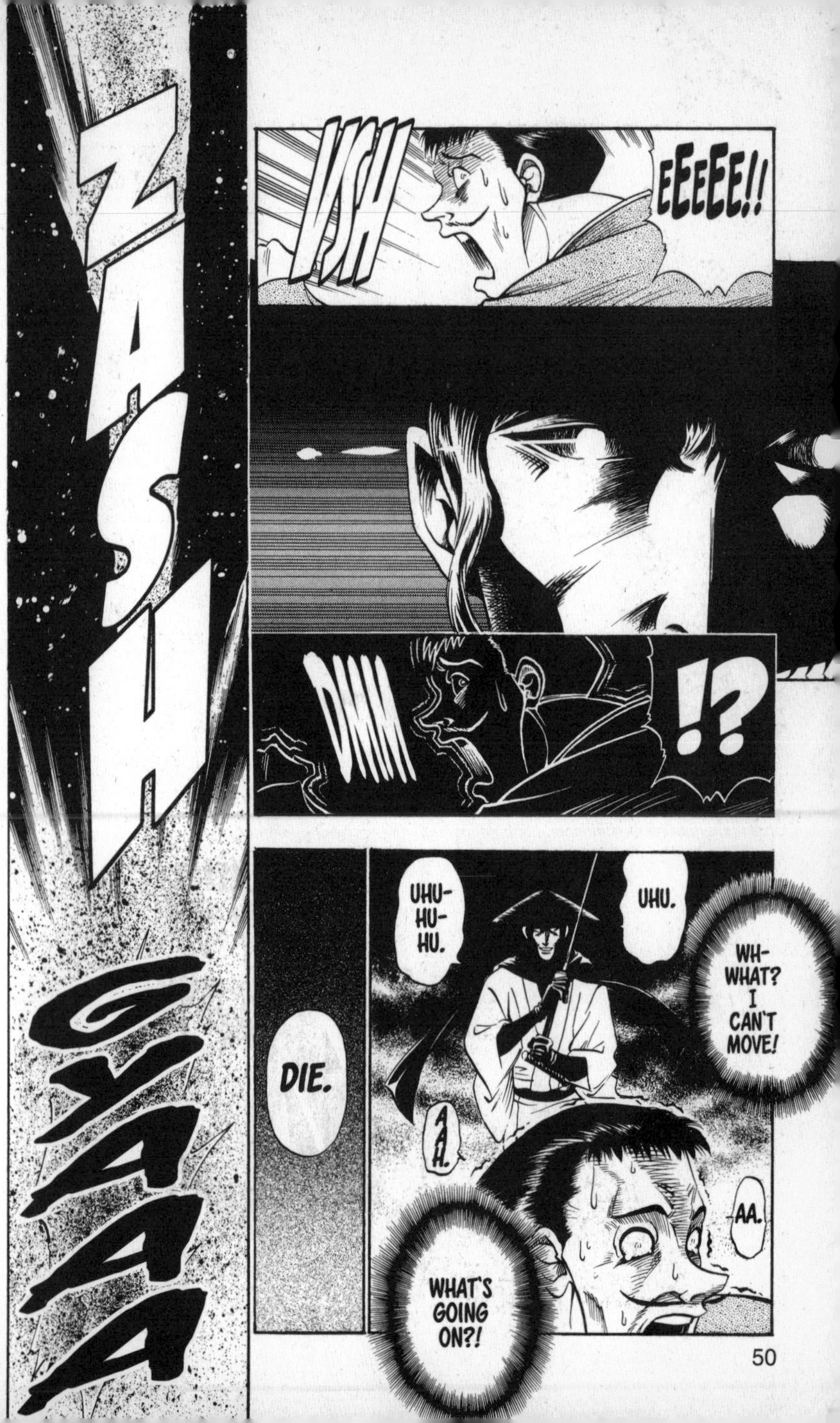
VISH
EEEEE!!
DNM
!?
WH-WHAT? I CAN'T MOVE!
UHU.
UHU-HU-HU.
AA.
AAH.
WHAT'S GOING ON?!
DIE.
ZASH
GYAAAA

READ THIS WAY

# Act 9 Kurogasa

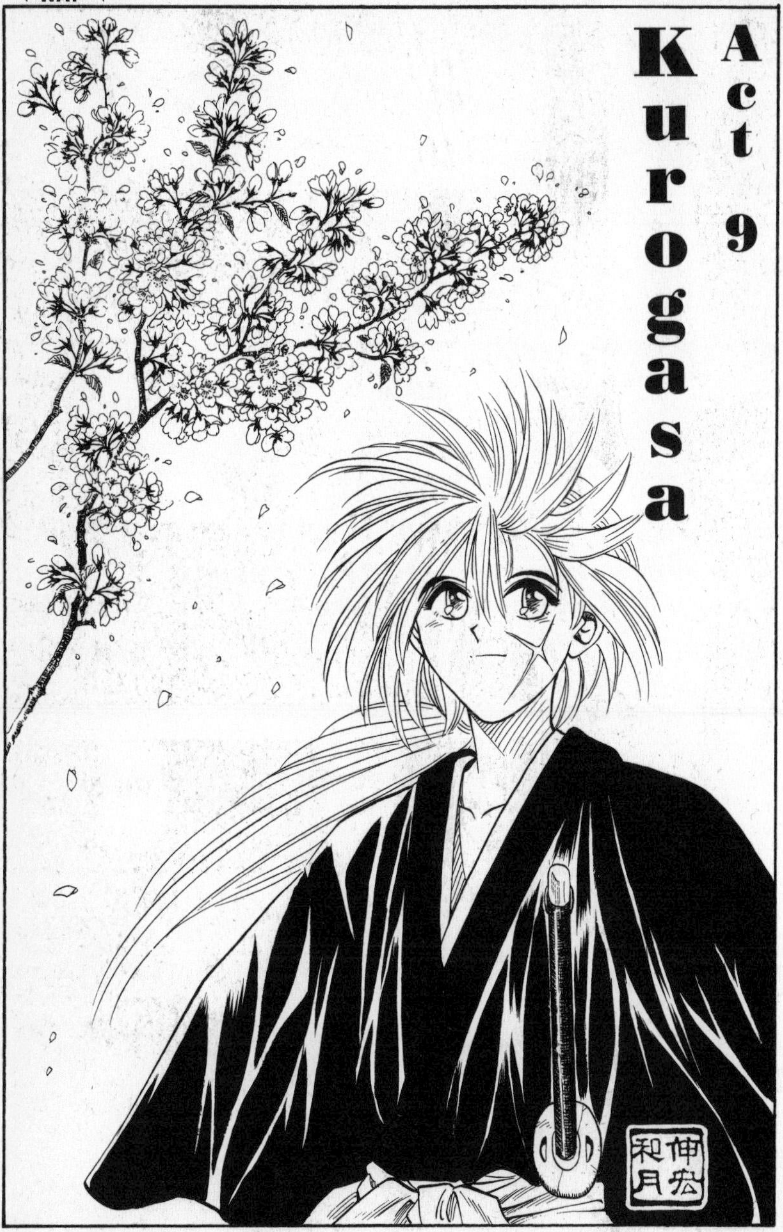
伸宏
和月

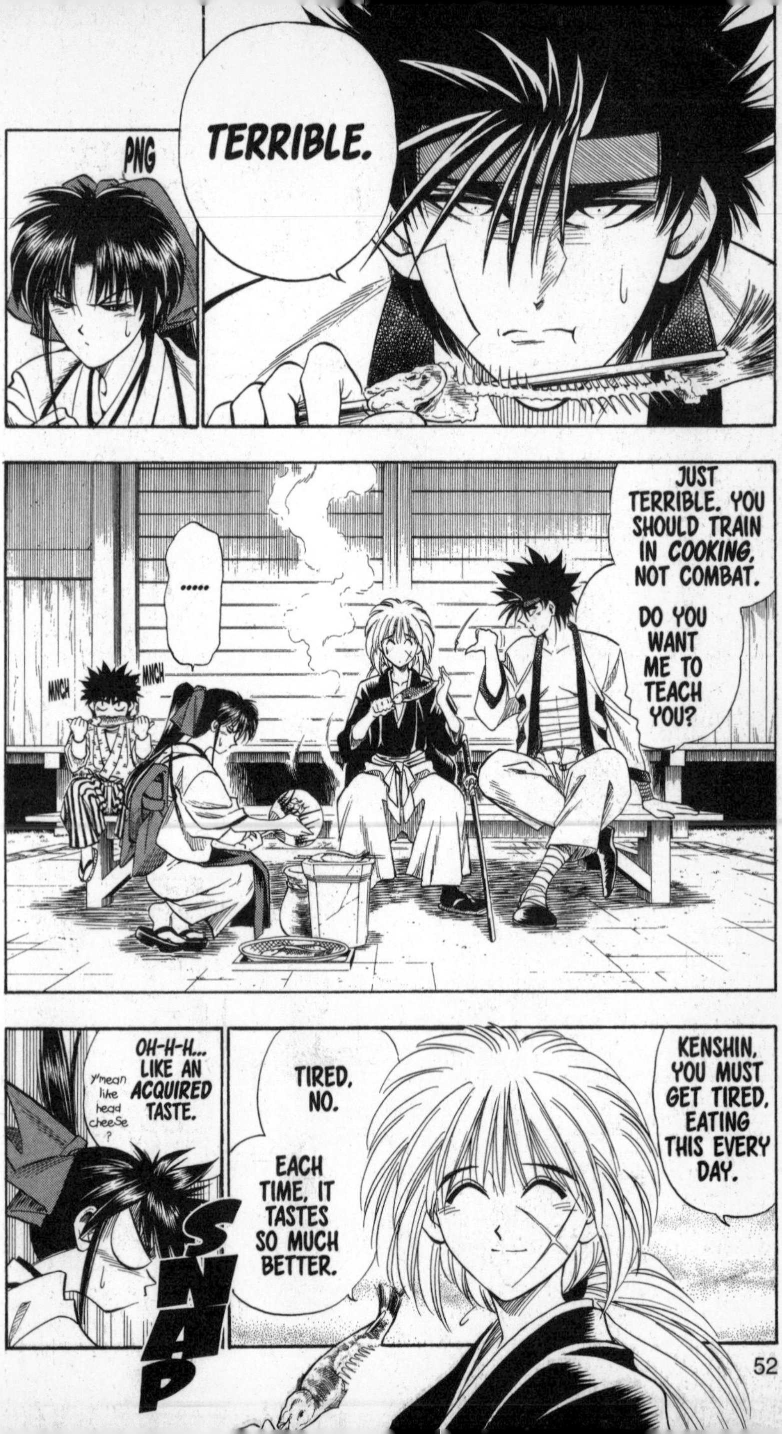
TERRIBLE.
PNG
JUST TERRIBLE. YOU SHOULD TRAIN IN *COOKING*, NOT COMBAT.
DO YOU WANT ME TO TEACH YOU?
......
MNCH
MNCH
KENSHIN, YOU MUST GET TIRED, EATING THIS EVERY DAY.
TIRED, NO.
EACH TIME, IT TASTES SO MUCH BETTER.
OH-H-H... LIKE AN ACQUIRED TASTE.
Y'mean like head cheese?
SNAP

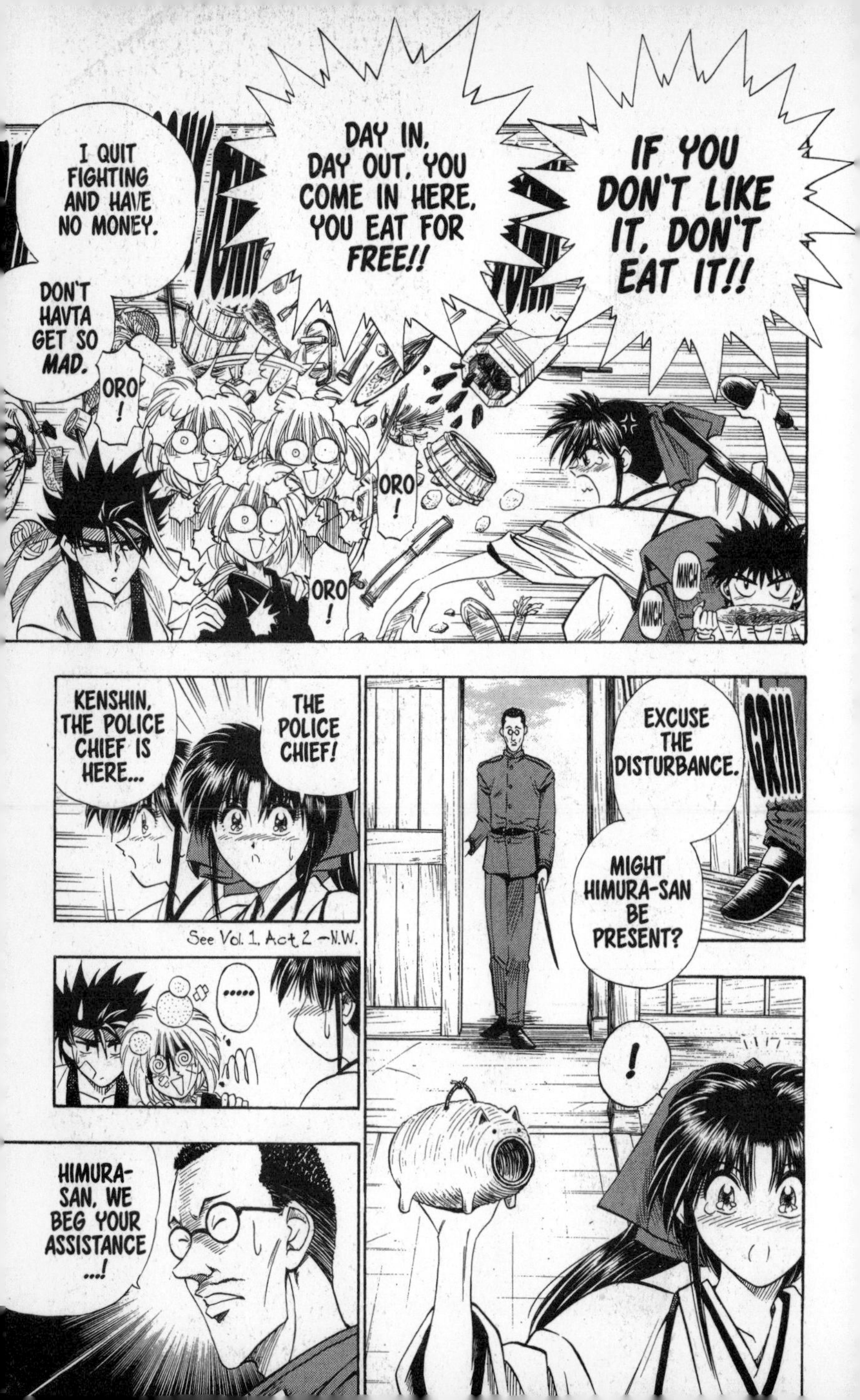
IF YOU DON'T LIKE IT, DON'T EAT IT!!
DAY IN, DAY OUT, YOU COME IN HERE, YOU EAT FOR FREE!!
I QUIT FIGHTING AND HAVE NO MONEY.
DON'T HAVTA GET SO MAD.
ORO!
ORO!
ORO!
MNCH
MNCH
GRIII
EXCUSE THE DISTURBANCE.
MIGHT HIMURA-SAN BE PRESENT?
THE POLICE CHIEF!
KENSHIN, THE POLICE CHIEF IS HERE...
See Vol. 1, Act 2 —N.W.
......
!
HIMURA-SAN, WE BEG YOUR ASSISTANCE ...!

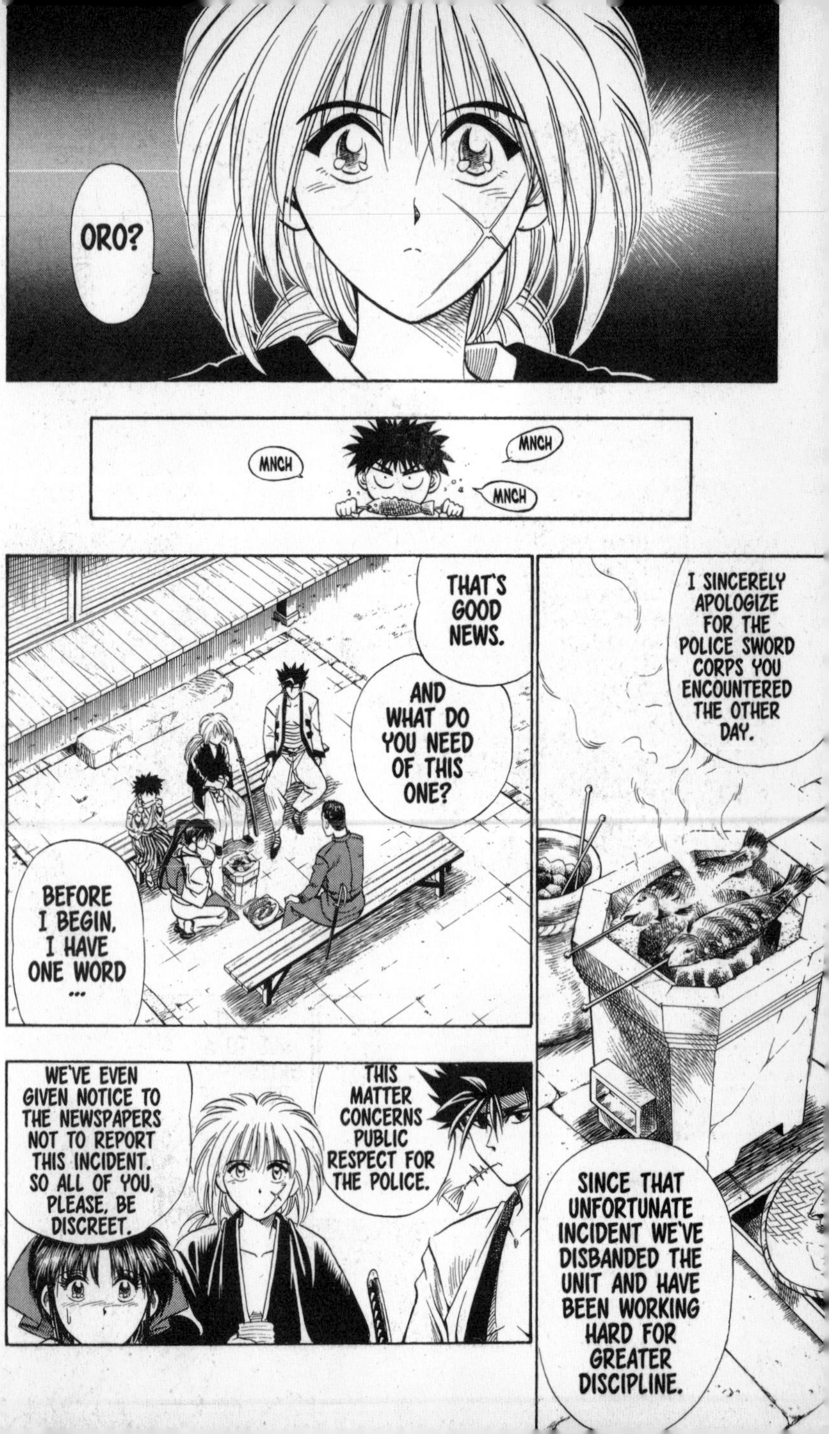

ORO?
MNCH
MNCH
MNCH
I SINCERELY APOLOGIZE FOR THE POLICE SWORD CORPS YOU ENCOUNTERED THE OTHER DAY.
SINCE THAT UNFORTUNATE INCIDENT WE'VE DISBANDED THE UNIT AND HAVE BEEN WORKING HARD FOR GREATER DISCIPLINE.
THAT'S GOOD NEWS.
AND WHAT DO YOU NEED OF THIS ONE?
BEFORE I BEGIN, I HAVE ONE WORD ...
THIS MATTER CONCERNS PUBLIC RESPECT FOR THE POLICE.
WE'VE EVEN GIVEN NOTICE TO THE NEWSPAPERS NOT TO REPORT THIS INCIDENT. SO ALL OF YOU, PLEASE, BE DISCREET.

READ THIS WAY

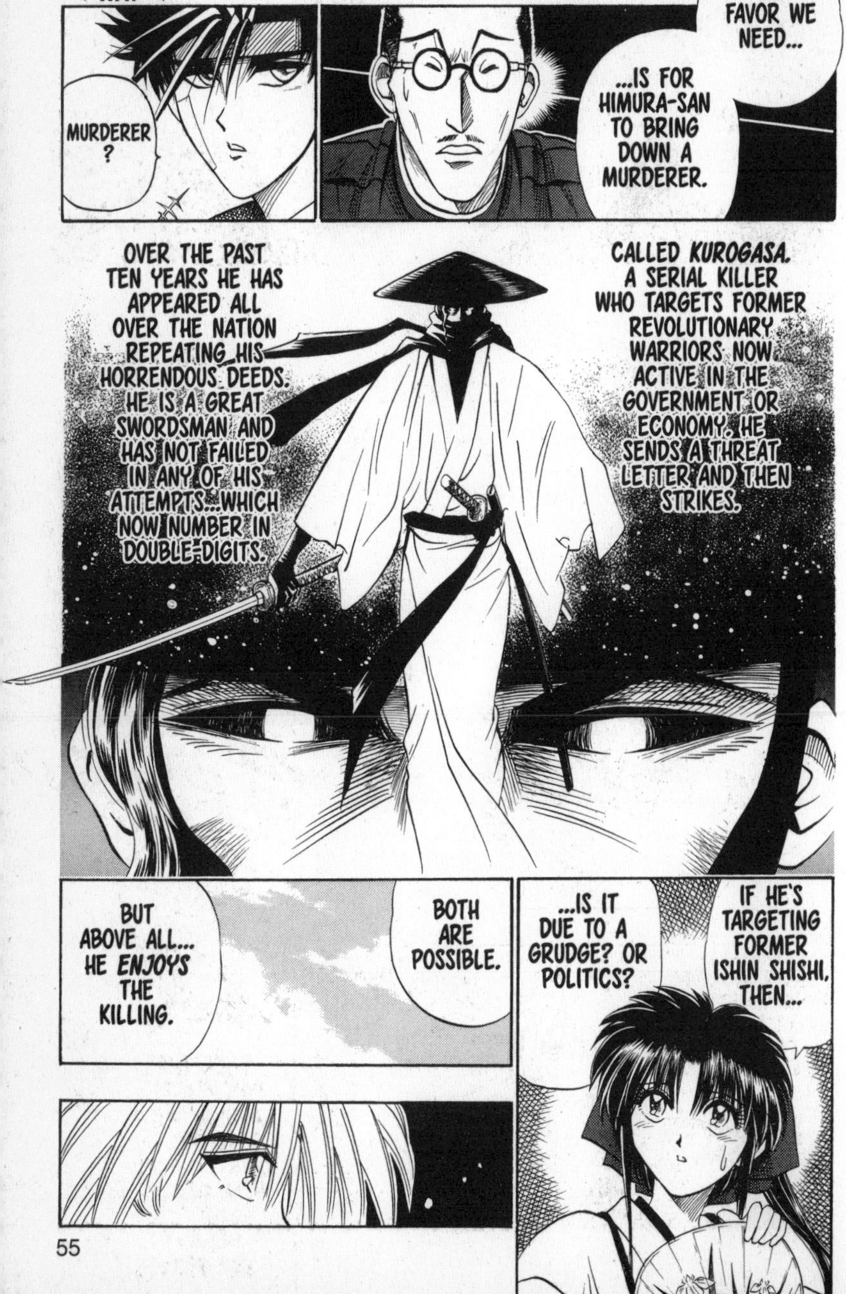

THE FAVOR WE NEED...
...IS FOR HIMURA-SAN TO BRING DOWN A MURDERER.
MURDERER?
CALLED *KUROGASA.* A SERIAL KILLER WHO TARGETS FORMER REVOLUTIONARY WARRIORS NOW ACTIVE IN THE GOVERNMENT OR ECONOMY. HE SENDS A THREAT LETTER AND THEN STRIKES.
OVER THE PAST TEN YEARS HE HAS APPEARED ALL OVER THE NATION REPEATING HIS HORRENDOUS DEEDS. HE IS A GREAT SWORDSMAN AND HAS NOT FAILED IN ANY OF HIS ATTEMPTS...WHICH NOW NUMBER IN DOUBLE-DIGITS.
IF HE'S TARGETING FORMER ISHIN SHISHI, THEN...
...IS IT DUE TO A GRUDGE? OR POLITICS?
BOTH ARE POSSIBLE.
BUT ABOVE ALL... HE *ENJOYS* THE KILLING.

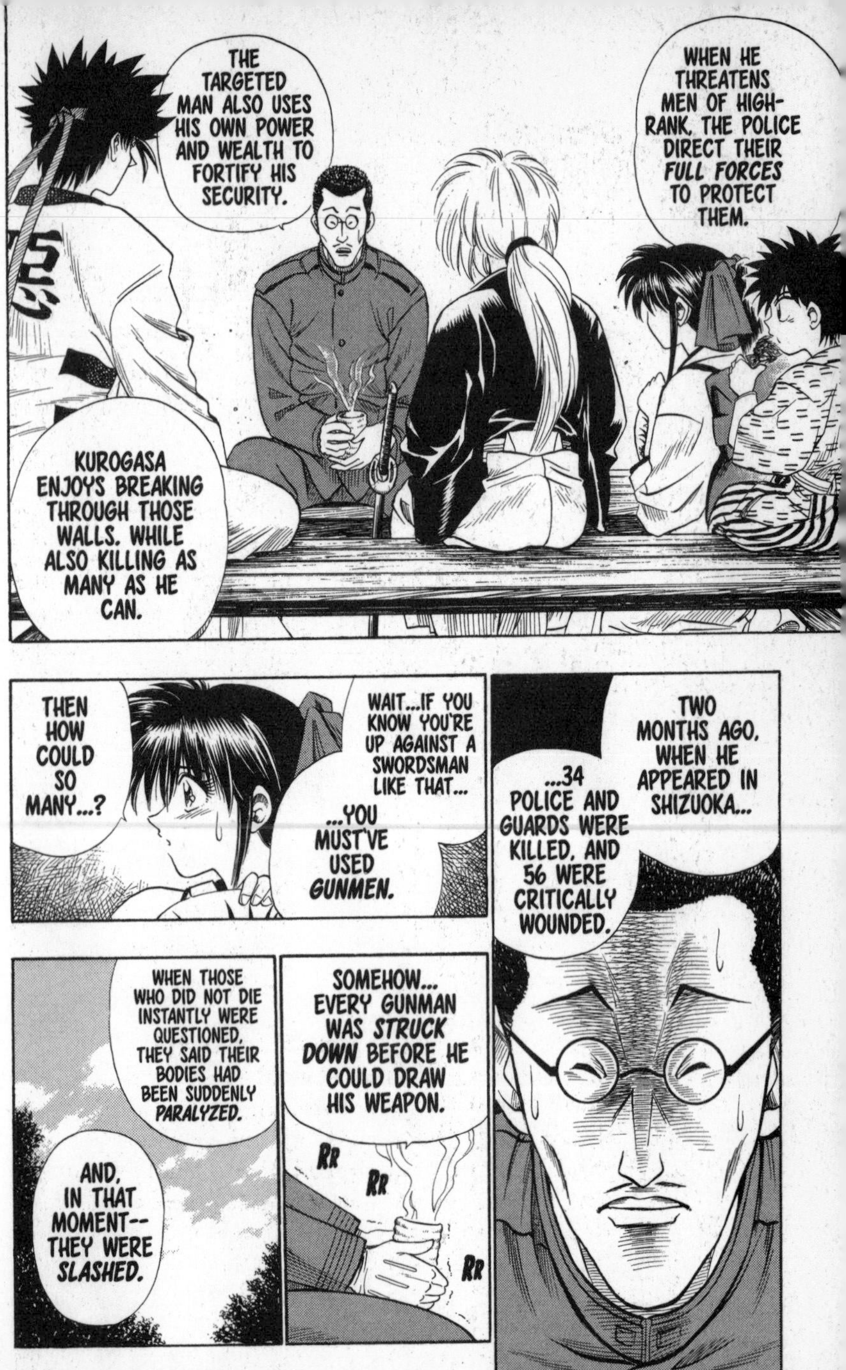
WHEN HE THREATENS MEN OF HIGH-RANK, THE POLICE DIRECT THEIR FULL FORCES TO PROTECT THEM.
THE TARGETED MAN ALSO USES HIS OWN POWER AND WEALTH TO FORTIFY HIS SECURITY.
KUROGASA ENJOYS BREAKING THROUGH THOSE WALLS. WHILE ALSO KILLING AS MANY AS HE CAN.
TWO MONTHS AGO, WHEN HE APPEARED IN SHIZUOKA...
...34 POLICE AND GUARDS WERE KILLED, AND 56 WERE CRITICALLY WOUNDED.
WAIT...IF YOU KNOW YOU'RE UP AGAINST A SWORDSMAN LIKE THAT...
...YOU MUST'VE USED GUNMEN.
THEN HOW COULD SO MANY...?
SOMEHOW... EVERY GUNMAN WAS STRUCK DOWN BEFORE HE COULD DRAW HIS WEAPON.
RR
RR
RR
WHEN THOSE WHO DID NOT DIE INSTANTLY WERE QUESTIONED, THEY SAID THEIR BODIES HAD BEEN SUDDENLY PARALYZED.
AND, IN THAT MOMENT-- THEY WERE SLASHED.

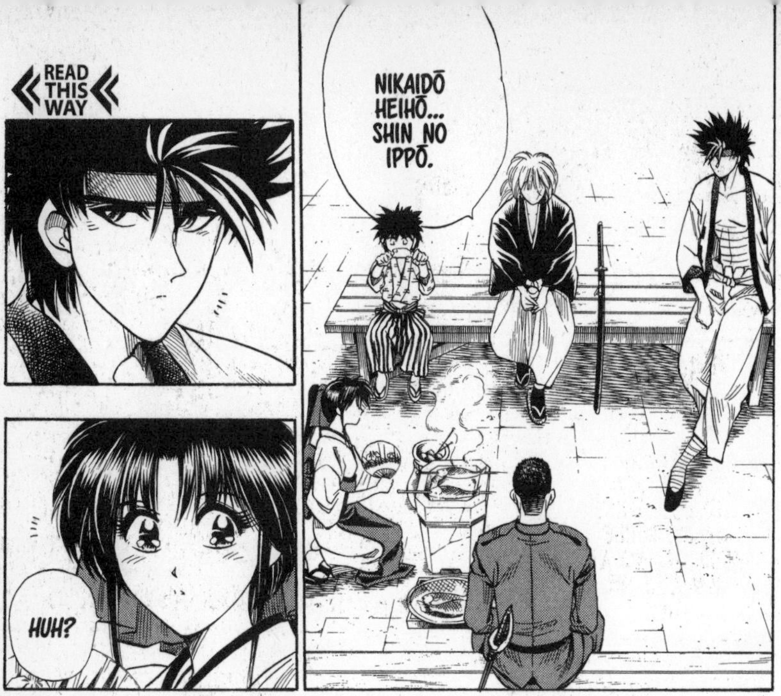
READ THIS WAY
NIKAIDŌ HEIHŌ... SHIN NO IPPŌ.
HUH?

The voice-actors of (the CD book) "Rurouni Kenshin":

| | |
|---|---|
| Himura Kenshin | Ogata Megumi |
| Kamiya Kaoru | Sakurai Tomo |
| Myōjin Yahiko | Takayama Minami |

Sanosuke's not in the group because the CD book is based on the first four manga chapters only. Sorry, Sanosuke fans! Even so, you should check it out. Really! Besides, with the start of the anime, you can check him out there. (You believe me, don't you?) Despite all my worries, then—and even though the casting was Watsuki-hands free! —I'm thinking it works.

伸宏和月

...to be continued

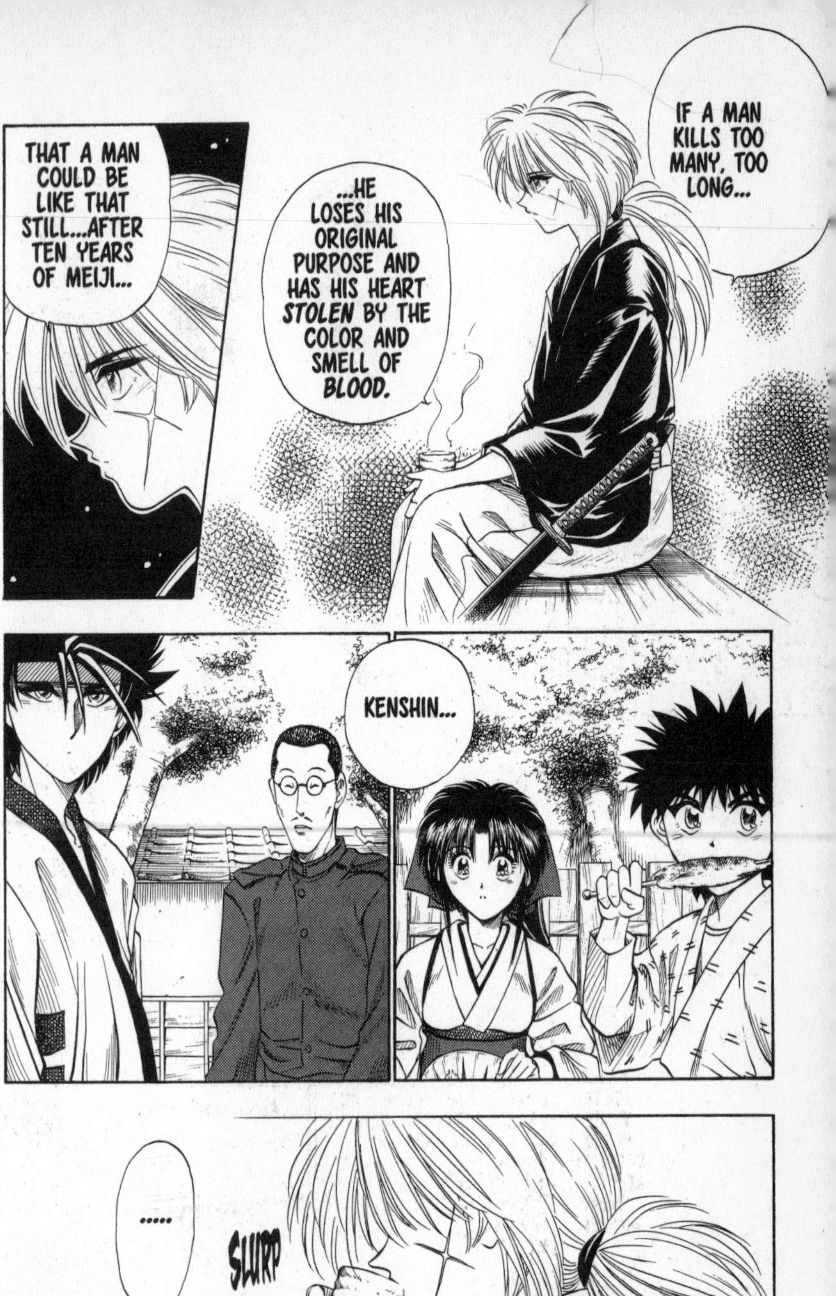
IF A MAN KILLS TOO MANY, TOO LONG...
...HE LOSES HIS ORIGINAL PURPOSE AND HAS HIS HEART STOLEN BY THE COLOR AND SMELL OF BLOOD.
THAT A MAN COULD BE LIKE THAT STILL...AFTER TEN YEARS OF MEIJI...
KENSHIN...
SLURP
......

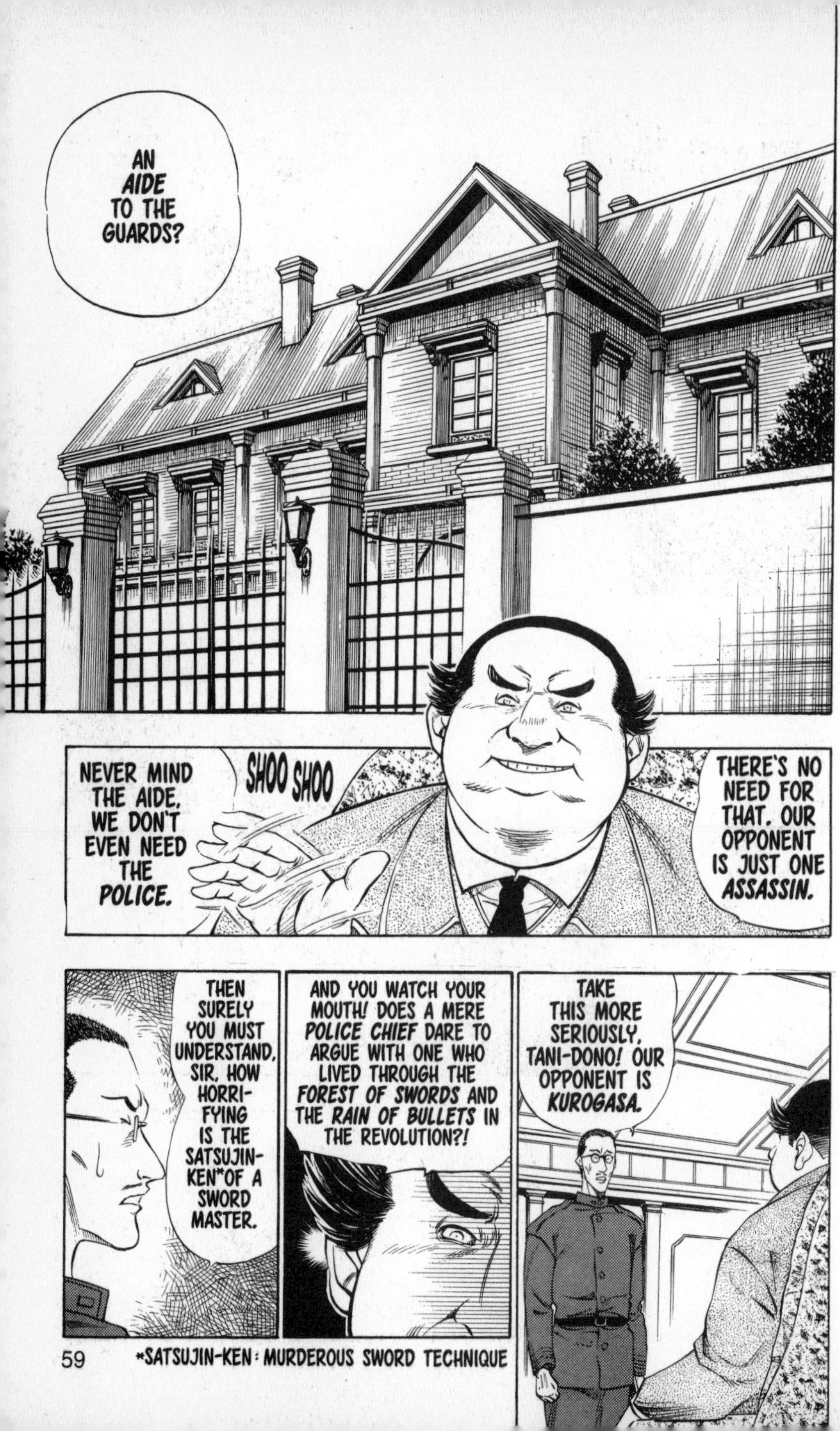
AN AIDE TO THE GUARDS?
THERE'S NO NEED FOR THAT. OUR OPPONENT IS JUST ONE ASSASSIN.
SHOO SHOO
NEVER MIND THE AIDE, WE DON'T EVEN NEED THE POLICE.
TAKE THIS MORE SERIOUSLY, TANI-DONO! OUR OPPONENT IS KUROGASA.
AND YOU WATCH YOUR MOUTH! DOES A MERE POLICE CHIEF DARE TO ARGUE WITH ONE WHO LIVED THROUGH THE FOREST OF SWORDS AND THE RAIN OF BULLETS IN THE REVOLUTION?!
THEN SURELY YOU MUST UNDERSTAND, SIR, HOW HORRI-FYING IS THE SATSUJIN-KEN* OF A SWORD MASTER.

*SATSUJIN-KEN: MURDEROUS SWORD TECHNIQUE

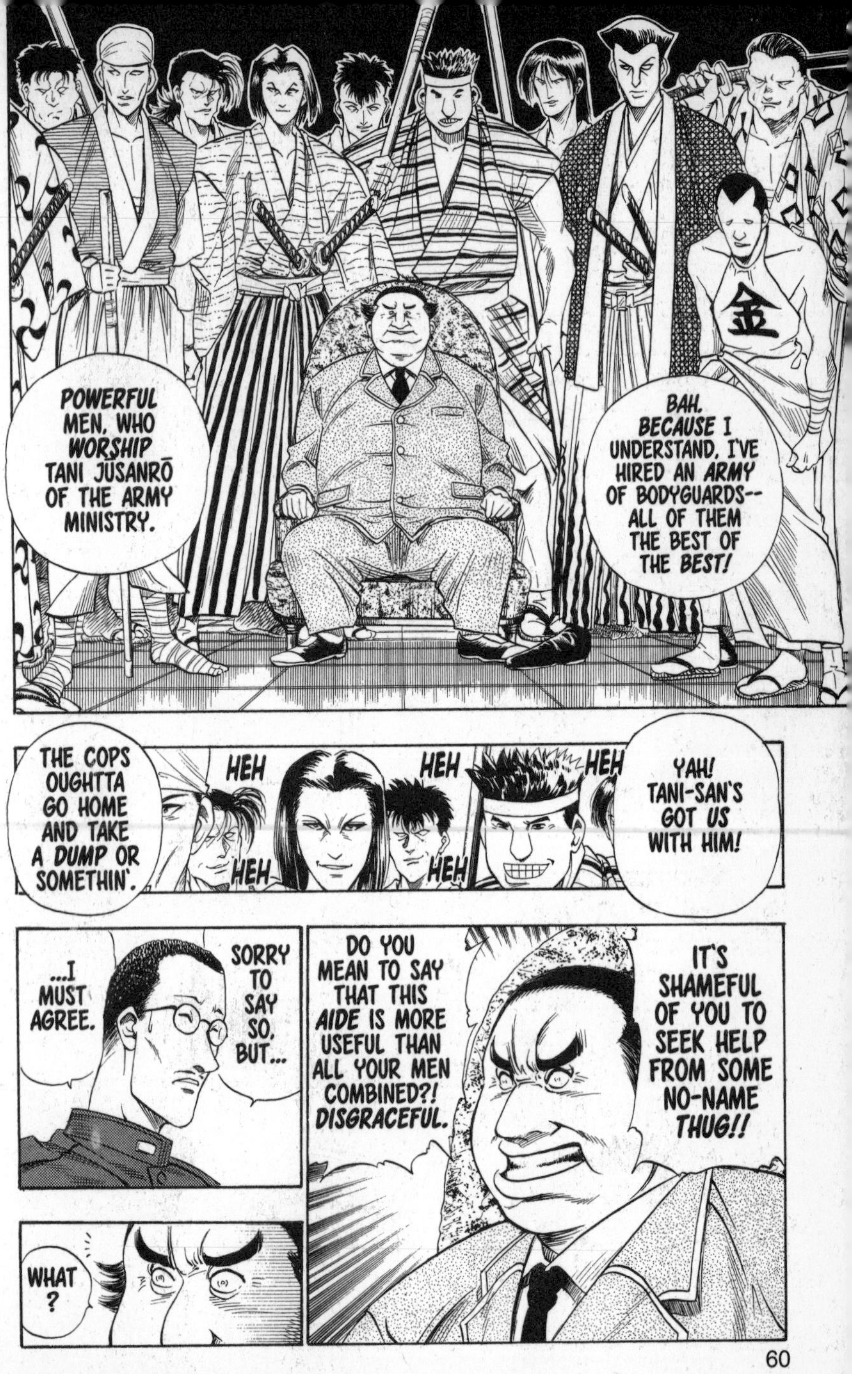
BAH. BECAUSE I UNDERSTAND, I'VE HIRED AN ARMY OF BODYGUARDS-- ALL OF THEM THE BEST OF THE BEST!
金
POWERFUL MEN, WHO WORSHIP TANI JŪSANRŌ OF THE ARMY MINISTRY.
YAH! TANI-SAN'S GOT US WITH HIM!
HEH
HEH
HEH
HEH
HEH
THE COPS OUGHTTA GO HOME AND TAKE A DUMP OR SOMETHIN'.
IT'S SHAMEFUL OF YOU TO SEEK HELP FROM SOME NO-NAME THUG!!
DO YOU MEAN TO SAY THAT THIS AIDE IS MORE USEFUL THAN ALL YOUR MEN COMBINED?! DISGRACEFUL.
SORRY TO SAY SO, BUT...
...I MUST AGREE.
WHAT?

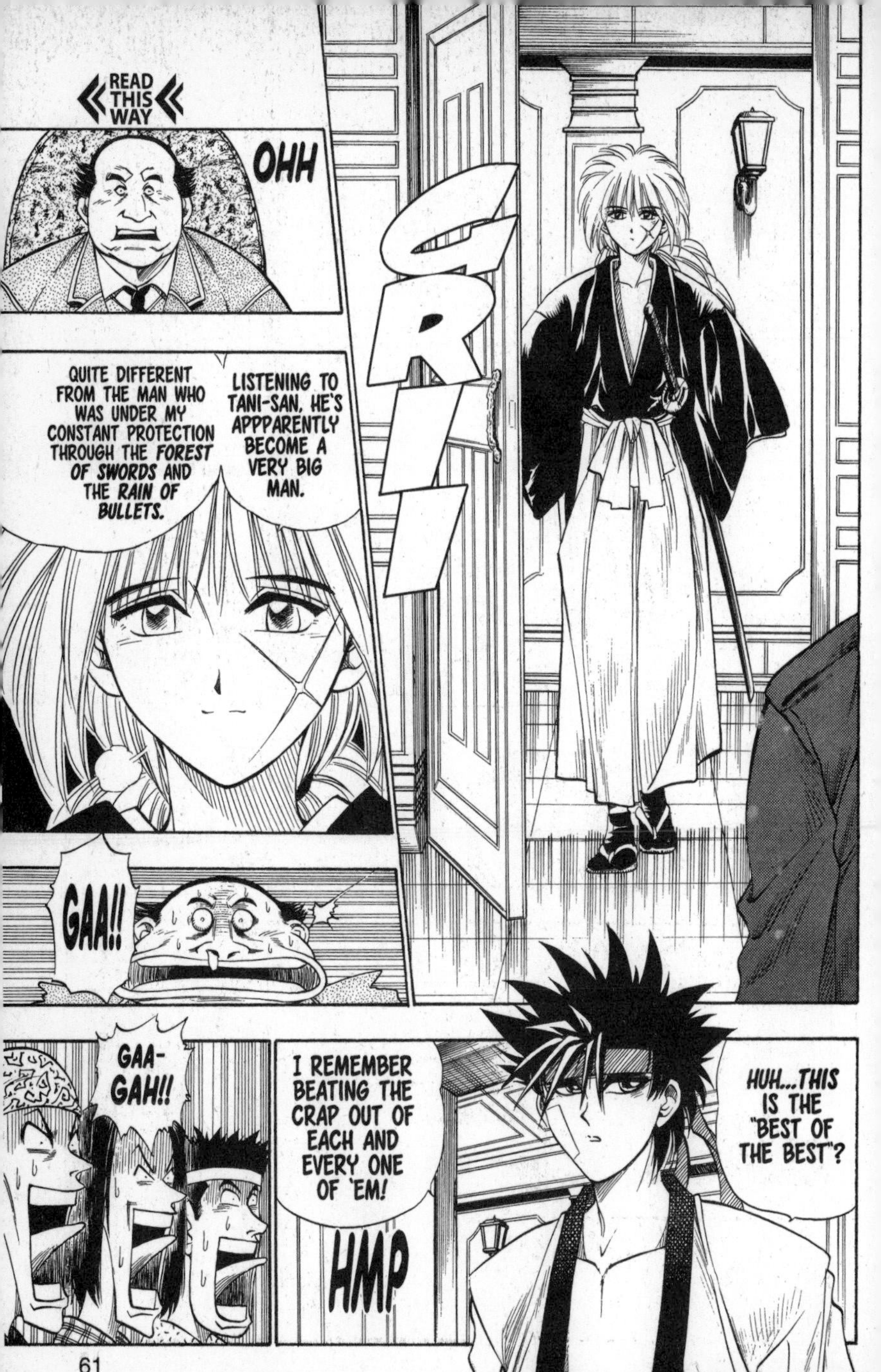
READ THIS WAY
CRII
OHH
LISTENING TO TANI-SAN, HE'S APPPARENTLY BECOME A VERY BIG MAN.
QUITE DIFFERENT FROM THE MAN WHO WAS UNDER MY CONSTANT PROTECTION THROUGH THE *FOREST OF SWORDS* AND THE *RAIN OF BULLETS*.
GAA!!
HUH...THIS IS THE "BEST OF THE BEST"?
I REMEMBER BEATING THE CRAP OUT OF EACH AND EVERY ONE OF 'EM!
HMP
GAA-GAH!!

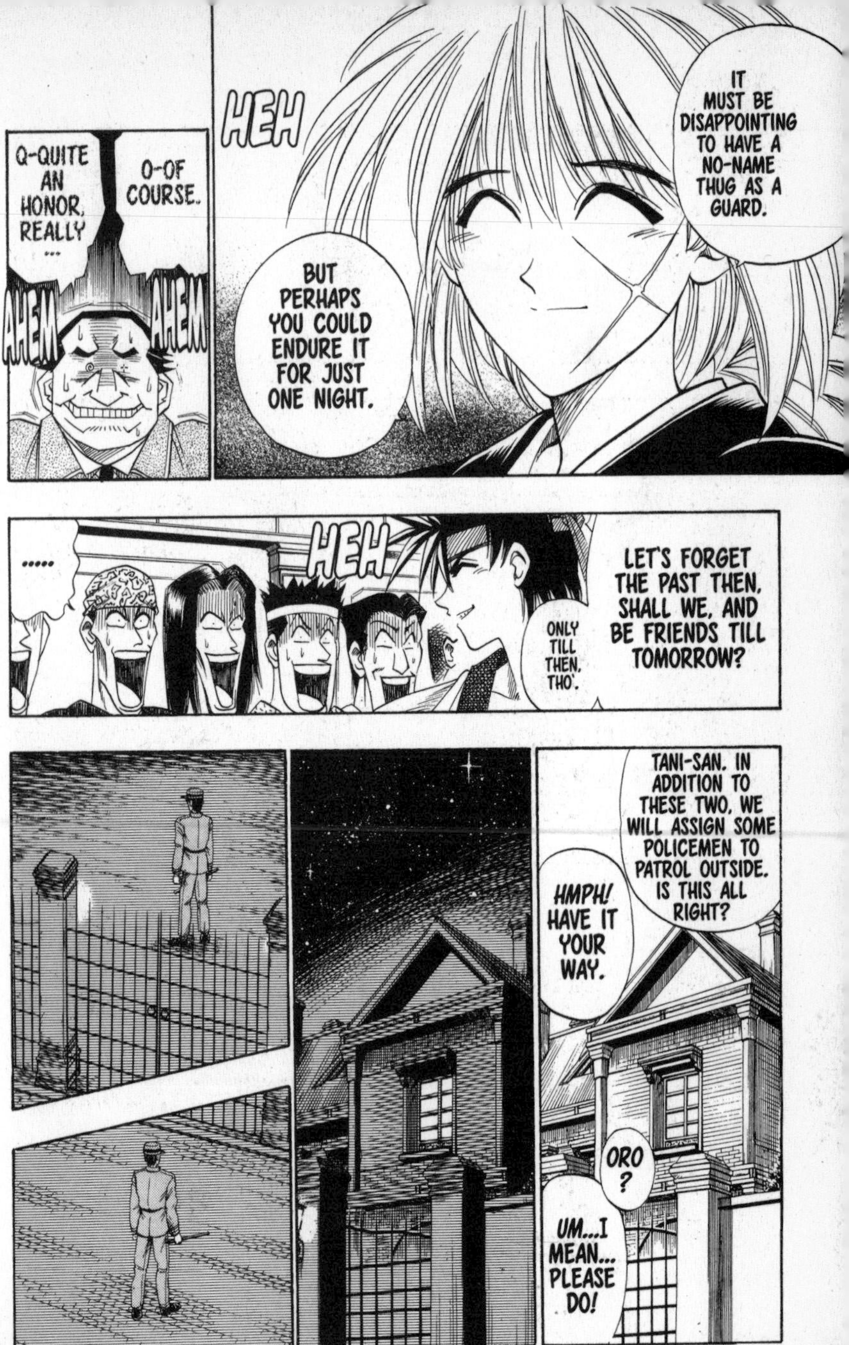
IT MUST BE DISAPPOINTING TO HAVE A NO-NAME THUG AS A GUARD.
HEH
BUT PERHAPS YOU COULD ENDURE IT FOR JUST ONE NIGHT.
O-OF COURSE..
Q-QUITE AN HONOR, REALLY ...
AHEM
AHEM
LET'S FORGET THE PAST THEN, SHALL WE, AND BE FRIENDS TILL TOMORROW?
ONLY TILL THEN, THO'.
HEH
......
TANI-SAN. IN ADDITION TO THESE TWO, WE WILL ASSIGN SOME POLICEMEN TO PATROL OUTSIDE. IS THIS ALL RIGHT?
HMPH! HAVE IT YOUR WAY.
ORO?
UM...I MEAN... PLEASE DO!

READ THIS WAY

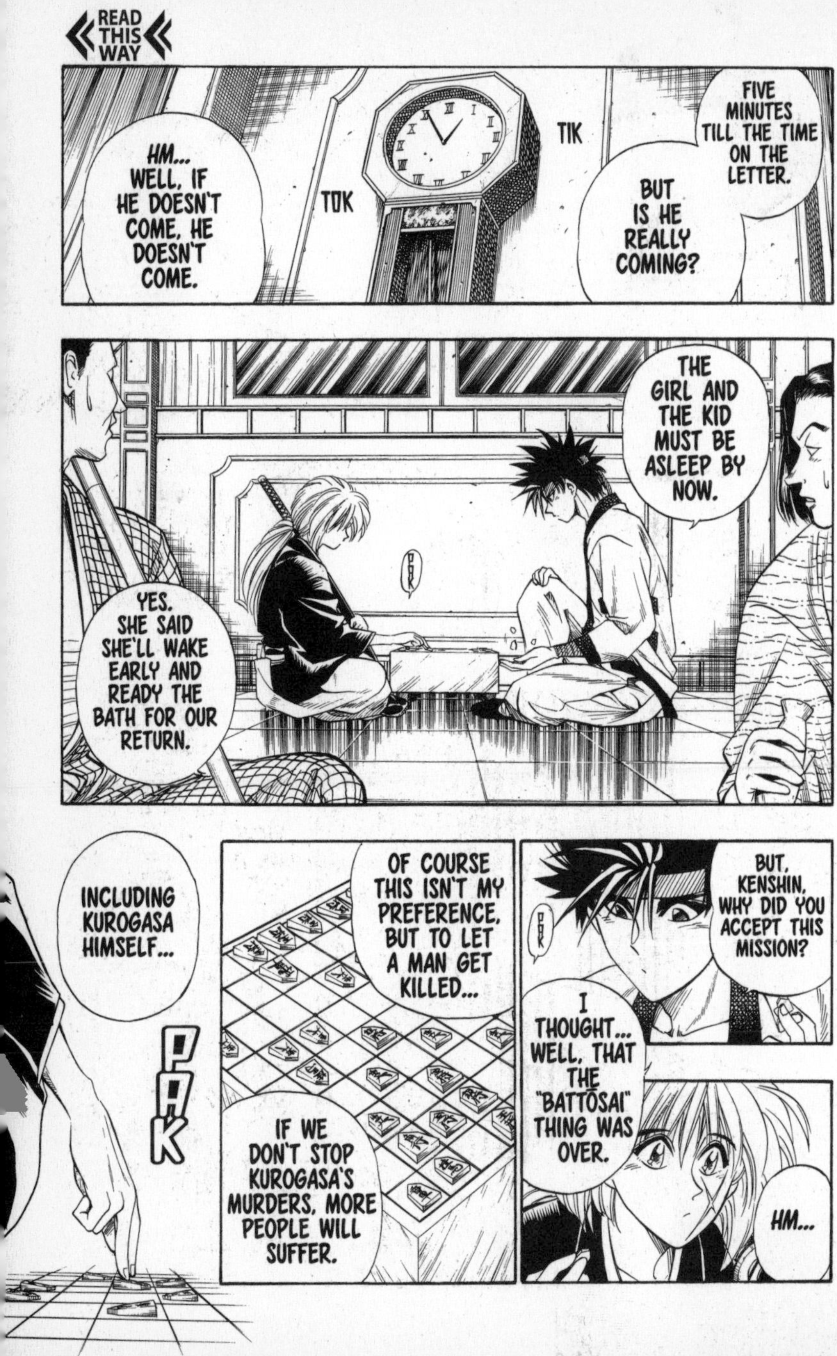
FIVE MINUTES TILL THE TIME ON THE LETTER.
BUT IS HE REALLY COMING?
TIK
TOK
HM... WELL, IF HE DOESN'T COME, HE DOESN'T COME.
THE GIRL AND THE KID MUST BE ASLEEP BY NOW.
YES. SHE SAID SHE'LL WAKE EARLY AND READY THE BATH FOR OUR RETURN.
BUT, KENSHIN, WHY DID YOU ACCEPT THIS MISSION?
I THOUGHT... WELL, THAT THE "BATTŌSAI" THING WAS OVER.
HM...
OF COURSE THIS ISN'T MY PREFERENCE, BUT TO LET A MAN GET KILLED...
IF WE DON'T STOP KUROGASA'S MURDERS, MORE PEOPLE WILL SUFFER.
INCLUDING KUROGASA HIMSELF...
PAK

READ THIS WAY

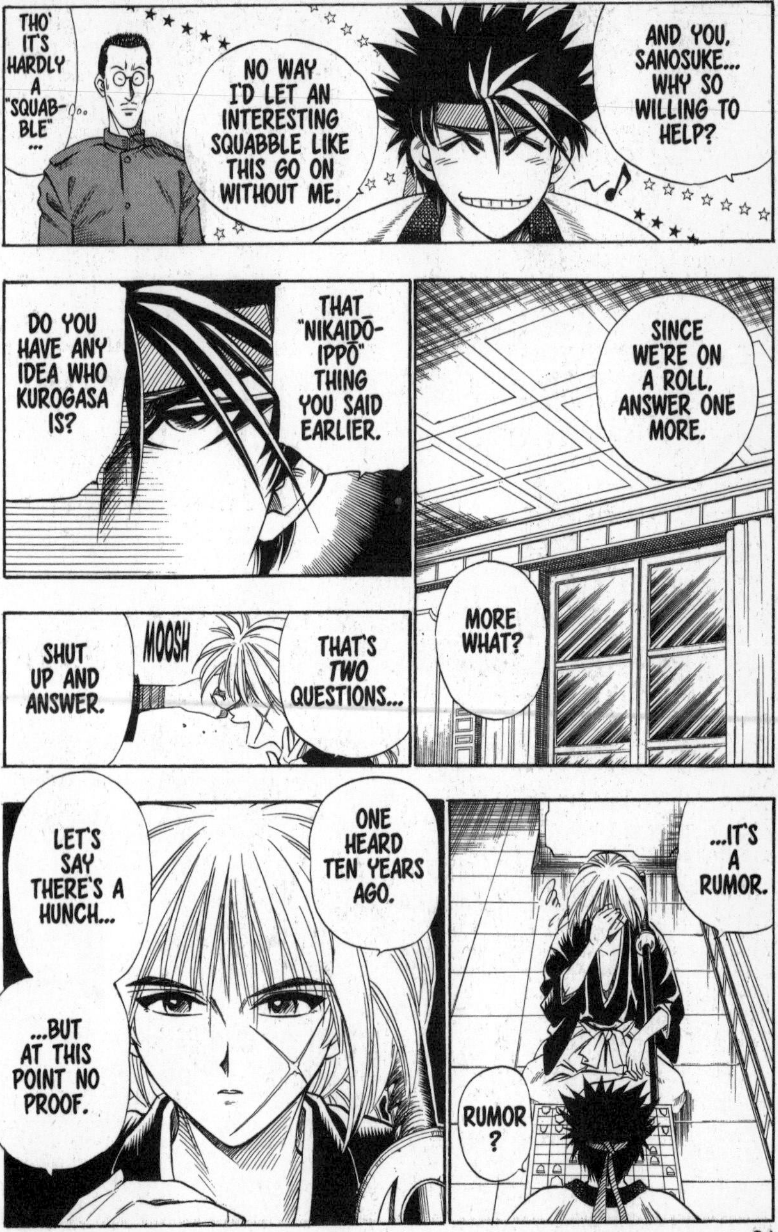
AND YOU, SANOSUKE... WHY SO WILLING TO HELP?
NO WAY I'D LET AN INTERESTING SQUABBLE LIKE THIS GO ON WITHOUT ME.
THO' IT'S HARDLY A "SQUAB-BLE" ...
SINCE WE'RE ON A ROLL, ANSWER ONE MORE.
MORE WHAT?
THAT "NIKAIDŌ-IPPŌ" THING YOU SAID EARLIER.
DO YOU HAVE ANY IDEA WHO KUROGASA IS?
THAT'S *TWO* QUESTIONS...
MOOSH
SHUT UP AND ANSWER.
...IT'S A RUMOR.
RUMOR?
ONE HEARD TEN YEARS AGO.
LET'S SAY THERE'S A HUNCH...
...BUT AT THIS POINT NO PROOF.

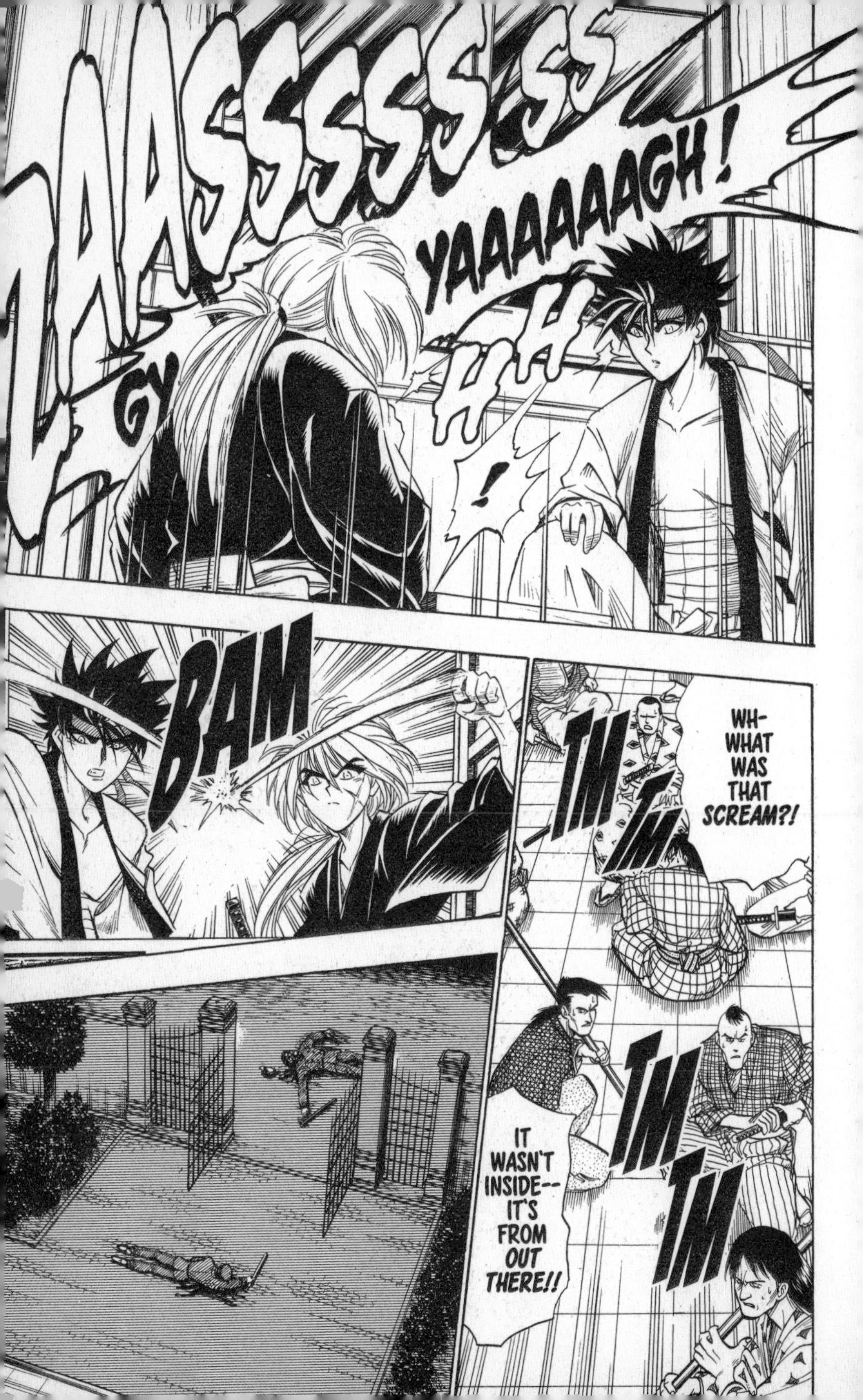
YAAAAAAGH!
WH-WHAT WAS THAT SCREAM?!
TM TM TM
IT WASN'T INSIDE-- IT'S FROM OUT THERE!!
TM TM TM
BAM

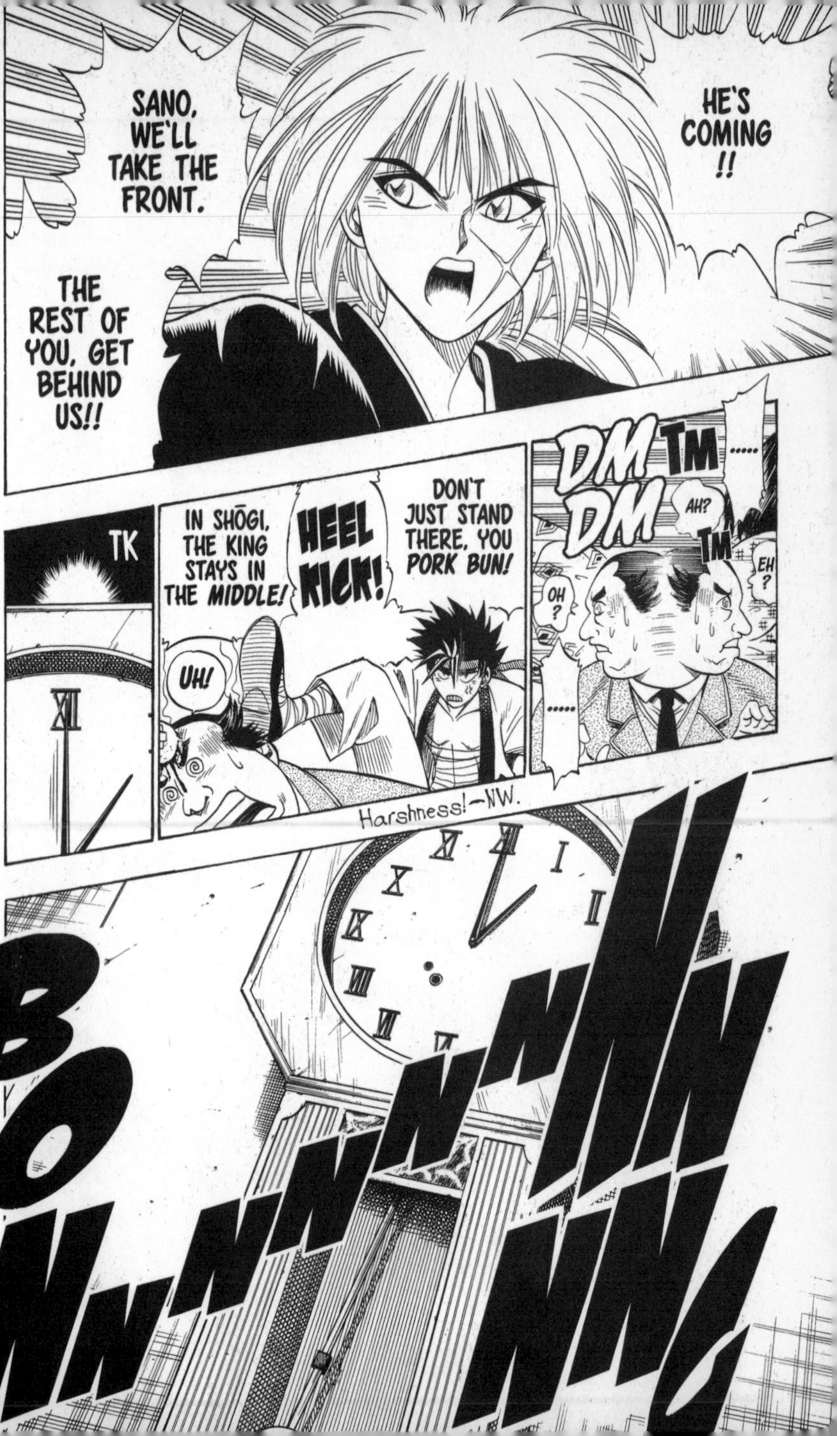
HE'S COMING!!
SANO, WE'LL TAKE THE FRONT.
THE REST OF YOU, GET BEHIND US!!
DM DM
TM .....
AH?
TM
EH?
OH?
.....
DON'T JUST STAND THERE, YOU PORK BUN!
HEEL KICK!
IN SHŌGI, THE KING STAYS IN THE MIDDLE!
UH!
Harshness!—NW.
TK
BONNNNNNNNNN!

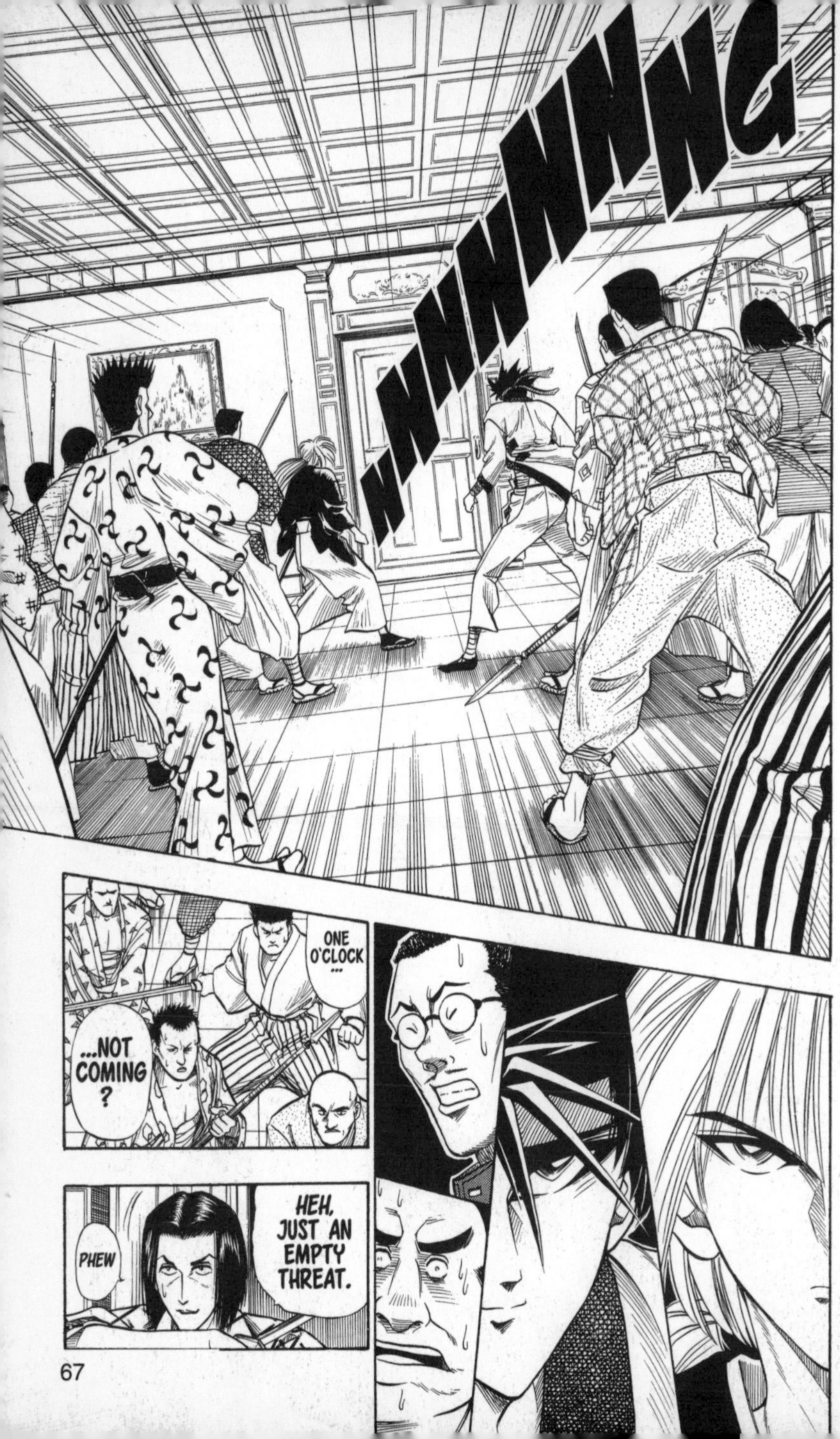
NNNNNNNG
ONE O'CLOCK...
...NOT COMING?
HEH, JUST AN EMPTY THREAT.
PHEW

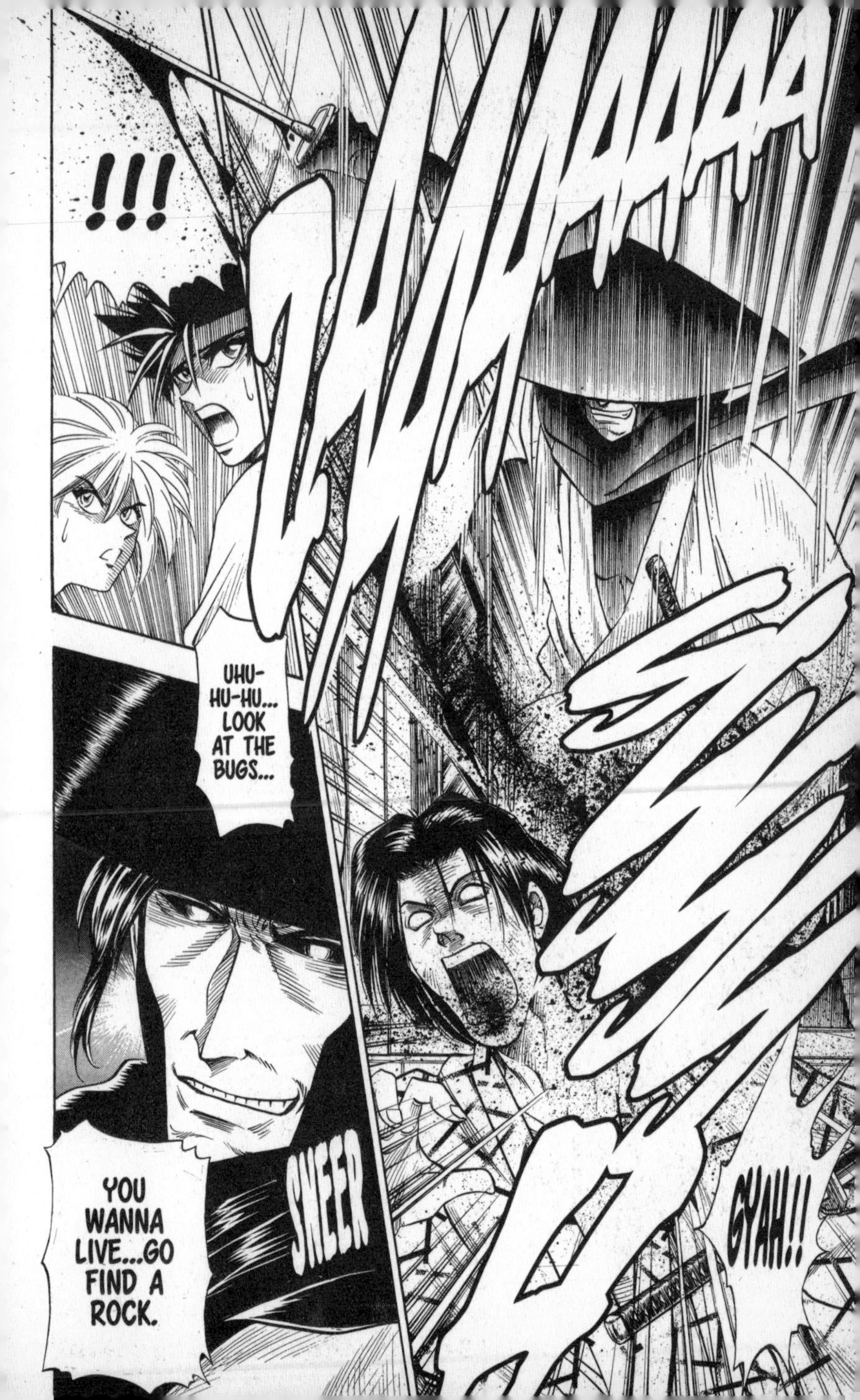
!!!
GYAH!!
UHU-HU-HU... LOOK AT THE BUGS...
SNEER
YOU WANNA LIVE...GO FIND A ROCK.

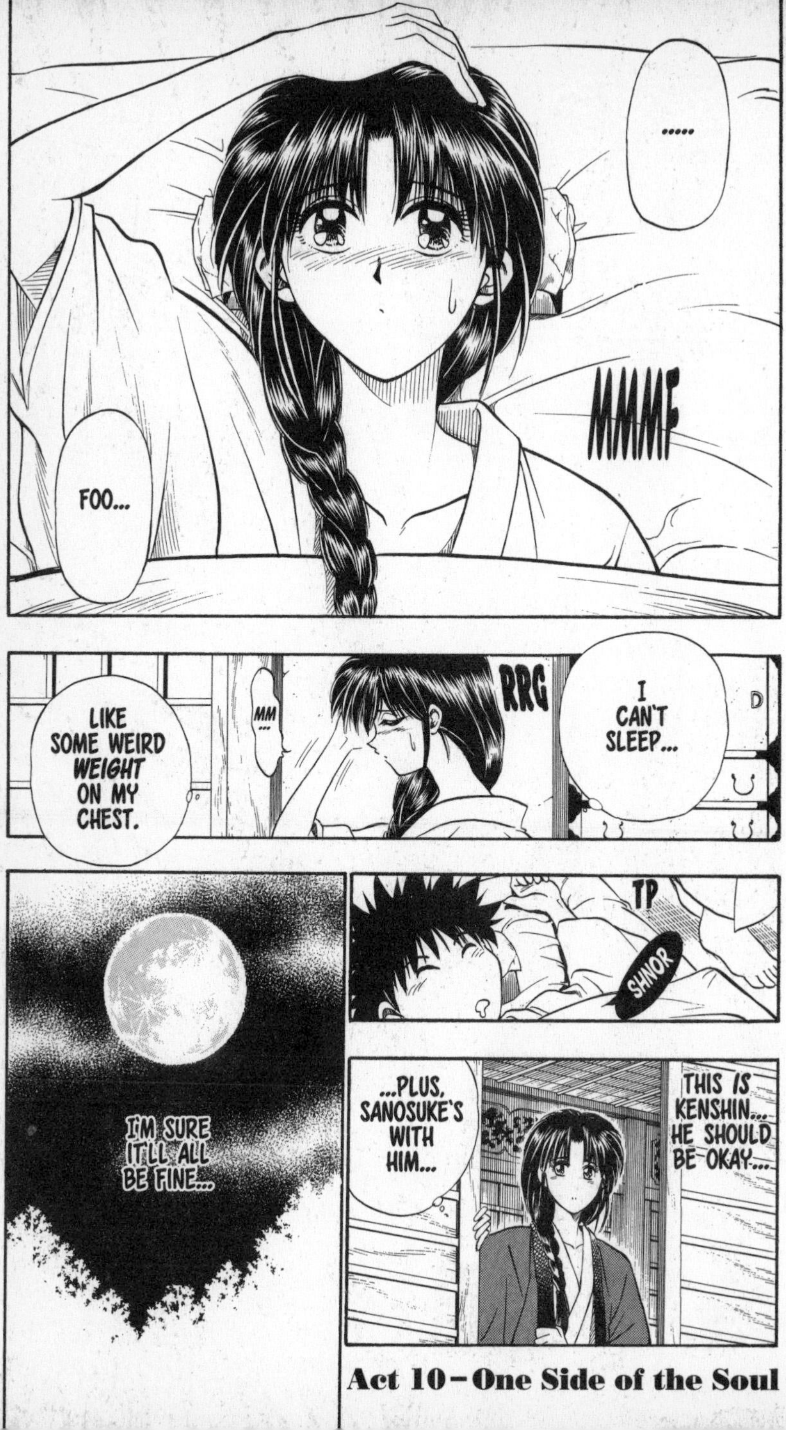
......
MMMF
FOO...
I CAN'T SLEEP...
RRG
MM...
LIKE SOME WEIRD WEIGHT ON MY CHEST.
TP
SHNOR
THIS IS KENSHIN... HE SHOULD BE OKAY...
...PLUS, SANOSUKE'S WITH HIM...
I'M SURE IT'LL ALL BE FINE...

## Act 10 – One Side of the Soul

READ THIS WAY

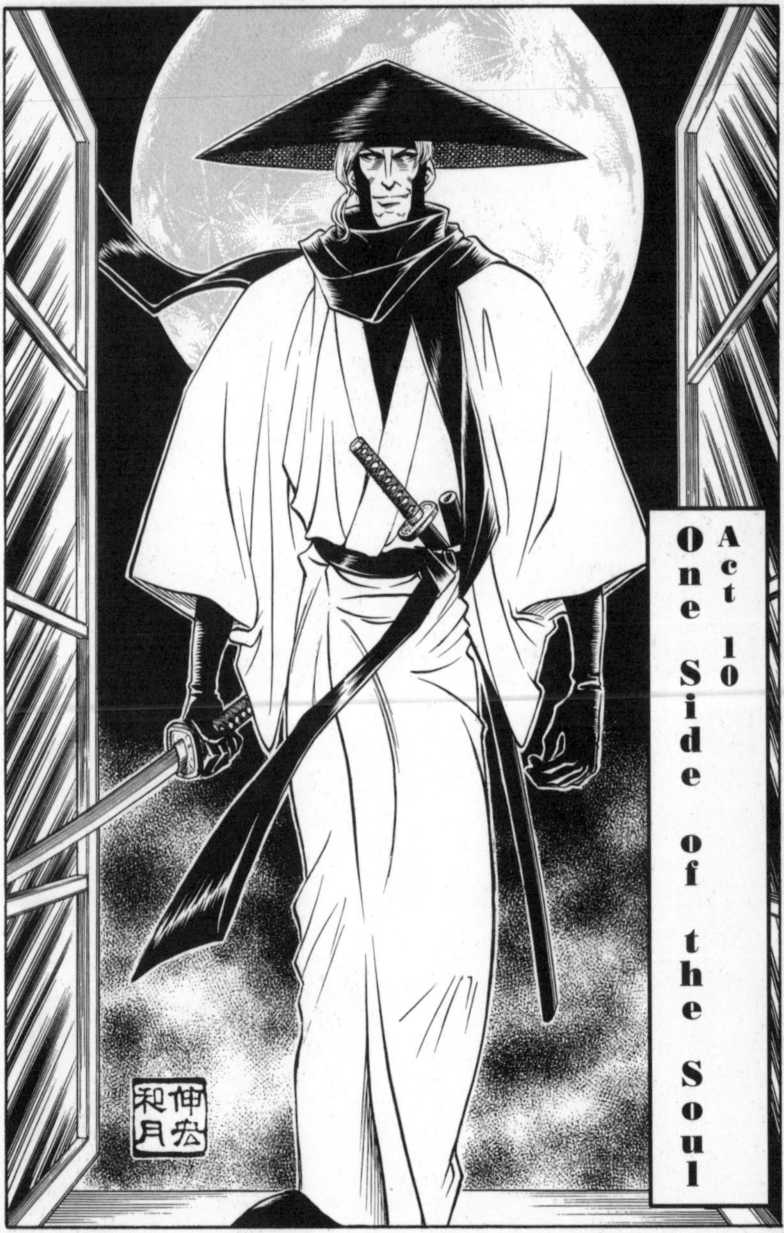
Act 10
One Side of the Soul
伸宏和月

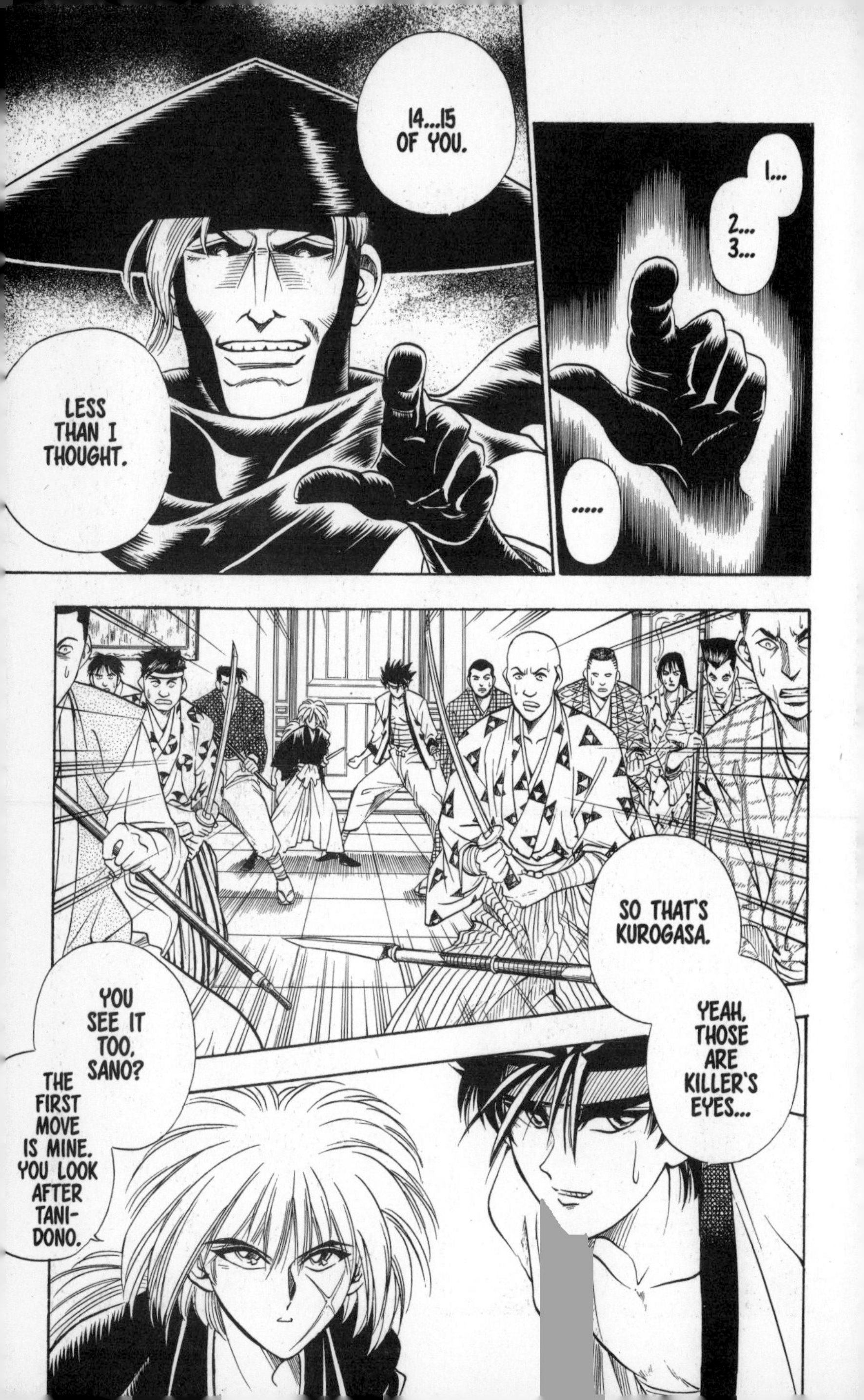
1...
2...
3...
......
14...15 OF YOU.
LESS THAN I THOUGHT.
SO THAT'S KUROGASA.
YEAH, THOSE ARE KILLER'S EYES...
YOU SEE IT TOO, SANO?
THE FIRST MOVE IS MINE. YOU LOOK AFTER TANI-DONO.

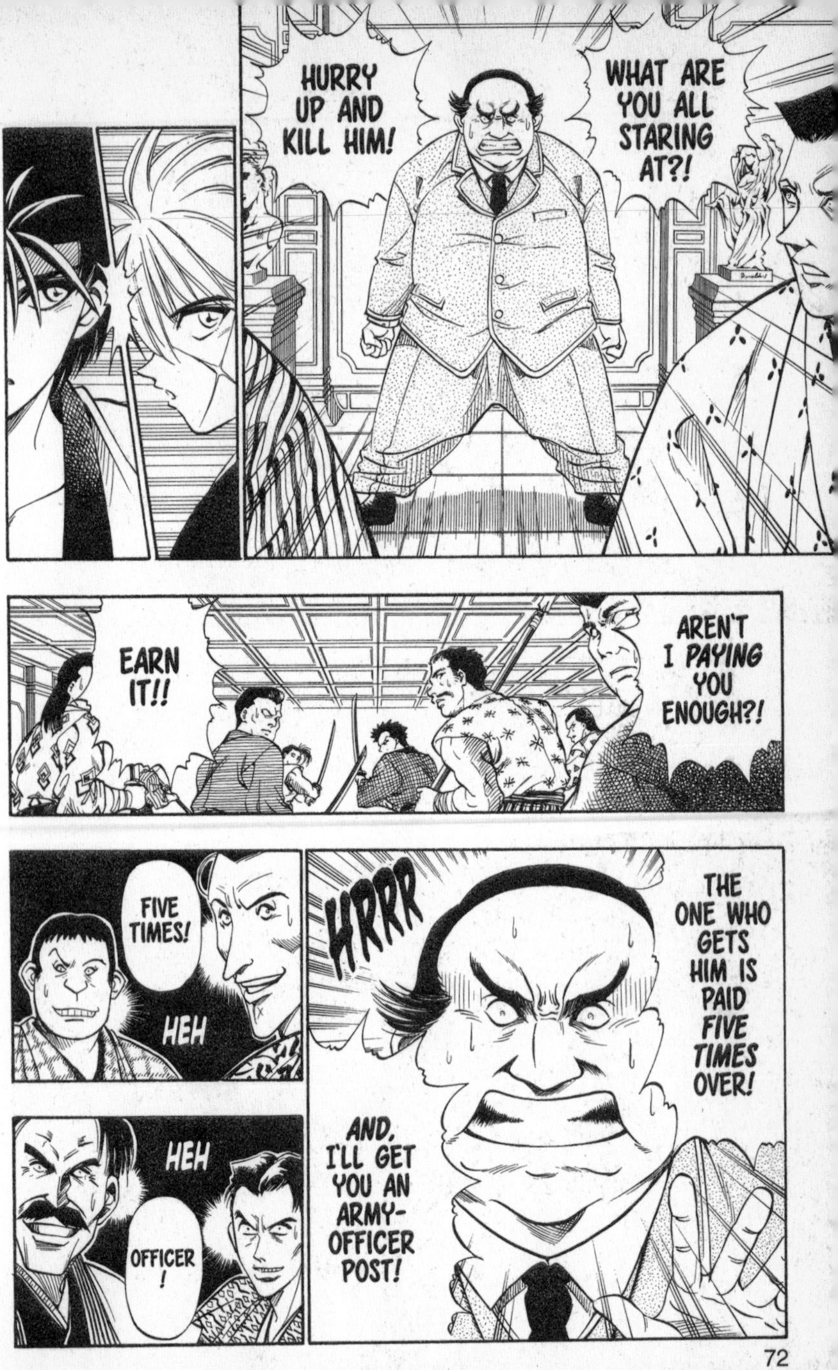
WHAT ARE YOU ALL STARING AT?!
HURRY UP AND KILL HIM!
AREN'T I *PAYING* YOU ENOUGH?!
EARN IT!!
HRRR
THE ONE WHO GETS HIM IS PAID *FIVE TIMES* OVER!
AND, I'LL GET YOU AN ARMY-OFFICER POST!
FIVE TIMES!
HEH
HEH
OFFICER!

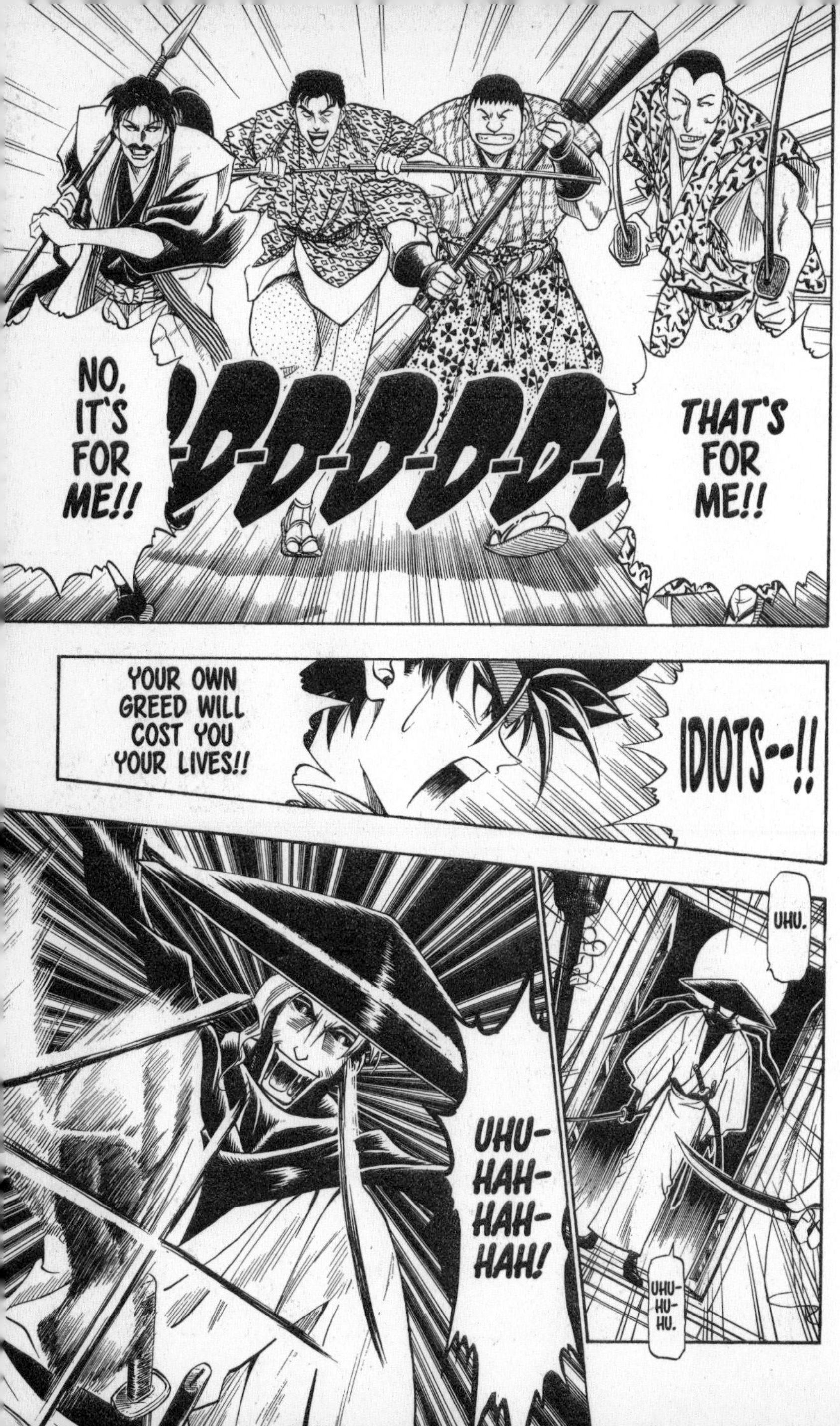
THAT'S FOR ME!!
NO, IT'S FOR ME!!
IDIOTS--!!
YOUR OWN GREED WILL COST YOU YOUR LIVES!!
UHU.
UHU-HU-HU.
UHU-HAH-HAH-HAH!

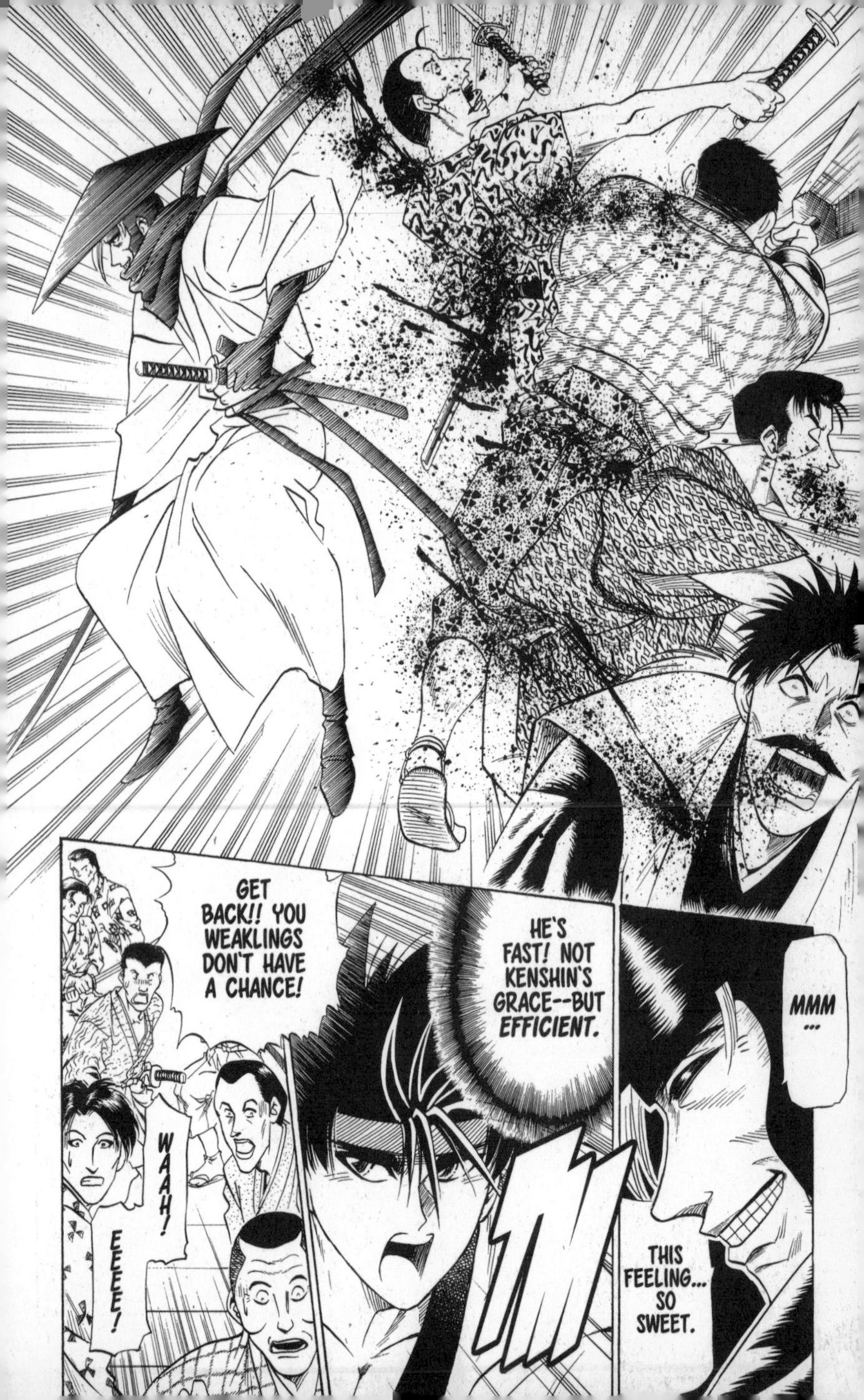
MMM...
THIS FEELING... SO SWEET.
HE'S FAST! NOT KENSHIN'S GRACE--BUT EFFICIENT.
GET BACK!! YOU WEAKLINGS DON'T HAVE A CHANCE!
WAAH!
EEEE!

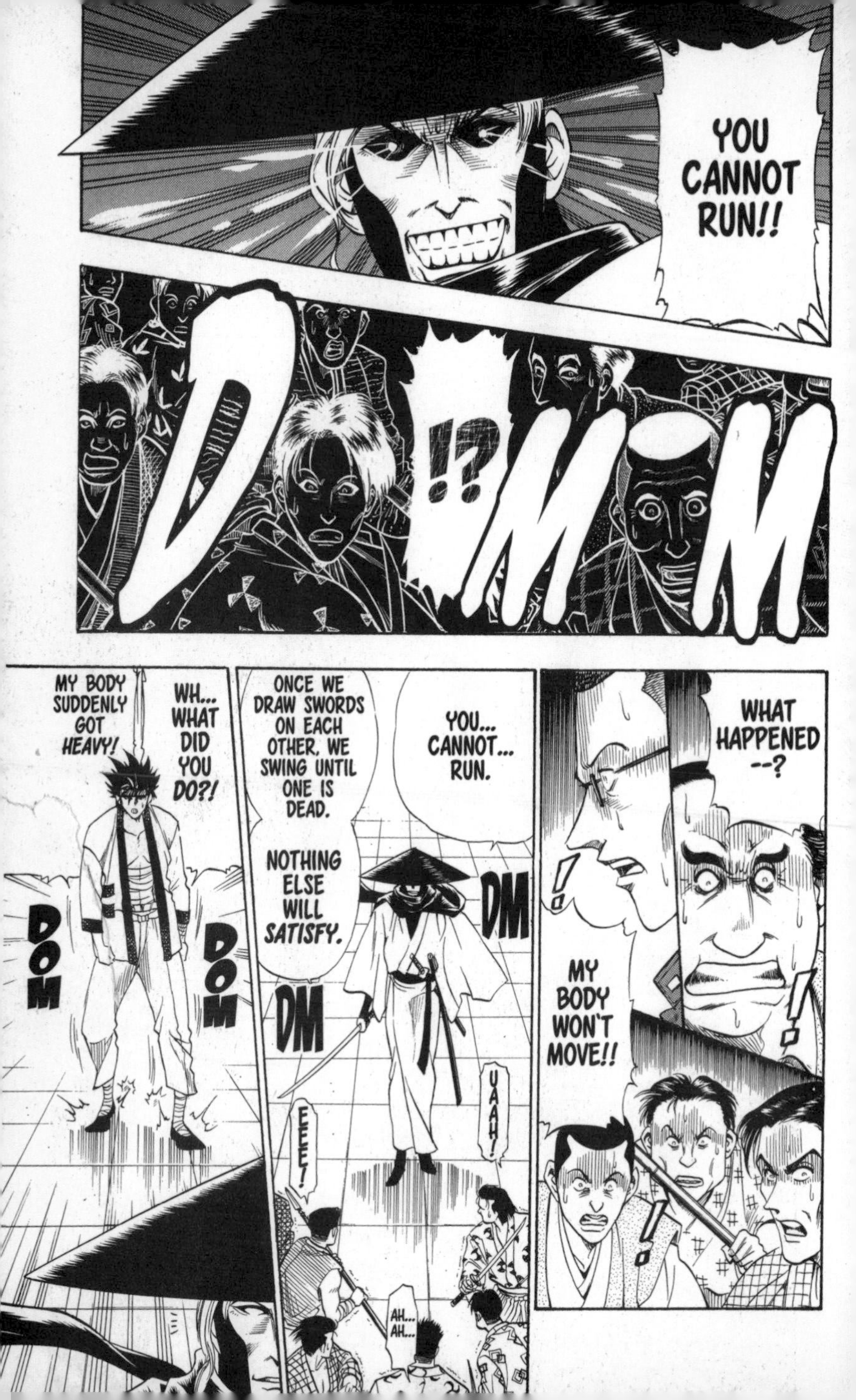
YOU CANNOT RUN!!
DMM
!?
WHAT HAPPENED --?
!
MY BODY WON'T MOVE!!
!
YOU... CANNOT... RUN.
ONCE WE DRAW SWORDS ON EACH OTHER, WE SWING UNTIL ONE IS DEAD.
NOTHING ELSE WILL SATISFY.
DM
DM
UAAH!
EEEE!
AH... AH...
WH... WHAT DID YOU DO?!
MY BODY SUDDENLY GOT HEAVY!
DOM
DOM

READ THIS WAY

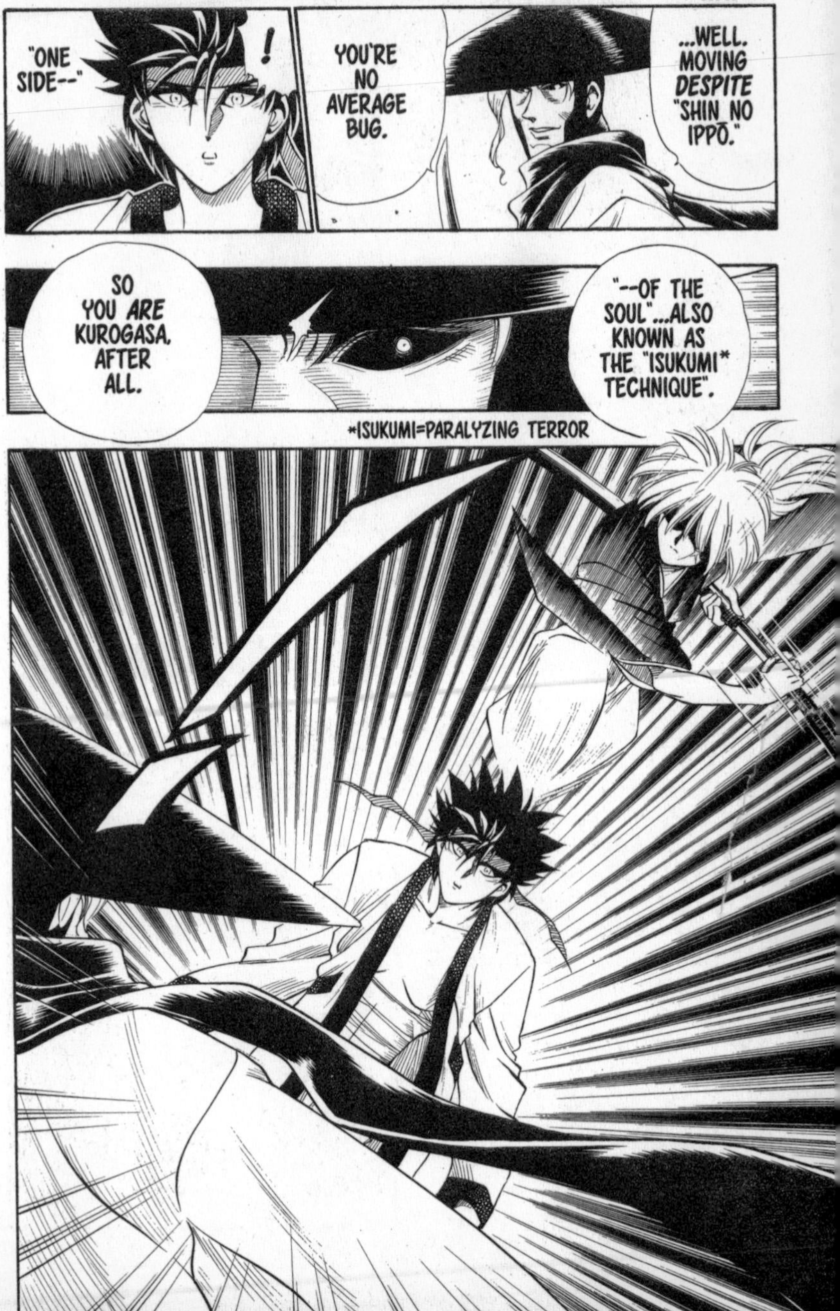
...WELL. MOVING DESPITE "SHIN NO IPPŌ."
YOU'RE NO AVERAGE BUG.
!
"ONE SIDE--"
"--OF THE SOUL"...ALSO KNOWN AS THE "ISUKUMI* TECHNIQUE".
SO YOU ARE KUROGASA, AFTER ALL.
*ISUKUMI=PARALYZING TERROR

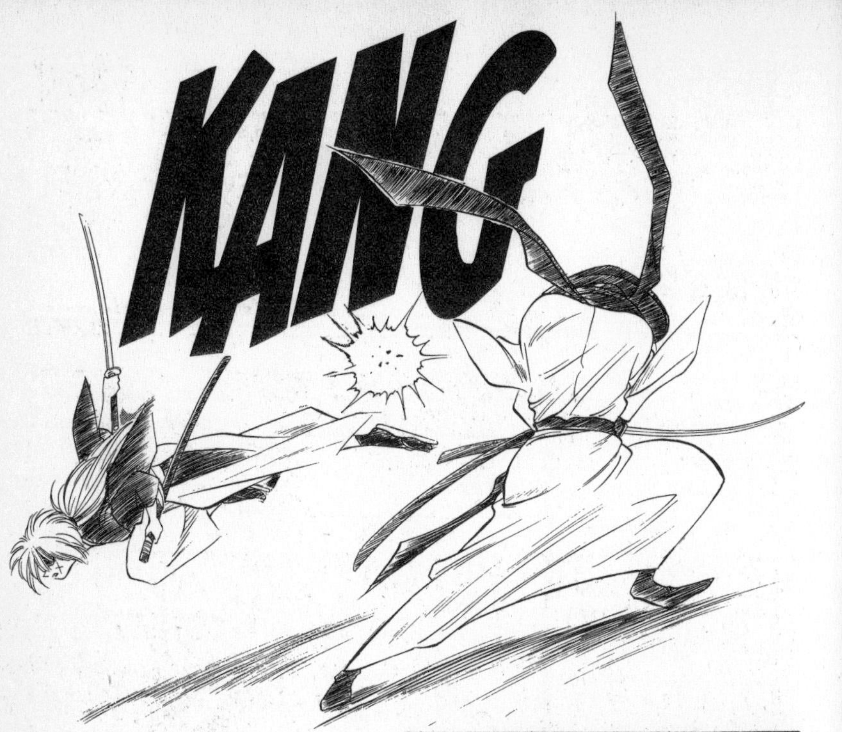
KANG

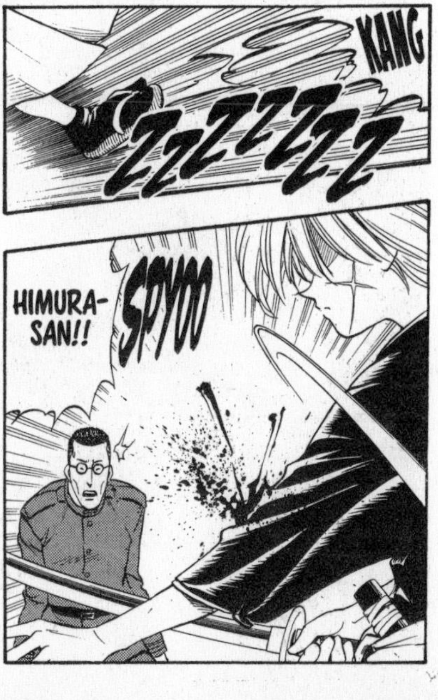
KANG
ZZZZZZZ
SPYOO
HIMURA-SAN!!

Even Watsuki, who watches anime yet knows little of anime voice-actors, knows (Kenshin "CD book" voice-actor) Ogata. That is how good and popular she is. To be fair, quite a few fan letters mention how well her voice fits (indicating, to me, how many "Kenshin" readers were also reading a certain, other, super-popular manga...and how sad and complicated a realization is that!). Given that Watsuki had imagined Kenshin's voice more "neutral," it's a good thing, having Ogata bring his voice to life.

伸宏
和月

...to be continued

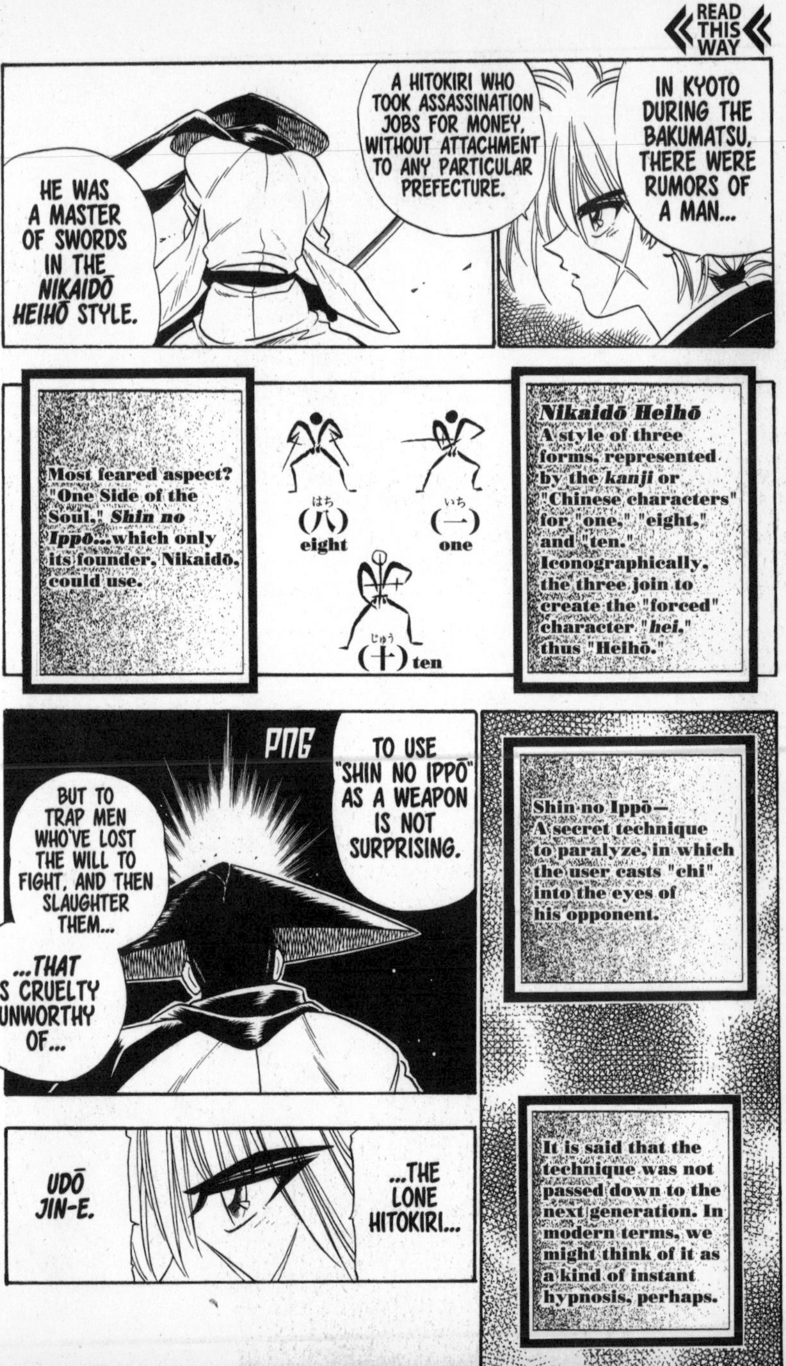
READ THIS WAY
IN KYOTO DURING THE BAKUMATSU, THERE WERE RUMORS OF A MAN...
A HITOKIRI WHO TOOK ASSASSINATION JOBS FOR MONEY, WITHOUT ATTACHMENT TO ANY PARTICULAR PREFECTURE.
HE WAS A MASTER OF SWORDS IN THE NIKAIDŌ HEIHŌ STYLE.
Nikaidō Heihō
A style of three forms, represented by the kanji or "Chinese characters" for "one," "eight," and "ten." Iconographically, the three join to create the "forced" character "hei," thus "Heihō."
いち (一) one
はち (八) eight
じゅう (十) ten
Most feared aspect? "One Side of the Soul," Shin no Ippō...which only its founder, Nikaidō, could use.
Shin no Ippō— A secret technique to paralyze, in which the user casts "chi" into the eyes of his opponent.
It is said that the technique was not passed down to the next generation. In modern terms, we might think of it as a kind of instant hypnosis, perhaps.
TO USE "SHIN NO IPPŌ" AS A WEAPON IS NOT SURPRISING.
PNG
BUT TO TRAP MEN WHO'VE LOST THE WILL TO FIGHT, AND THEN SLAUGHTER THEM...
...THAT IS CRUELTY UNWORTHY OF...
...THE LONE HITOKIRI...
UDŌ JIN-E.

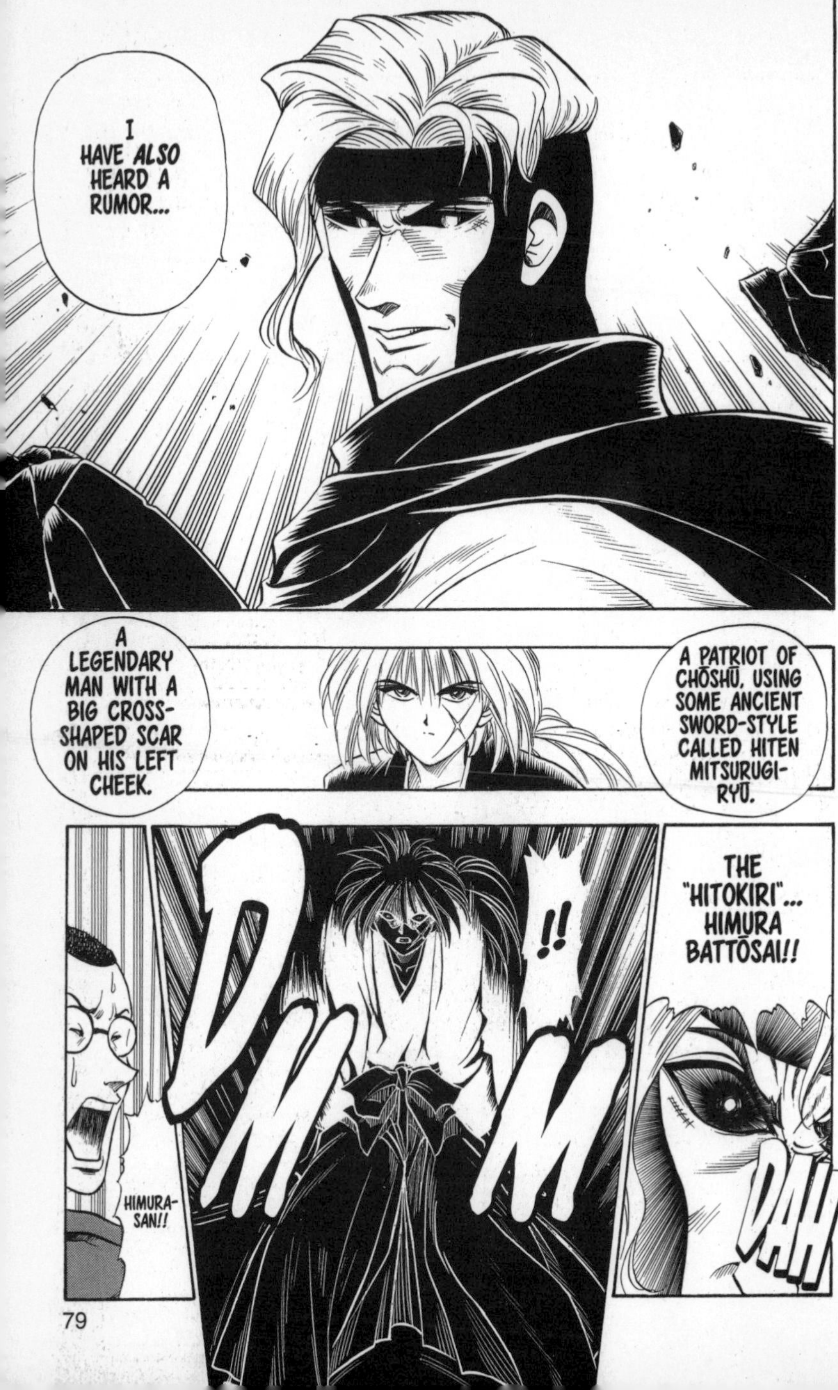
I HAVE *ALSO* HEARD A RUMOR...
A PATRIOT OF CHŌSHŪ, USING SOME ANCIENT SWORD-STYLE CALLED HITEN MITSURUGI-RYŪ.
A LEGENDARY MAN WITH A BIG CROSS-SHAPED SCAR ON HIS LEFT CHEEK.
THE "HITOKIRI"... HIMURA BATTŌSAI!!
DAH
!!
HIMURA-SAN!!

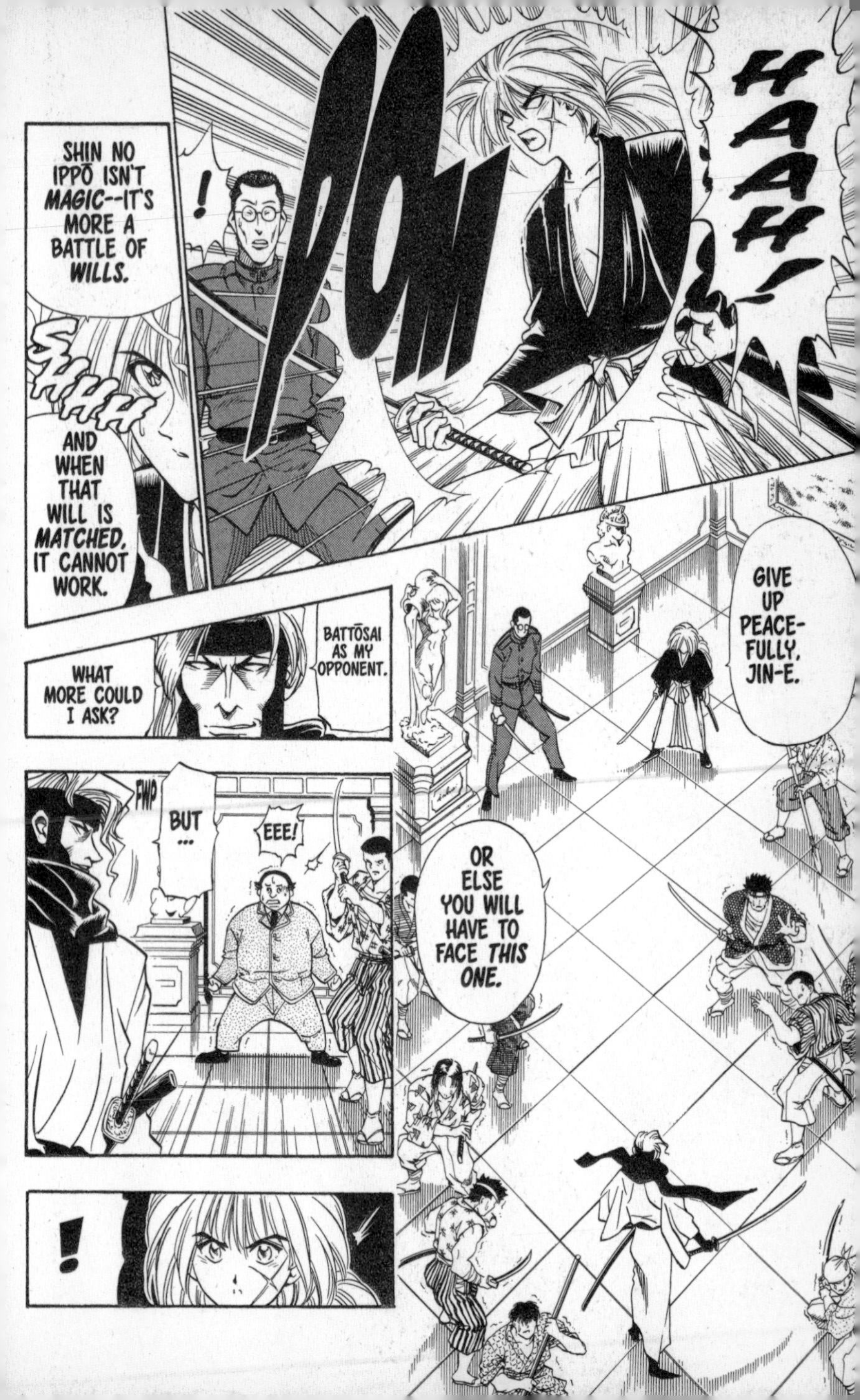
HAAH!
POW
!
SHIN NO IPPŌ ISN'T MAGIC--IT'S MORE A BATTLE OF WILLS.
SHHH
AND WHEN THAT WILL IS MATCHED, IT CANNOT WORK.
GIVE UP PEACEFULLY, JIN-E.
OR ELSE YOU WILL HAVE TO FACE THIS ONE.
BATTŌSAI AS MY OPPONENT.
WHAT MORE COULD I ASK?
FWP
EEE!
BUT ...
!

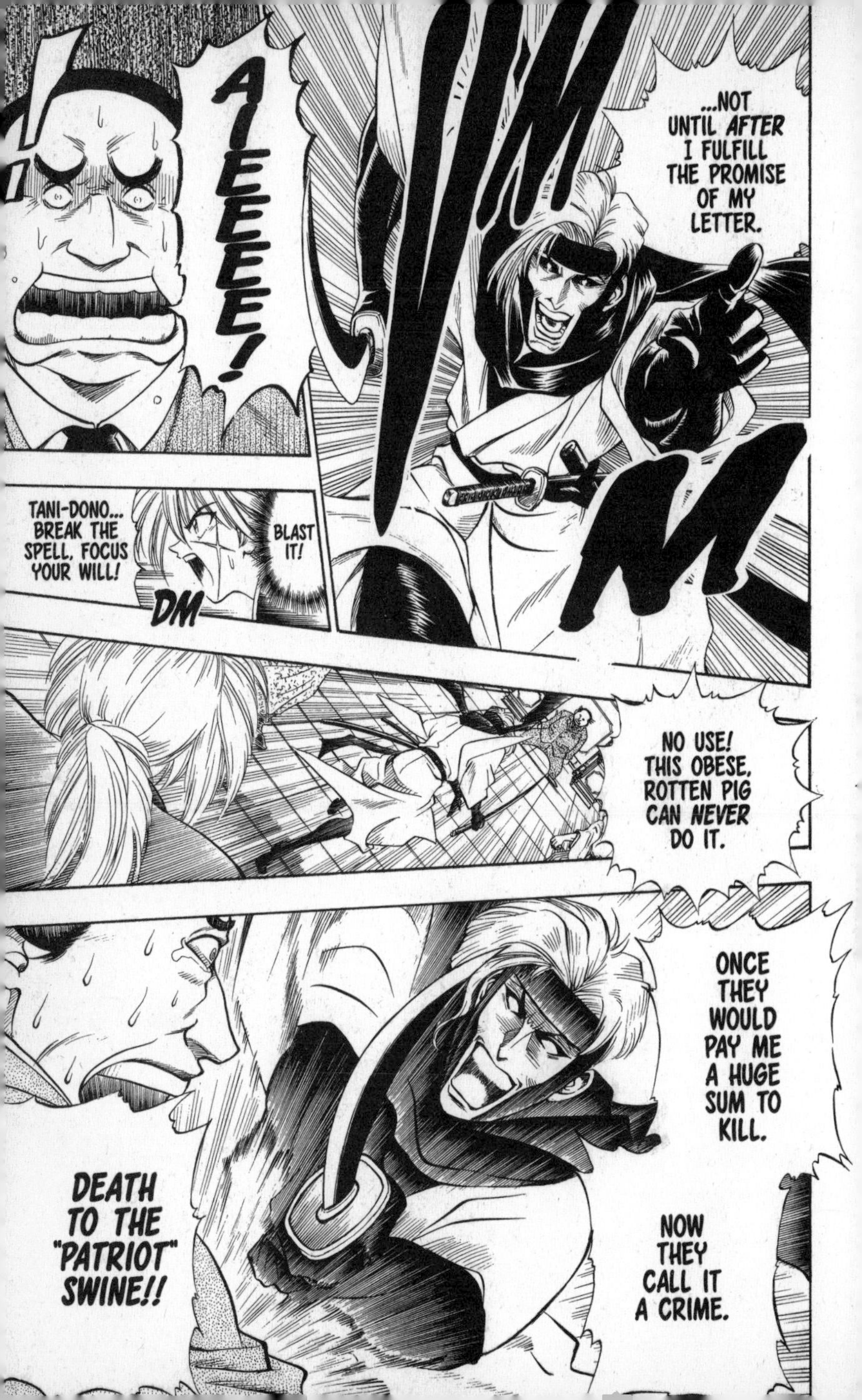
...NOT UNTIL AFTER I FULFILL THE PROMISE OF MY LETTER.
AIEEEEE!
BLAST IT!
TANI-DONO... BREAK THE SPELL, FOCUS YOUR WILL!
DM
NO USE! THIS OBESE, ROTTEN PIG CAN NEVER DO IT.
ONCE THEY WOULD PAY ME A HUGE SUM TO KILL.
NOW THEY CALL IT A CRIME.
DEATH TO THE "PATRIOT" SWINE!!

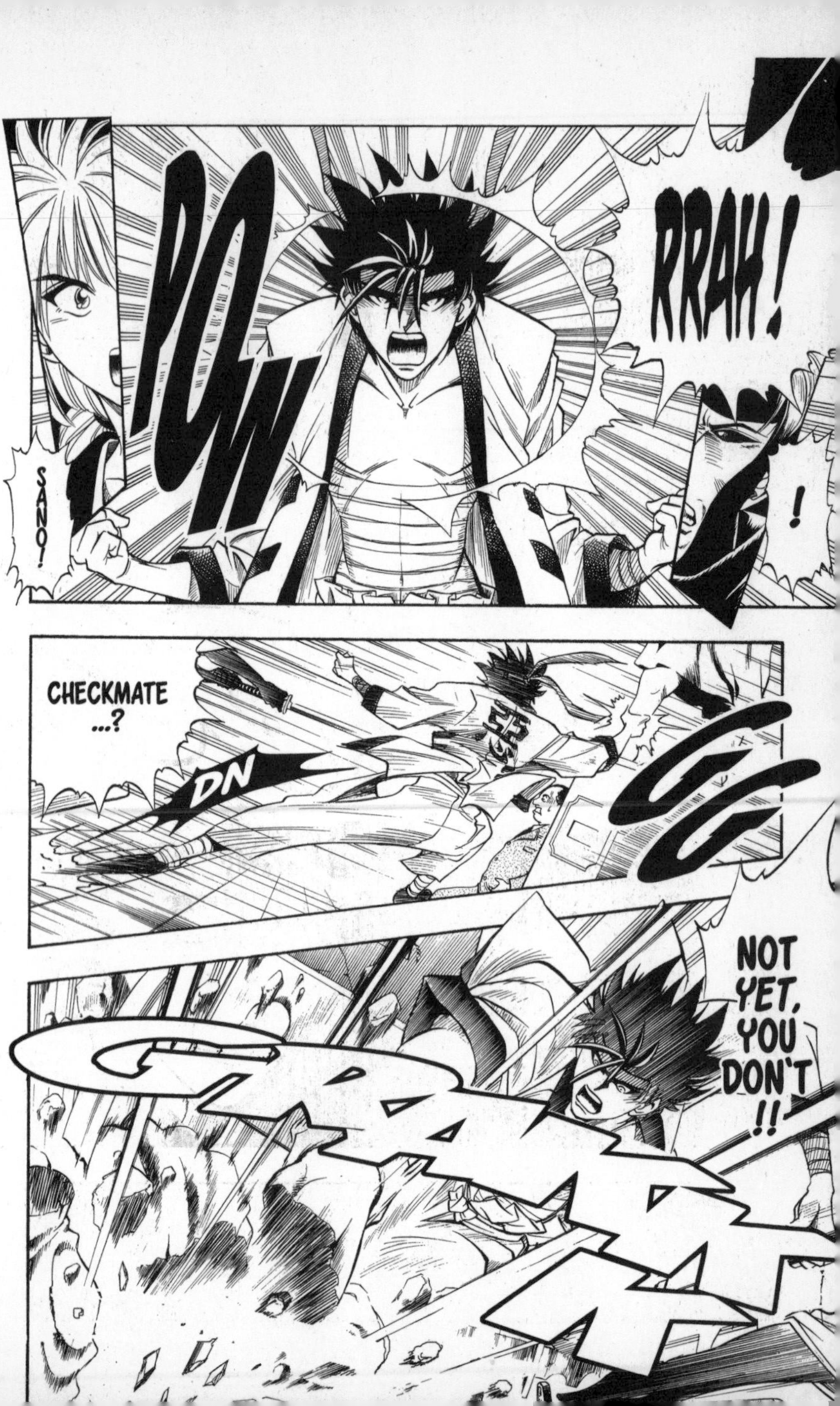
RRAH!
!
POW
SANO!
GG
DN
CHECKMATE ...?
NOT YET, YOU DON'T!!

READ THIS WAY

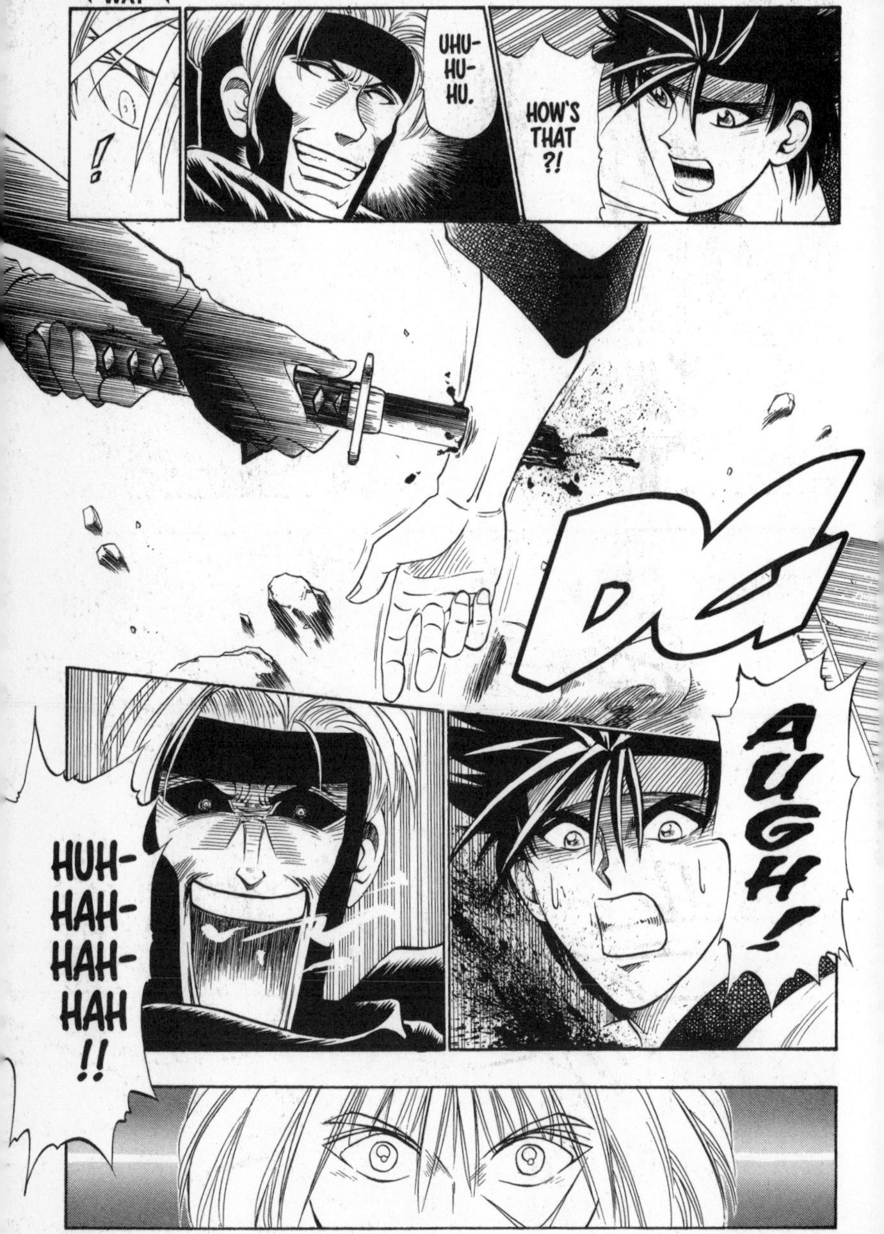
HOW'S THAT ?!
UHU- HU- HU.
!
DO
AUGH!
HUH- HAH- HAH- HAH !!

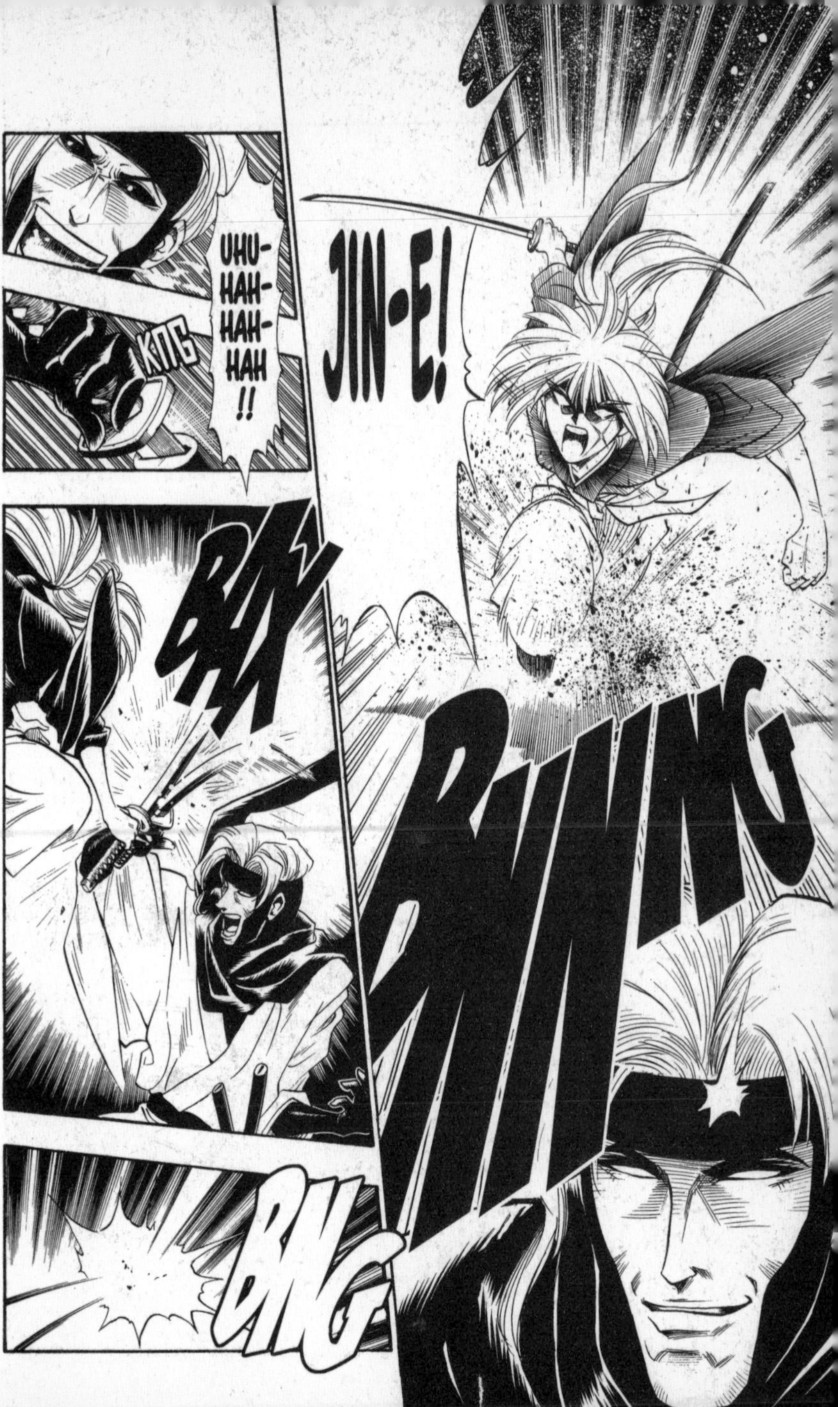
JIN-E!
BWIING
KTNG
UHU-HAH-HAH-HAH!!
BAN
BANG

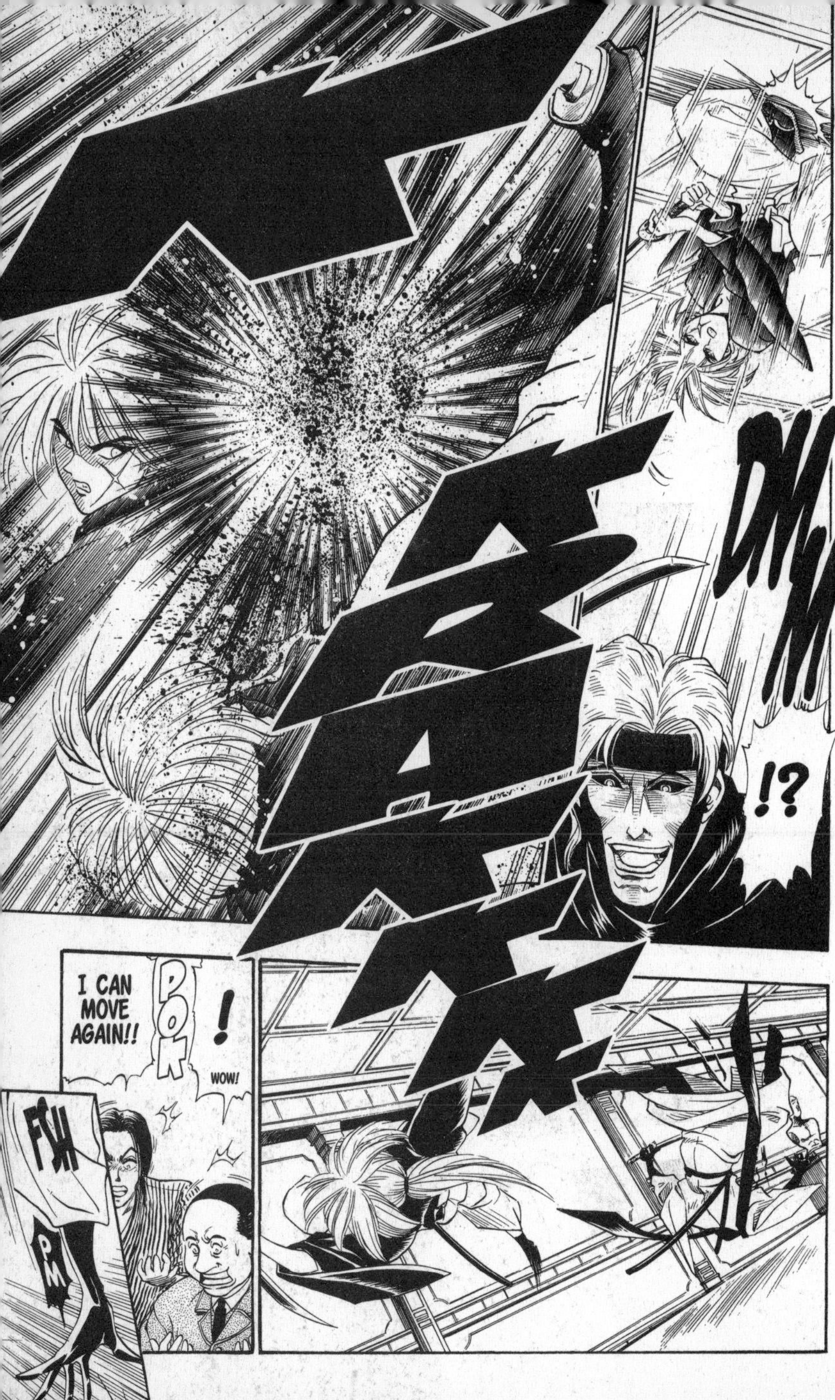
DMM
!?
!
POK
I CAN MOVE AGAIN!!
WOW!
FSH
PM

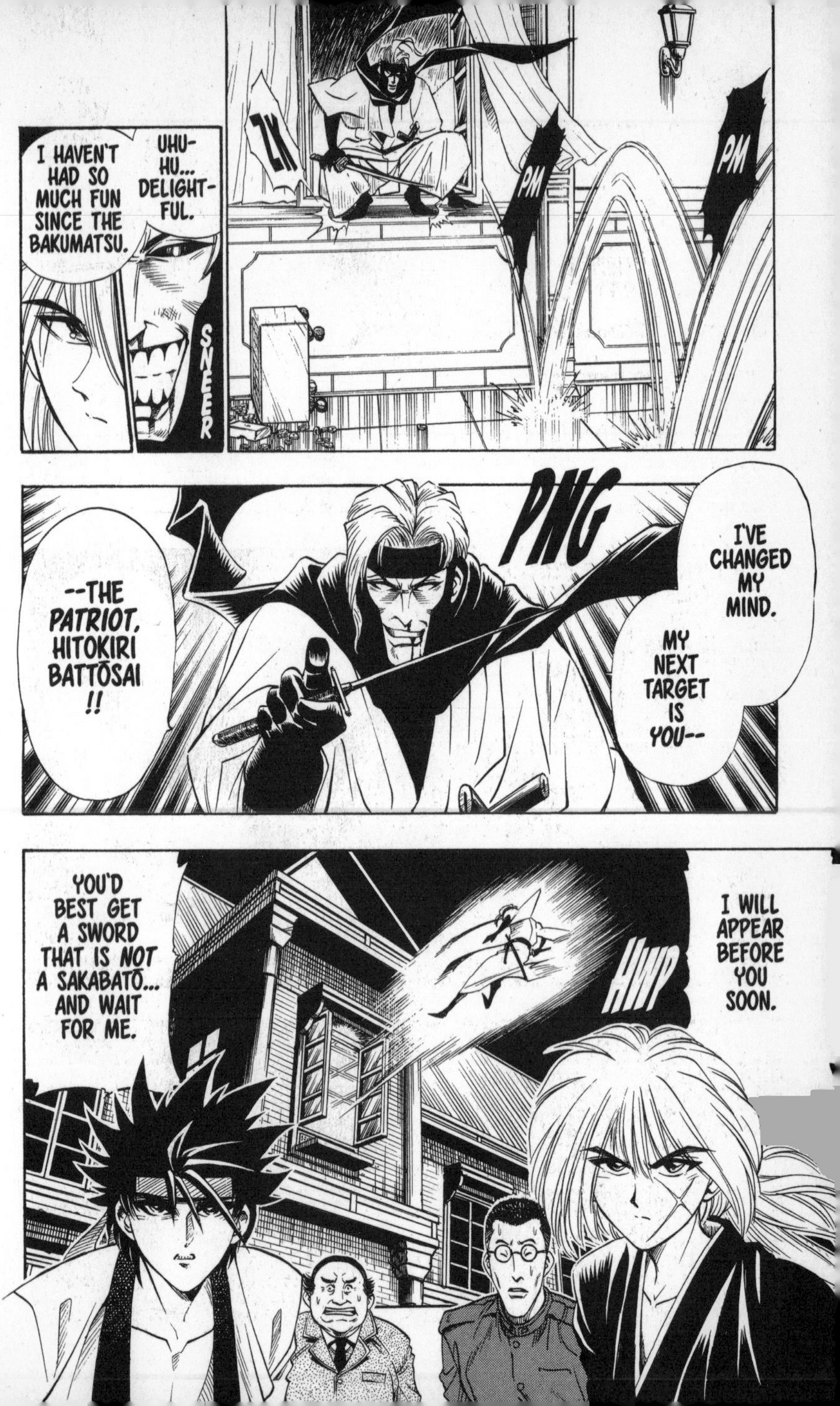
ZK
PM
PM
UHU-HU... DELIGHTFUL.
I HAVEN'T HAD SO MUCH FUN SINCE THE BAKUMATSU.
SNEER
PNG
I'VE CHANGED MY MIND.
MY NEXT TARGET IS *YOU*--
--THE *PATRIOT*, HITOKIRI BATTŌSAI !!
I WILL APPEAR BEFORE YOU SOON.
HWP
YOU'D BEST GET A SWORD THAT IS *NOT* A SAKABATŌ... AND WAIT FOR ME.

READ THIS WAY

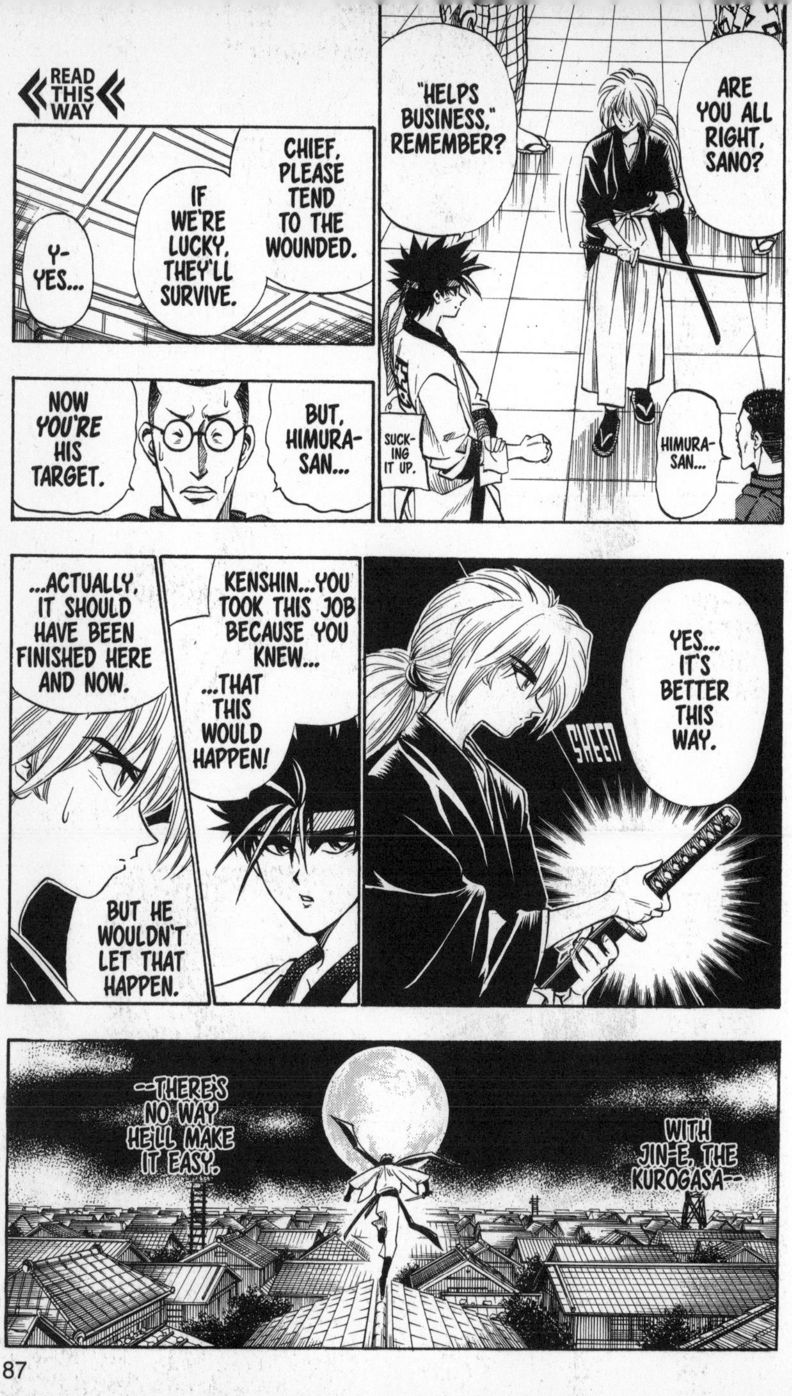
ARE YOU ALL RIGHT, SANO?
"HELPS BUSINESS," REMEMBER?
HIMURA-SAN...
SUCKING IT UP.
CHIEF, PLEASE TEND TO THE WOUNDED.
IF WE'RE LUCKY, THEY'LL SURVIVE.
Y-YES...
BUT, HIMURA-SAN...
NOW *YOU'RE* HIS TARGET.
YES... IT'S BETTER THIS WAY.
SHEEN
KENSHIN...YOU TOOK THIS JOB BECAUSE YOU KNEW...
...THAT THIS WOULD HAPPEN!
...ACTUALLY, IT SHOULD HAVE BEEN FINISHED HERE AND NOW.
BUT HE WOULDN'T LET THAT HAPPEN.
WITH JIN-E, THE KUROGASA--
--THERE'S NO WAY HE'LL MAKE IT EASY.

READ THIS WAY

# Act 11 – The Ribbon That Binds

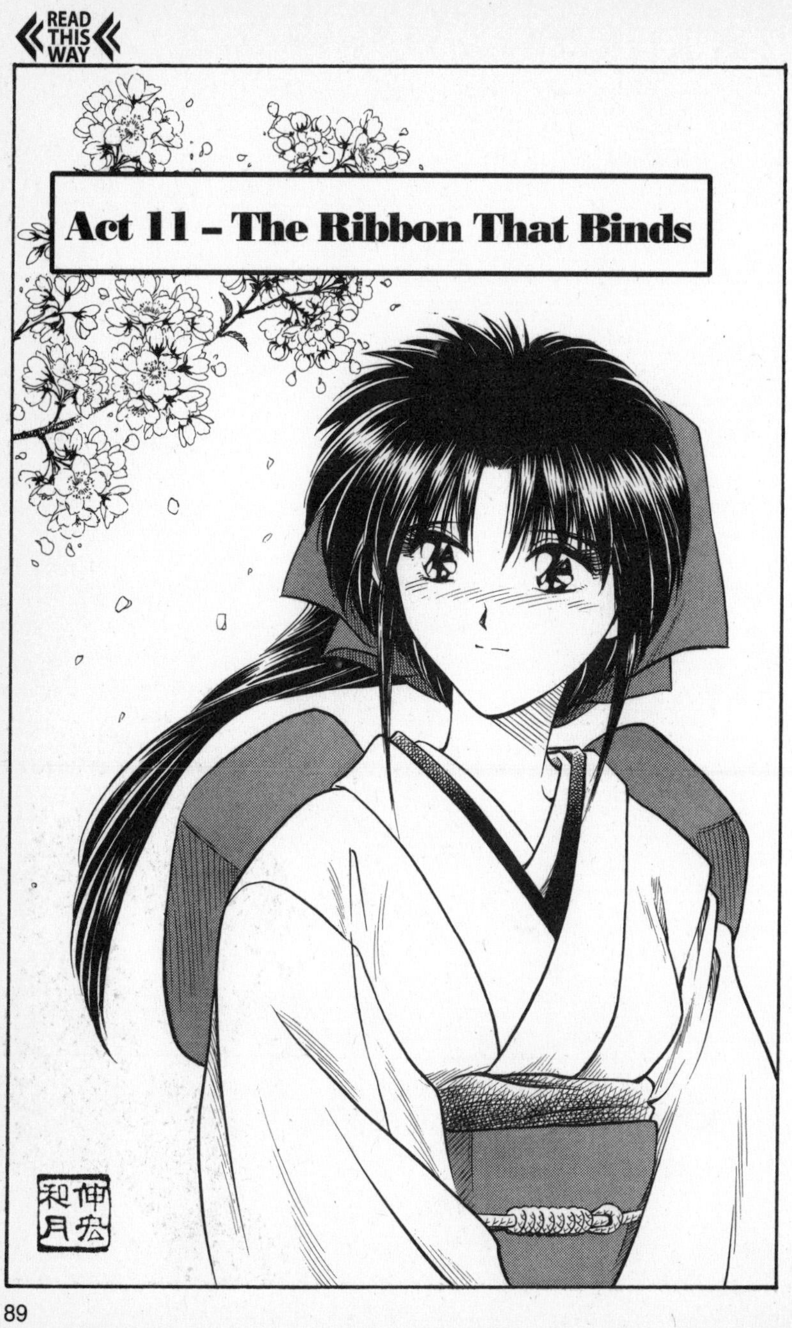
伸宏
和月

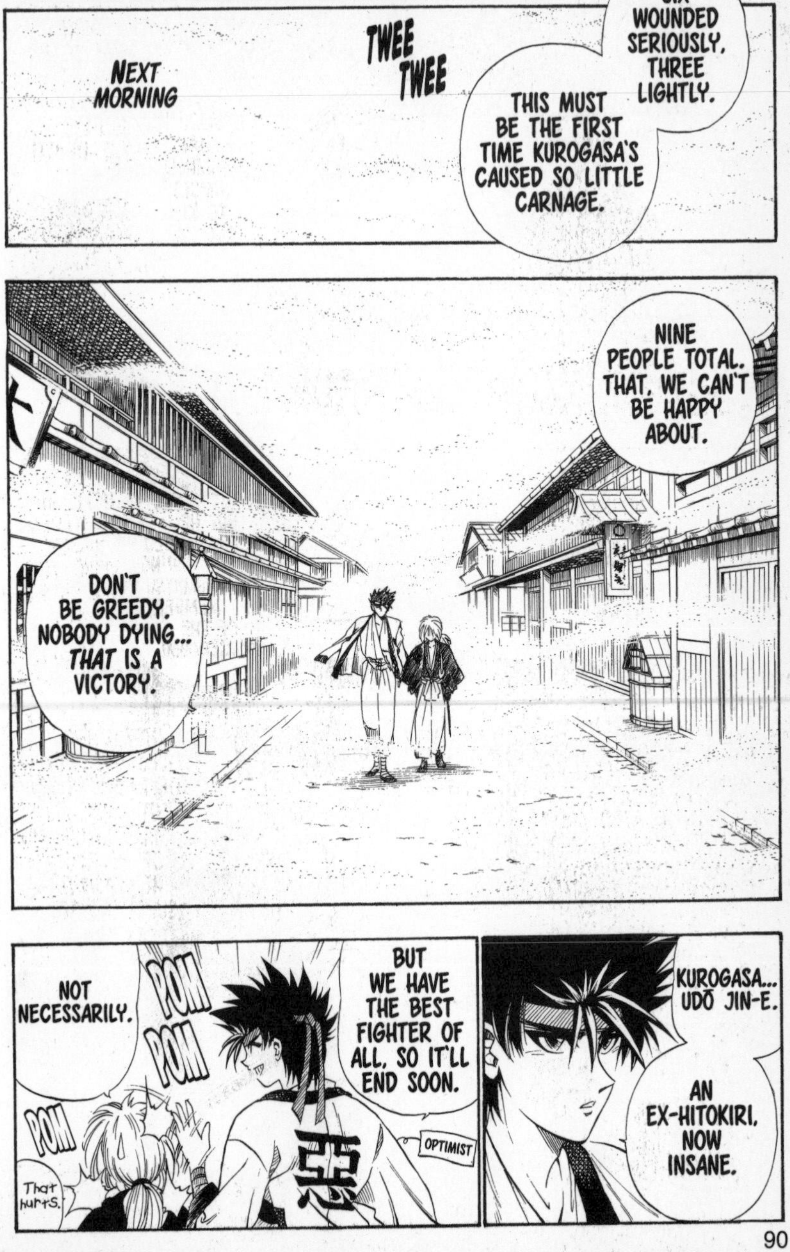
SIX WOUNDED SERIOUSLY, THREE LIGHTLY.
THIS MUST BE THE FIRST TIME KUROGASA'S CAUSED SO LITTLE CARNAGE.
TWEE TWEE
NEXT MORNING
NINE PEOPLE TOTAL. THAT, WE CAN'T BE HAPPY ABOUT.
DON'T BE GREEDY. NOBODY DYING... *THAT* IS A VICTORY.
KUROGASA... UDŌ JIN-E.
AN EX-HITOKIRI. NOW INSANE.
BUT WE HAVE THE BEST FIGHTER OF ALL, SO IT'LL END SOON.
OPTIMIST
POM POM
NOT NECESSARILY.
POM
That hurts.

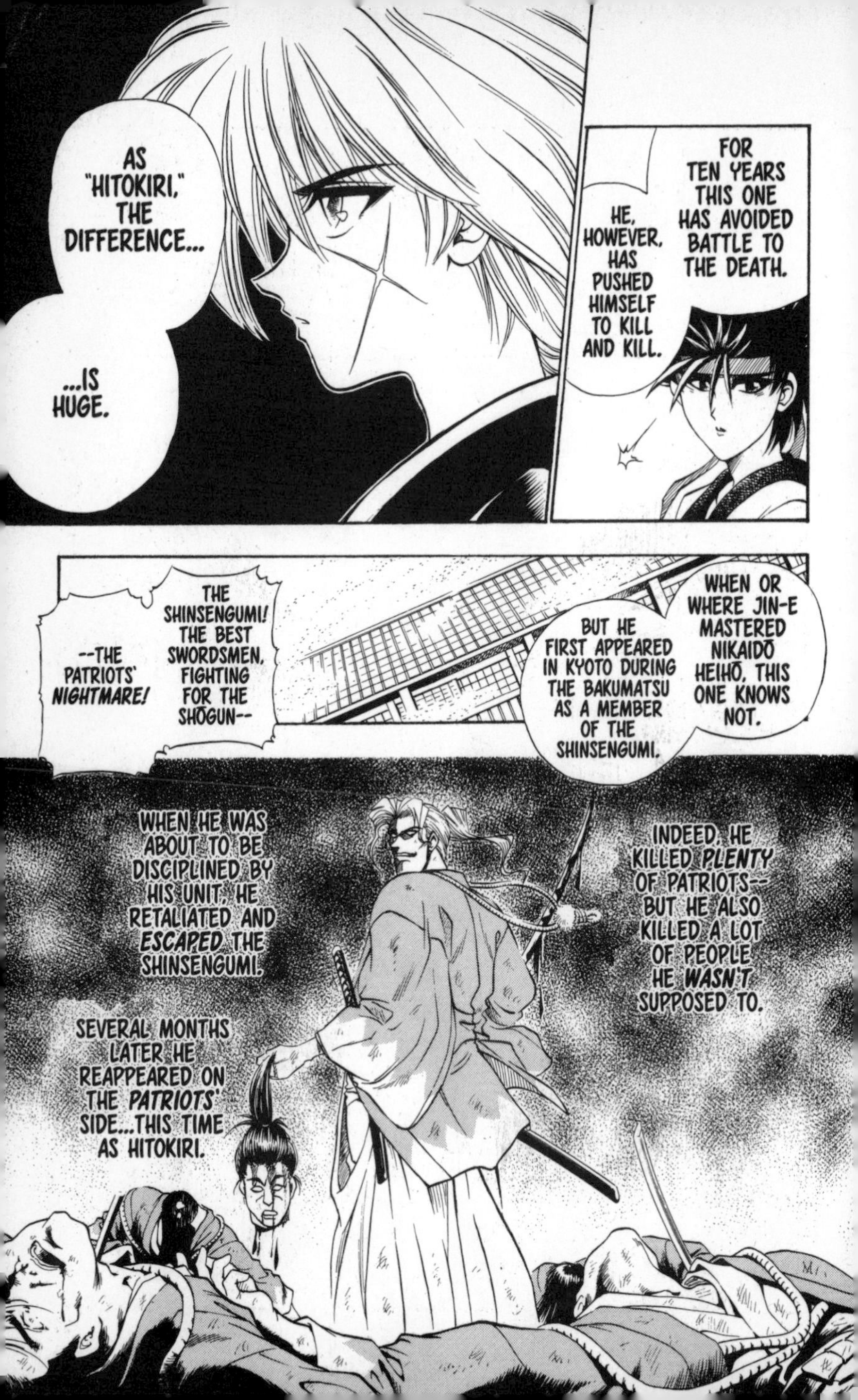
FOR TEN YEARS THIS ONE HAS AVOIDED BATTLE TO THE DEATH.
HE, HOWEVER, HAS PUSHED HIMSELF TO KILL AND KILL.
AS "HITOKIRI," THE DIFFERENCE...
...IS HUGE.
WHEN OR WHERE JIN-E MASTERED NIKAIDŌ HEIHŌ, THIS ONE KNOWS NOT.
BUT HE FIRST APPEARED IN KYOTO DURING THE BAKUMATSU AS A MEMBER OF THE SHINSENGUMI.
THE SHINSENGUMI! THE BEST SWORDSMEN, FIGHTING FOR THE SHŌGUN--
--THE PATRIOTS' *NIGHTMARE!*
INDEED, HE KILLED *PLENTY* OF PATRIOTS-- BUT HE ALSO KILLED A LOT OF PEOPLE HE *WASN'T* SUPPOSED TO.
WHEN HE WAS ABOUT TO BE DISCIPLINED BY HIS UNIT, HE RETALIATED AND *ESCAPED* THE SHINSENGUMI.
SEVERAL MONTHS LATER HE REAPPEARED ON THE *PATRIOTS'* SIDE...THIS TIME AS HITOKIRI.

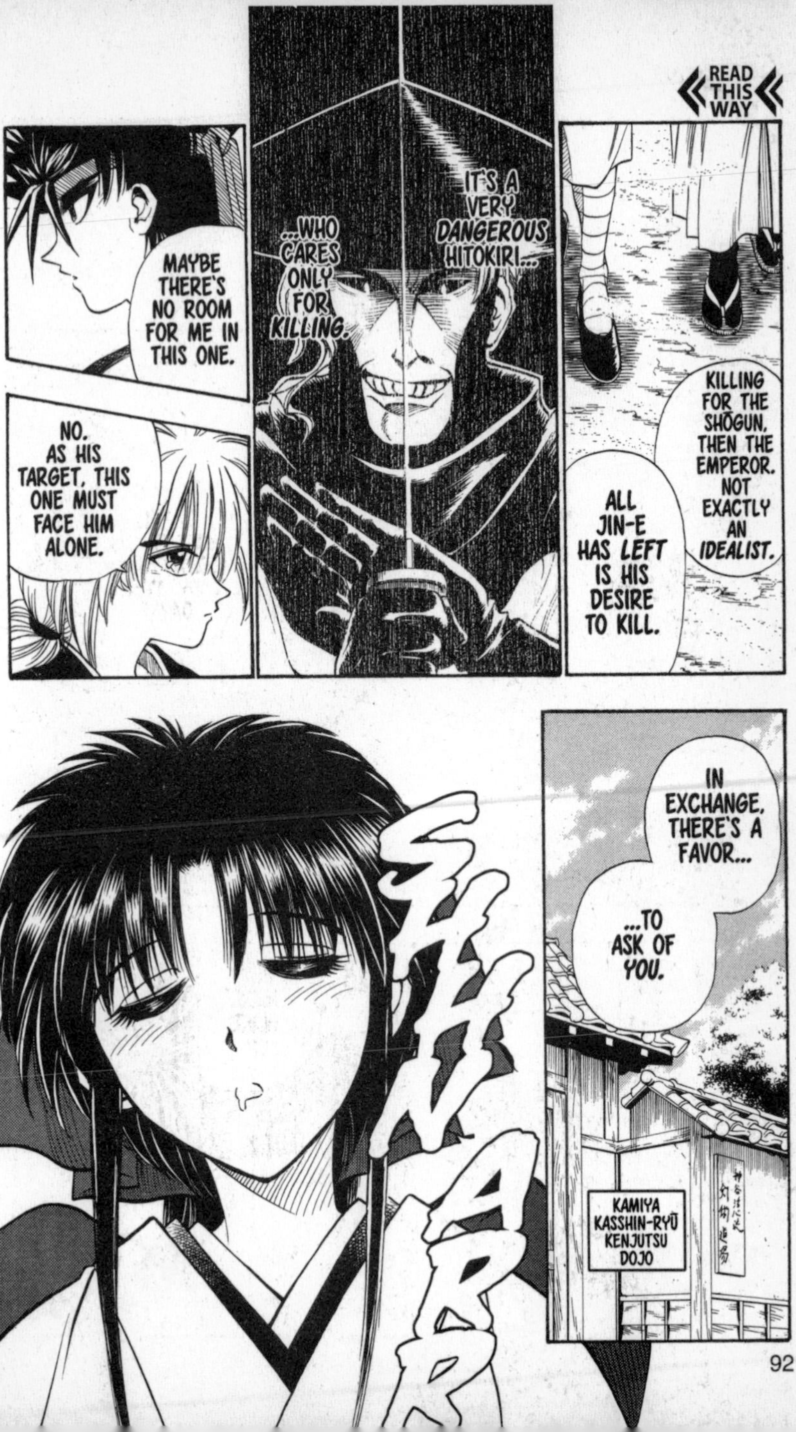
KILLING FOR THE SHŌGUN, THEN THE EMPEROR. NOT EXACTLY AN IDEALIST.
ALL JIN-E HAS LEFT IS HIS DESIRE TO KILL.
IT'S A VERY DANGEROUS HITOKIRI...
...WHO CARES ONLY FOR KILLING.
MAYBE THERE'S NO ROOM FOR ME IN THIS ONE.
NO. AS HIS TARGET, THIS ONE MUST FACE HIM ALONE.
IN EXCHANGE, THERE'S A FAVOR...
...TO ASK OF YOU.
KAMIYA KASSHIN-RYŪ KENJUTSU DOJO

READ THIS WAY

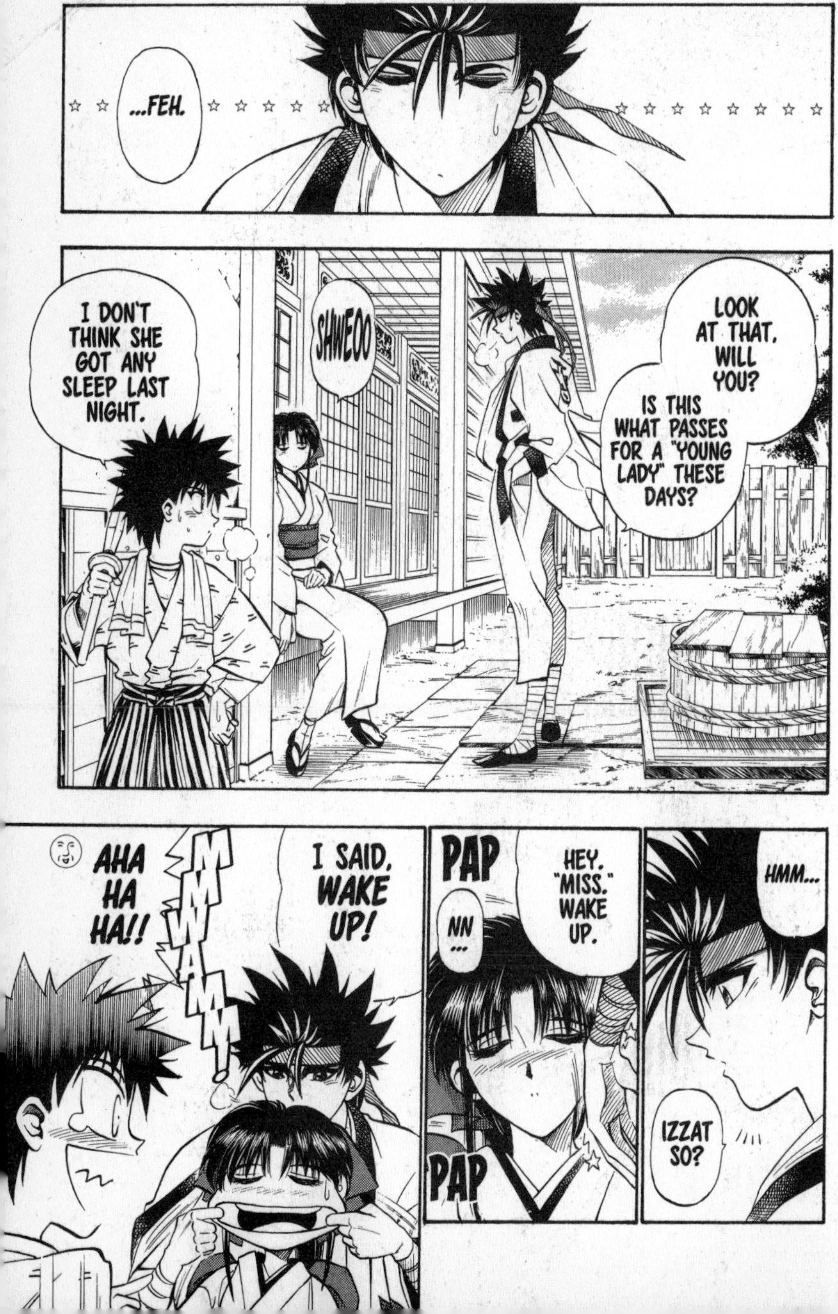
...FEH.
LOOK AT THAT, WILL YOU?
IS THIS WHAT PASSES FOR A "YOUNG LADY" THESE DAYS?
SHWEOO
I DON'T THINK SHE GOT ANY SLEEP LAST NIGHT.
HMM...
IZZAT SO?
PAP
HEY. "MISS." WAKE UP.
NN...
PAP
I SAID, WAKE UP!
MWAMM!
AHA HA HA!!

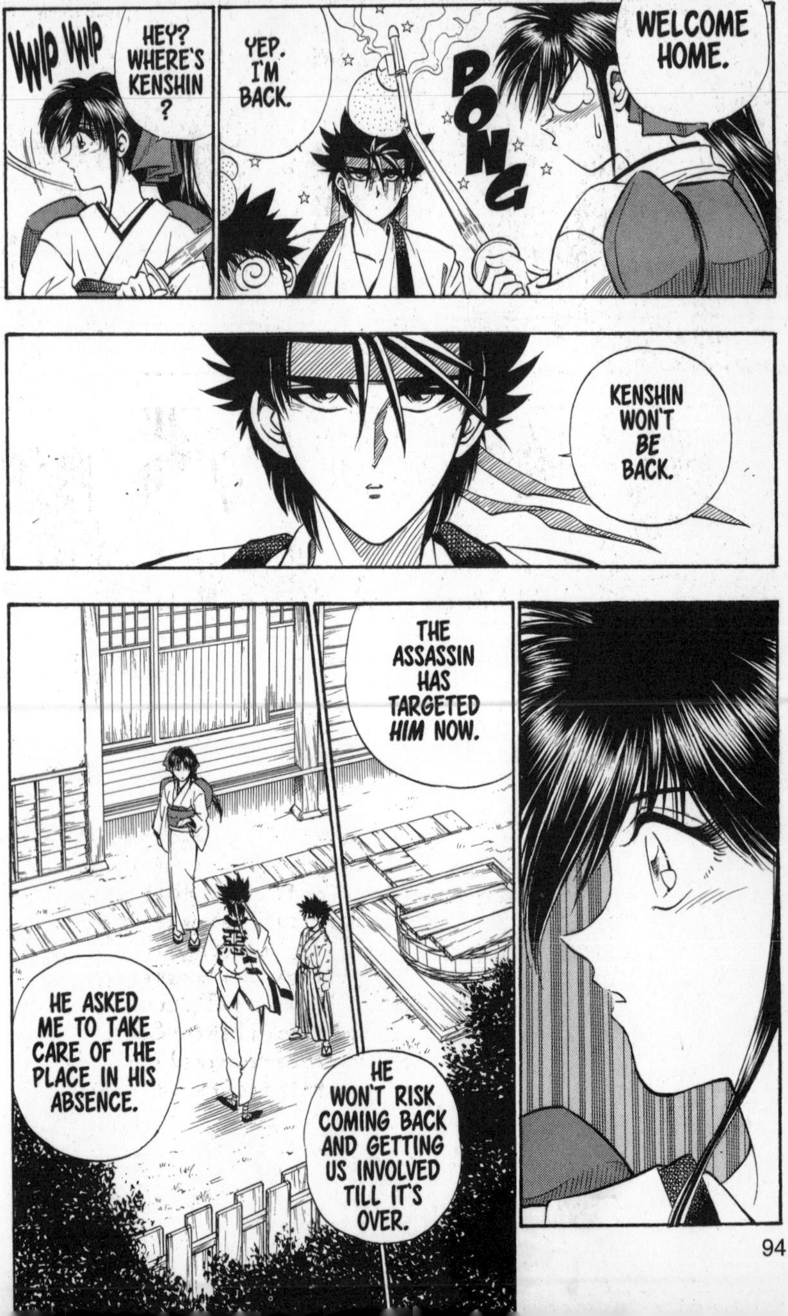
WELCOME HOME.
PONG
YEP. I'M BACK.
VWIP VWIP
HEY? WHERE'S KENSHIN ?
KENSHIN WON'T BE BACK.
THE ASSASSIN HAS TARGETED *HIM* NOW.
HE WON'T RISK COMING BACK AND GETTING US INVOLVED TILL IT'S OVER.
HE ASKED ME TO TAKE CARE OF THE PLACE IN HIS ABSENCE.

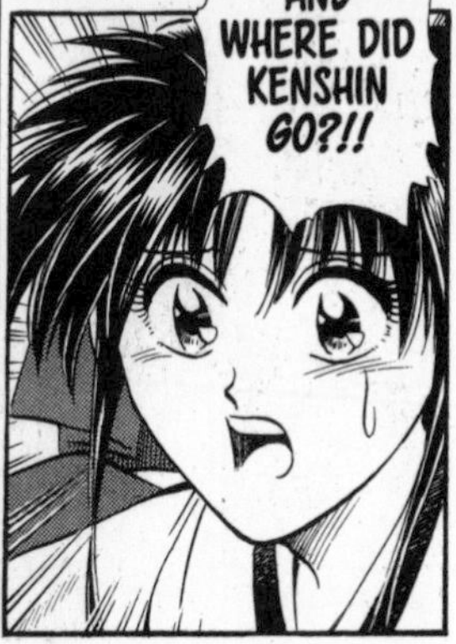
AND WHERE DID KENSHIN GO?!!

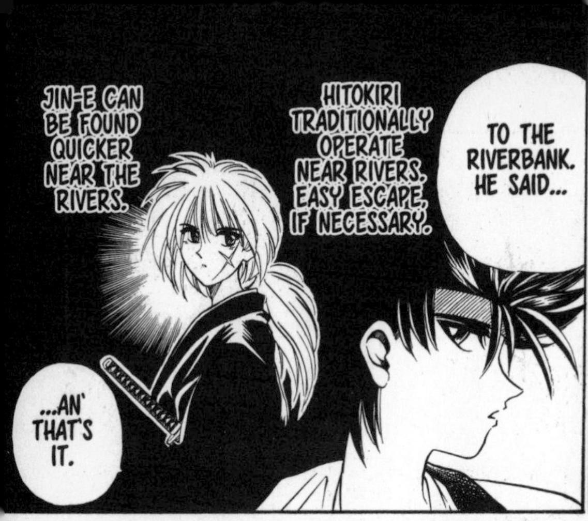
TO THE RIVERBANK. HE SAID...
HITOKIRI TRADITIONALLY OPERATE NEAR RIVERS. EASY ESCAPE, IF NECESSARY.
JIN-E CAN BE FOUND QUICKER NEAR THE RIVERS.
...AN' THAT'S IT.

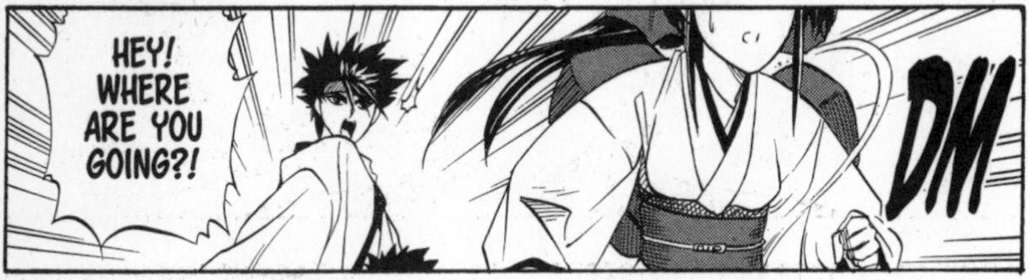
DM
HEY! WHERE ARE YOU GOING?!

I didn't know who Sakurai was—sorry, my bad!—so, when I asked a friend, I found out she was also voicing the heroine of a new anime series to start that fall. Eventually, I watched it, and thought she was good—not too high, not too low. That "not too airhead-y" tone was close to what Watsuki had imagined for Kaoru's voice..."bang on," I'd thought. Takayama, they tell me, is "Kiki" in "The Witch's Delivery Service" (I'm sorry, I really do not know voice-actors). She's got a lot of energy, and is a great fit for "the kid," Yahiko.

...to be continued

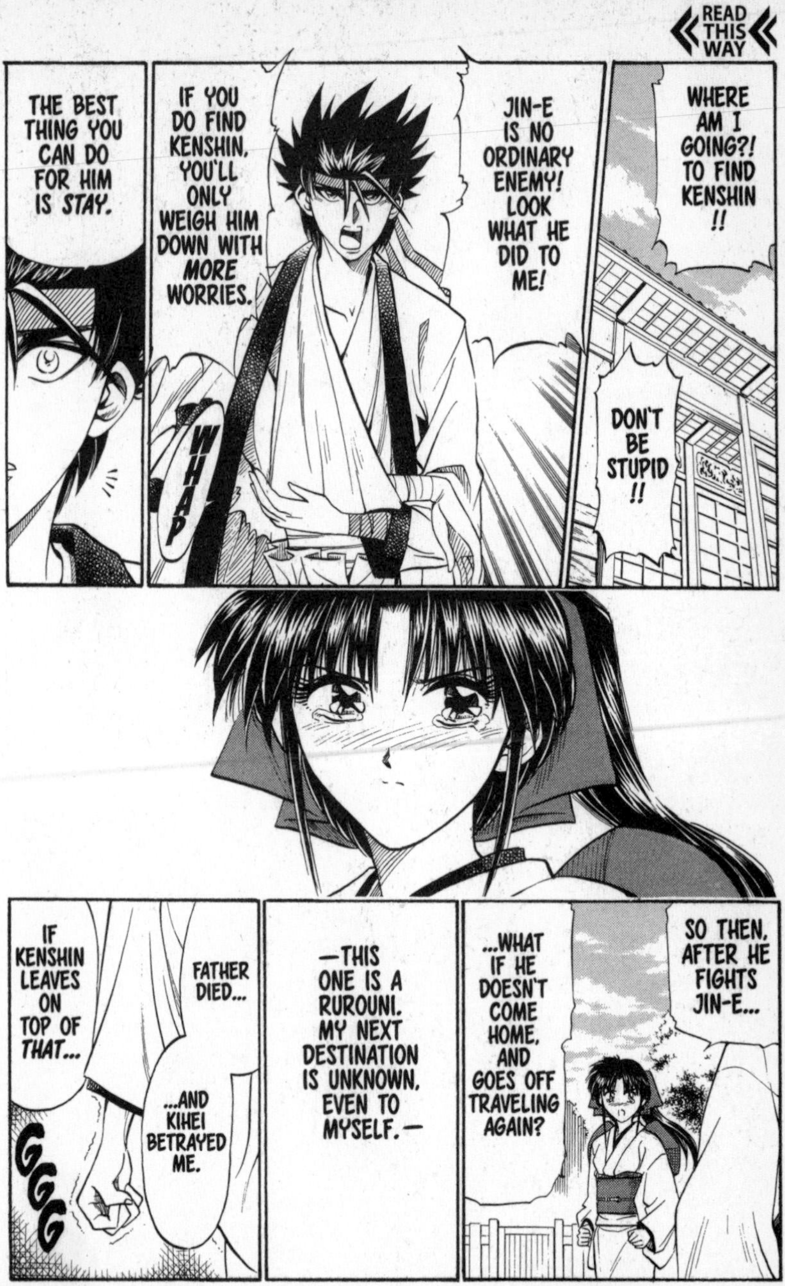
READ THIS WAY
WHERE AM I GOING?! TO FIND KENSHIN!!
DON'T BE STUPID!!
JIN-E IS NO ORDINARY ENEMY! LOOK WHAT HE DID TO ME!
IF YOU DO FIND KENSHIN, YOU'LL ONLY WEIGH HIM DOWN WITH *MORE* WORRIES.
WHAP
THE BEST THING YOU CAN DO FOR HIM IS *STAY*.
SO THEN, AFTER HE FIGHTS JIN-E...
...WHAT IF HE DOESN'T COME HOME, AND GOES OFF TRAVELING AGAIN?
—THIS ONE IS A RUROUNI. MY NEXT DESTINATION IS UNKNOWN, EVEN TO MYSELF.—
FATHER DIED...
IF KENSHIN LEAVES ON TOP OF *THAT*...
...AND KIHEI BETRAYED ME.
GGG

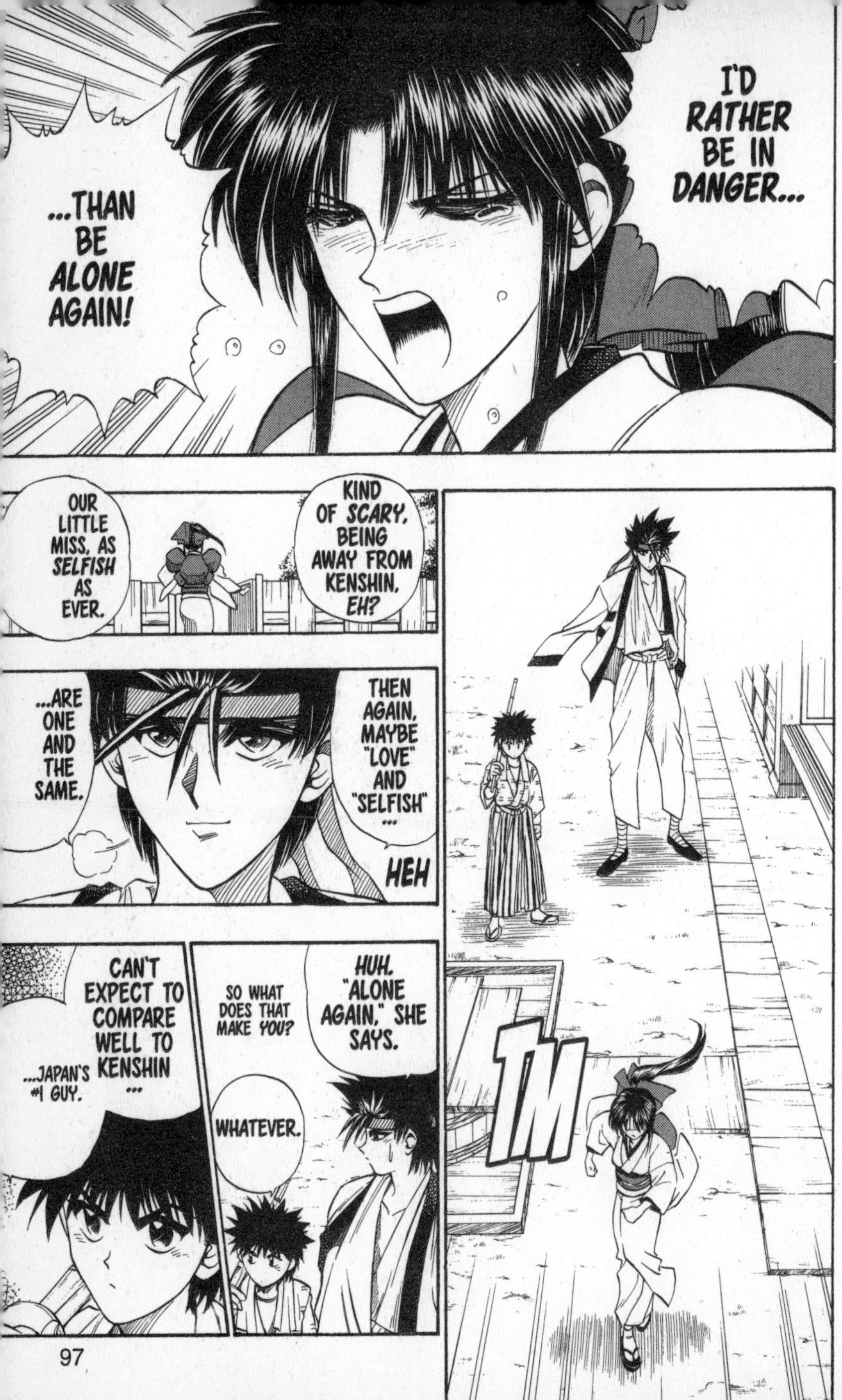
I'D RATHER BE IN DANGER...
...THAN BE ALONE AGAIN!
TM
KIND OF SCARY, BEING AWAY FROM KENSHIN, EH?
OUR LITTLE MISS, AS SELFISH AS EVER.
THEN AGAIN, MAYBE "LOVE" AND "SELFISH"...
HEH
...ARE ONE AND THE SAME.
HUH. "ALONE AGAIN," SHE SAYS.
SO WHAT DOES THAT MAKE YOU?
WHATEVER.
CAN'T EXPECT TO COMPARE WELL TO KENSHIN...
...JAPAN'S #1 GUY.

READ THIS WAY

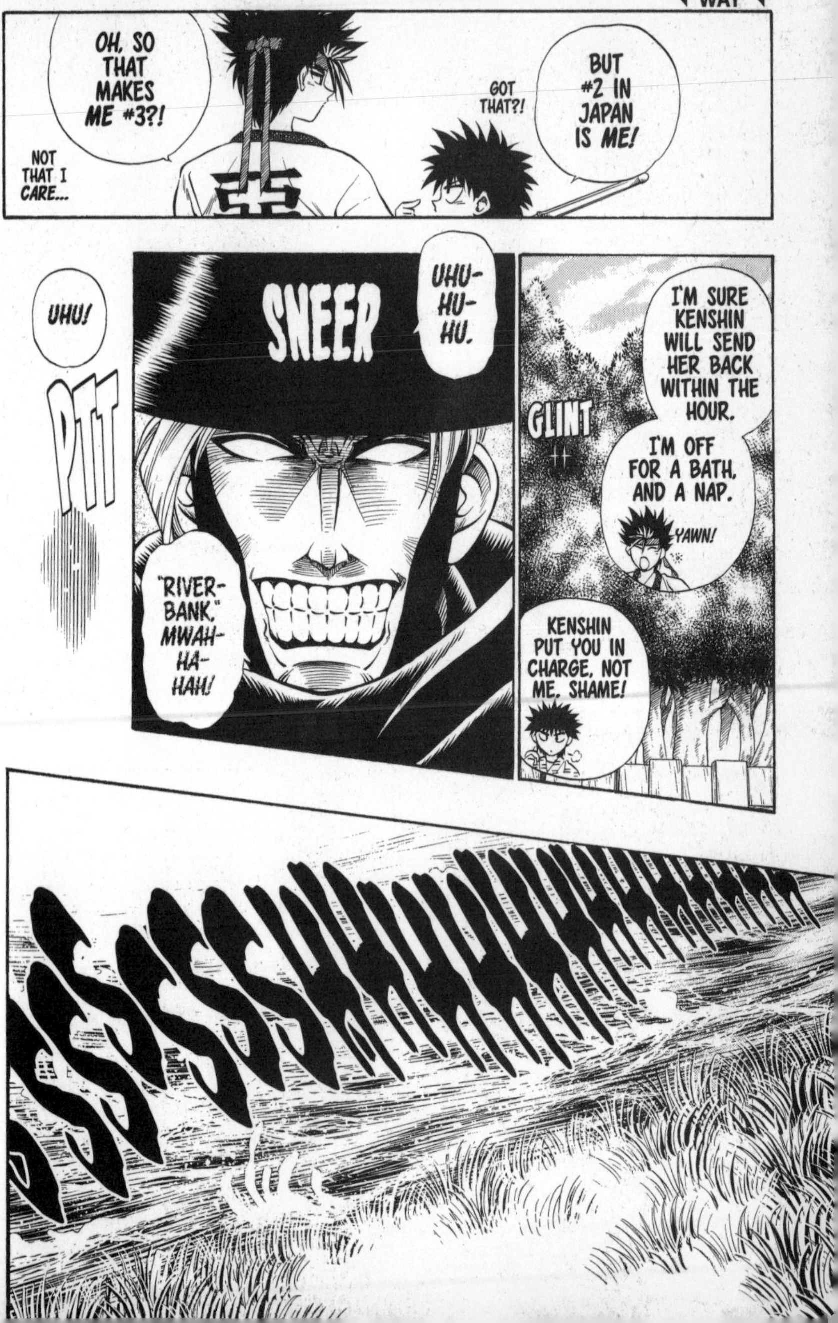
BUT #2 IN JAPAN IS ME!
GOT THAT?!
OH, SO THAT MAKES ME #3?!
NOT THAT I CARE...
I'M SURE KENSHIN WILL SEND HER BACK WITHIN THE HOUR.
GLINT
I'M OFF FOR A BATH, AND A NAP.
YAWN!
KENSHIN PUT YOU IN CHARGE, NOT ME. SHAME!
UHU-HU-HU.
SNEER
"RIVER-BANK," MWAH-HA-HAH!
UHU!
PTT
SSSSSHHHHHHHHHHHHH

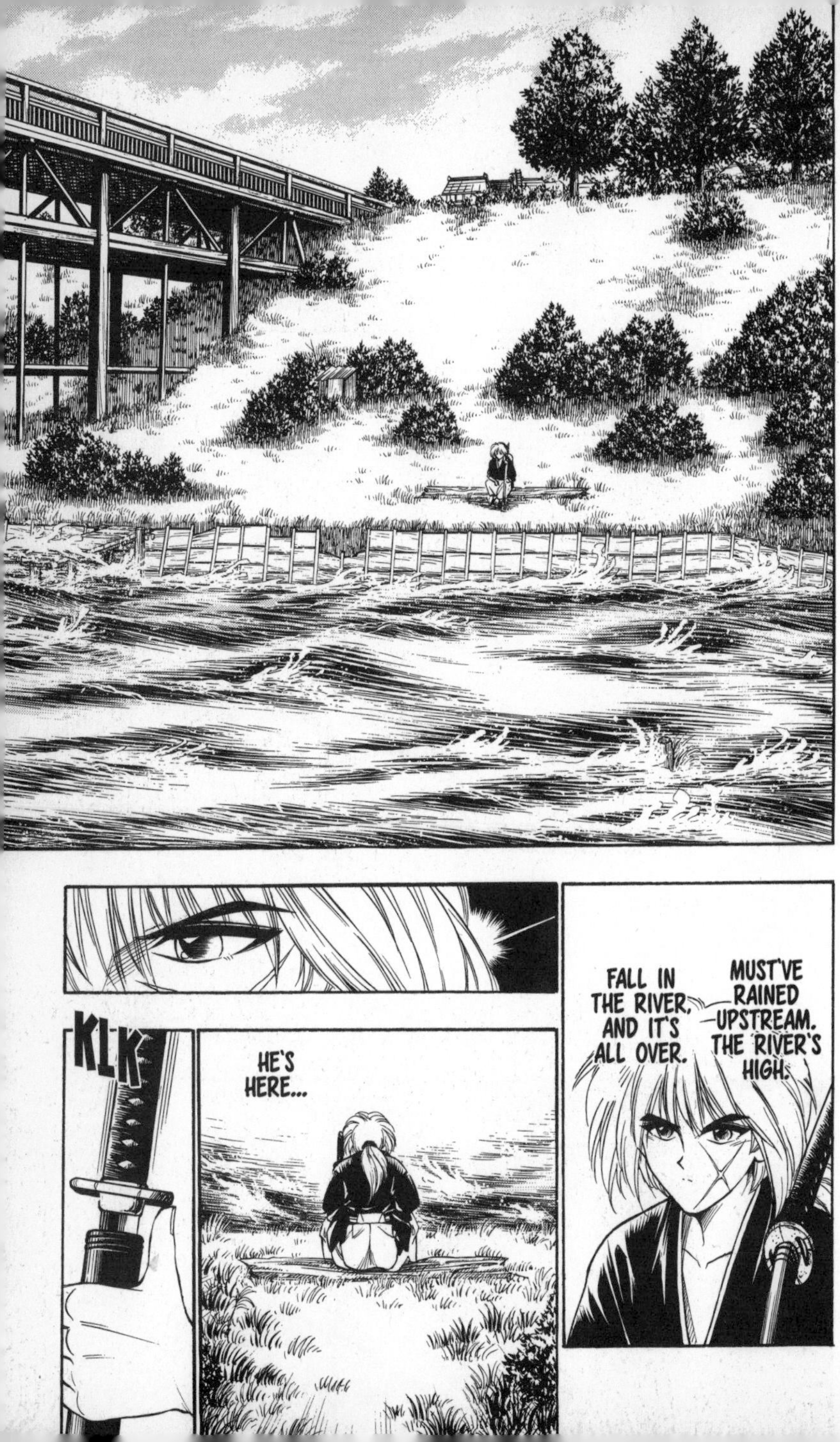
MUST'VE RAINED UPSTREAM. THE RIVER'S HIGH.
FALL IN THE RIVER, AND IT'S ALL OVER.
HE'S HERE...
KLIK

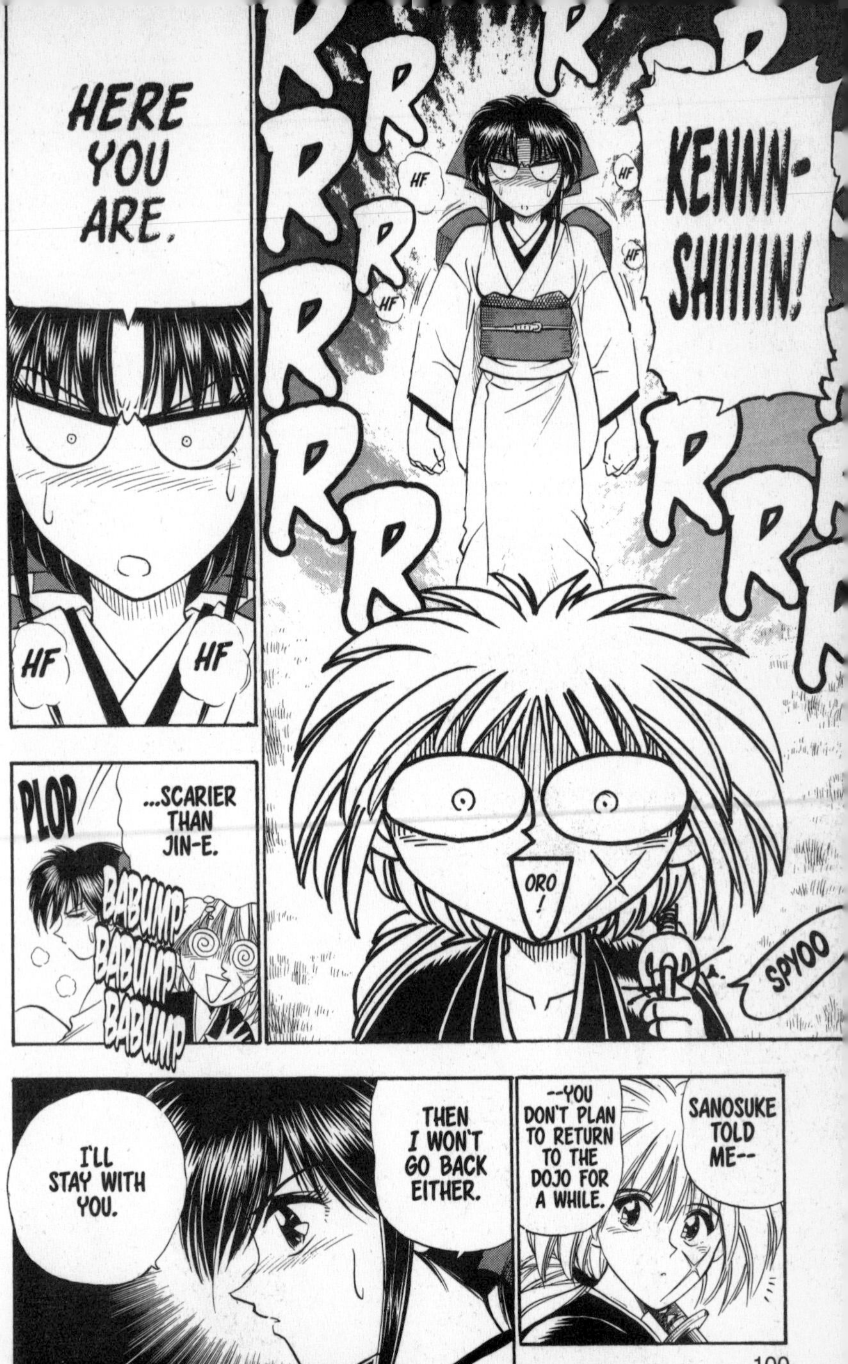
KENNN-SHIIIIN!
KRRRRRRRR
HF HF HF HF
ORO!
SPYOO
HERE YOU ARE.
HF HF
PLOP
...SCARIER THAN JIN-E.
BABUMP BABUMP BABUMP
SANOSUKE TOLD ME--
--YOU DON'T PLAN TO RETURN TO THE DOJO FOR A WHILE.
THEN I WON'T GO BACK EITHER.
I'LL STAY WITH YOU.

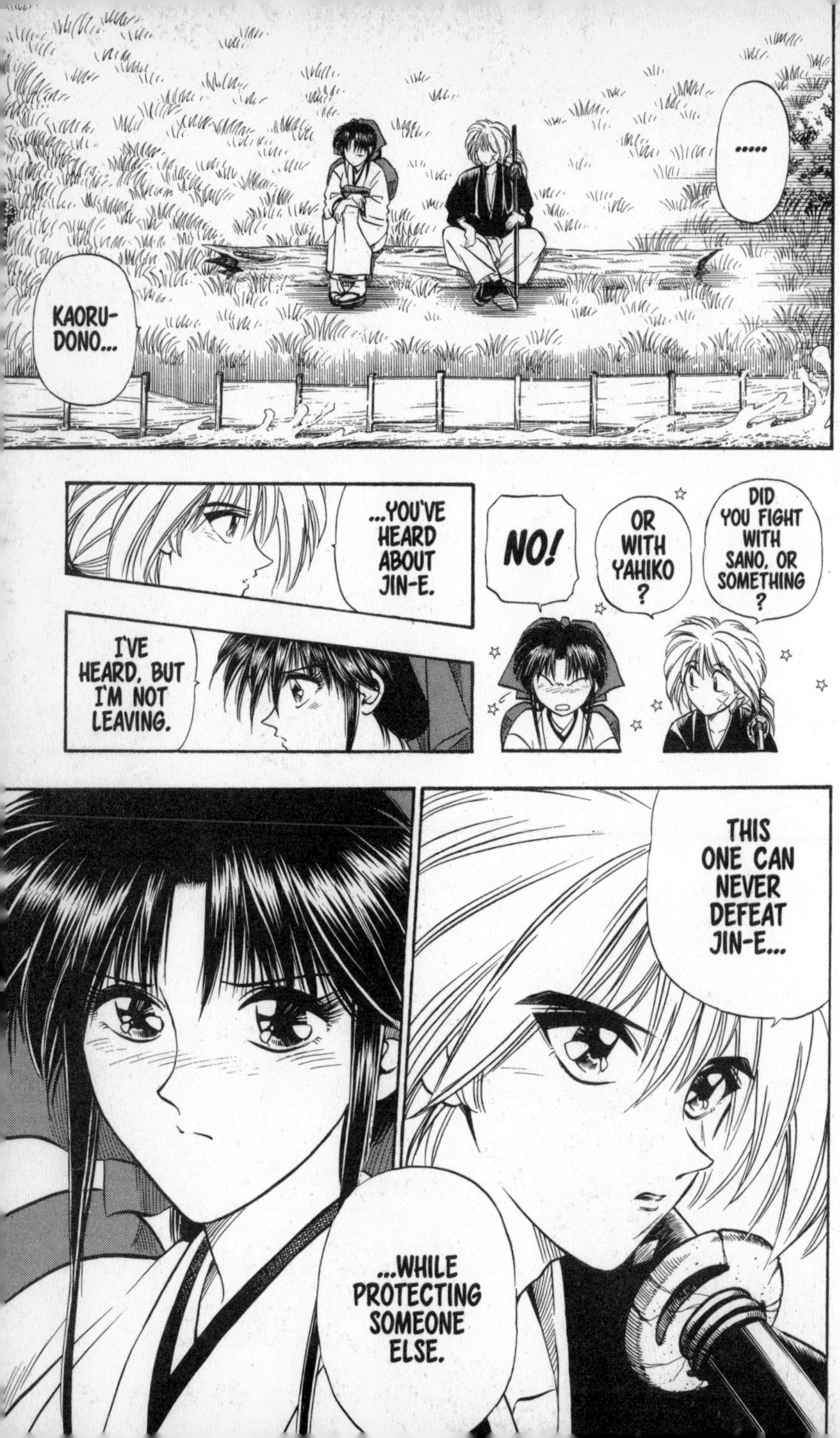
.....
KAORU-DONO...
DID YOU FIGHT WITH SANO, OR SOMETHING?
OR WITH YAHIKO?
NO!
...YOU'VE HEARD ABOUT JIN-E.
I'VE HEARD, BUT I'M NOT LEAVING.
THIS ONE CAN NEVER DEFEAT JIN-E...
...WHILE PROTECTING SOMEONE ELSE.

READ THIS WAY

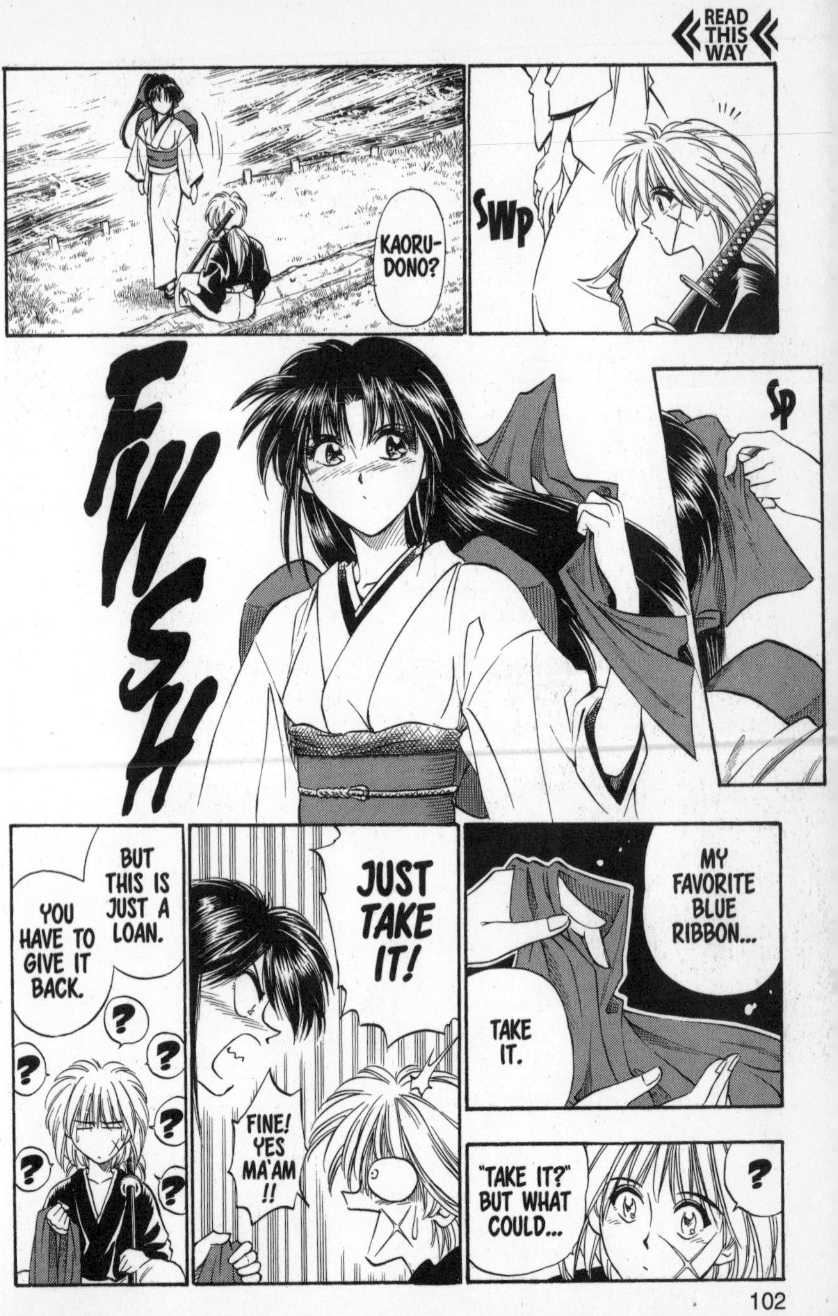
SWP
KAORU-DONO?
SP
FWSH
MY FAVORITE BLUE RIBBON...
TAKE IT.
?
"TAKE IT?" BUT WHAT COULD...
JUST TAKE IT!
FINE! YES MA'AM!!
BUT THIS IS JUST A LOAN.
YOU HAVE TO GIVE IT BACK.
? ? ? ? ? ?

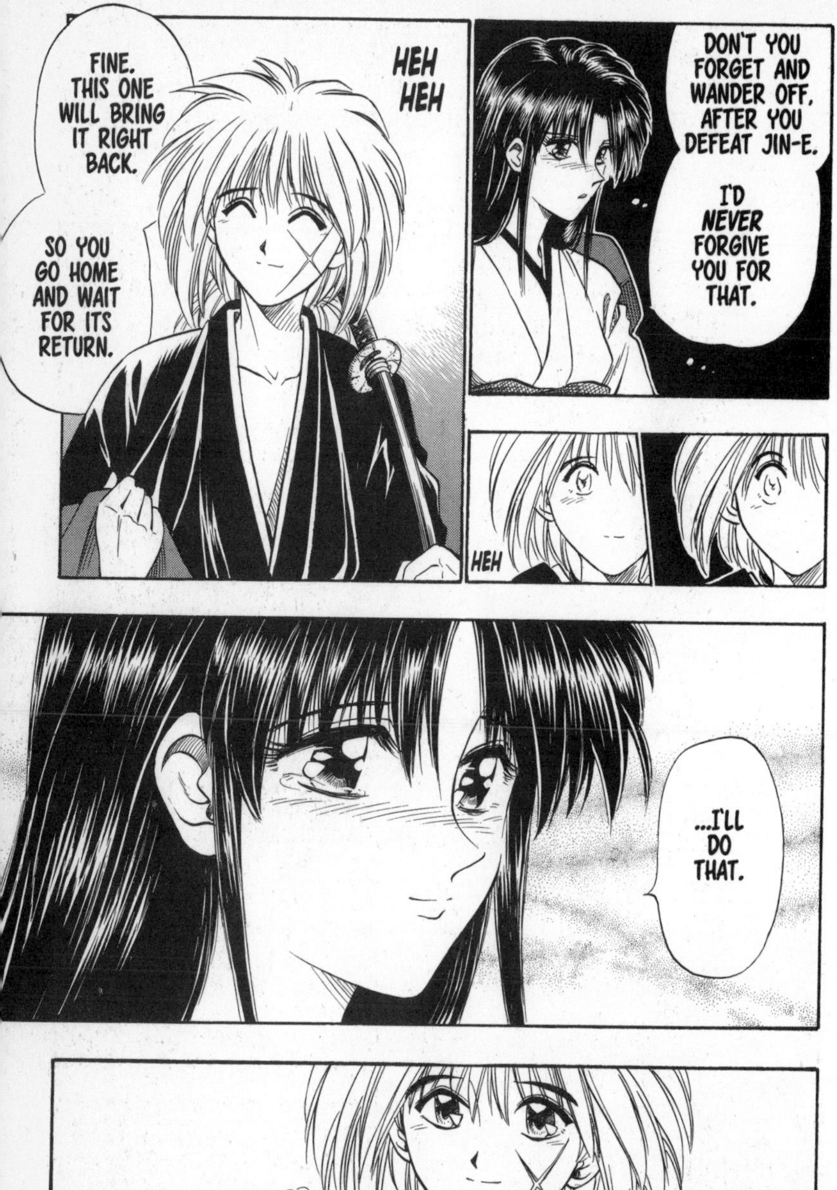
DON'T YOU FORGET AND WANDER OFF, AFTER YOU DEFEAT JIN-E.
I'D NEVER FORGIVE YOU FOR THAT.
HEH
FINE. THIS ONE WILL BRING IT RIGHT BACK.
HEH HEH
SO YOU GO HOME AND WAIT FOR ITS RETURN.
...I'LL DO THAT.

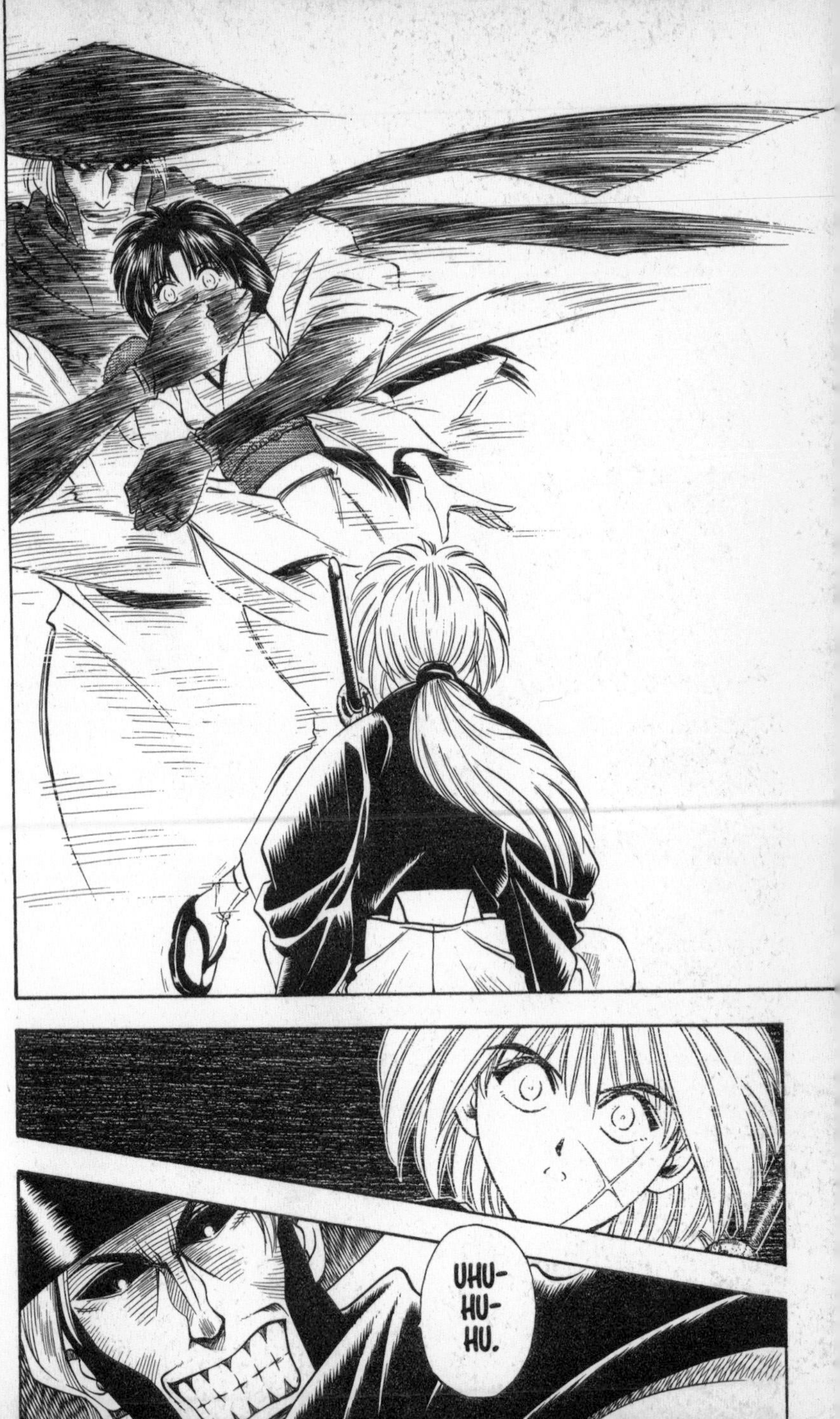
UHU-HU-HU.

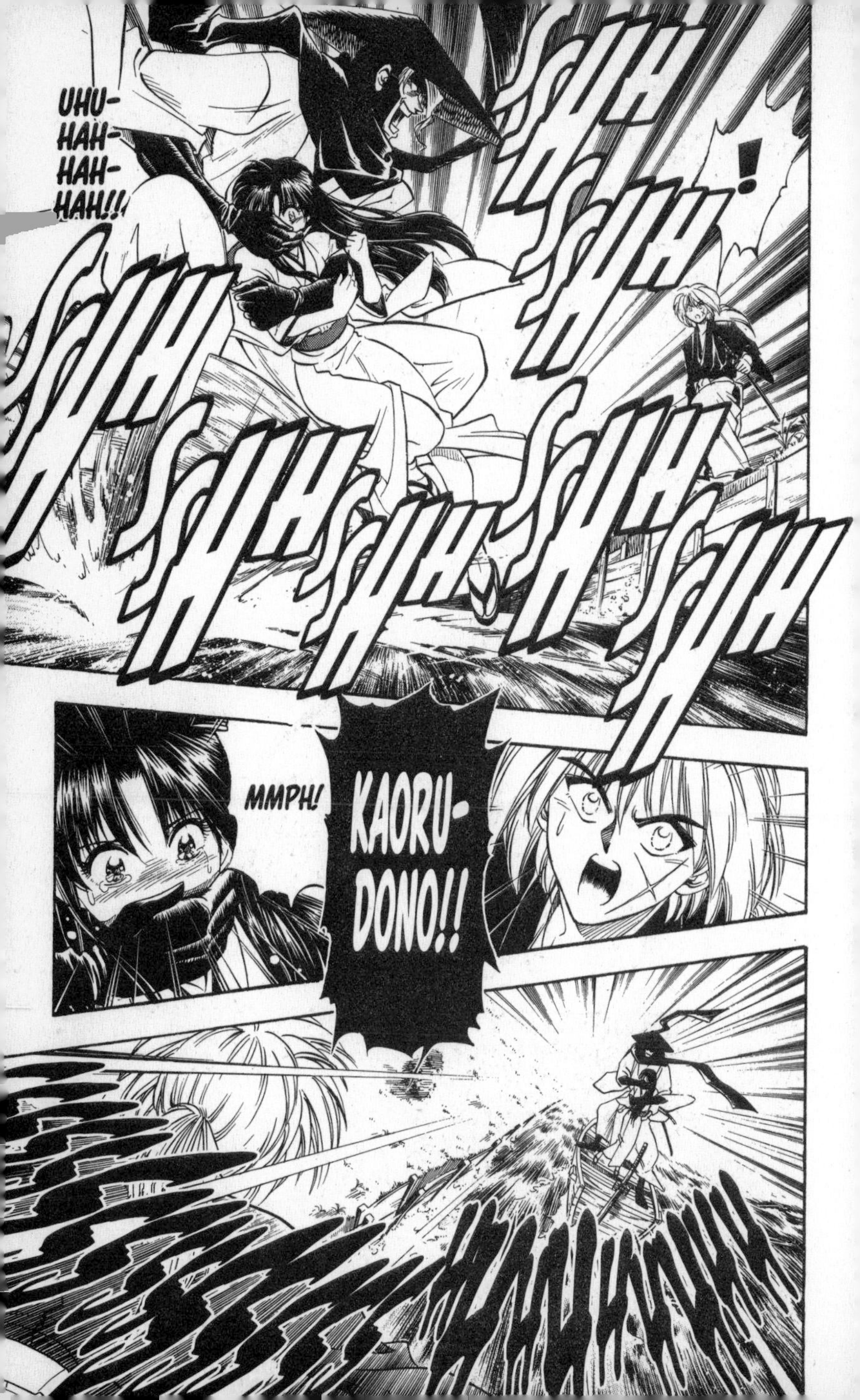
UHU-HAH-HAH-HAH!!
KAORU-DONO!!
MMPH!

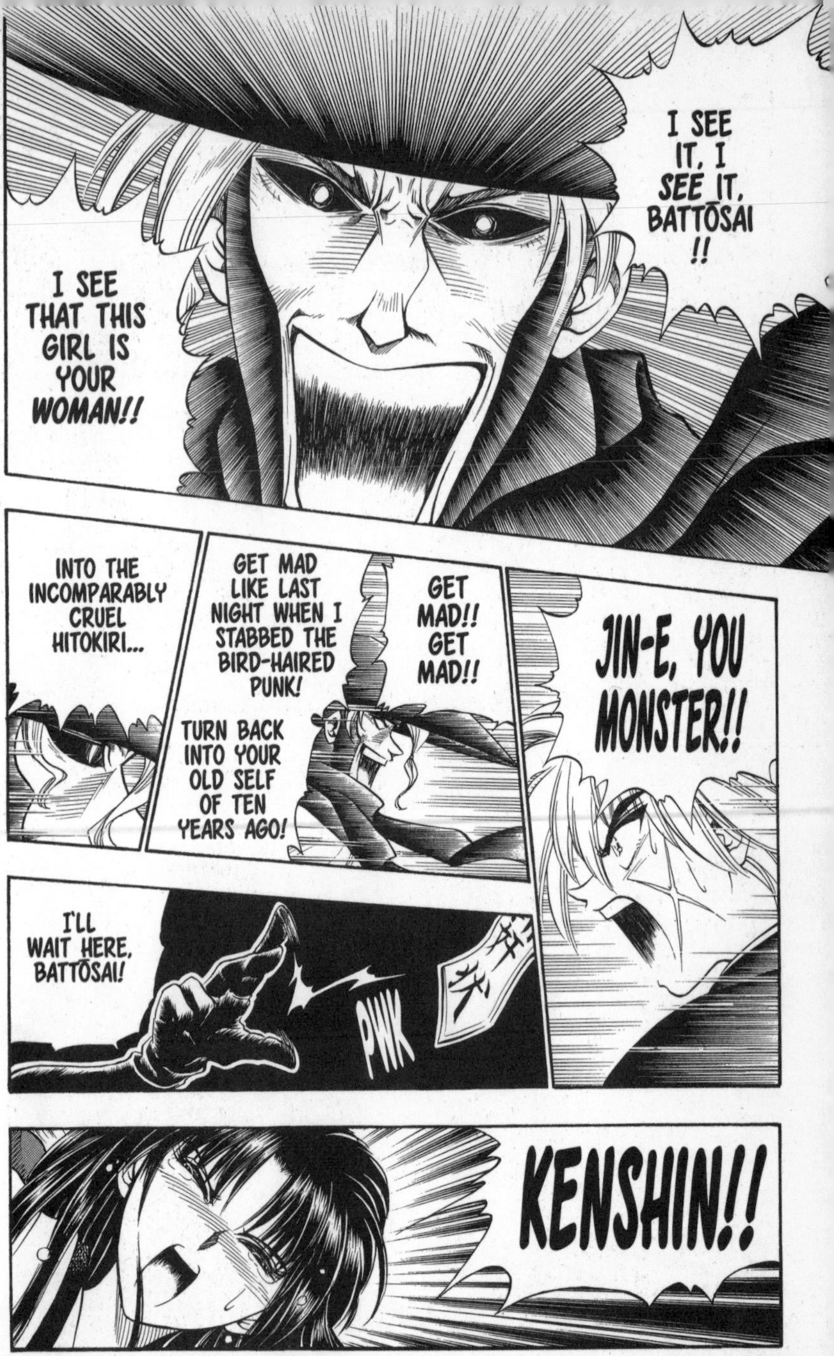
I SEE IT, I SEE IT, BATTŌSAI!!
I SEE THAT THIS GIRL IS YOUR WOMAN!!
JIN-E, YOU MONSTER!!
GET MAD!! GET MAD!!
GET MAD LIKE LAST NIGHT WHEN I STABBED THE BIRD-HAIRED PUNK!
TURN BACK INTO YOUR OLD SELF OF TEN YEARS AGO!
INTO THE INCOMPARABLY CRUEL HITOKIRI...
I'LL WAIT HERE, BATTŌSAI!
PWK
KENSHIN!!

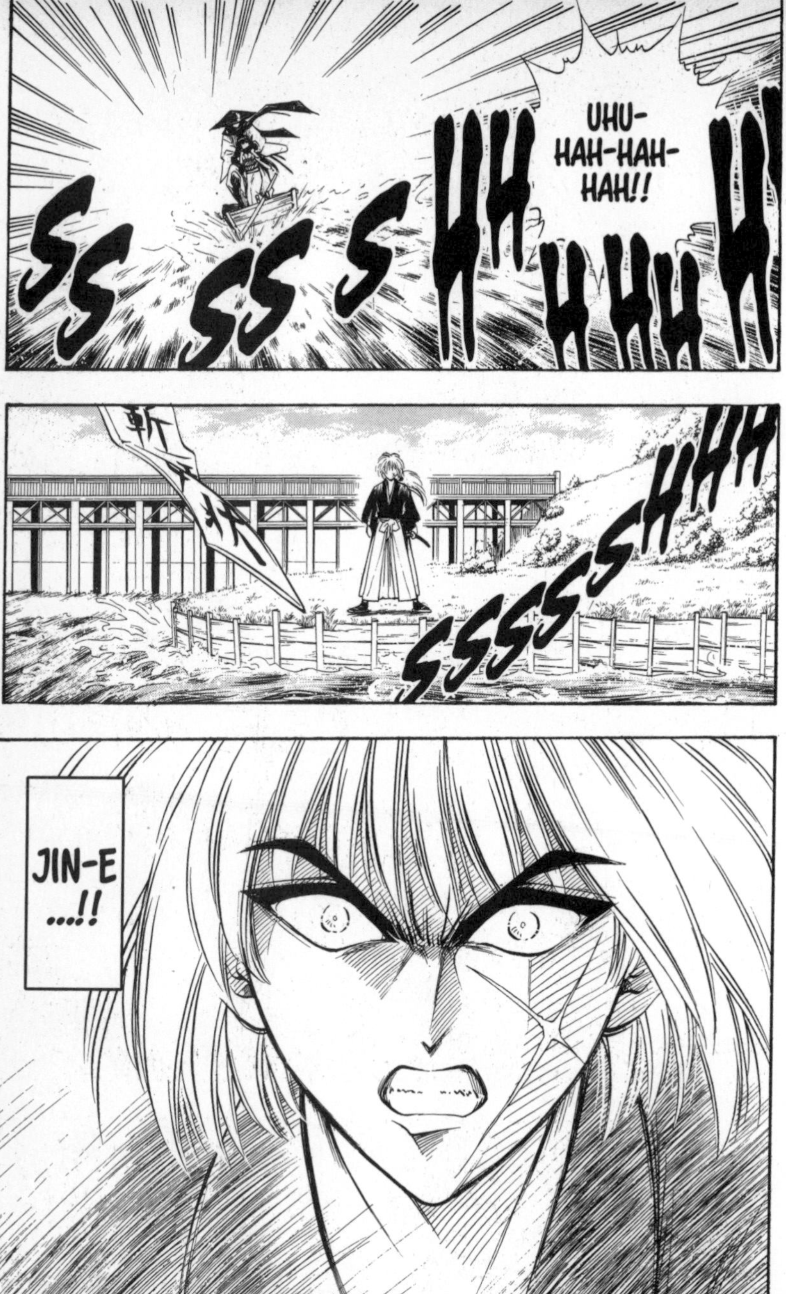
UHU-HAH-HAH-HAH!!
SSSSSHHHHHHH
SSSSSHHHH
JIN-E ...!!

# Act 12 — The Two Hitokiri

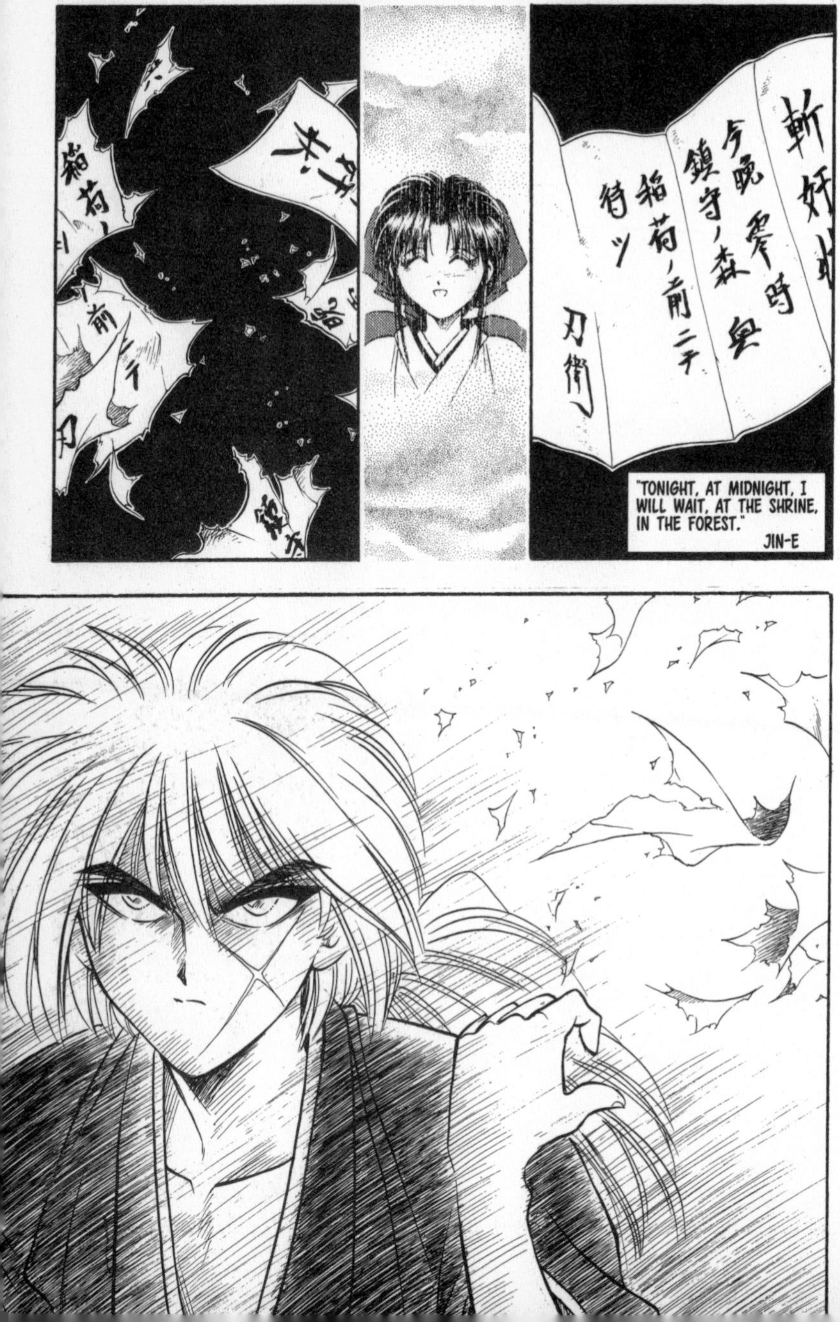
斬奸
今晩 零時
鎮守ノ森 奥
稲荷ノ前ニテ
待ツ
刃衛
"TONIGHT, AT MIDNIGHT, I WILL WAIT, AT THE SHRINE, IN THE FOREST."
JIN-E

READ THIS WAY

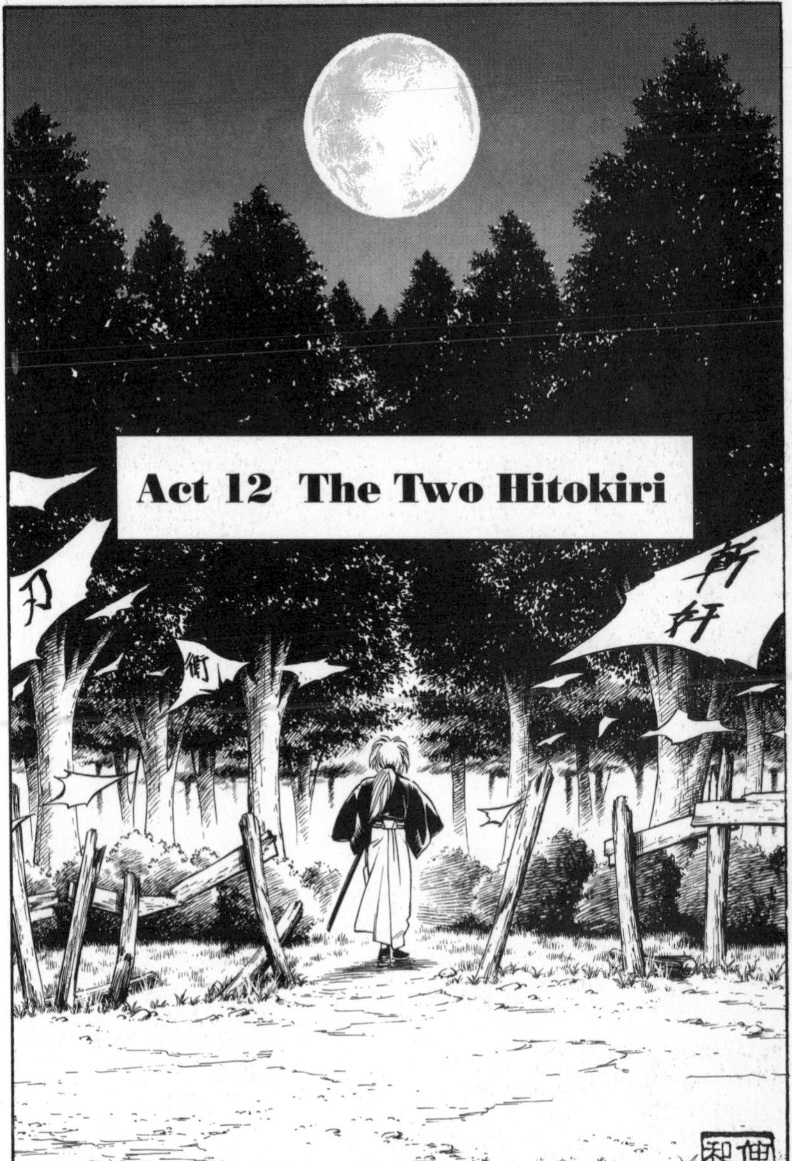
Act 12 The Two Hitokiri

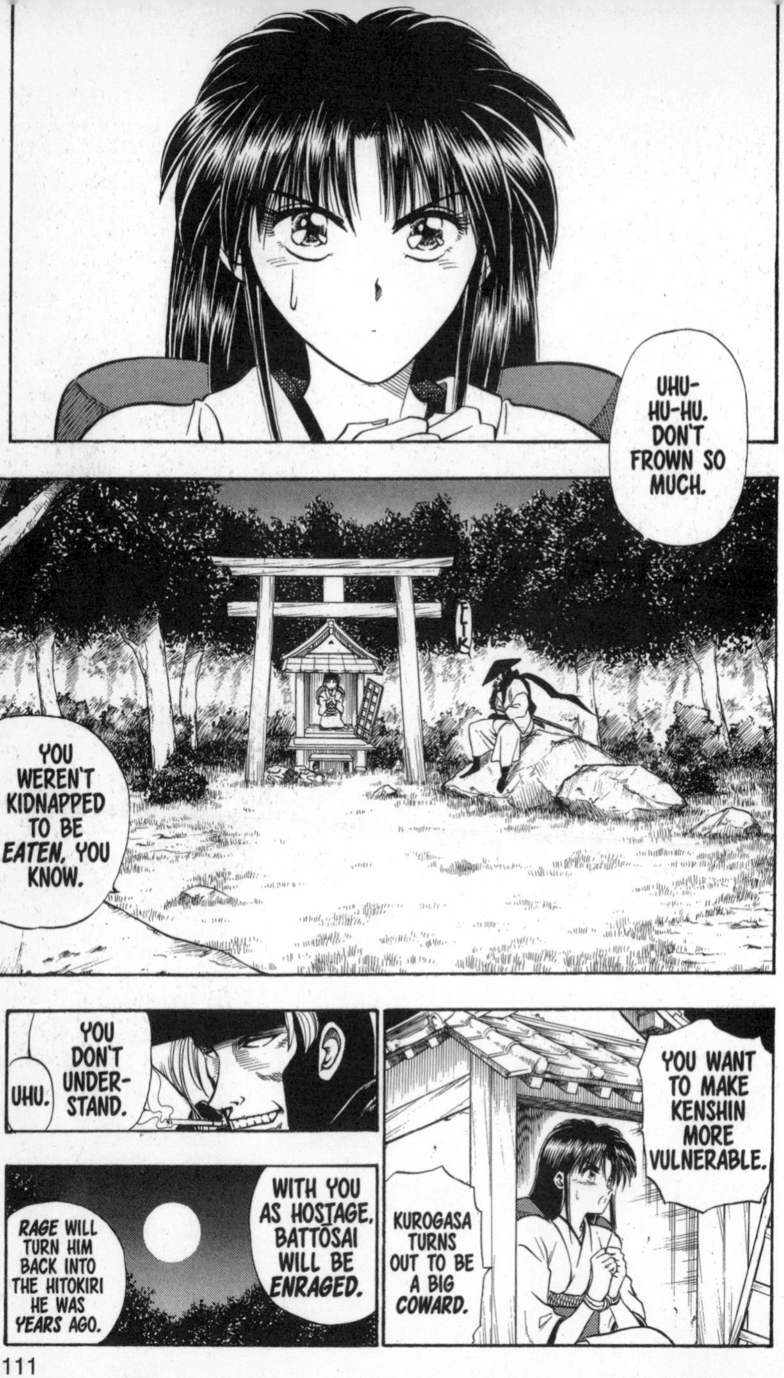
UHU-HU-HU. DON'T FROWN SO MUCH.
FLIK
YOU WEREN'T KIDNAPPED TO BE EATEN, YOU KNOW.
YOU WANT TO MAKE KENSHIN MORE VULNERABLE.
KUROGASA TURNS OUT TO BE A BIG COWARD.
YOU DON'T UNDER-STAND.
UHU.
WITH YOU AS HOSTAGE, BATTOSAI WILL BE ENRAGED.
RAGE WILL TURN HIM BACK INTO THE HITOKIRI HE WAS YEARS AGO.

READ THIS WAY

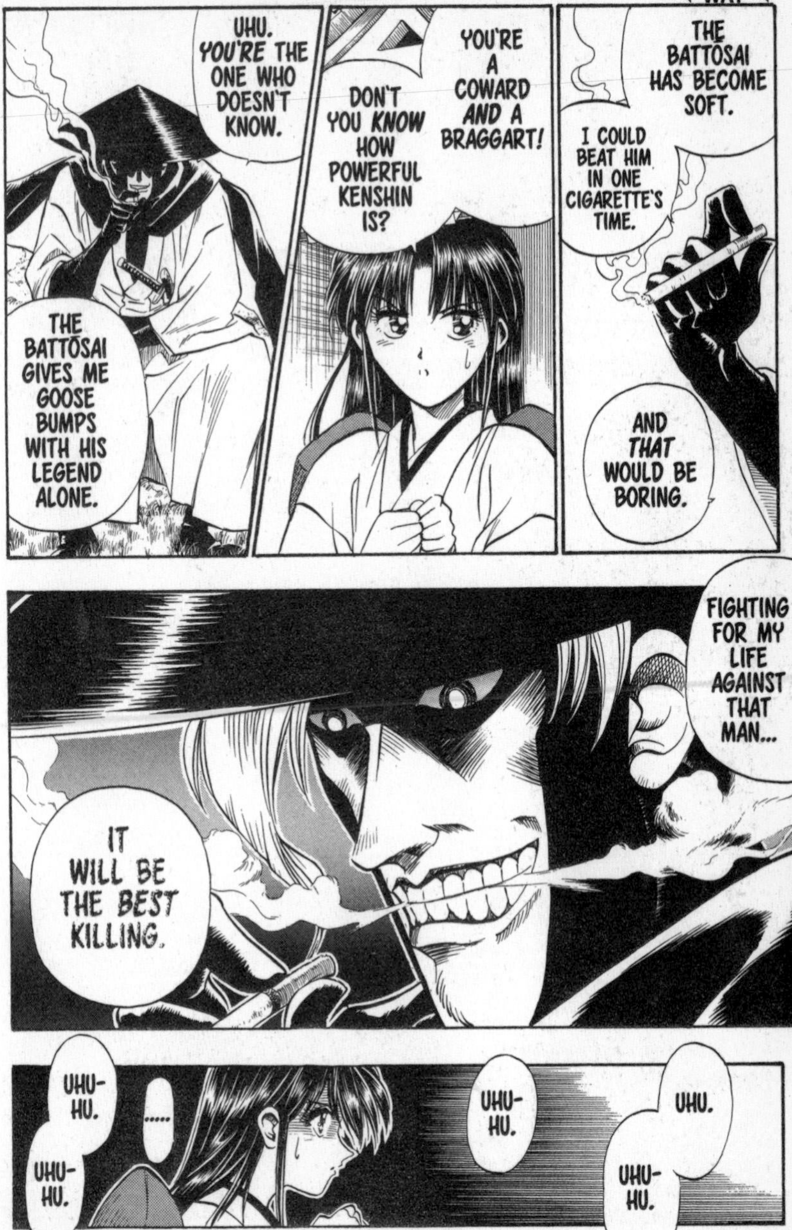
THE BATTŌSAI HAS BECOME SOFT.
I COULD BEAT HIM IN ONE CIGARETTE'S TIME.
AND THAT WOULD BE BORING.
YOU'RE A COWARD AND A BRAGGART!
DON'T YOU KNOW HOW POWERFUL KENSHIN IS?
UHU. YOU'RE THE ONE WHO DOESN'T KNOW.
THE BATTŌSAI GIVES ME GOOSE BUMPS WITH HIS LEGEND ALONE.
FIGHTING FOR MY LIFE AGAINST THAT MAN...
IT WILL BE THE BEST KILLING.
UHU.
UHU-HU.
UHU-HU.
......
UHU-HU.
UHU-HU.

READ THIS WAY

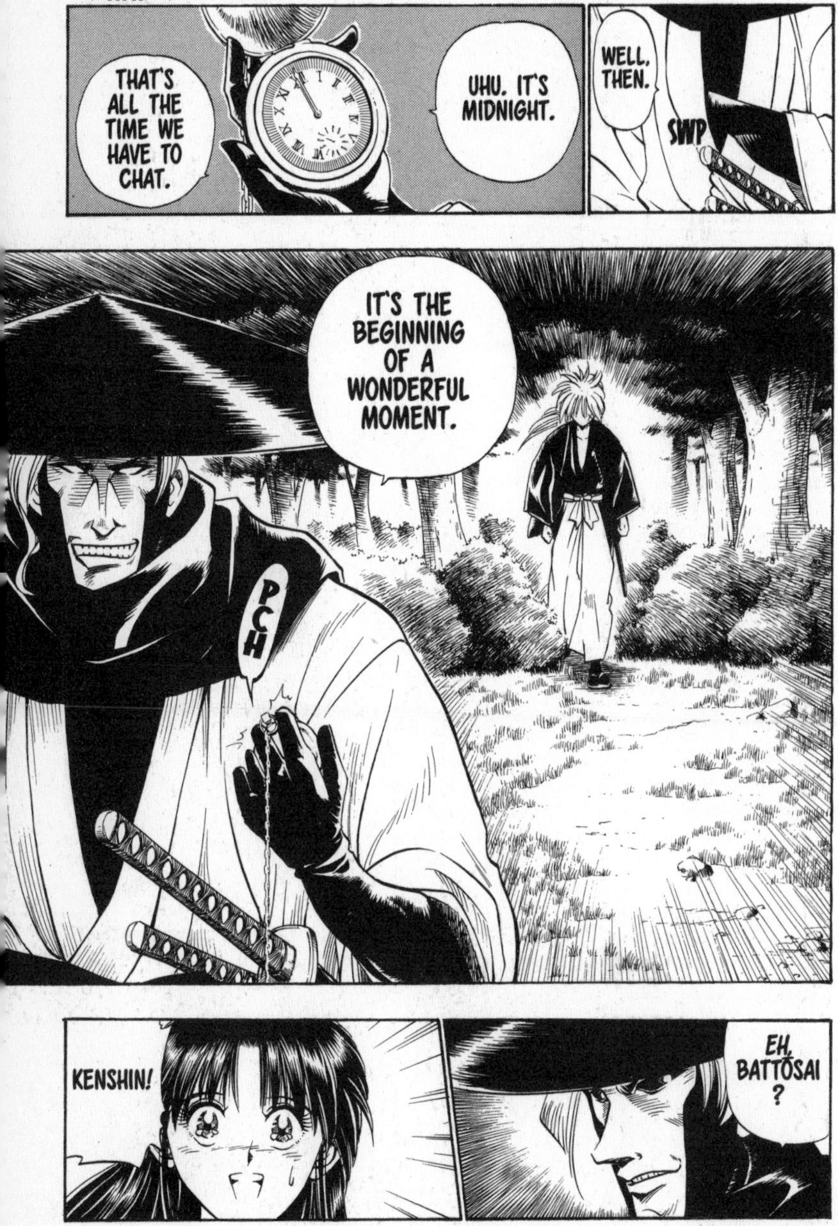

WELL, THEN.
SWP
UHU. IT'S MIDNIGHT.
THAT'S ALL THE TIME WE HAVE TO CHAT.
IT'S THE BEGINNING OF A WONDERFUL MOMENT.
PCH
EH, BATTŌSAI ?
KENSHIN!

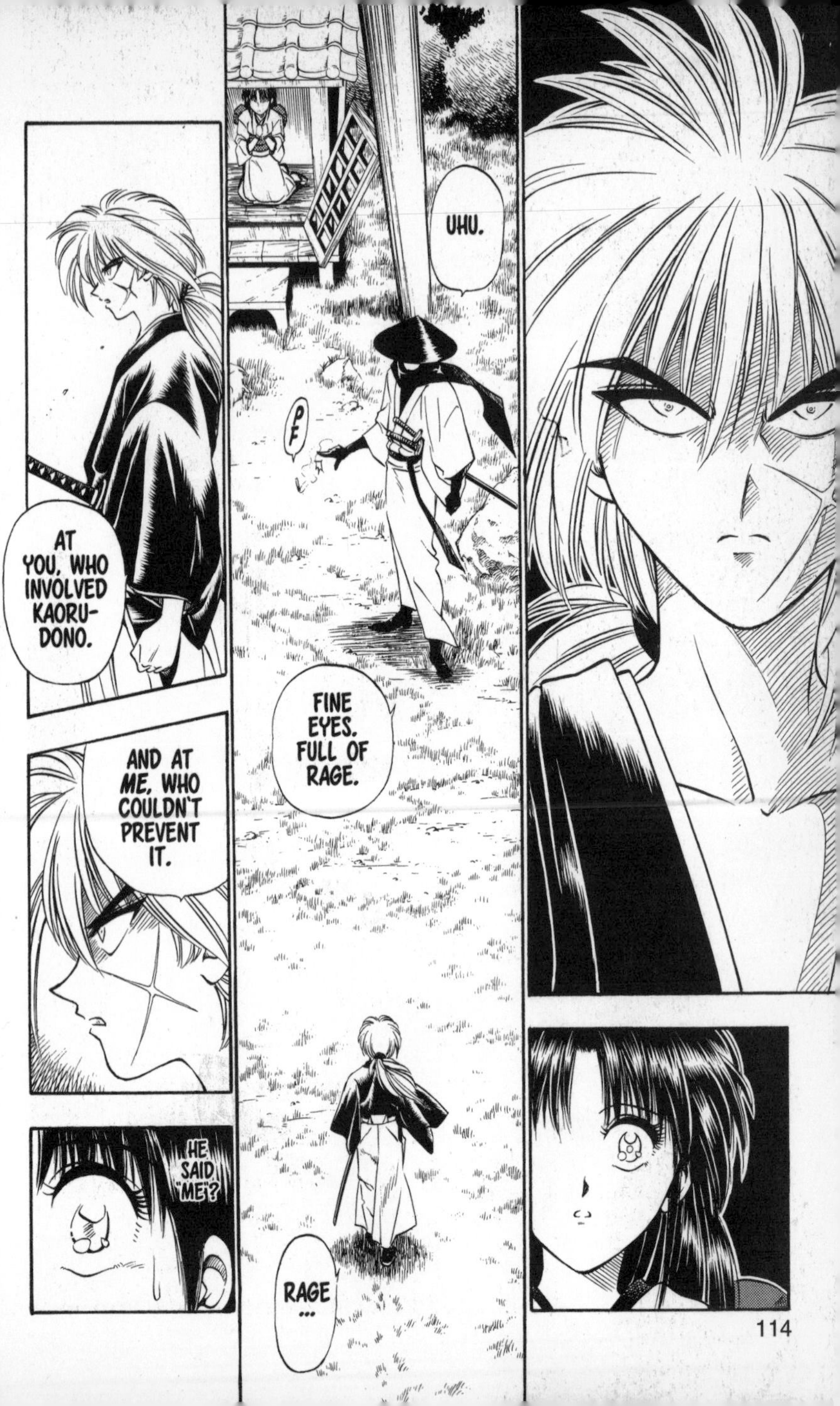
UHU.
PF
FINE EYES. FULL OF RAGE.
RAGE...
AT YOU, WHO INVOLVED KAORU-DONO.
AND AT ME, WHO COULDN'T PREVENT IT.
HE SAID "ME"?

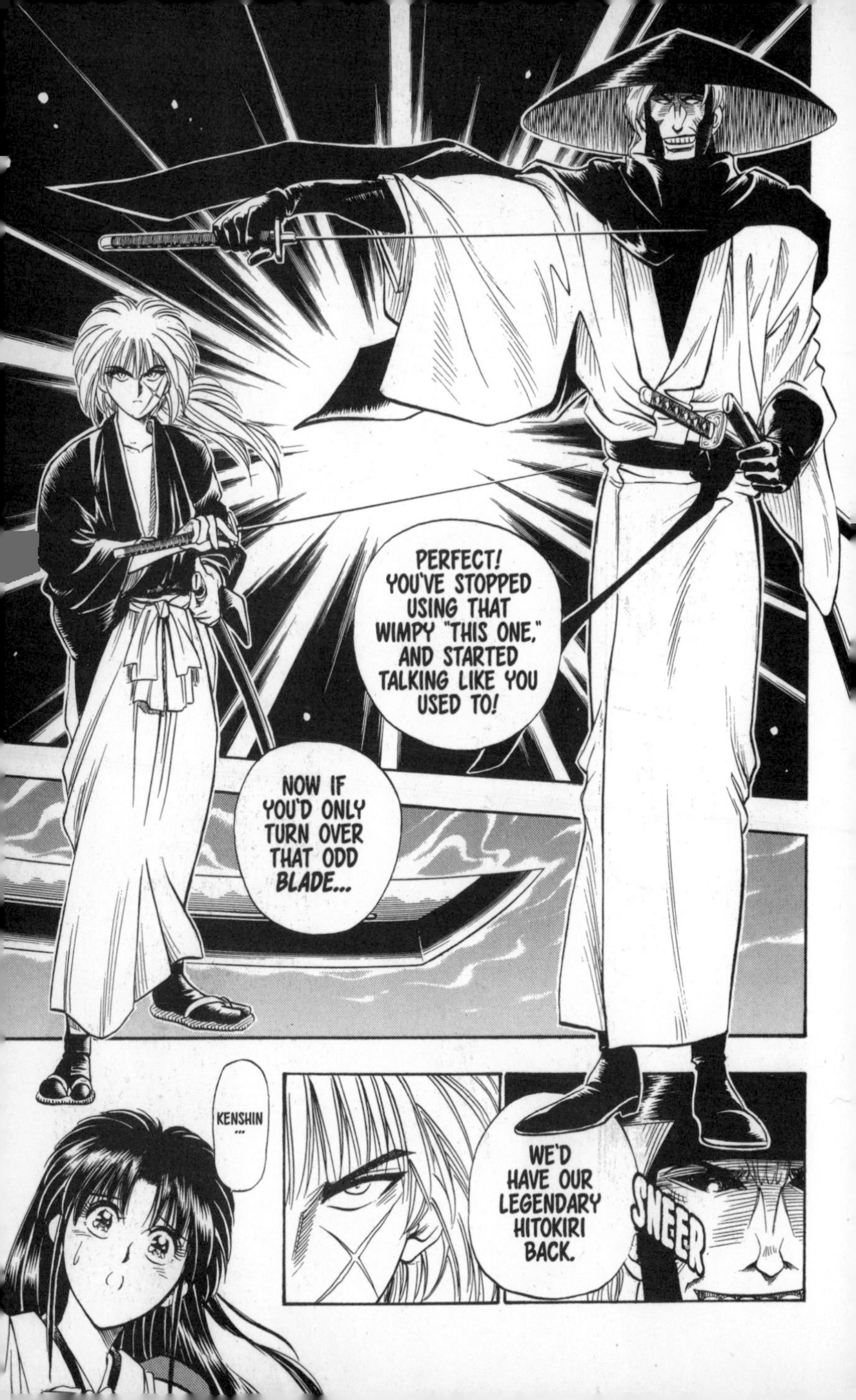
PERFECT! YOU'VE STOPPED USING THAT WIMPY "THIS ONE," AND STARTED TALKING LIKE YOU USED TO!
NOW IF YOU'D ONLY TURN OVER THAT ODD BLADE...
WE'D HAVE OUR LEGENDARY HITOKIRI BACK.
SNEER
KENSHIN ...

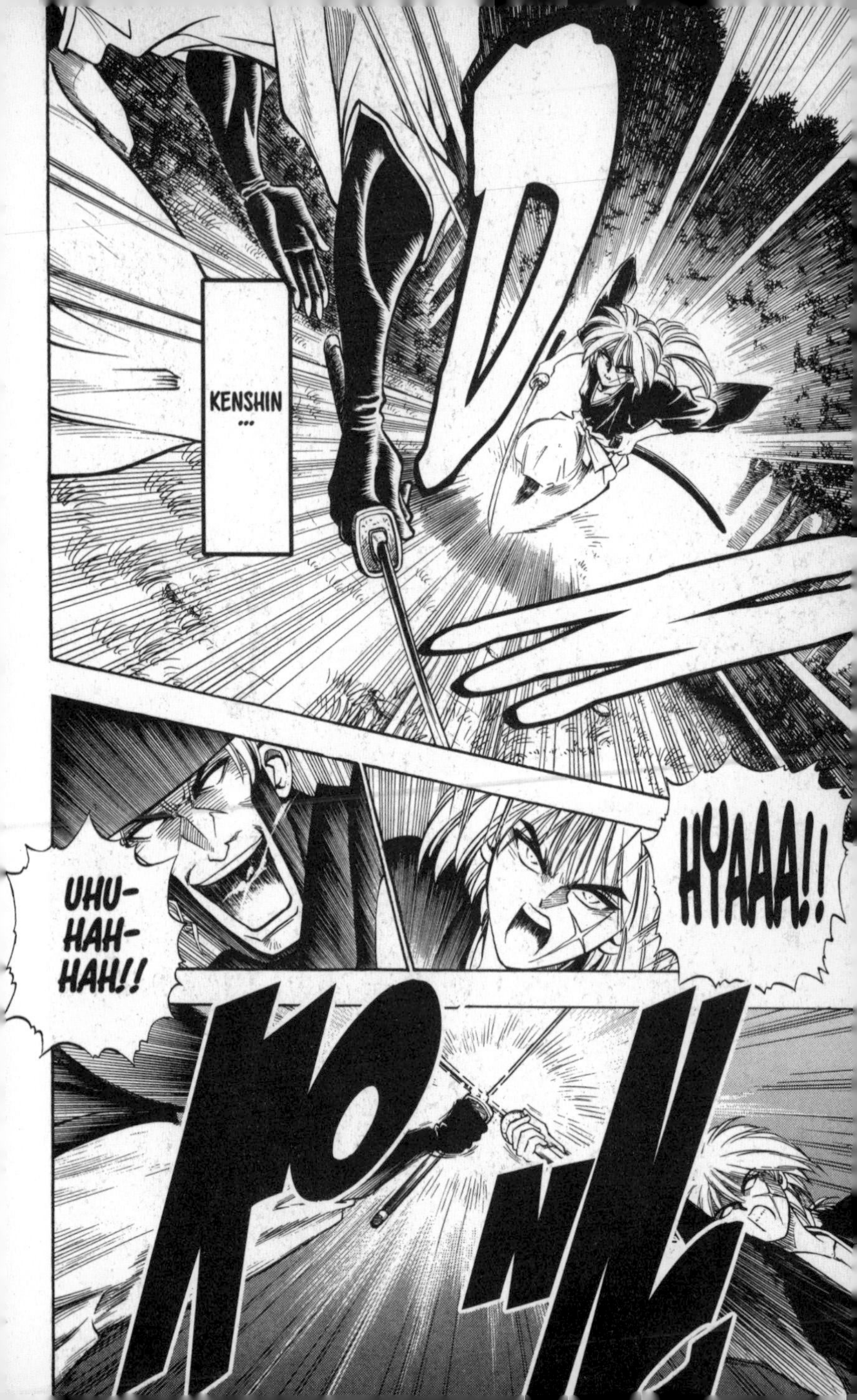
KENSHIN
...
HYAAA!!
UHU-
HAH-
HAH!!

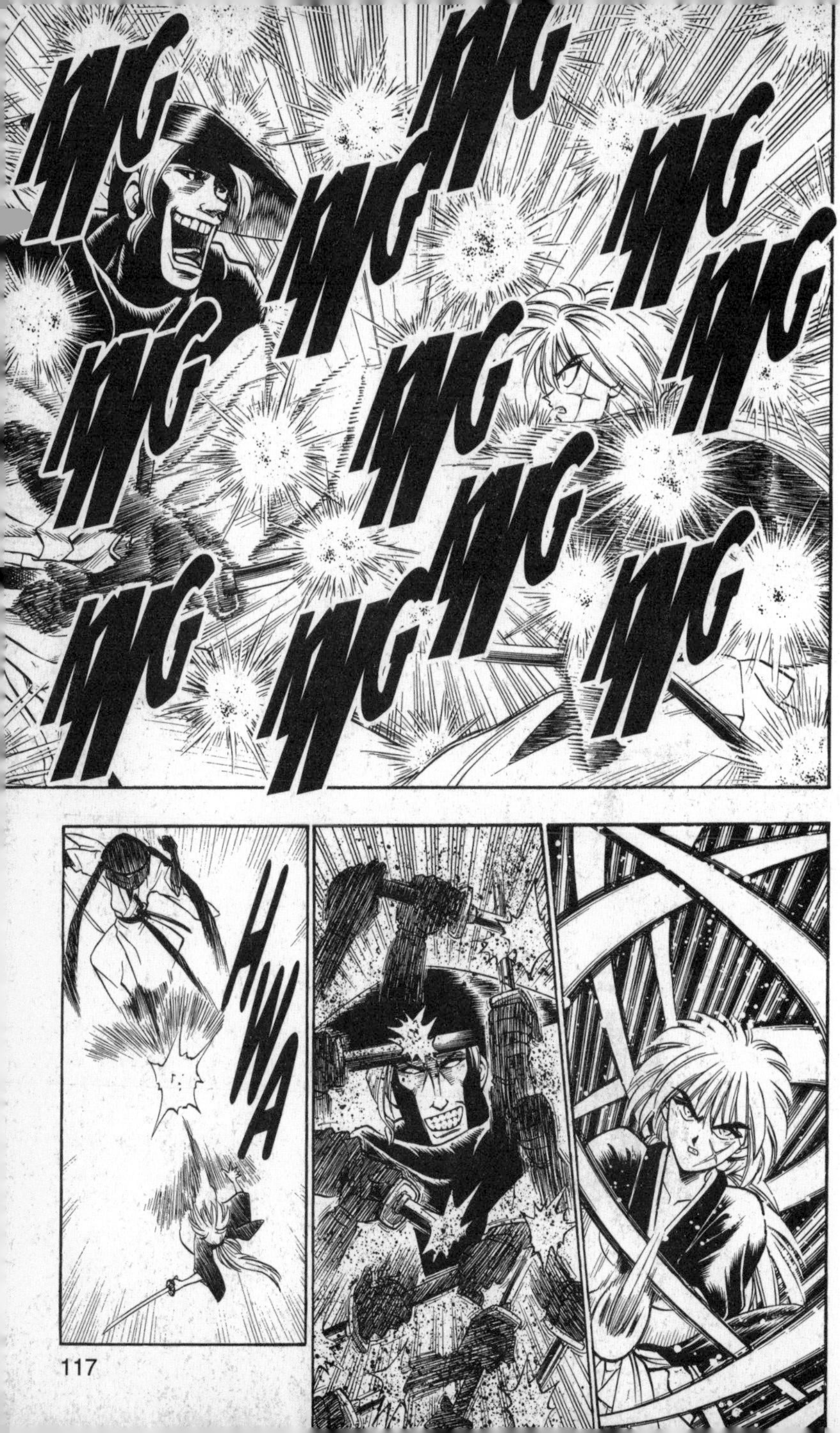
NNG
NNG
NNG
NNG
NNG
NNG
NNG
NNG
NNG
NNG
NNG
HWA

READ THIS WAY

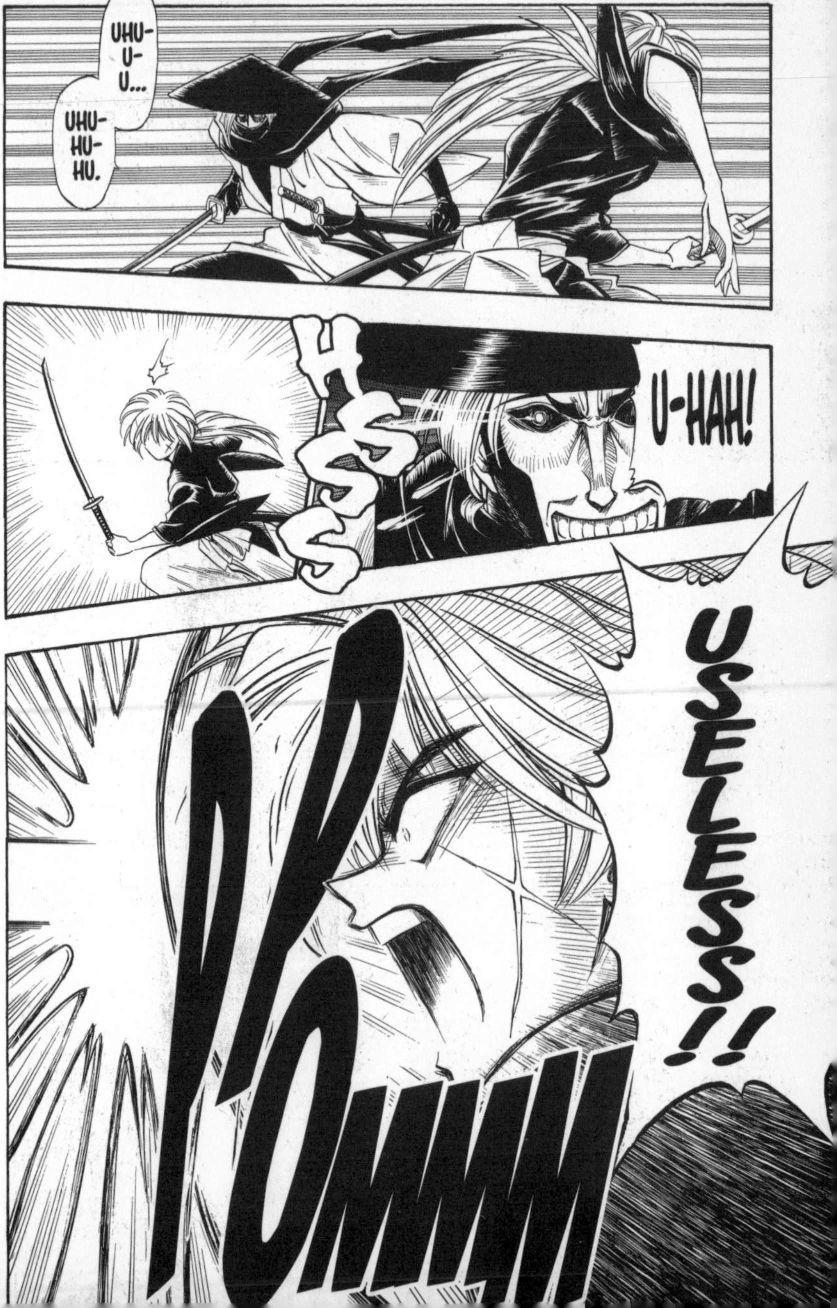
UHU-U-U...
UHU-HU-HU.
U-HAH!
HSSSS
USELESS!!

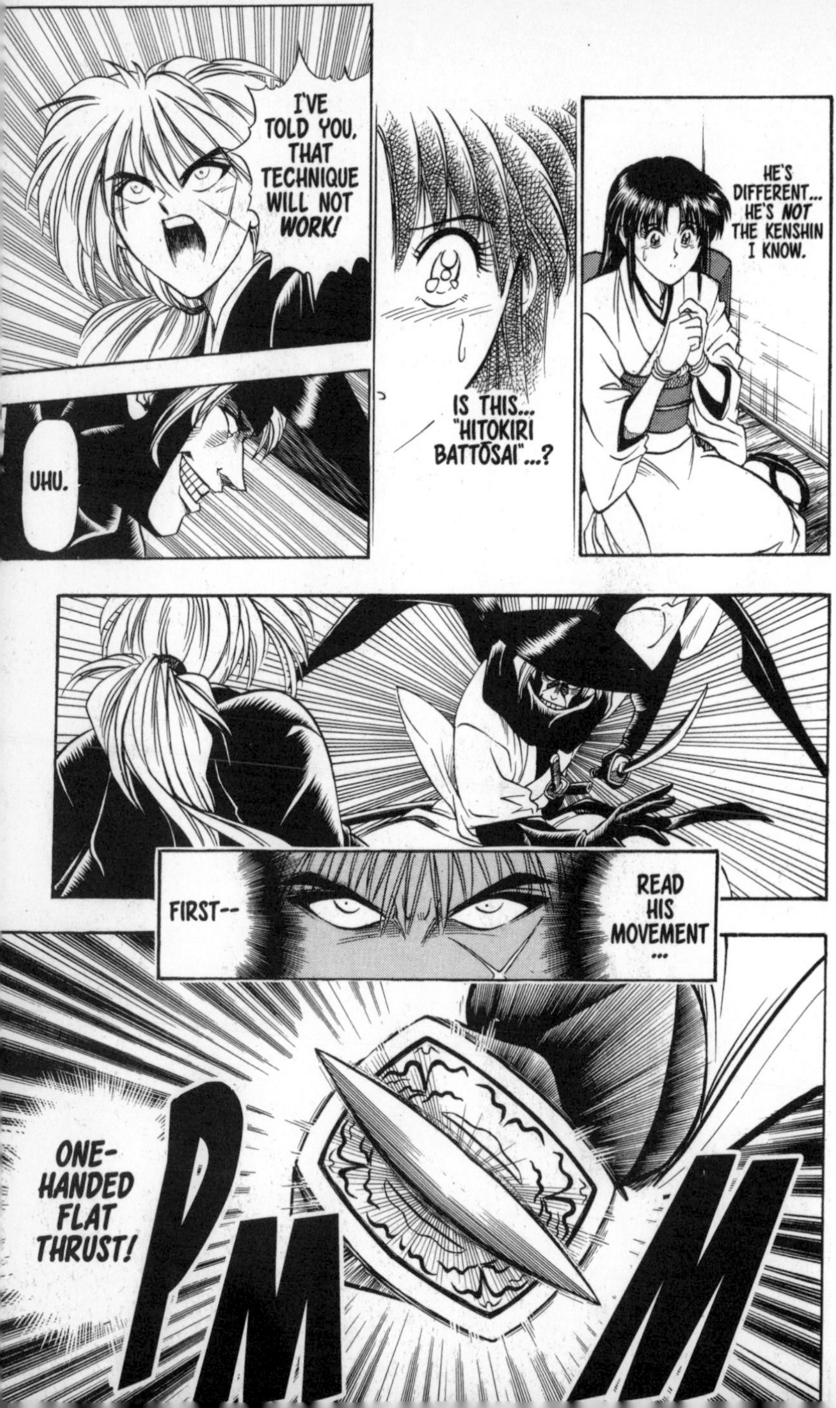
HE'S DIFFERENT... HE'S *NOT* THE KENSHIN I KNOW.
IS THIS... "HITOKIRI BATTŌSAI"...?
I'VE TOLD YOU, THAT TECHNIQUE WILL NOT *WORK!*
UHU.
FIRST--
READ HIS MOVEMENT...
ONE-HANDED FLAT THRUST!
PMM

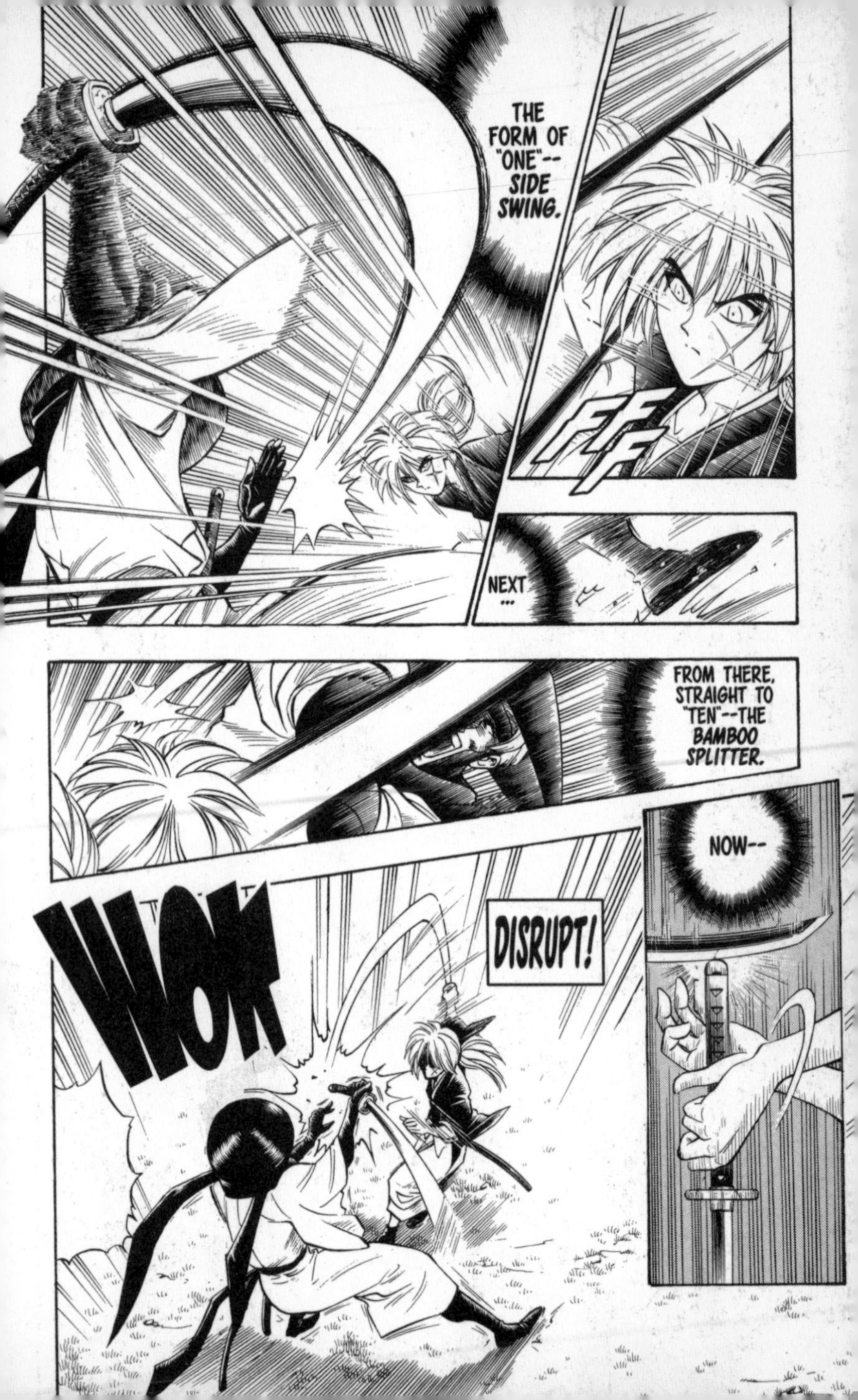
THE FORM OF "ONE"-- SIDE SWING.
FFF
NEXT...
FROM THERE, STRAIGHT TO "TEN"--THE BAMBOO SPLITTER.
NOW--
DISRUPT!
WOK

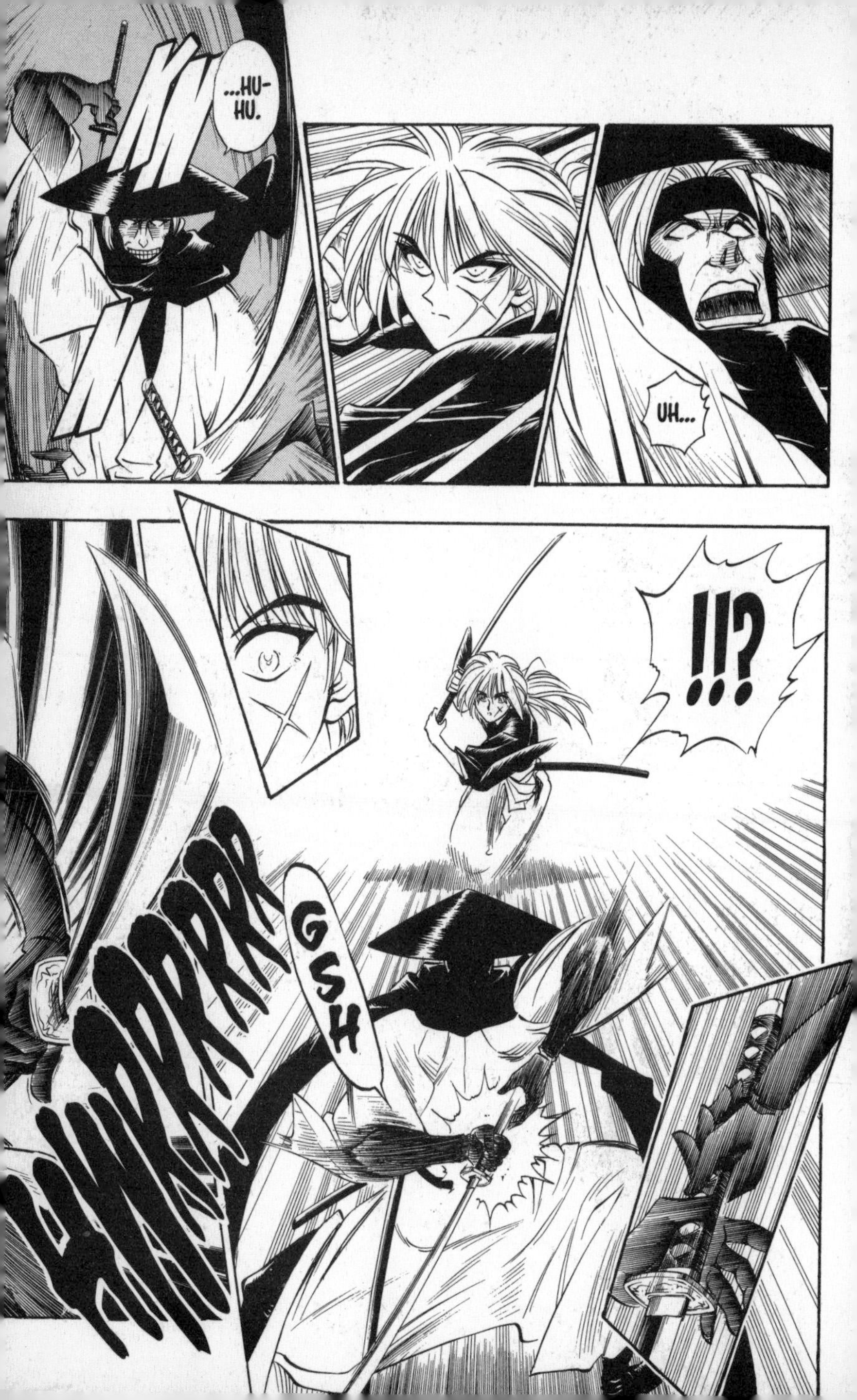
UH...
...HU-HU.
!!?
GSH

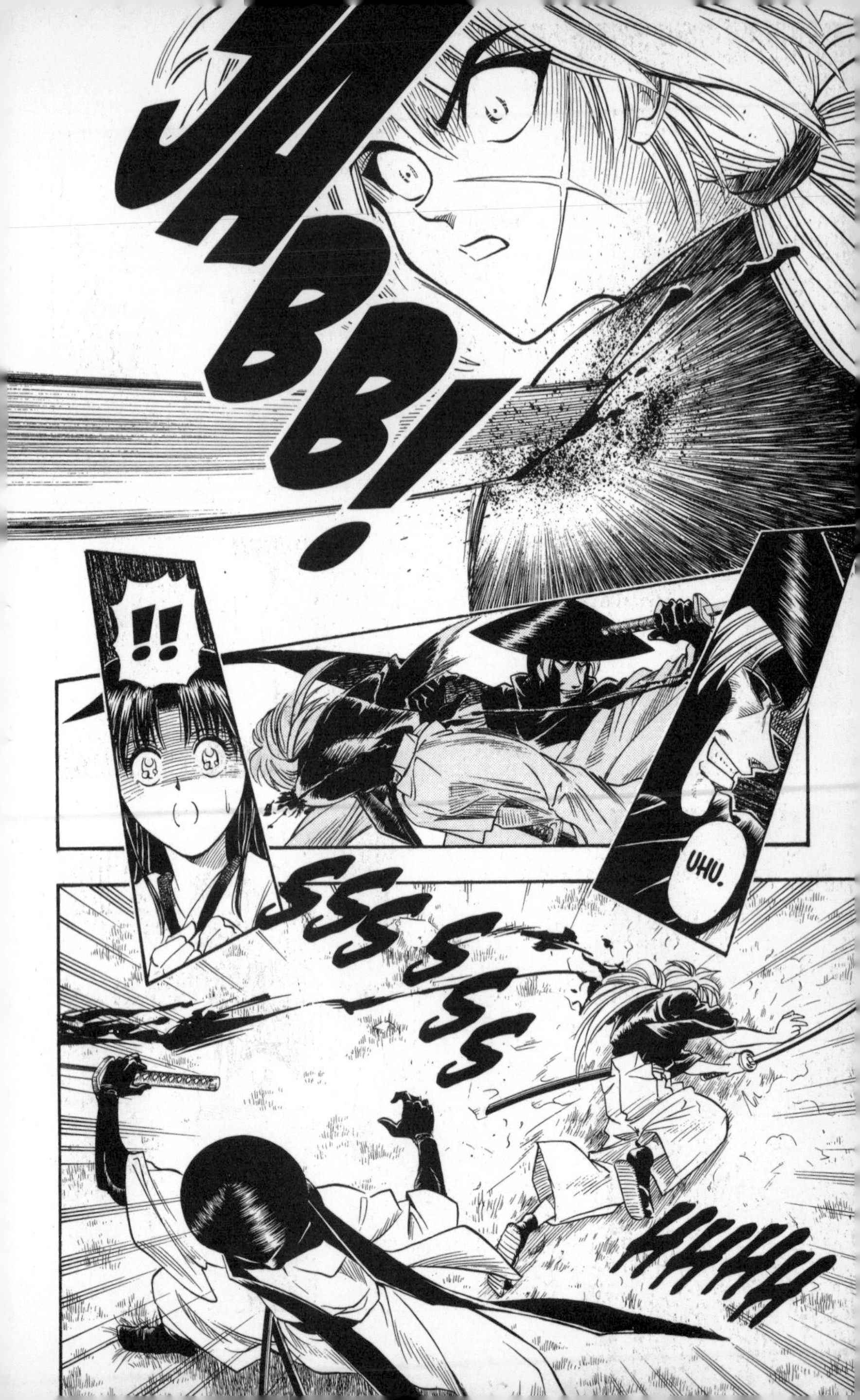
JABB!
UHU.
!!
SSSSSSSS
HHHH

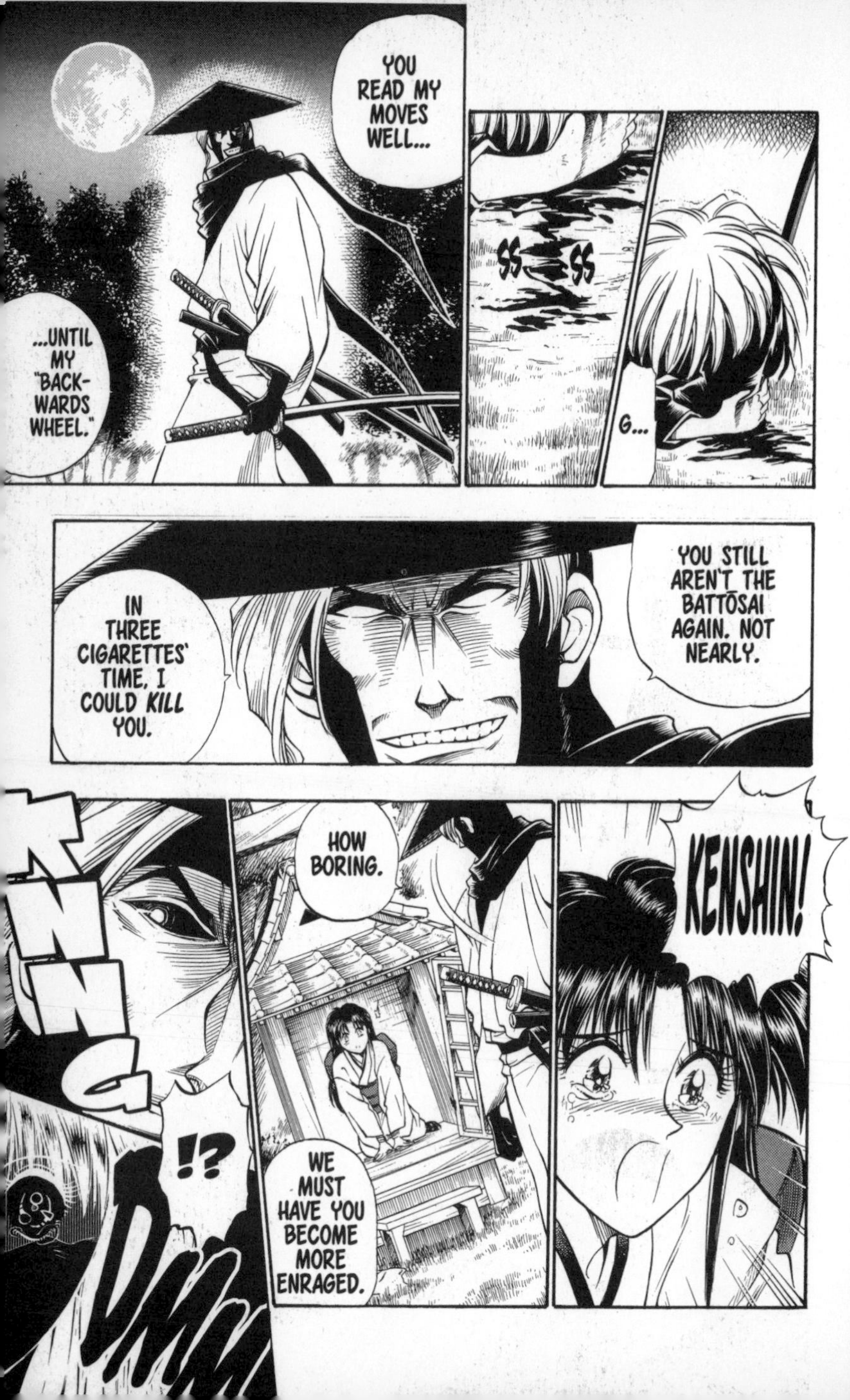
G...
SS SS
YOU READ MY MOVES WELL...
...UNTIL MY "BACKWARDS WHEEL."
YOU STILL AREN'T THE BATTŌSAI AGAIN. NOT NEARLY.
IN THREE CIGARETTES' TIME, I COULD KILL YOU.
KENSHIN!
HOW BORING.
WE MUST HAVE YOU BECOME MORE ENRAGED.
!?

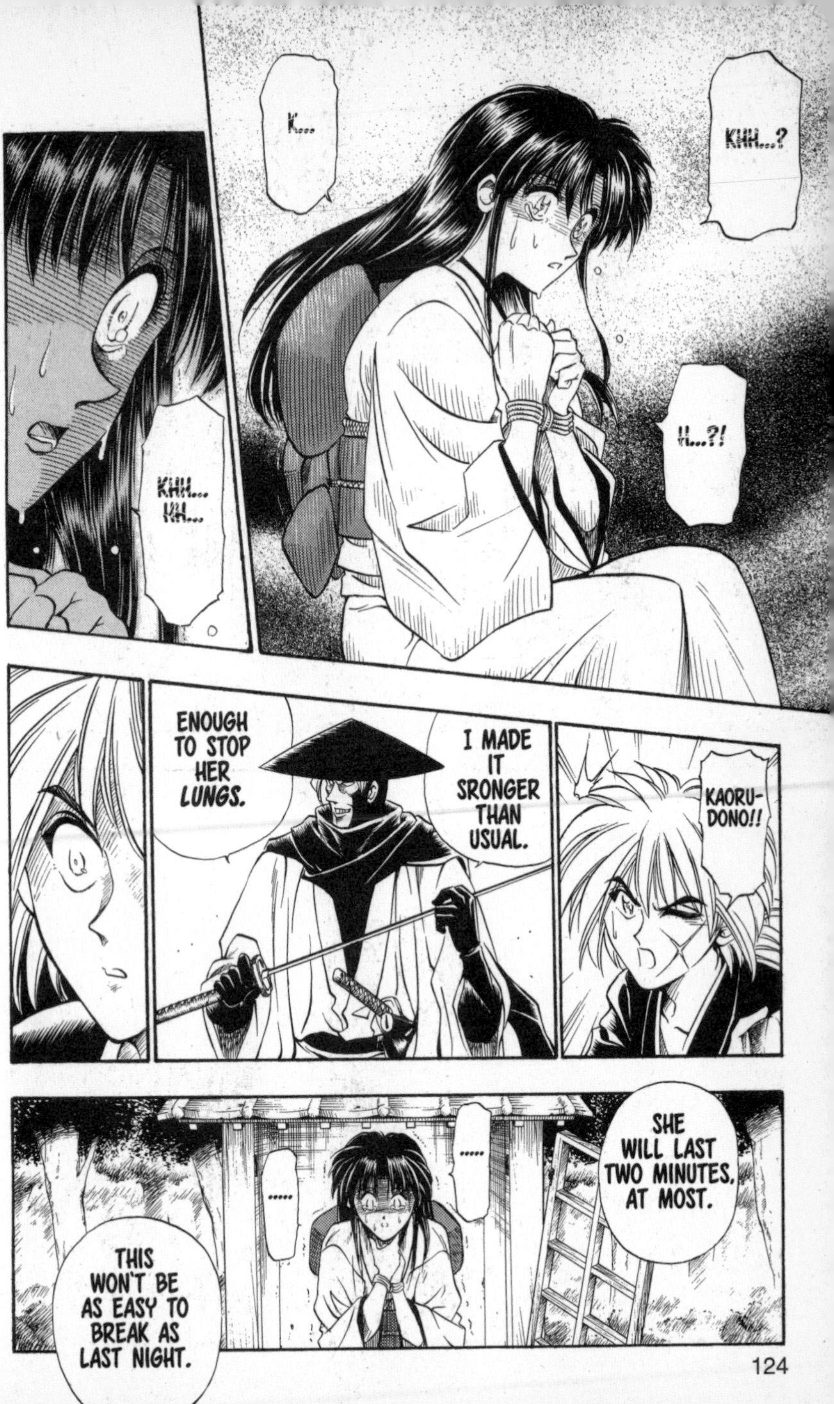
KHH...?
K...
U...?!
KHH... NH...
KAORU-DONO!!
I MADE IT SRONGER THAN USUAL.
ENOUGH TO STOP HER LUNGS.
SHE WILL LAST TWO MINUTES, AT MOST.
.....
.....
THIS WON'T BE AS EASY TO BREAK AS LAST NIGHT.

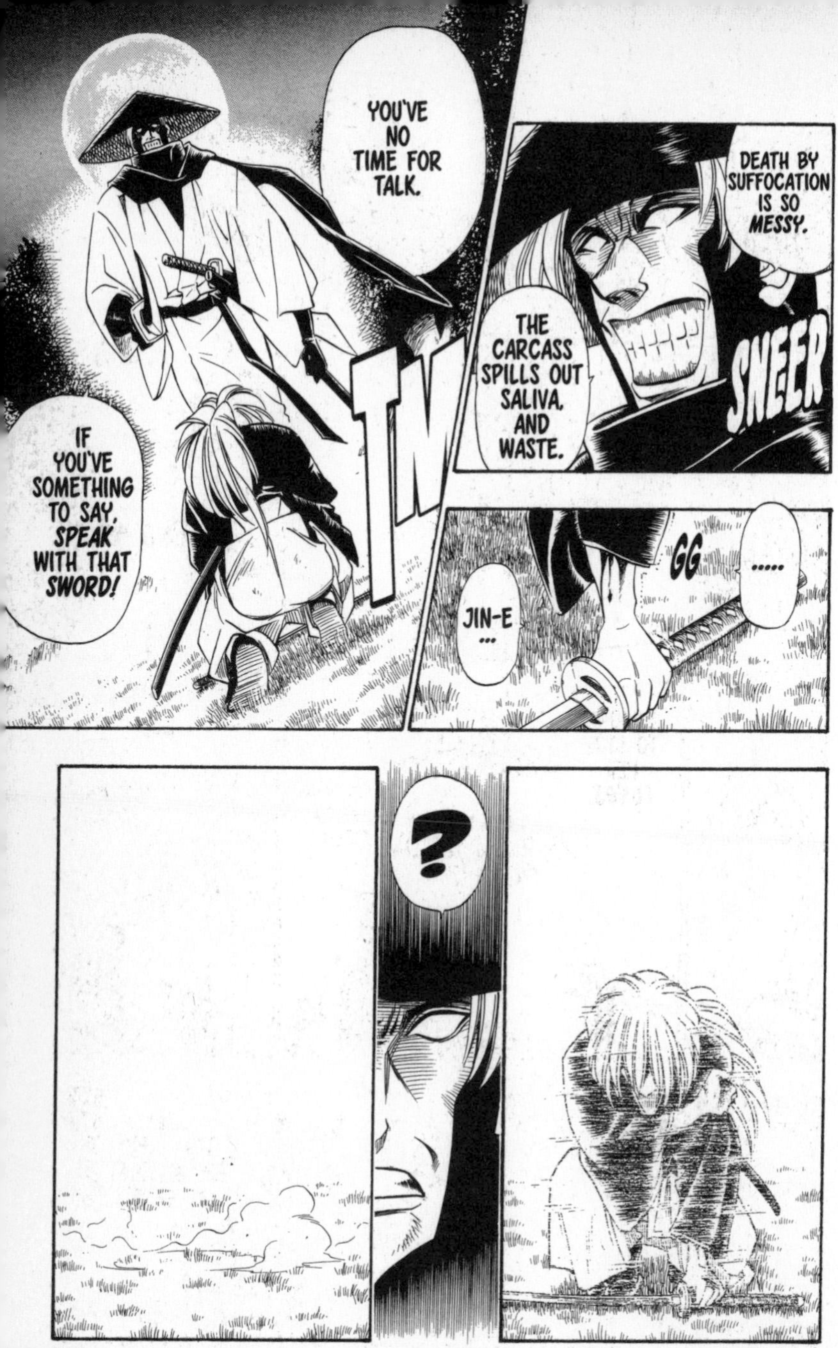
DEATH BY SUFFOCATION IS SO MESSY.
THE CARCASS SPILLS OUT SALIVA, AND WASTE.
SNEER
......
GG
JIN-E ...
YOU'VE NO TIME FOR TALK.
TM
IF YOU'VE SOMETHING TO SAY, SPEAK WITH THAT SWORD!
?

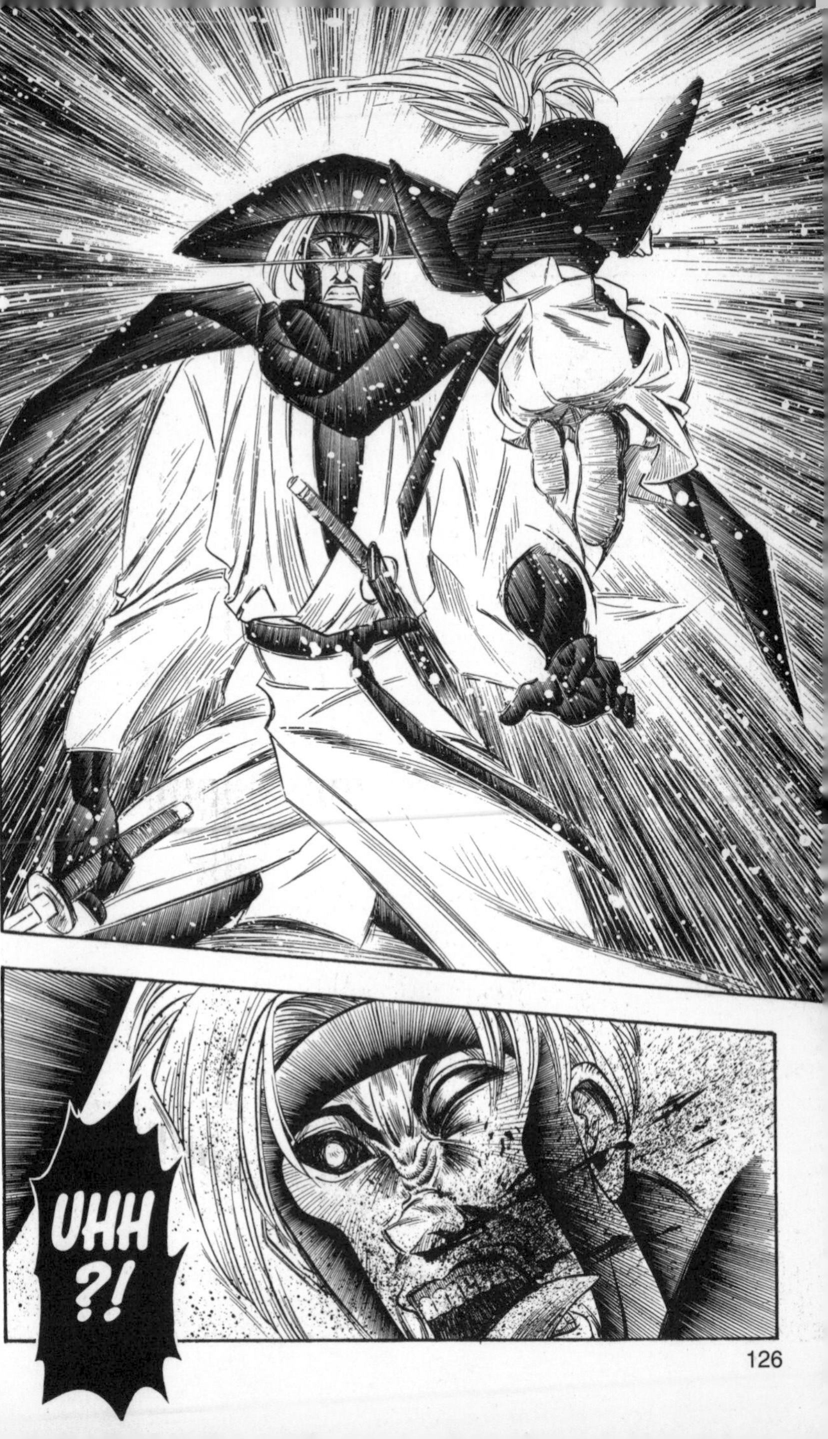
UHH ?!

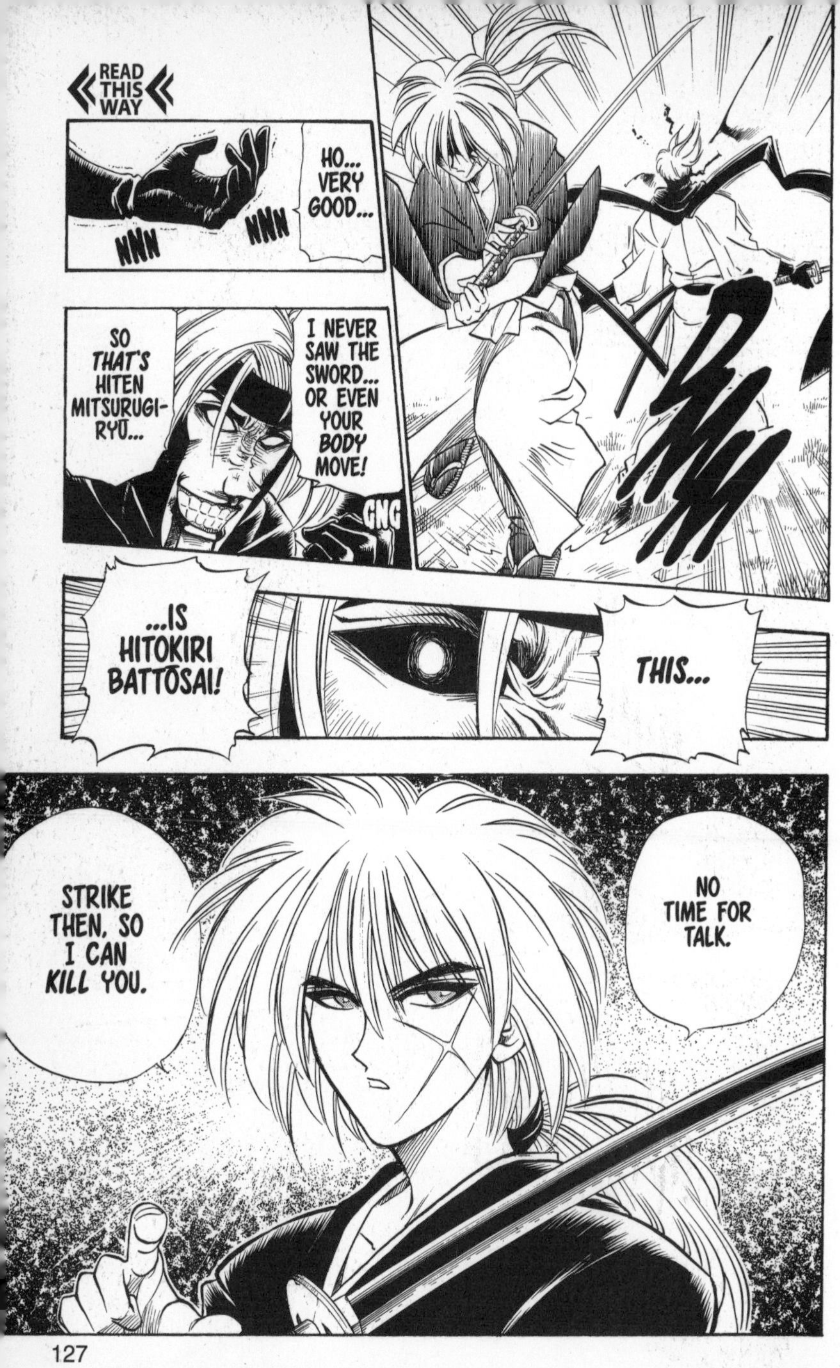
READ THIS WAY
HO... VERY GOOD...
NNN
NNN
I NEVER SAW THE SWORD... OR EVEN YOUR BODY MOVE!
SO THAT'S HITEN MITSURUGI-RYŪ...
GNG
THIS...
...IS HITOKIRI BATTŌSAI!
NO TIME FOR TALK.
STRIKE THEN, SO I CAN KILL YOU.

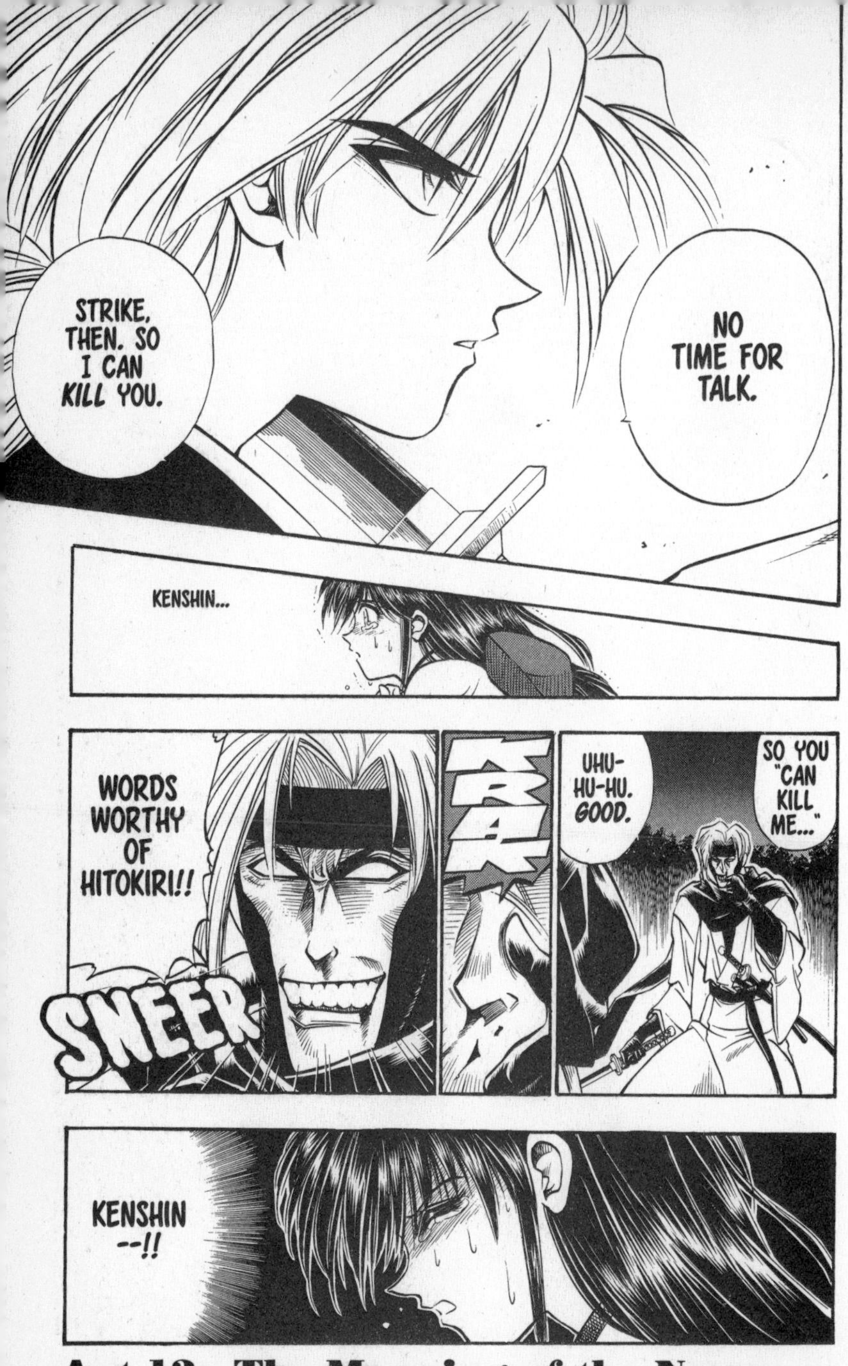
NO TIME FOR TALK.
STRIKE, THEN. SO I CAN KILL YOU.
KENSHIN...
SO YOU "CAN KILL ME..."
UHU-HU-HU. GOOD.
KRAK
WORDS WORTHY OF HITOKIRI!!
SNEER
KENSHIN --!!

## Act 13 – The Meaning of the Name

READ THIS WAY

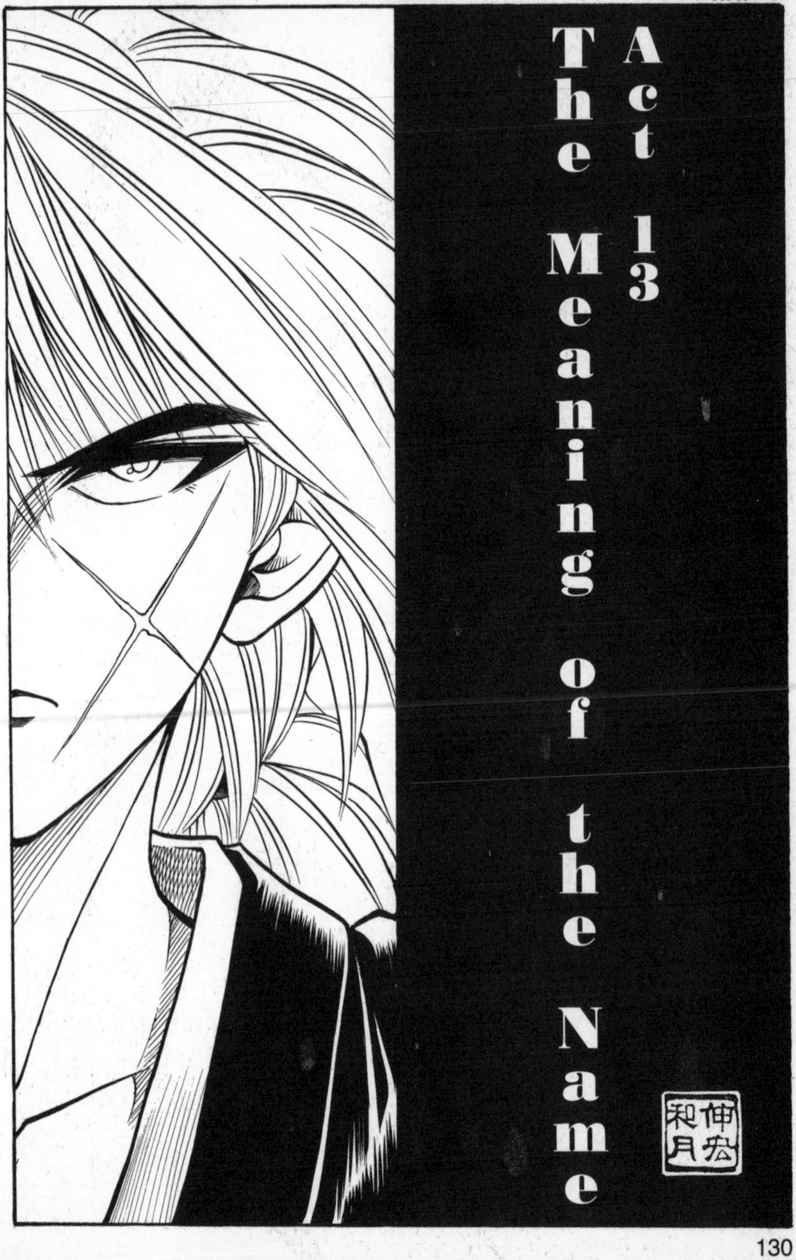
Act 13
The Meaning of the Name
伸宏和月

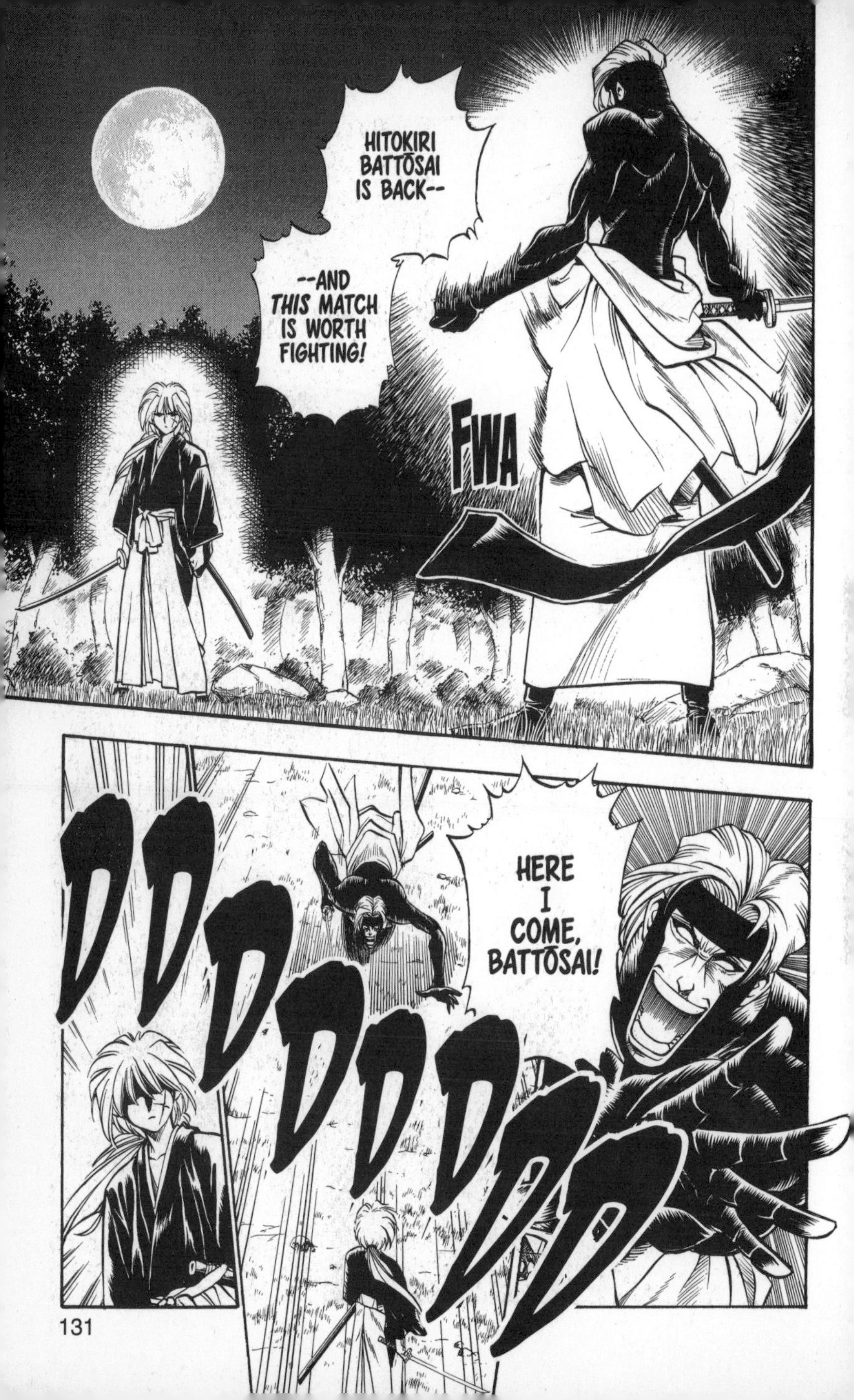
HITOKIRI BATTŌSAI IS BACK--
--AND THIS MATCH IS WORTH FIGHTING!
FWA
HERE I COME, BATTŌSAI!
DDDDDDDDDDD

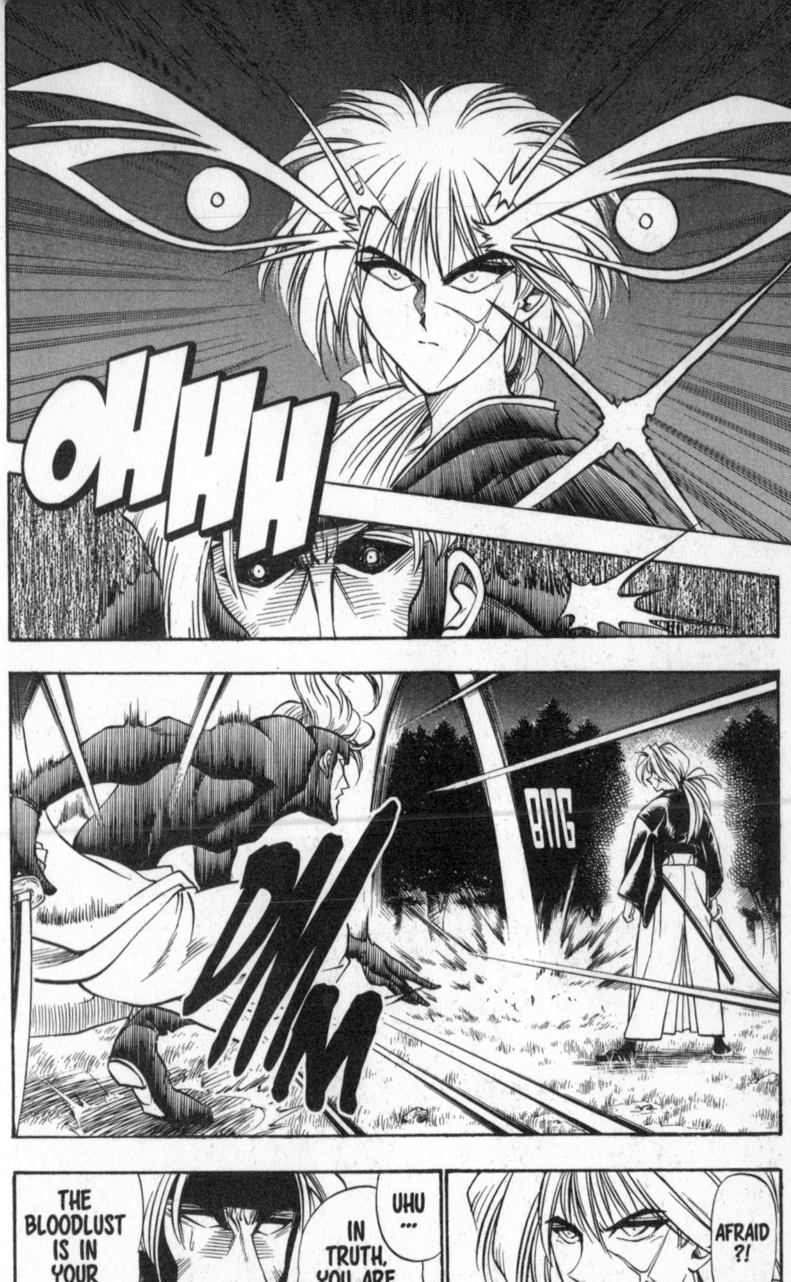
OHHHH
BNG
DMM
AFRAID ?!
UHU ...
IN TRUTH, YOU ARE HE...
THE BLOODLUST IS IN YOUR EYES.

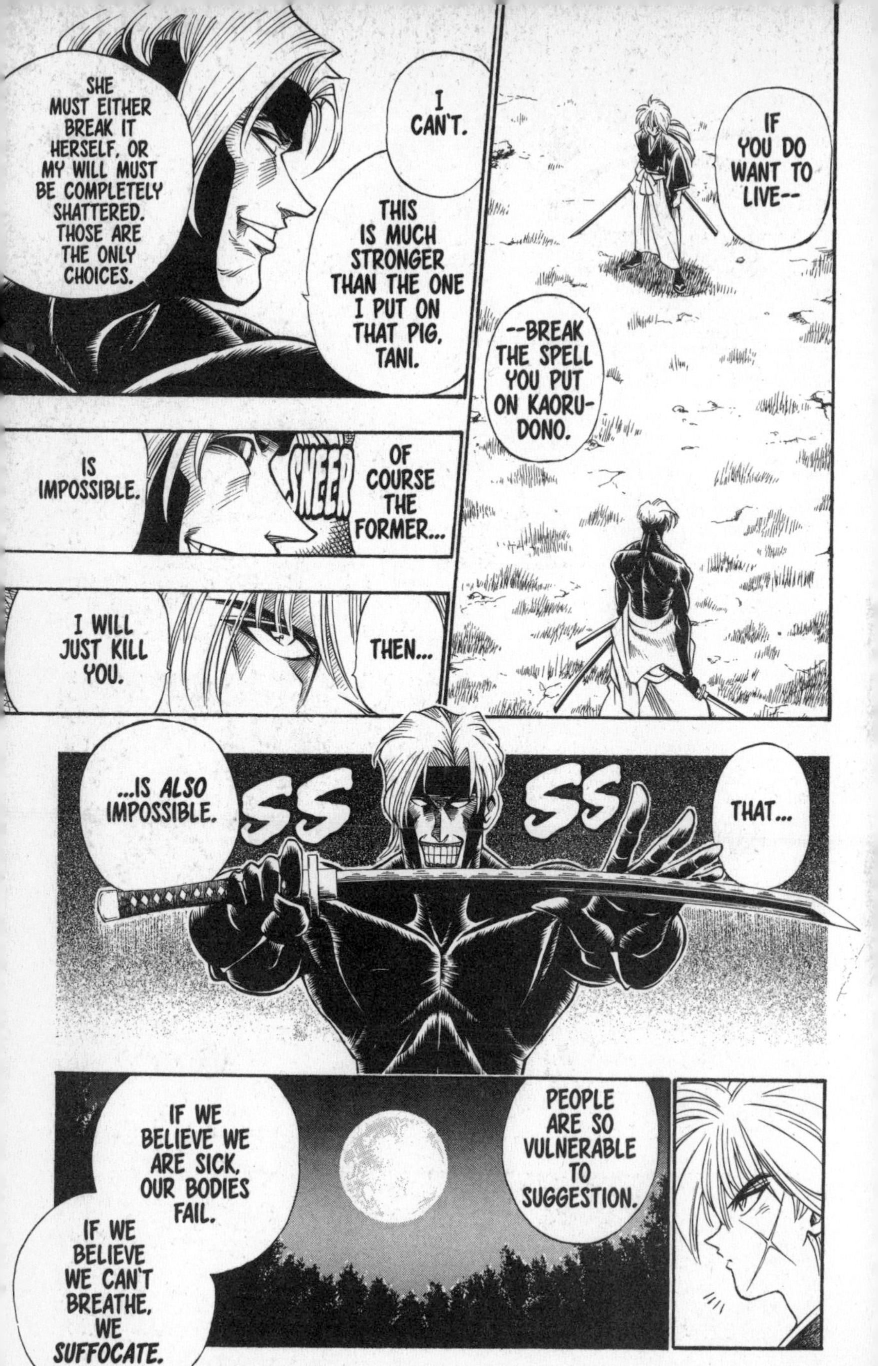
IF YOU DO WANT TO LIVE--
--BREAK THE SPELL YOU PUT ON KAORU-DONO.
I CAN'T.
THIS IS MUCH STRONGER THAN THE ONE I PUT ON THAT PIG, TANI.
SHE MUST EITHER BREAK IT HERSELF, OR MY WILL MUST BE COMPLETELY SHATTERED. THOSE ARE THE ONLY CHOICES.
OF COURSE THE FORMER...
SNEER
IS IMPOSSIBLE.
THEN...
I WILL JUST KILL YOU.
THAT...
SS
SS
...IS *ALSO* IMPOSSIBLE.
PEOPLE ARE SO VULNERABLE TO SUGGESTION.
IF WE BELIEVE WE ARE SICK, OUR BODIES FAIL.
IF WE BELIEVE WE CAN'T BREATHE, WE *SUFFOCATE*.

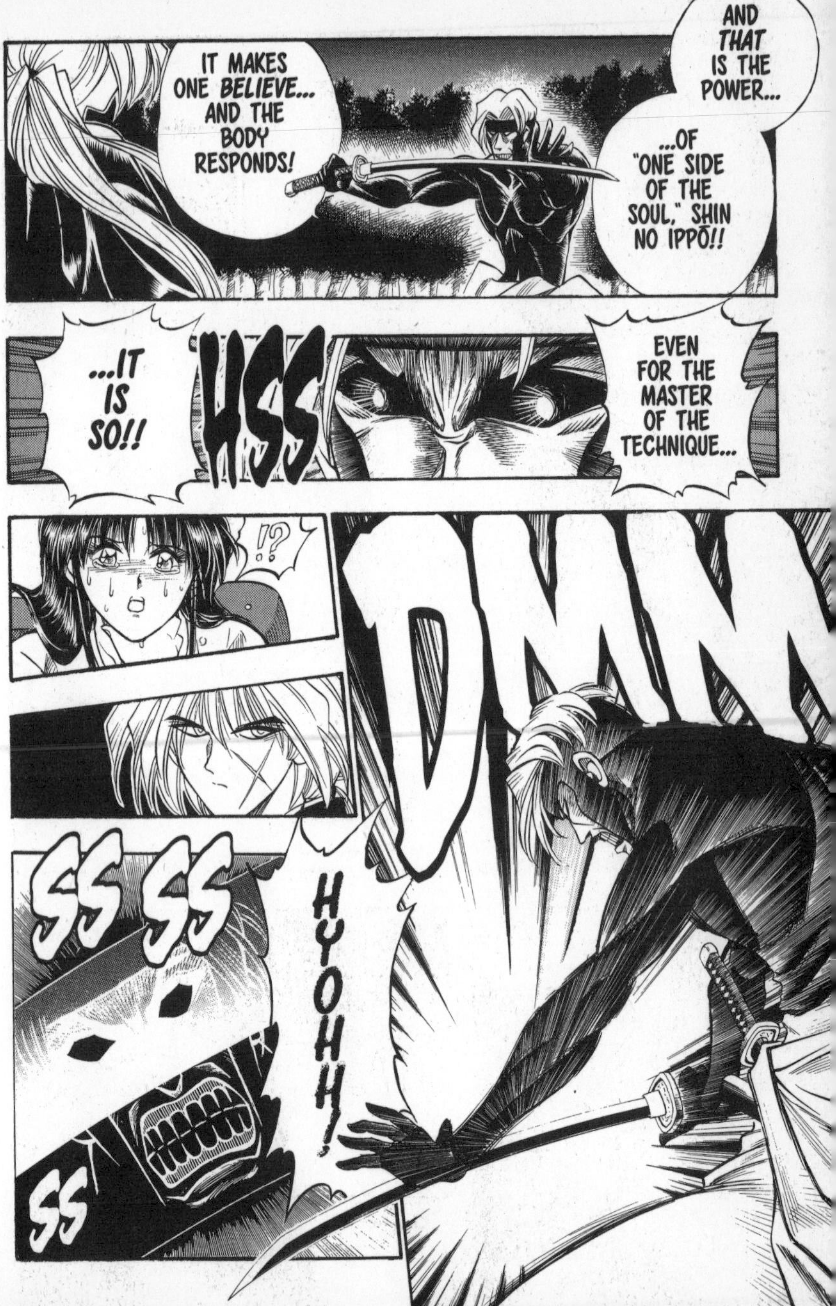
AND THAT IS THE POWER...
...OF "ONE SIDE OF THE SOUL," SHIN NO IPPŌ!!
IT MAKES ONE BELIEVE... AND THE BODY RESPONDS!
EVEN FOR THE MASTER OF THE TECHNIQUE...
HSS
...IT IS SO!!
DMM
!?
SS SS
HYOHH!
SS

READ THIS WAY

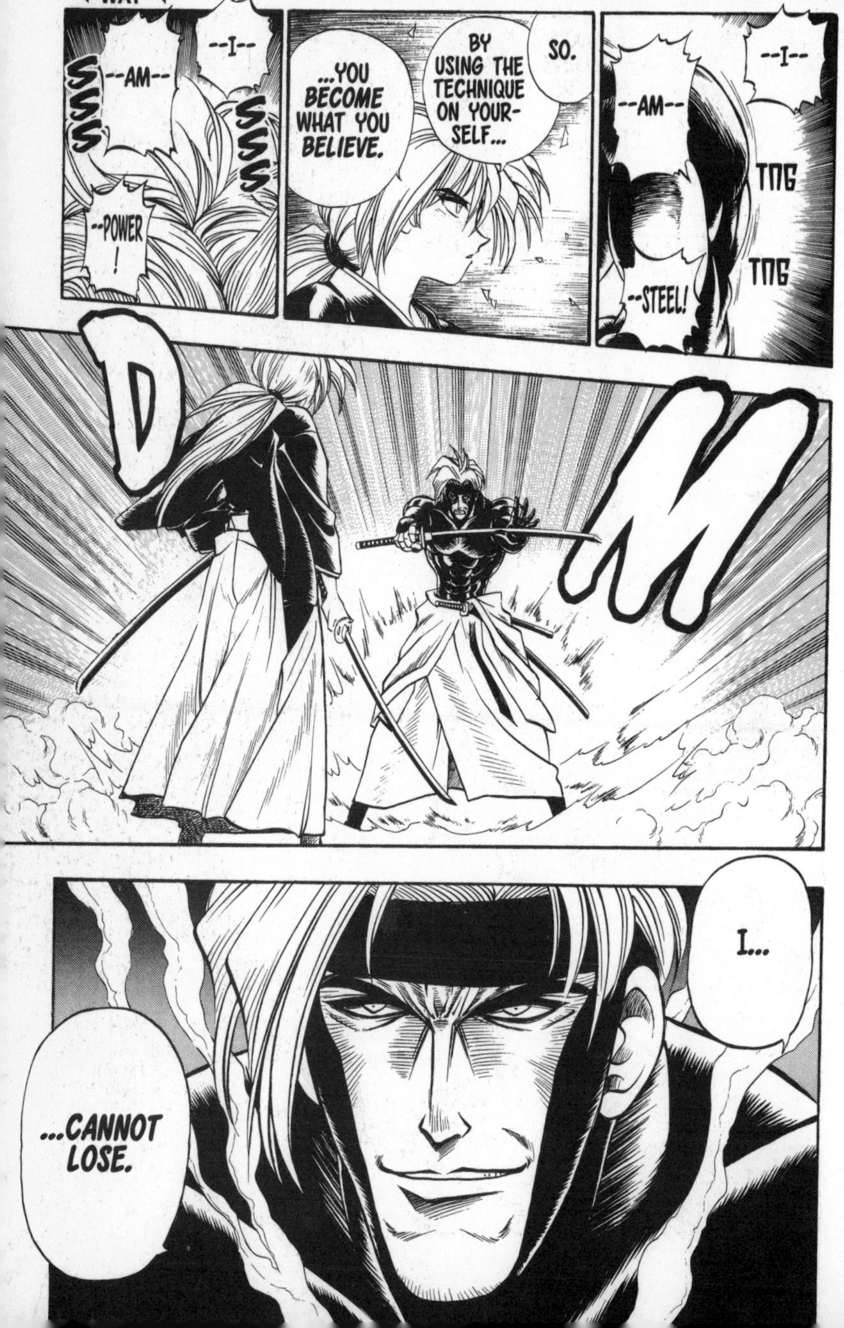

--I--
--AM--
TNG
TNG
--STEEL!
SO.
BY USING THE TECHNIQUE ON YOURSELF...
...YOU BECOME WHAT YOU BELIEVE.
--I--
--AM--
SSS
SSS
--POWER!
M
D
I...
...CANNOT LOSE.

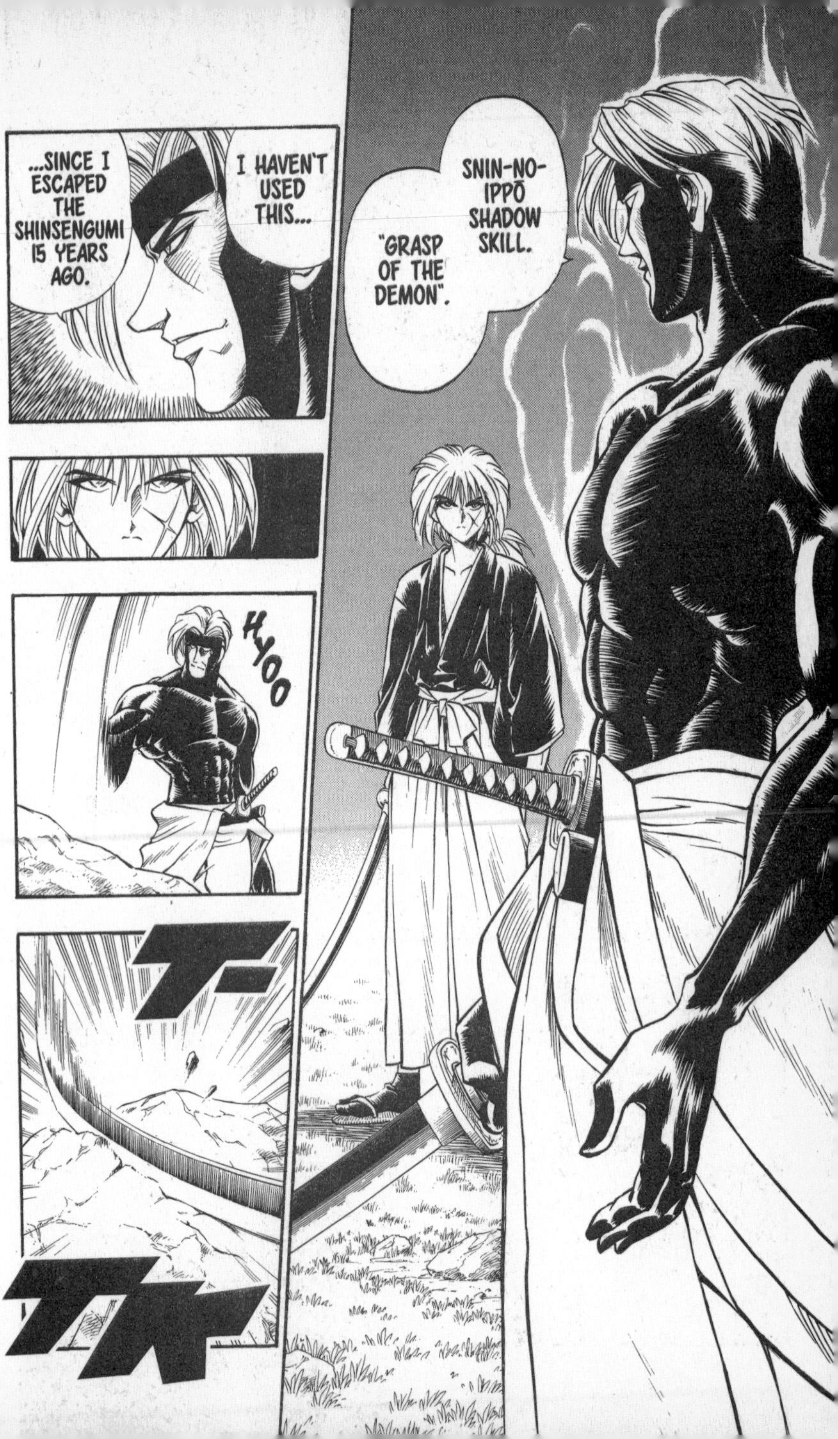
SNIN-NO-IPPŌ SHADOW SKILL.
"GRASP OF THE DEMON".
I HAVEN'T USED THIS...
...SINCE I ESCAPED THE SHINSENGUMI 15 YEARS AGO.
HYOO

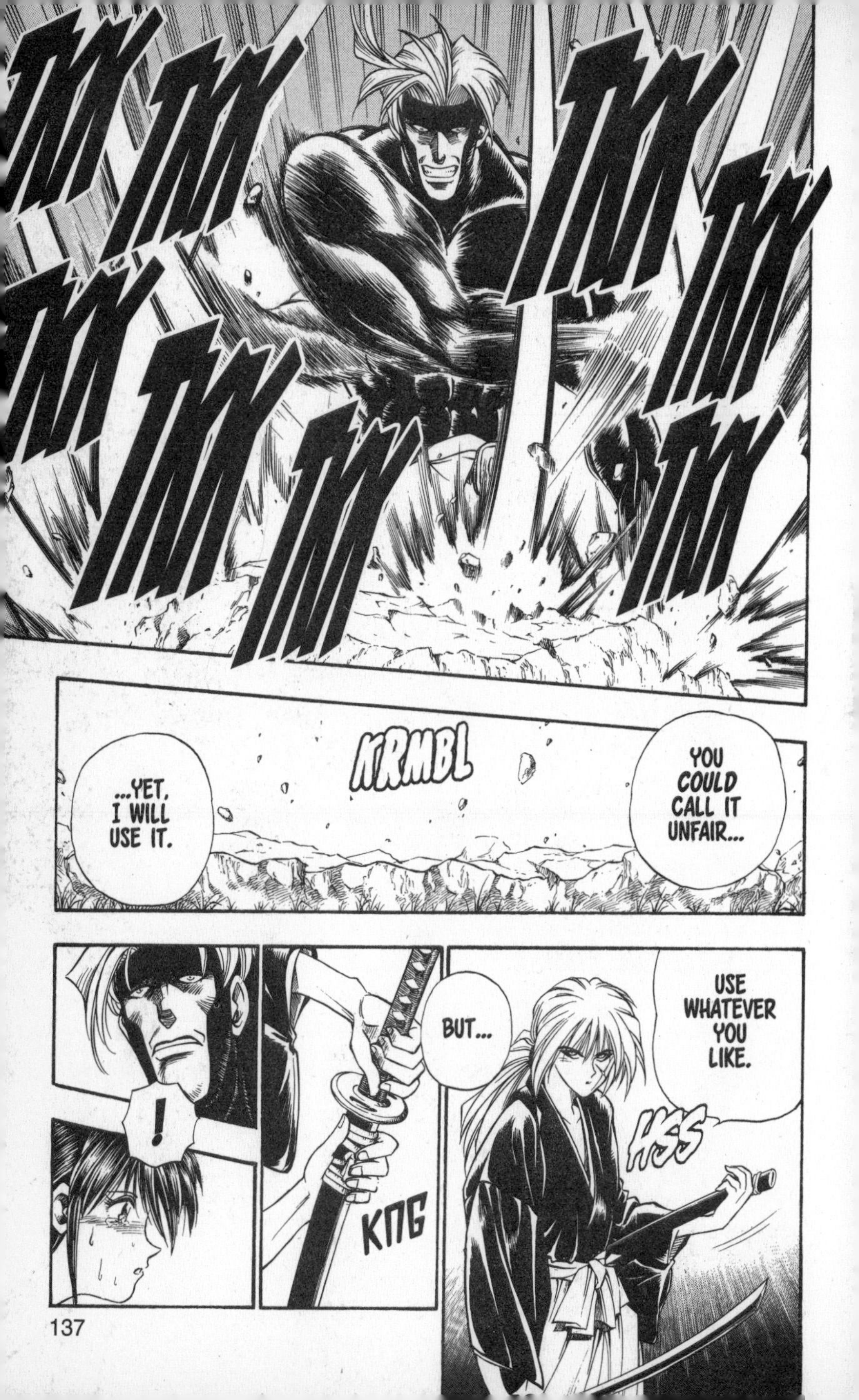
YOU COULD CALL IT UNFAIR...
KRMBL
...YET, I WILL USE IT.
USE WHATEVER YOU LIKE.
HSS
BUT...
KNG
!

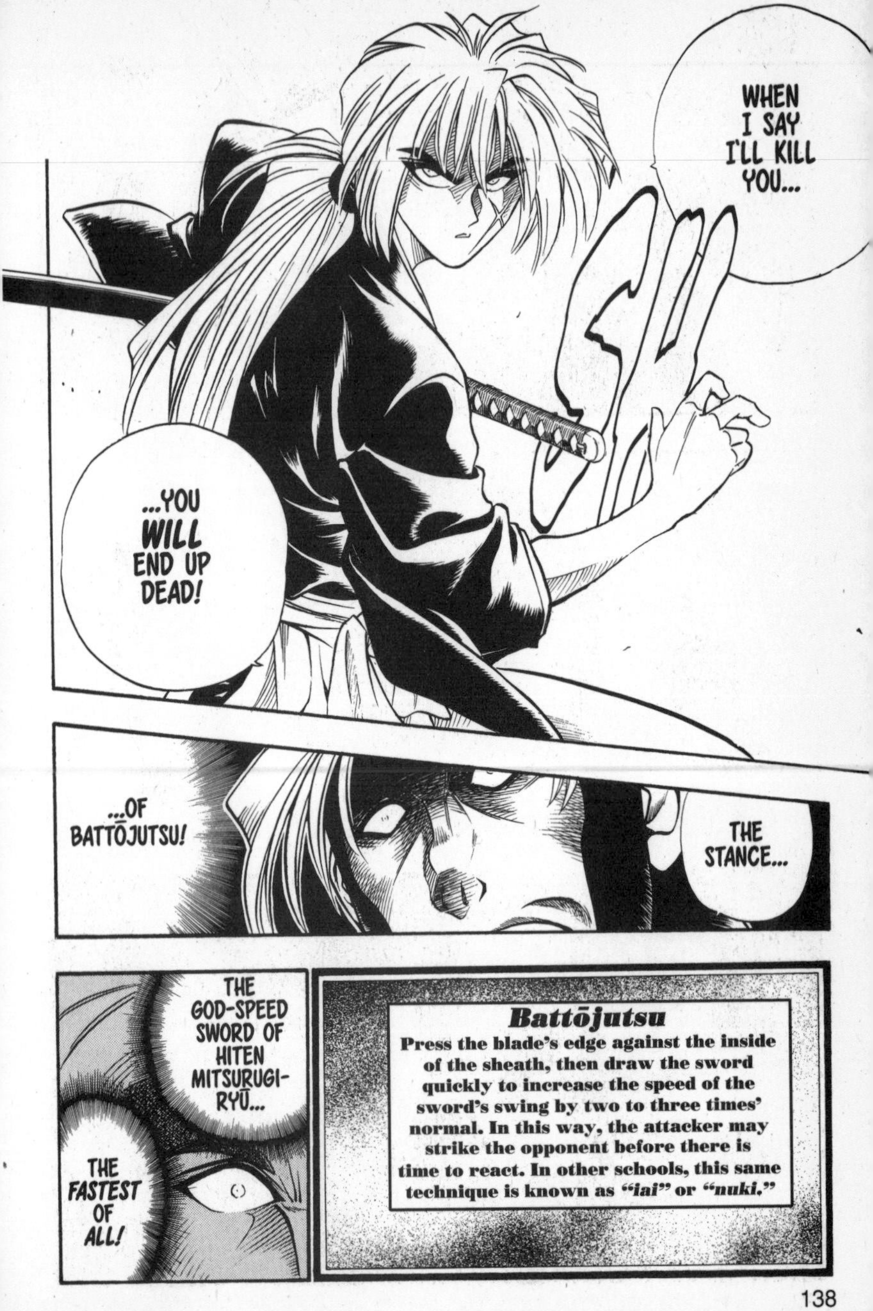
WHEN I SAY I'LL KILL YOU...
...YOU *WILL* END UP DEAD!
THE STANCE...
...OF BATTŌJUTSU!
**Battōjutsu**
Press the blade's edge against the inside of the sheath, then draw the sword quickly to increase the speed of the sword's swing by two to three times' normal. In this way, the attacker may strike the opponent before there is time to react. In other schools, this same technique is known as "*iai*" or "*nuki*."
THE GOD-SPEED SWORD OF HITEN MITSURUGI-RYŪ...
THE FASTEST OF ALL!

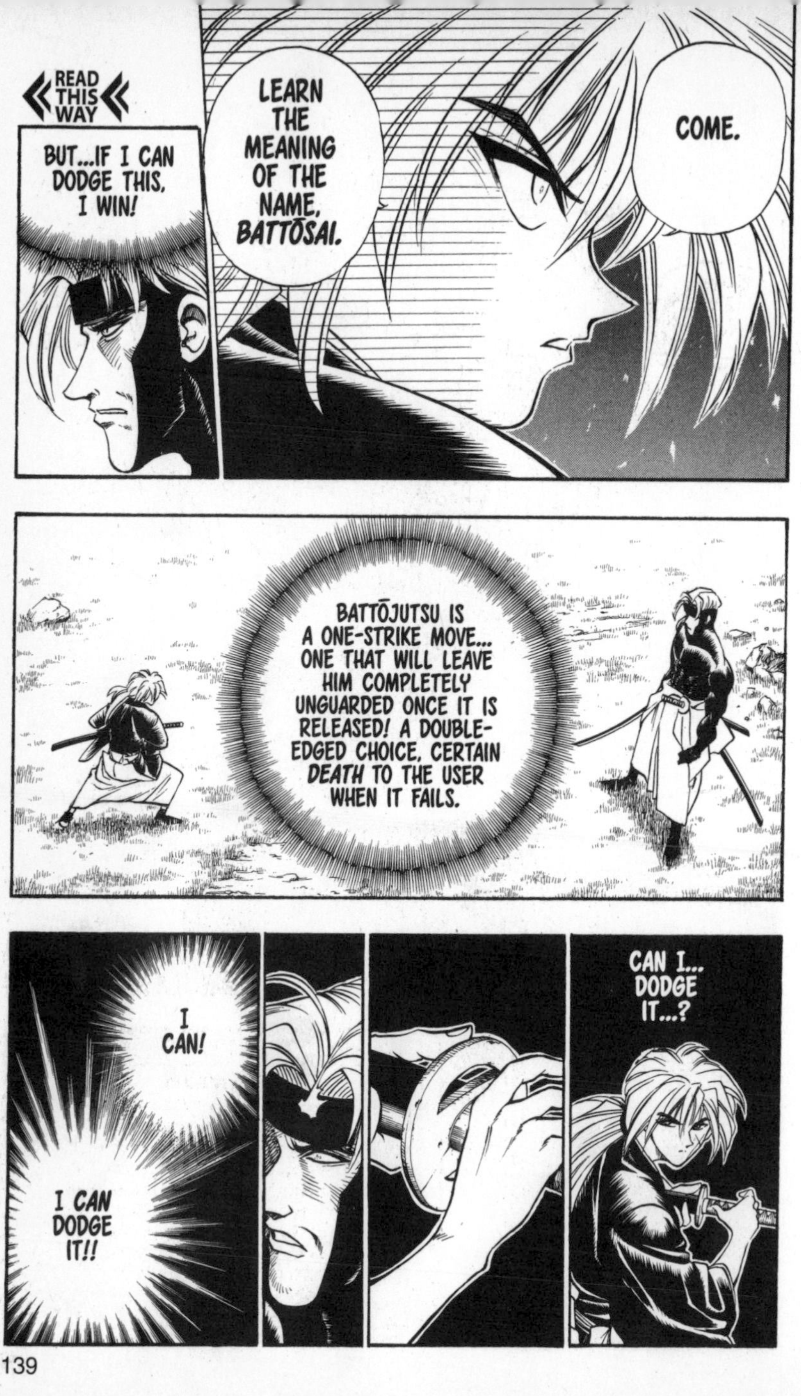
READ THIS WAY
COME.
LEARN THE MEANING OF THE NAME, BATTŌSAI.
BUT...IF I CAN DODGE THIS, I WIN!
BATTŌJUTSU IS A ONE-STRIKE MOVE... ONE THAT WILL LEAVE HIM COMPLETELY UNGUARDED ONCE IT IS RELEASED! A DOUBLE-EDGED CHOICE, CERTAIN *DEATH* TO THE USER WHEN IT FAILS.
CAN I... DODGE IT...?
I CAN!
I *CAN* DODGE IT!!

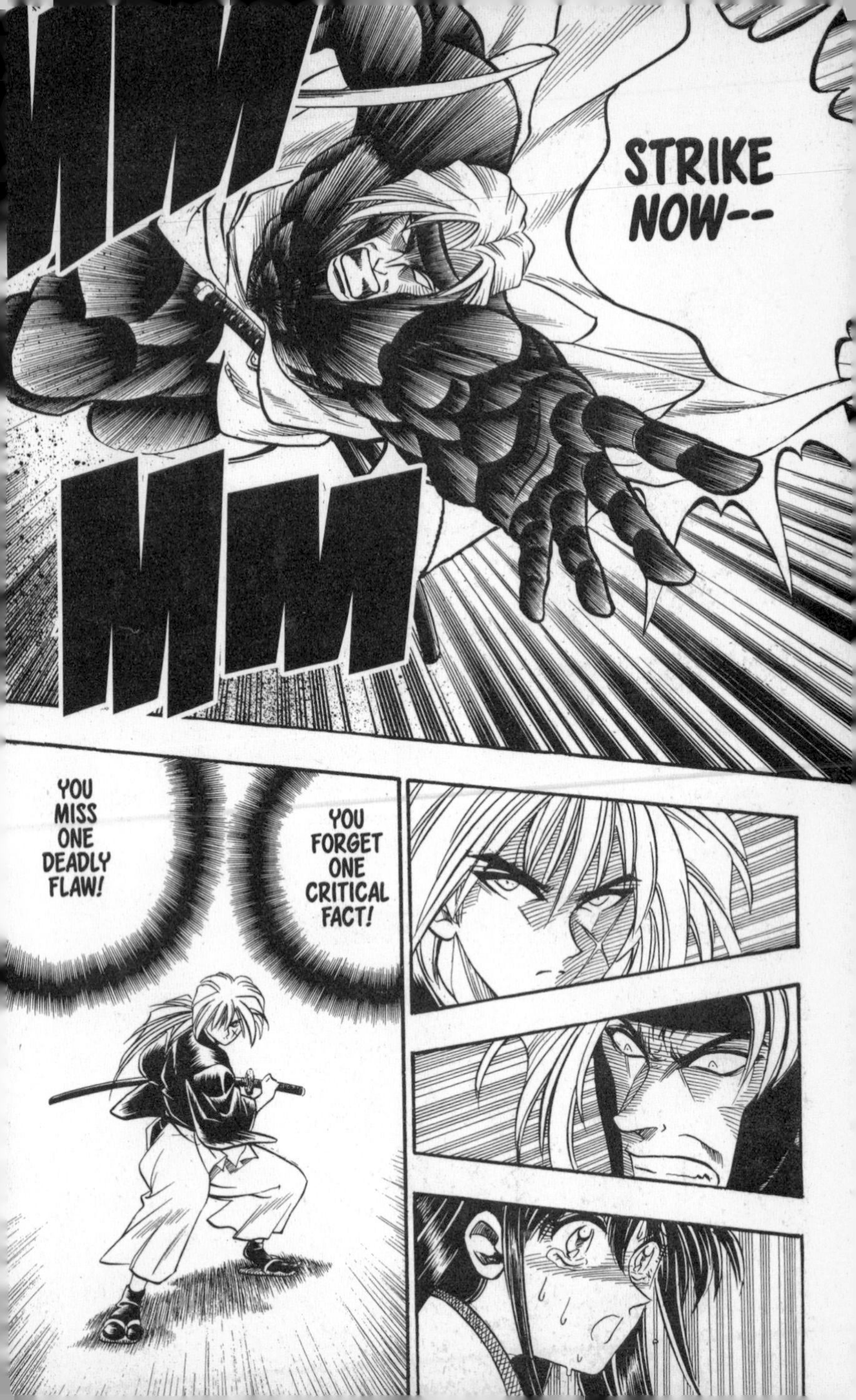
STRIKE NOW--
MMM
YOU FORGET ONE CRITICAL FACT!
YOU MISS ONE DEADLY FLAW!

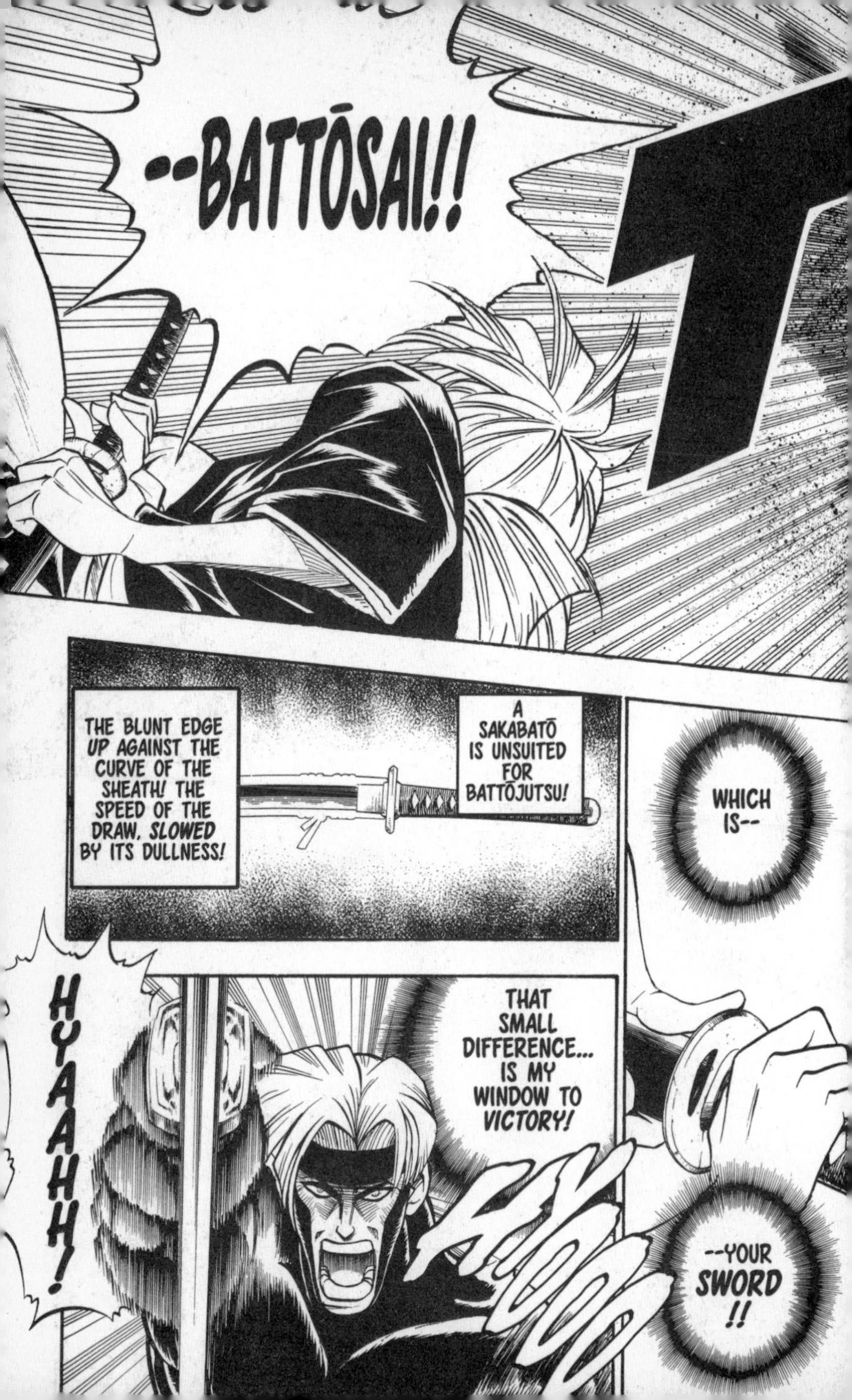
--BATTŌSAI!!
WHICH IS--
--YOUR SWORD!!
A SAKABATŌ IS UNSUITED FOR BATTŌJUTSU!
THE BLUNT EDGE UP AGAINST THE CURVE OF THE SHEATH! THE SPEED OF THE DRAW, SLOWED BY ITS DULLNESS!
THAT SMALL DIFFERENCE... IS MY WINDOW TO VICTORY!
HYAAAHH!

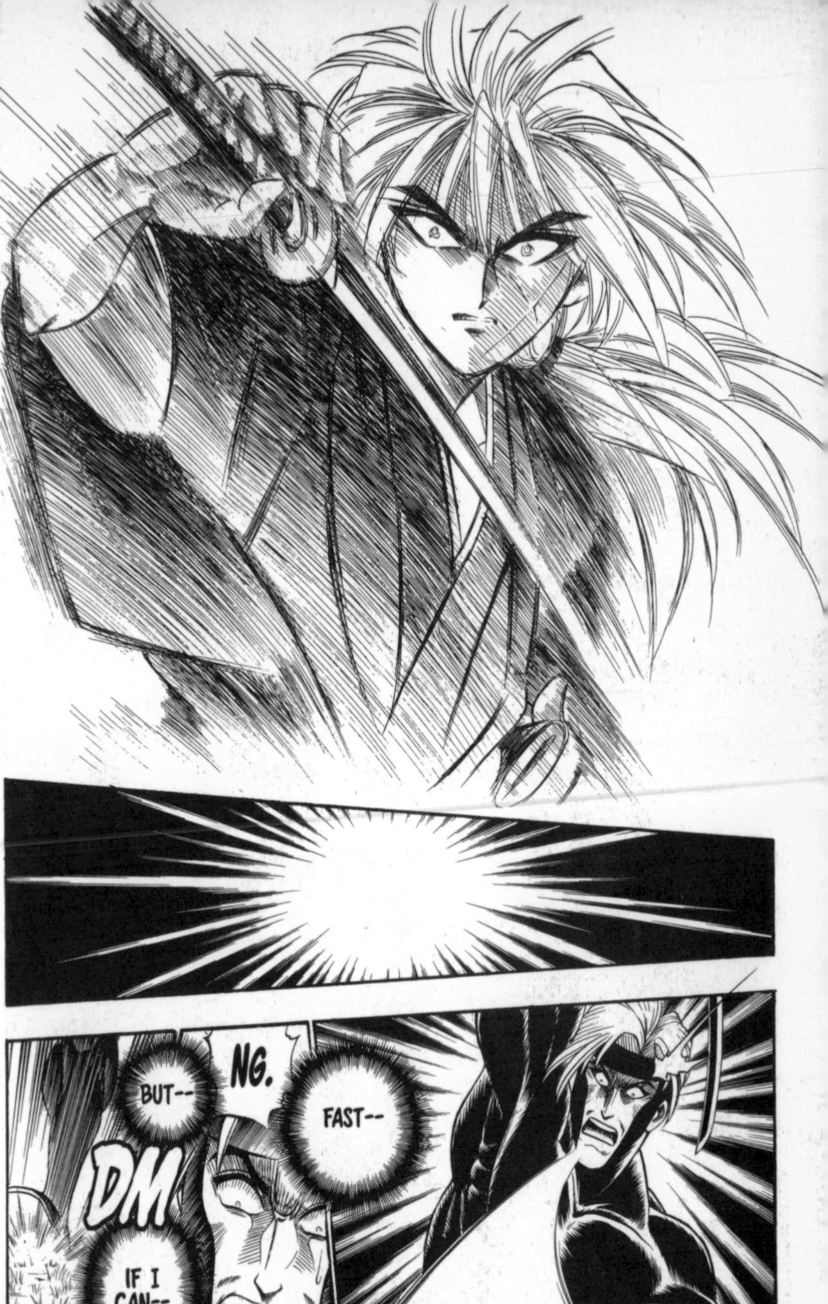
NG.
FAST--
BUT--
DM
IF I CAN--

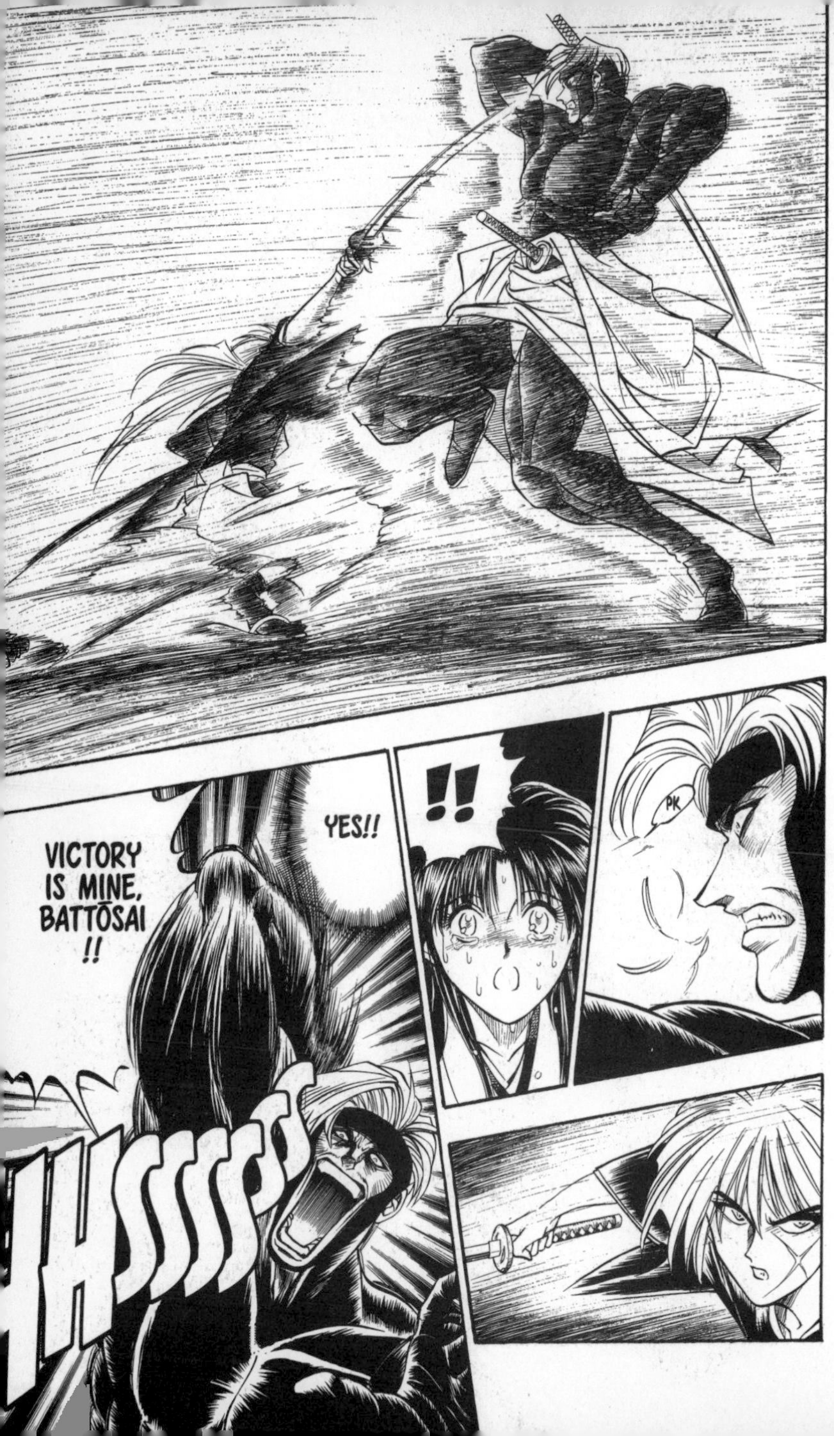
PK
!!
YES!!
VICTORY IS MINE, BATTŌSAI !!
HSSSSS

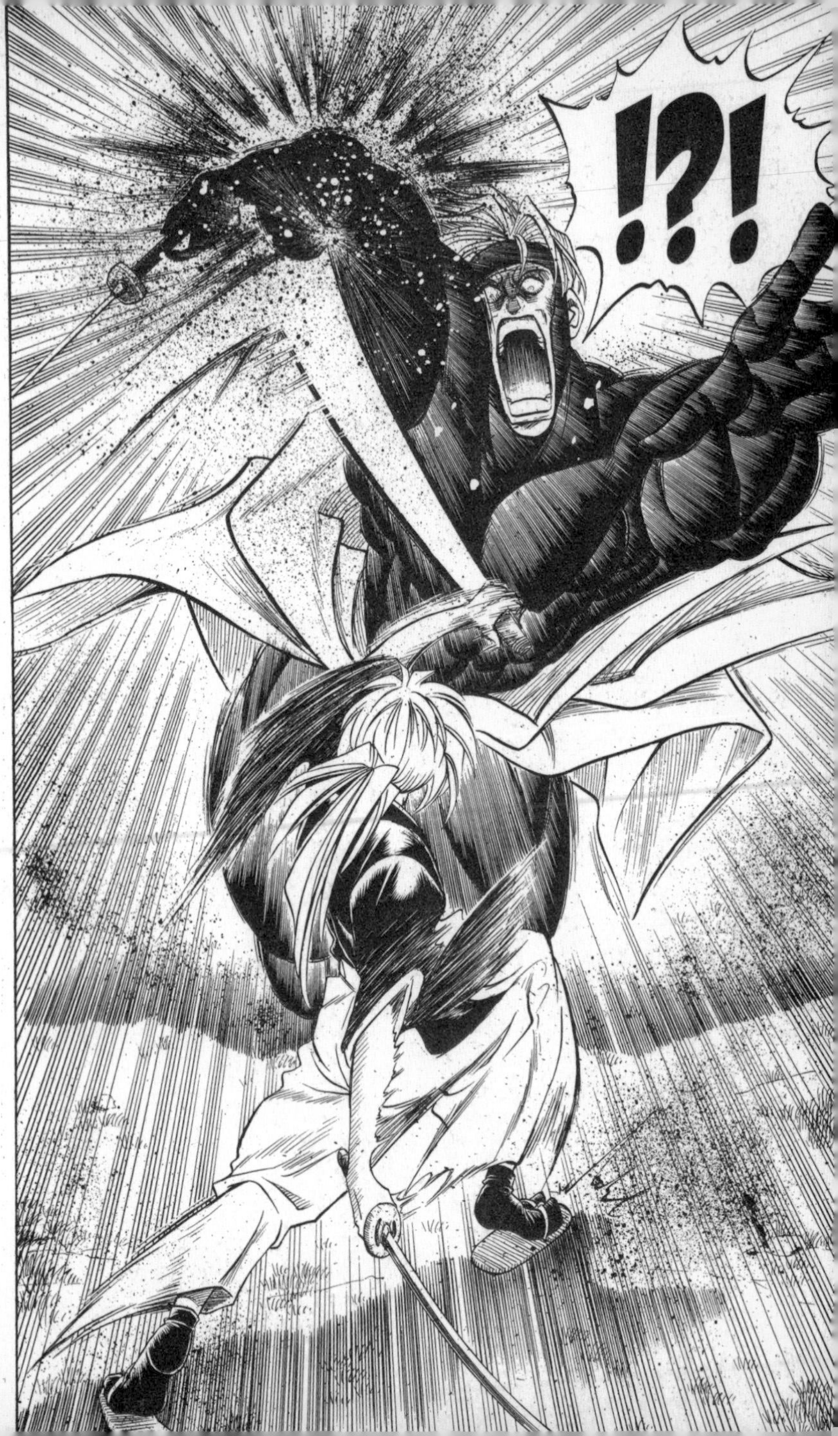
!?!

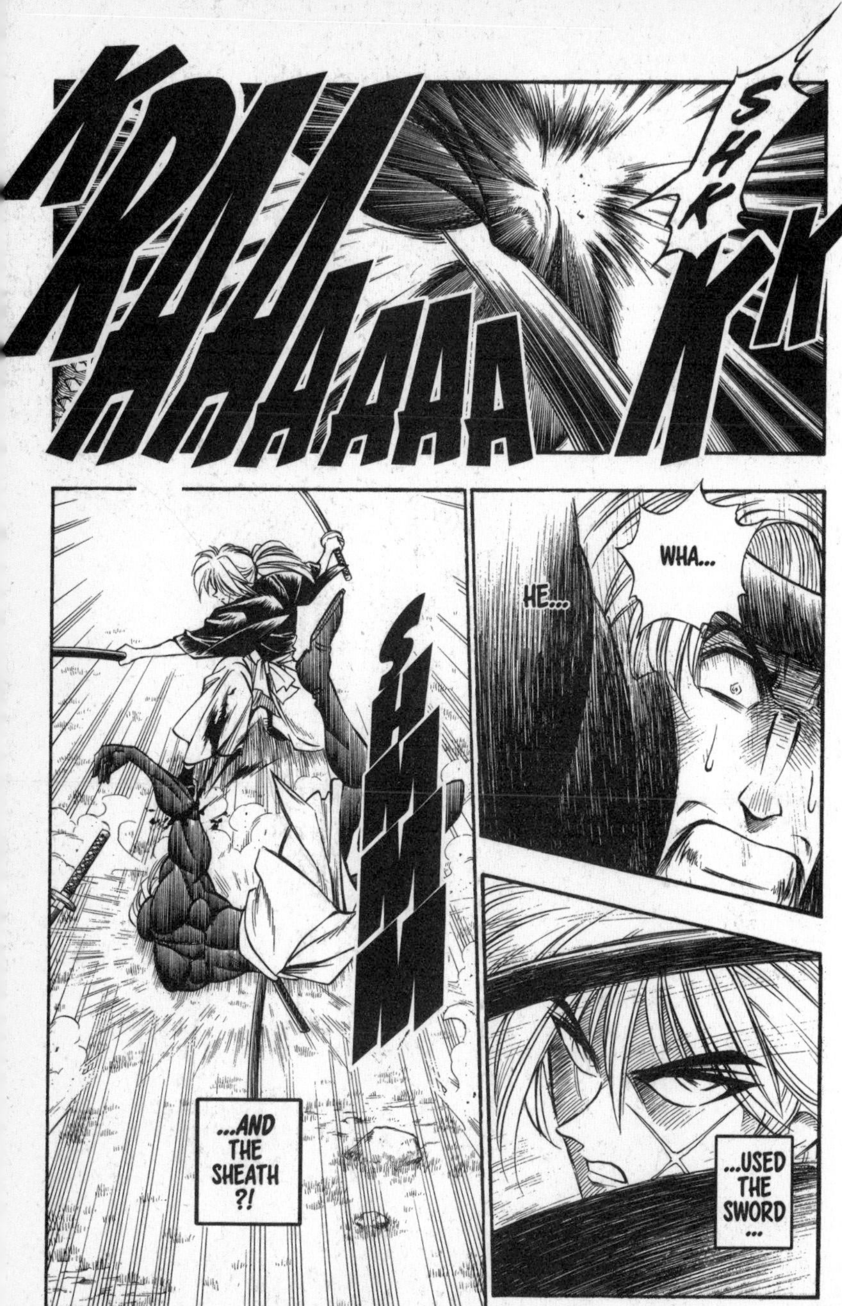
SHK
WHA...
HE...
...USED THE SWORD...
...AND THE SHEATH ?!

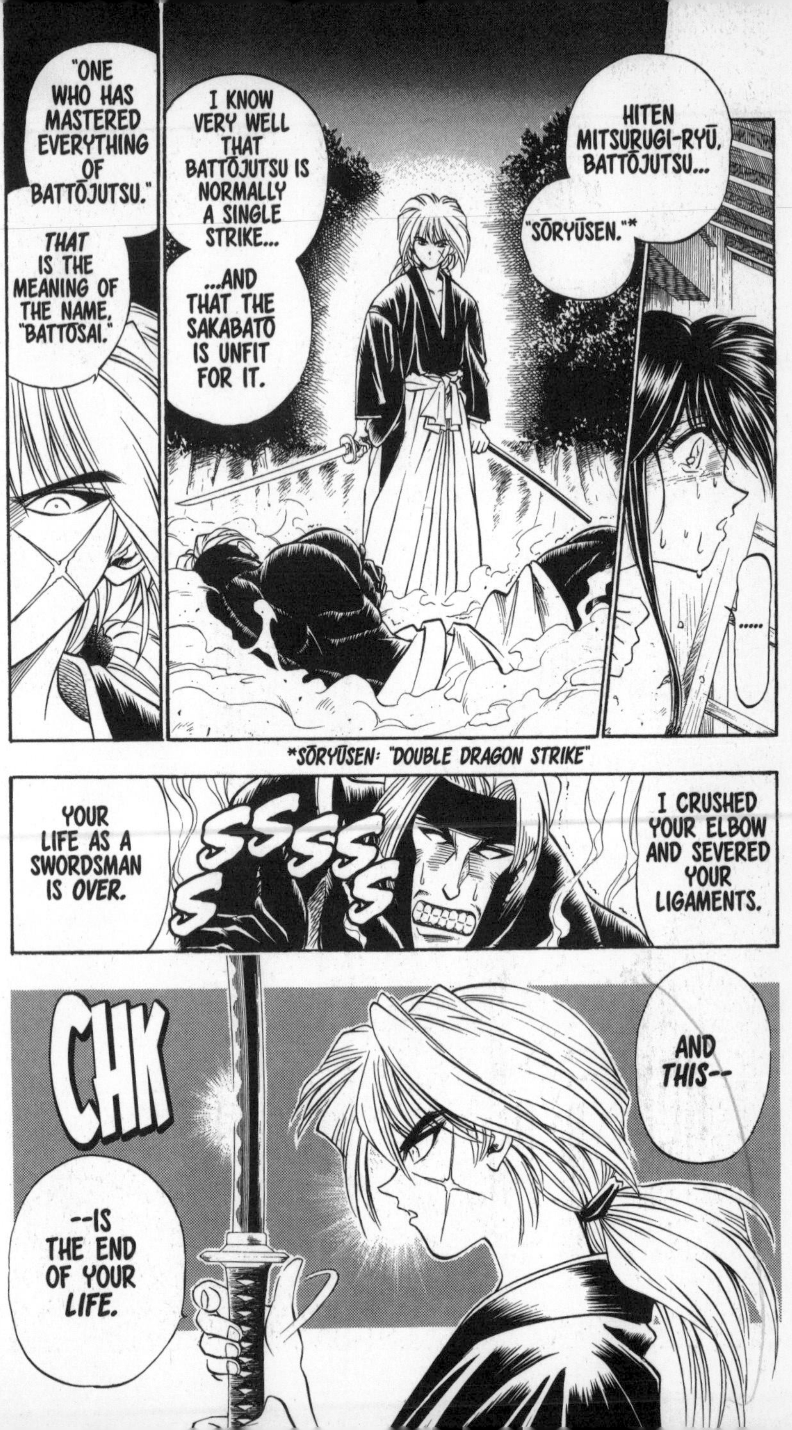
HITEN MITSURUGI-RYŪ, BATTŌJUTSU...
"SŌRYŪSEN."*
......
I KNOW VERY WELL THAT BATTŌJUTSU IS NORMALLY A SINGLE STRIKE...
...AND THAT THE SAKABATŌ IS UNFIT FOR IT.
"ONE WHO HAS MASTERED EVERYTHING OF BATTŌJUTSU."
*THAT* IS THE MEANING OF THE NAME, "BATTŌSAI."
I CRUSHED YOUR ELBOW AND SEVERED YOUR LIGAMENTS.
SSSSS
YOUR LIFE AS A SWORDSMAN IS *OVER.*
AND *THIS*--
CHK
--IS THE END OF YOUR *LIFE.*

*SŌRYŪSEN: "DOUBLE DRAGON STRIKE"

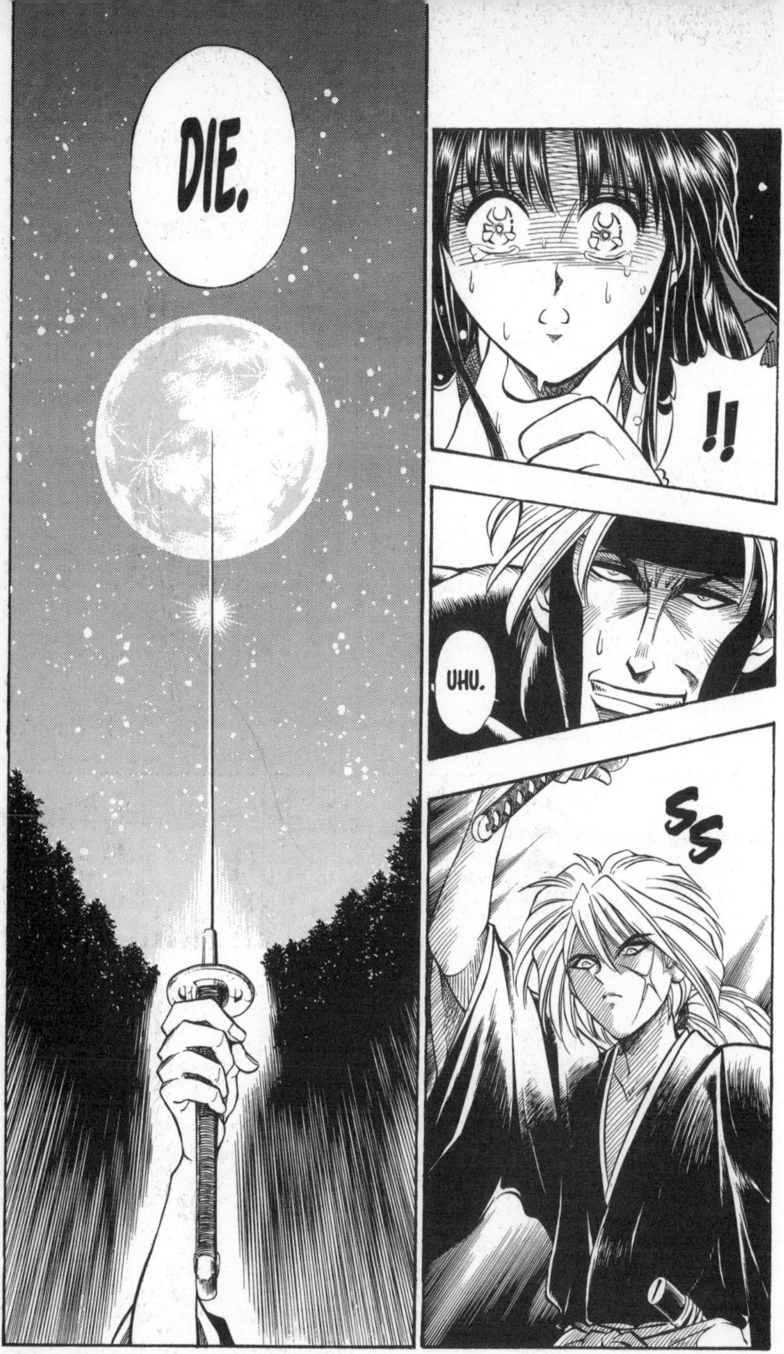
!!
UHU.
SS
DIE.

READ THIS WAY

# Act 14 End Beneath the Moon

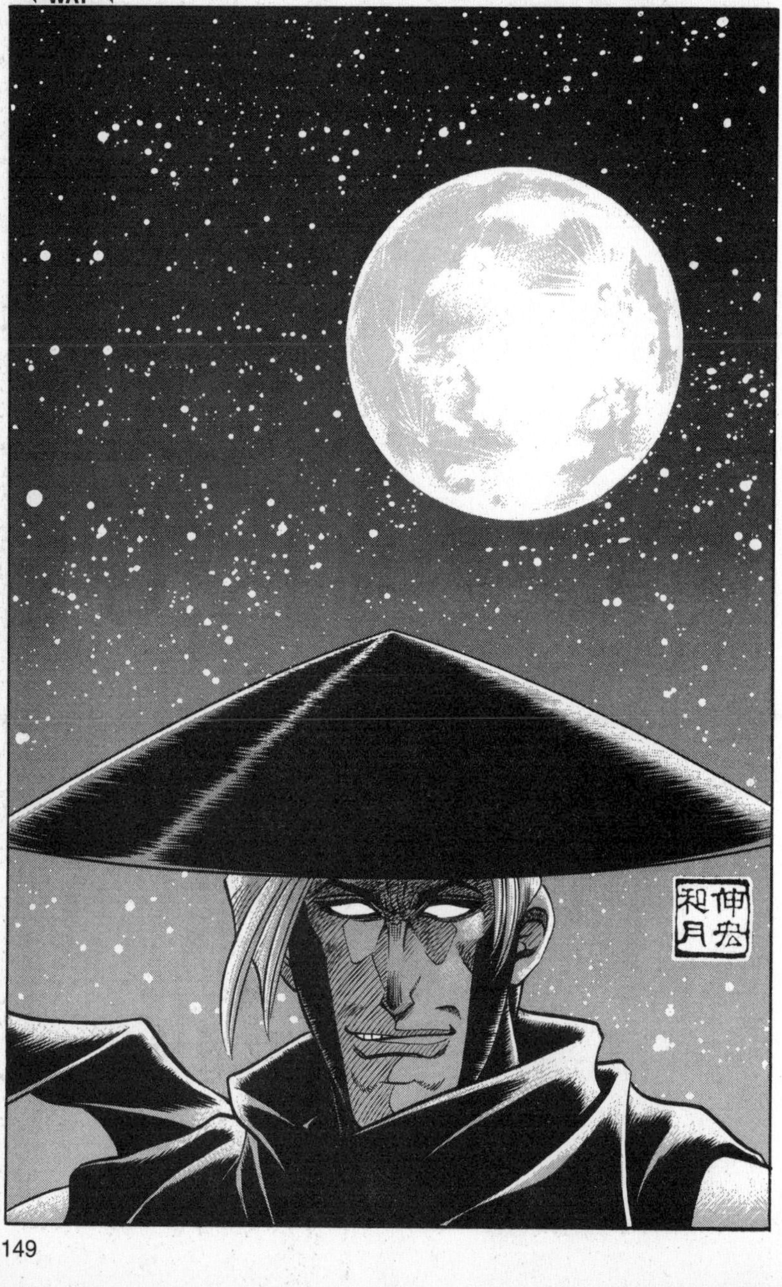
伸宏
和月

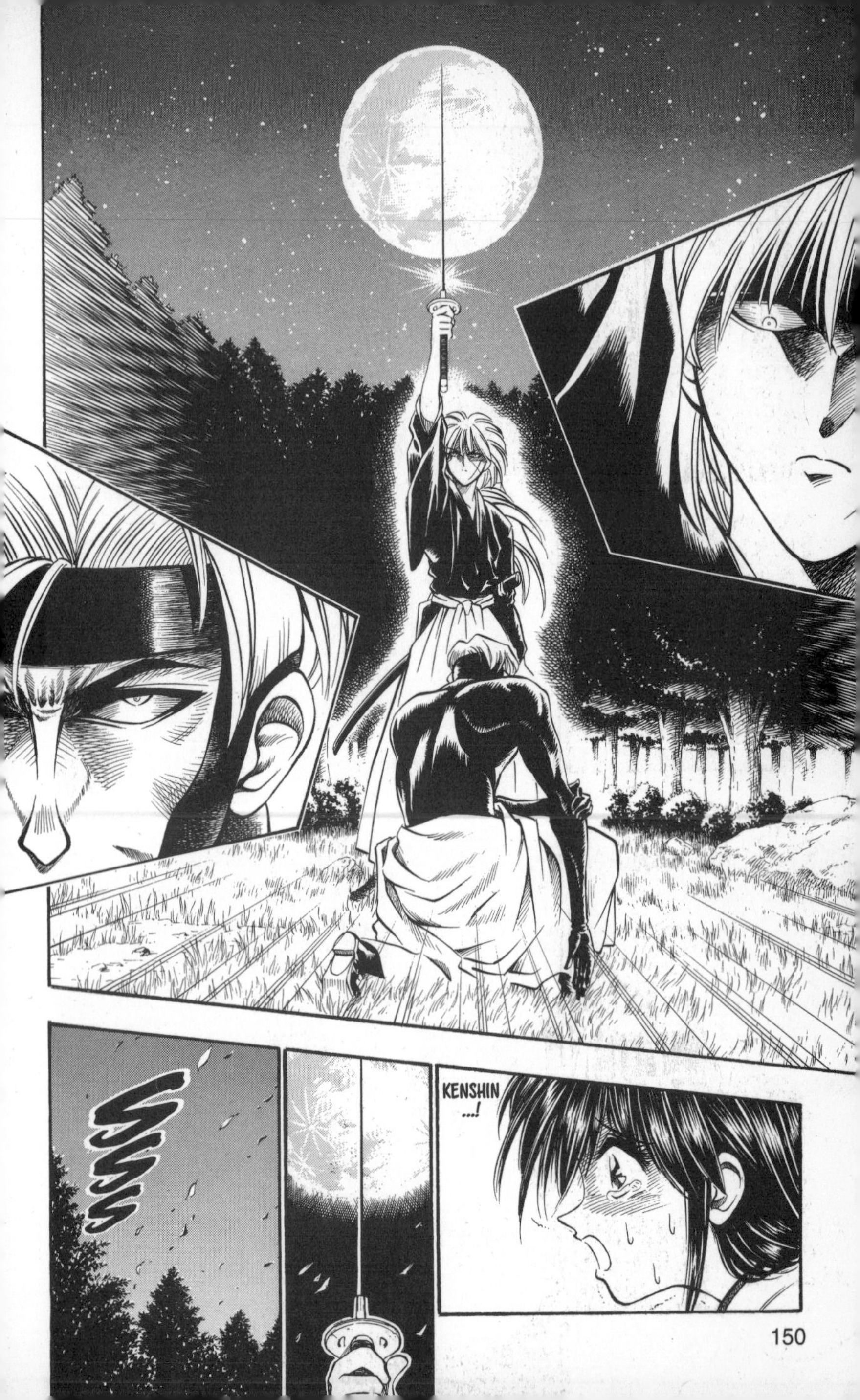
KENSHIN ...!
SSSS

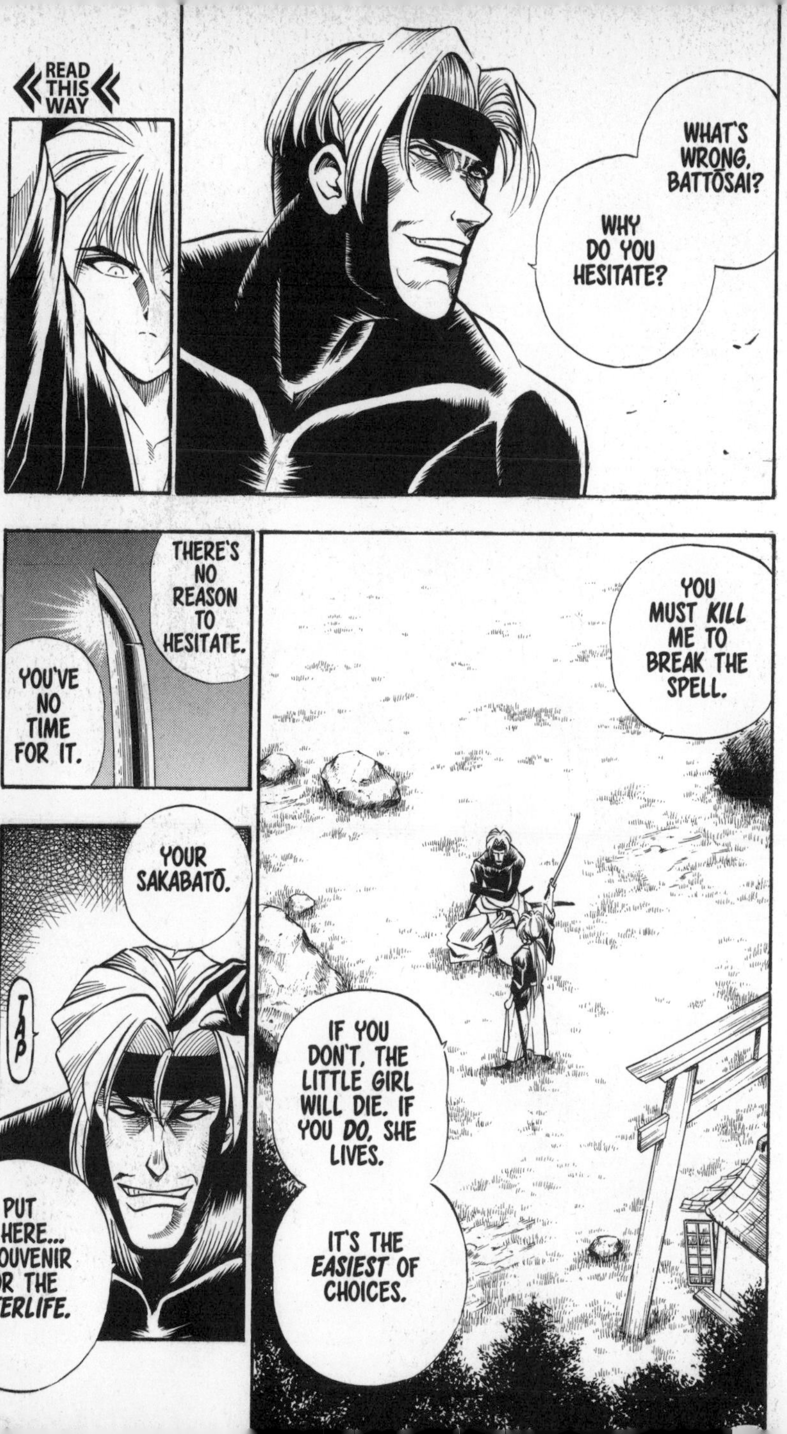
READ THIS WAY
WHAT'S WRONG, BATTŌSAI?
WHY DO YOU HESITATE?
YOU MUST *KILL* ME TO BREAK THE SPELL.
IF YOU DON'T, THE LITTLE GIRL WILL DIE. IF YOU *DO*, SHE LIVES.
IT'S THE *EASIEST* OF CHOICES.
THERE'S NO REASON TO HESITATE.
YOU'VE NO TIME FOR IT.
YOUR SAKABATŌ.
TAP
PUT IT HERE... A SOUVENIR FOR THE *AFTERLIFE*.

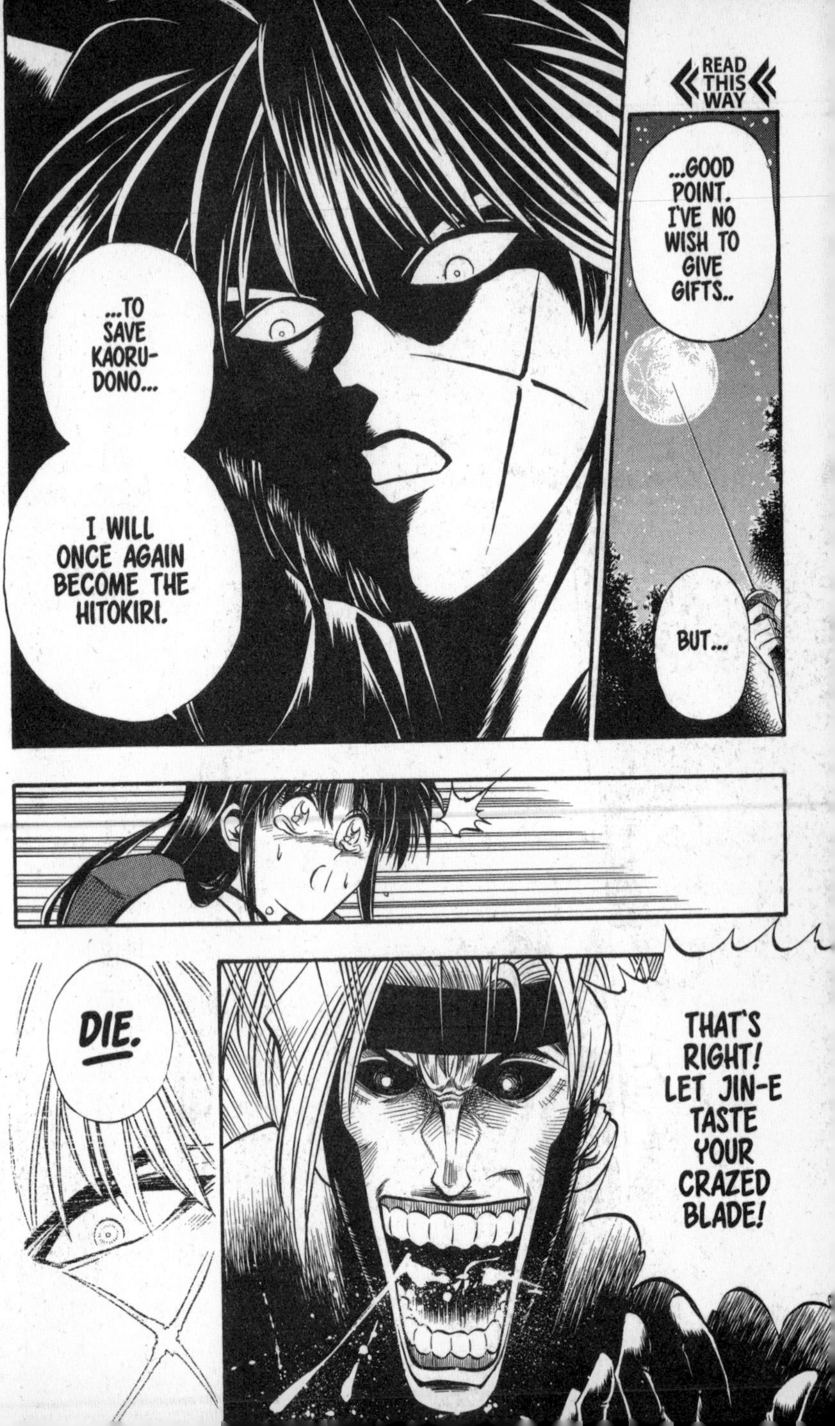
READ THIS WAY
...GOOD POINT. I'VE NO WISH TO GIVE GIFTS..
BUT...
...TO SAVE KAORU-DONO...
I WILL ONCE AGAIN BECOME THE HITOKIRI.
THAT'S RIGHT! LET JIN-E TASTE YOUR CRAZED BLADE!
DIE.

READ THIS WAY

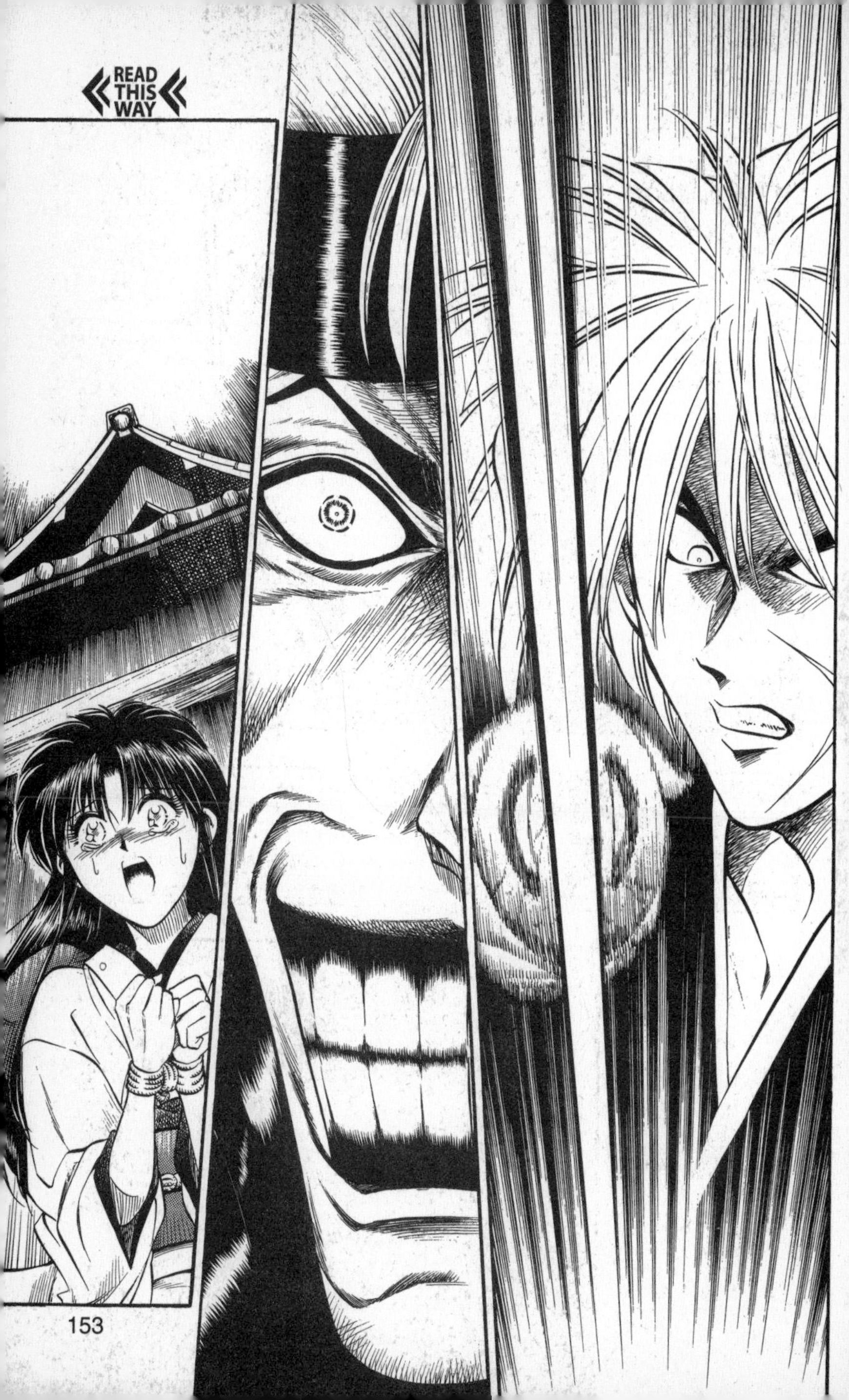

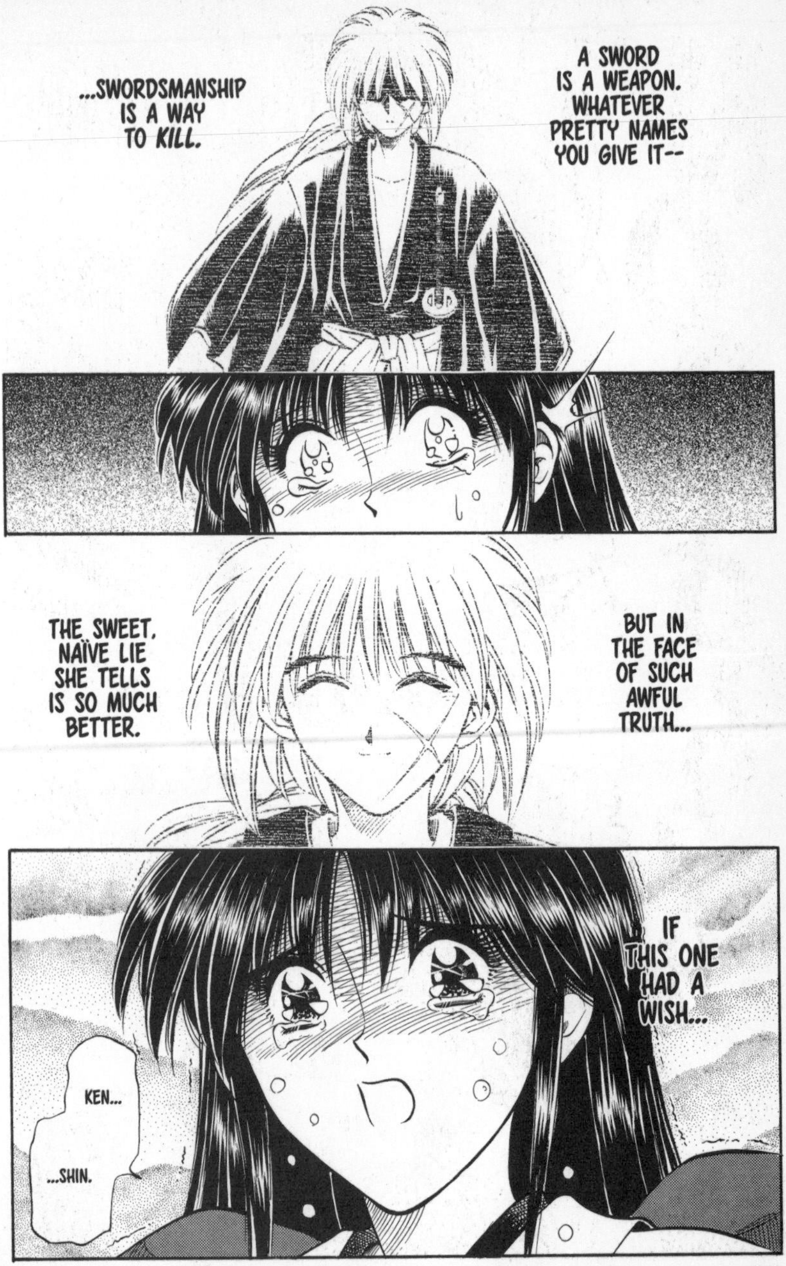
A SWORD IS A WEAPON. WHATEVER PRETTY NAMES YOU GIVE IT--
...SWORDSMANSHIP IS A WAY TO KILL.
BUT IN THE FACE OF SUCH AWFUL TRUTH...
THE SWEET, NAÏVE LIE SHE TELLS IS SO MUCH BETTER.
IF THIS ONE HAD A WISH...
KEN...
...SHIN.

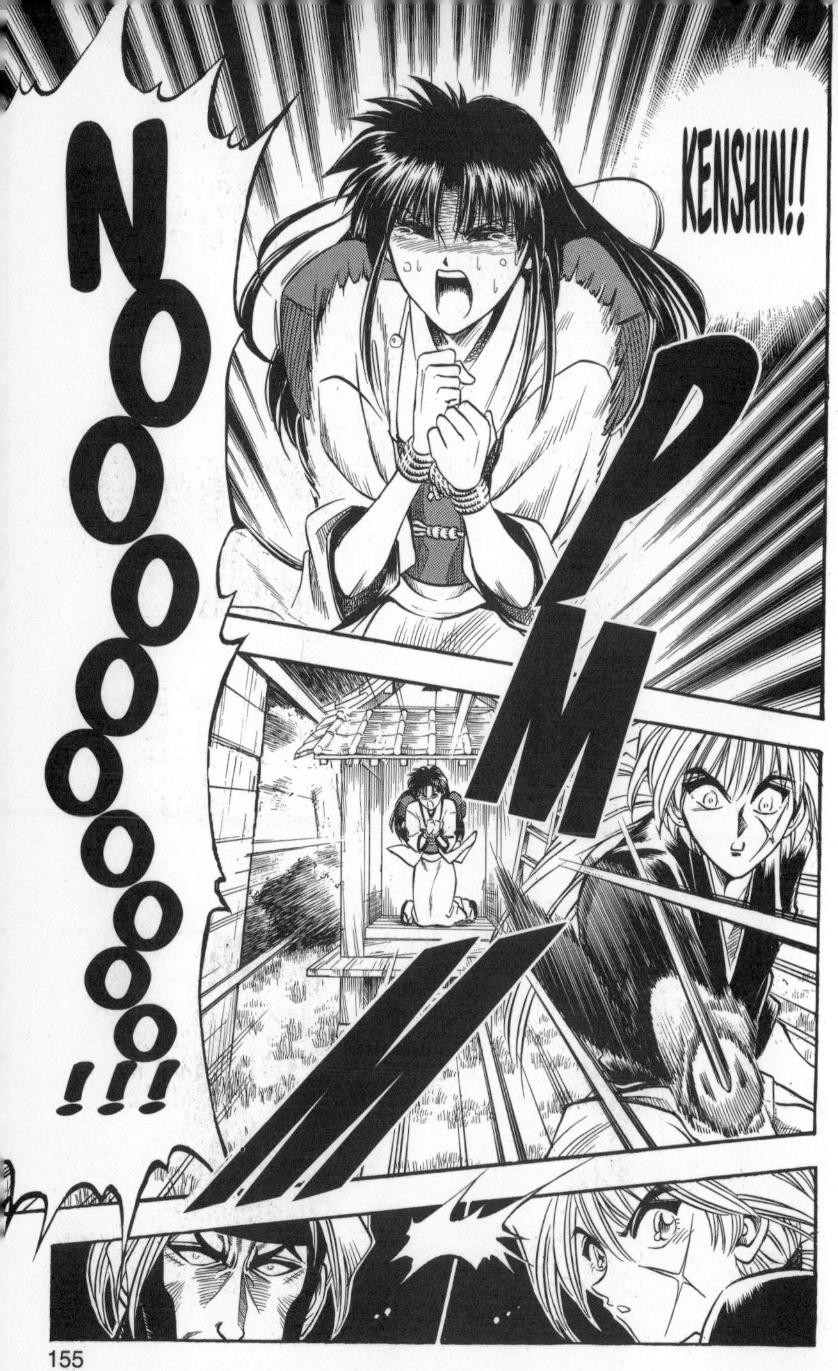
KENSHIN!!
NOOOOOOOOOO!!!
DOMM

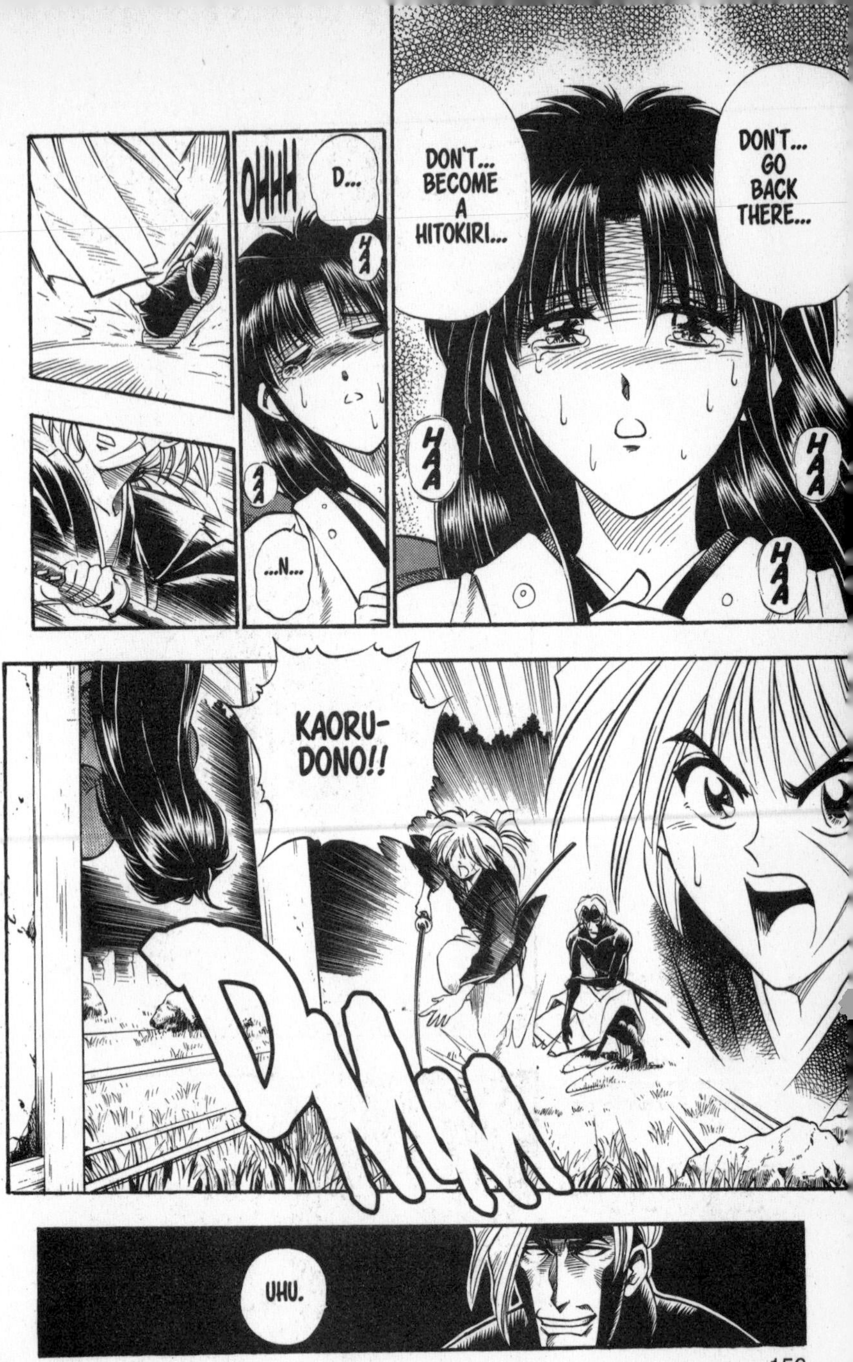
DON'T... GO BACK THERE...
HAA
HAA
DON'T... BECOME A HITOKIRI...
HAA
D...
OHHH
HAA
HAA
...N...
KAORU-DONO!!
UHU.

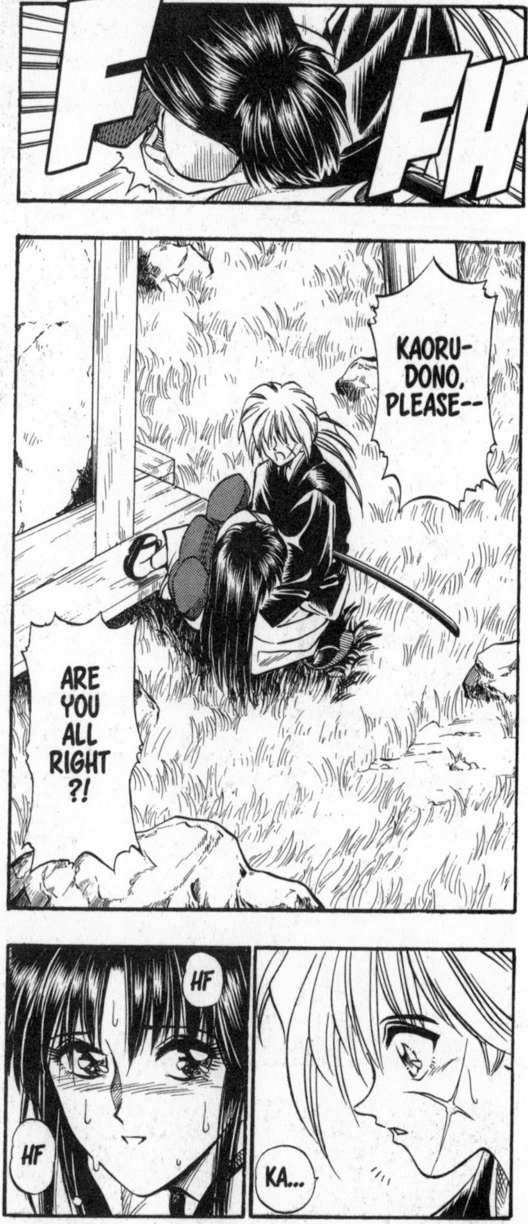
F
EH
KAORU-DONO, PLEASE--
ARE YOU ALL RIGHT?!
KA...
HF
HF

Okay! So! The "CD book" version of "Rurouni Kenshin"...! The recording script looks great and I'm really excited. I just wish I weren't so busy with work so I could sit in on the recording...But... is this real? Is "Rurouni Kenshin" REALLY real?

I think I may be dreaming....We'll find out, I guess. Hoping you're enjoying this as much as I am (I'm a little scared, myself...).

Watsuki

伸宏
和月

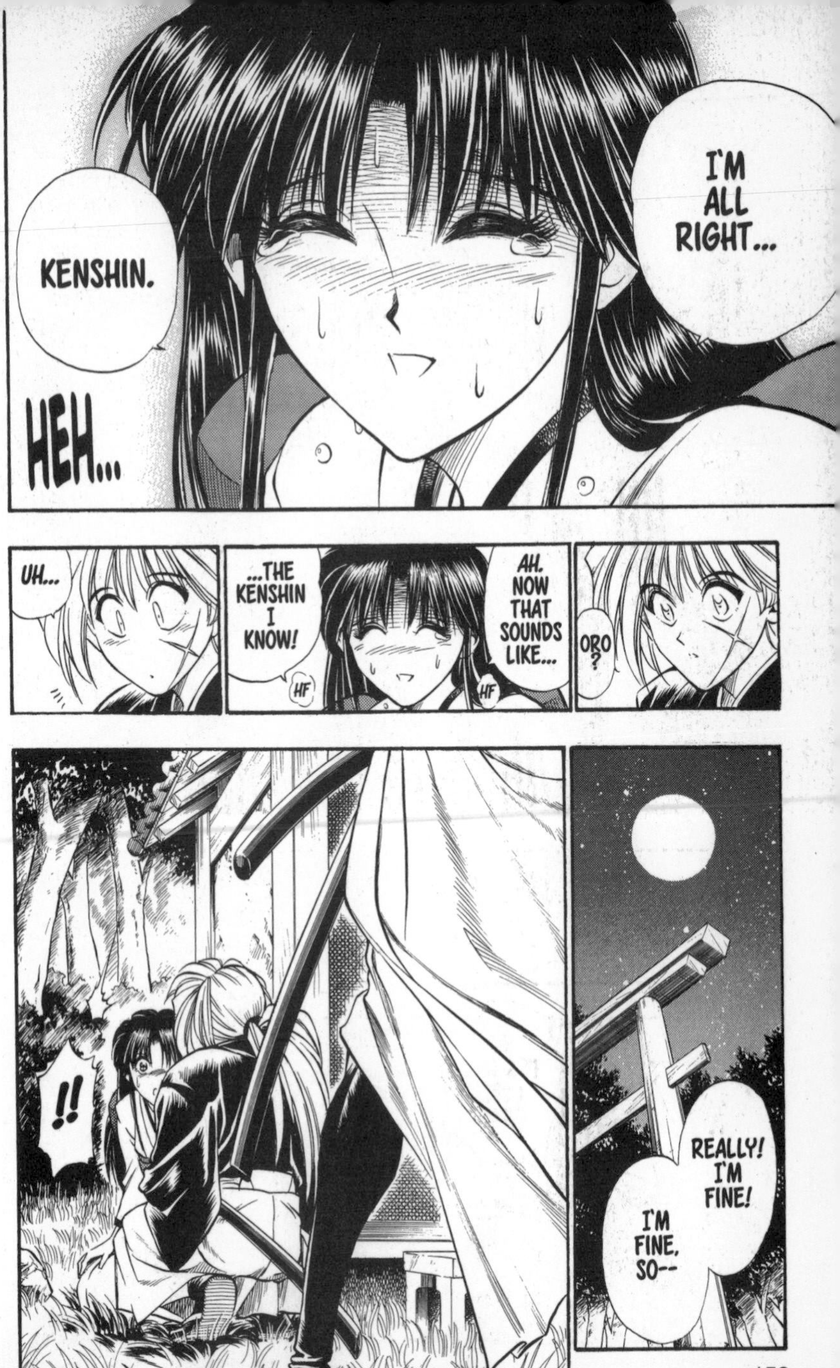
I'M ALL RIGHT...
KENSHIN.
HEH...
ORO ?
AH. NOW THAT SOUNDS LIKE...
...THE KENSHIN I KNOW!
HF
HF
UH...
REALLY! I'M FINE!
I'M FINE, SO--
!!

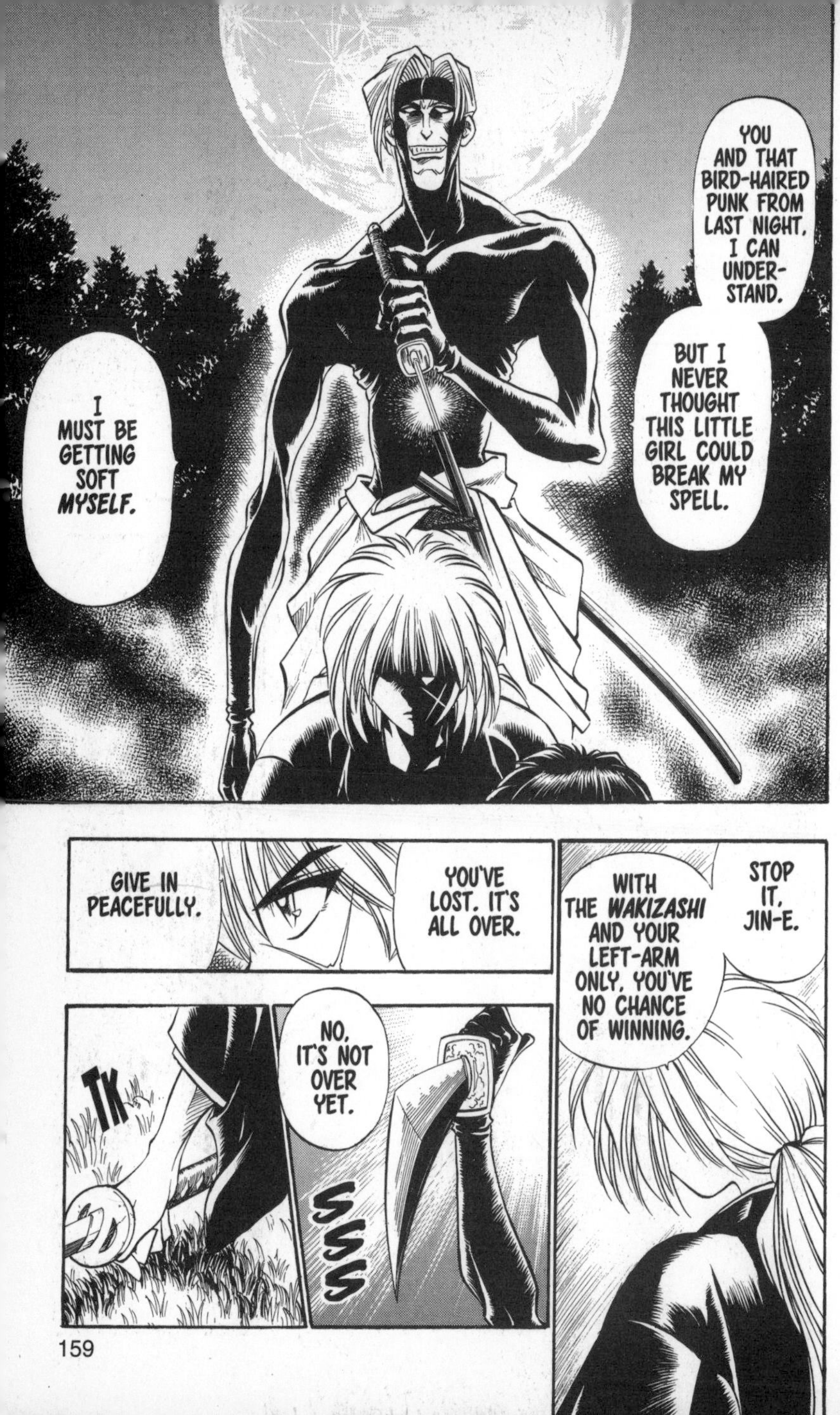
YOU AND THAT BIRD-HAIRED PUNK FROM LAST NIGHT, I CAN UNDER-STAND.
BUT I NEVER THOUGHT THIS LITTLE GIRL COULD BREAK MY SPELL.
I MUST BE GETTING SOFT *MYSELF.*
STOP IT, JIN-E.
WITH THE *WAKIZASHI* AND YOUR LEFT-ARM ONLY, YOU'VE NO CHANCE OF WINNING.
YOU'VE LOST. IT'S ALL OVER.
GIVE IN PEACEFULLY.
NO, IT'S NOT OVER YET.
SSS
TK

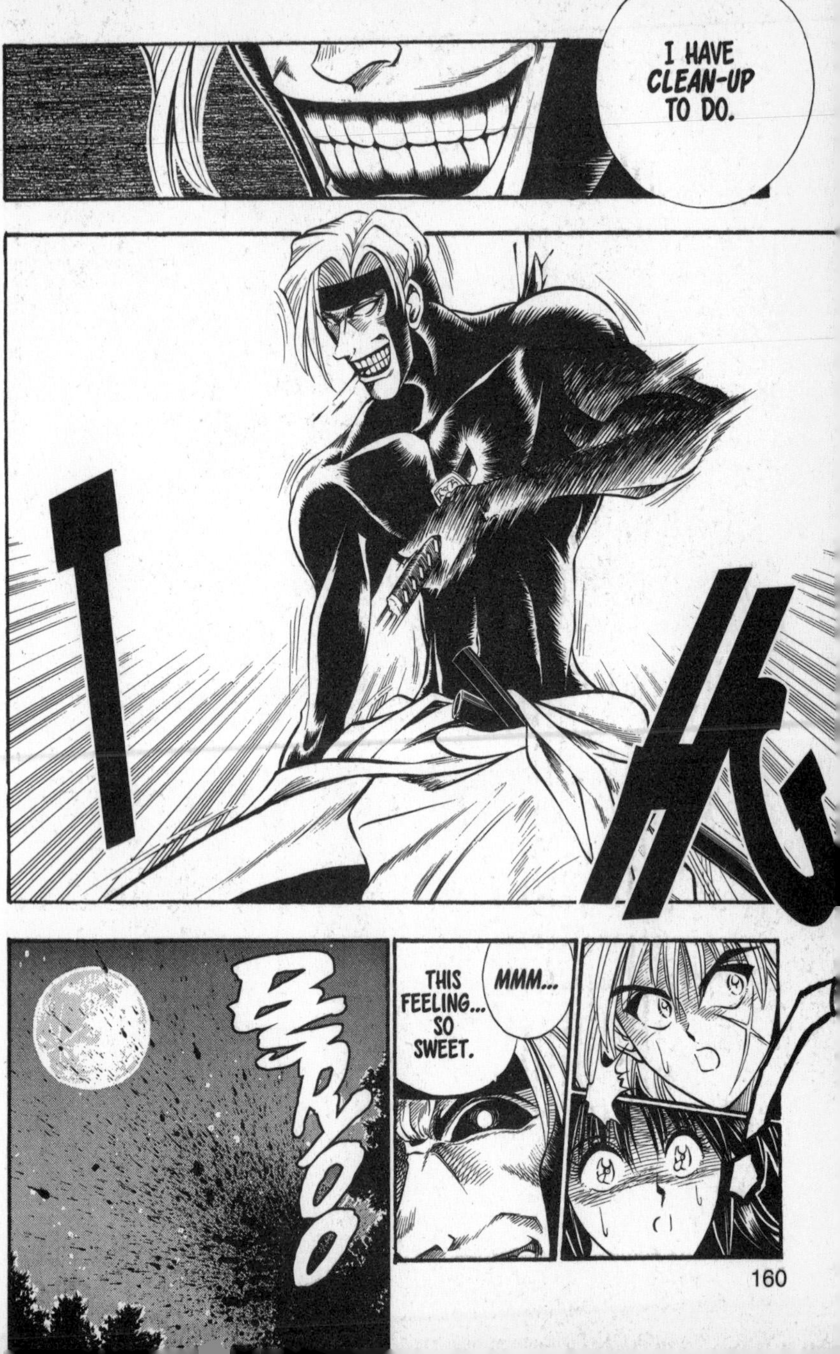
I HAVE CLEAN-UP TO DO.
MMM...
THIS FEELING... SO SWEET.

READ THIS WAY

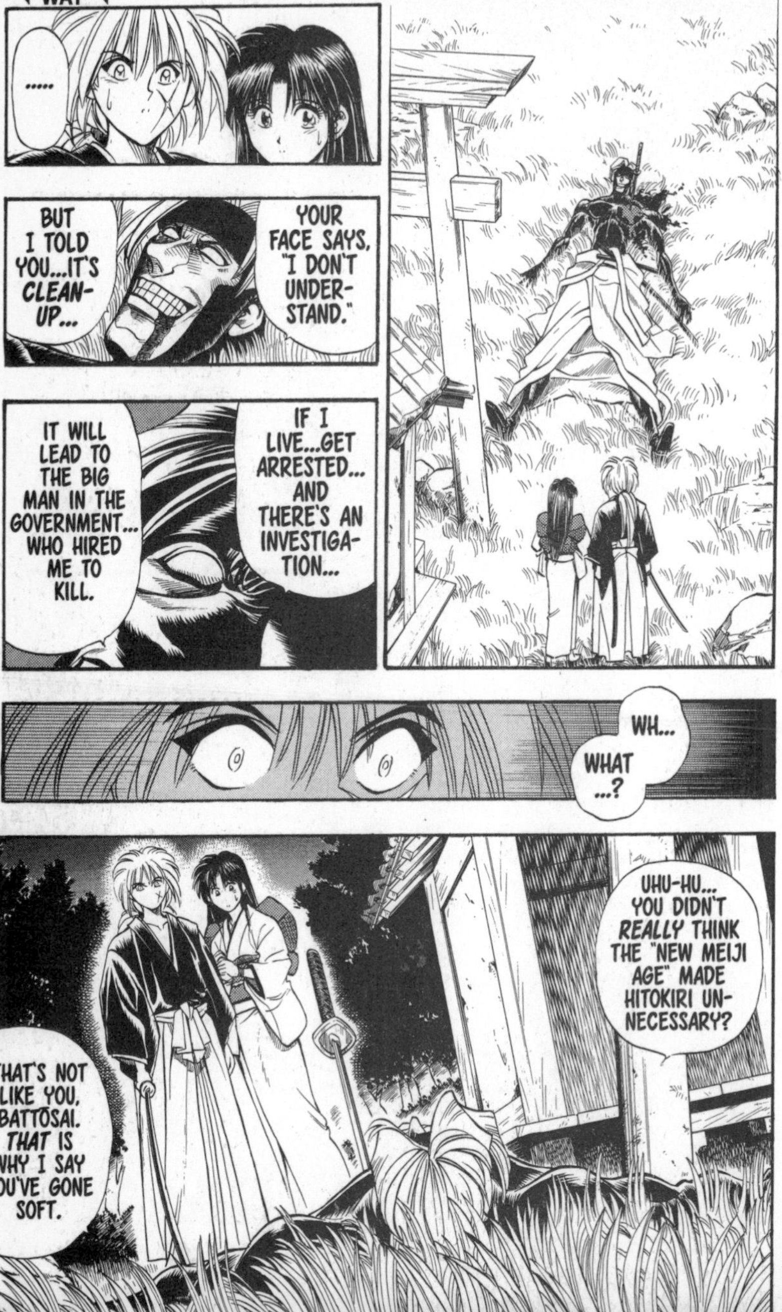

.....
YOUR FACE SAYS, "I DON'T UNDERSTAND."
BUT I TOLD YOU...IT'S *CLEAN-UP*...
IF I LIVE...GET ARRESTED... AND THERE'S AN INVESTIGATION...
IT WILL LEAD TO THE BIG MAN IN THE GOVERNMENT... WHO HIRED ME TO KILL.
WH... WHAT ...?
UHU-HU... YOU DIDN'T *REALLY* THINK THE "NEW MEIJI AGE" MADE HITOKIRI UNNECESSARY?
THAT'S NOT LIKE YOU, BATTOSAI. *THAT* IS WHY I SAY YOU'VE GONE SOFT.

READ THIS WAY

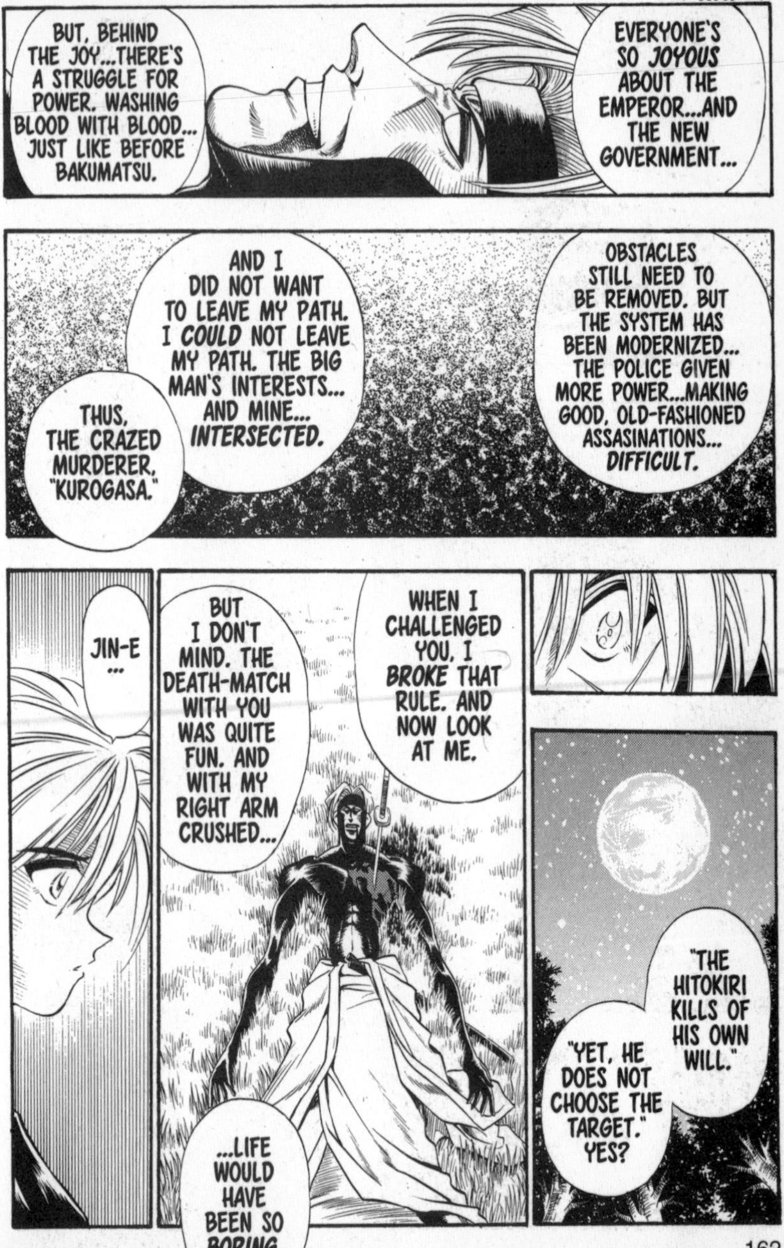
EVERYONE'S SO JOYOUS ABOUT THE EMPEROR...AND THE NEW GOVERNMENT...
BUT, BEHIND THE JOY...THERE'S A STRUGGLE FOR POWER. WASHING BLOOD WITH BLOOD... JUST LIKE BEFORE BAKUMATSU.
OBSTACLES STILL NEED TO BE REMOVED. BUT THE SYSTEM HAS BEEN MODERNIZED... THE POLICE GIVEN MORE POWER...MAKING GOOD, OLD-FASHIONED ASSASINATIONS... DIFFICULT.
AND I DID NOT WANT TO LEAVE MY PATH. I COULD NOT LEAVE MY PATH. THE BIG MAN'S INTERESTS... AND MINE... INTERSECTED.
THUS, THE CRAZED MURDERER, "KUROGASA."
"THE HITOKIRI KILLS OF HIS OWN WILL."
"YET, HE DOES NOT CHOOSE THE TARGET." YES?
WHEN I CHALLENGED YOU, I BROKE THAT RULE. AND NOW LOOK AT ME.
BUT I DON'T MIND. THE DEATH-MATCH WITH YOU WAS QUITE FUN. AND WITH MY RIGHT ARM CRUSHED...
...LIFE WOULD HAVE BEEN SO BORING.
JIN-E ...

READ THIS WAY

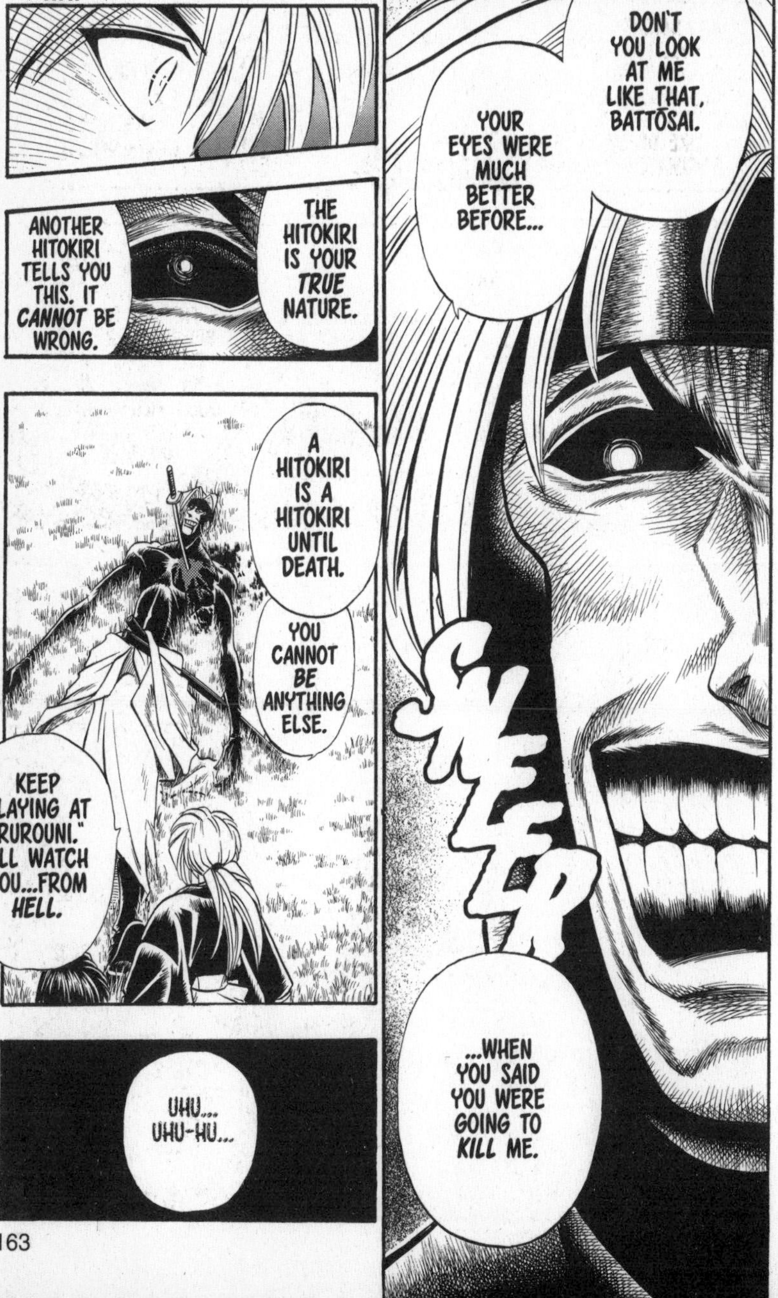
DON'T YOU LOOK AT ME LIKE THAT, BATTŌSAI.
YOUR EYES WERE MUCH BETTER BEFORE...
SNEER
...WHEN YOU SAID YOU WERE GOING TO KILL ME.
THE HITOKIRI IS YOUR TRUE NATURE.
ANOTHER HITOKIRI TELLS YOU THIS. IT CANNOT BE WRONG.
A HITOKIRI IS A HITOKIRI UNTIL DEATH.
YOU CANNOT BE ANYTHING ELSE.
KEEP PLAYING AT "RUROUNI." I'LL WATCH YOU...FROM HELL.
UHU... UHU-HU...

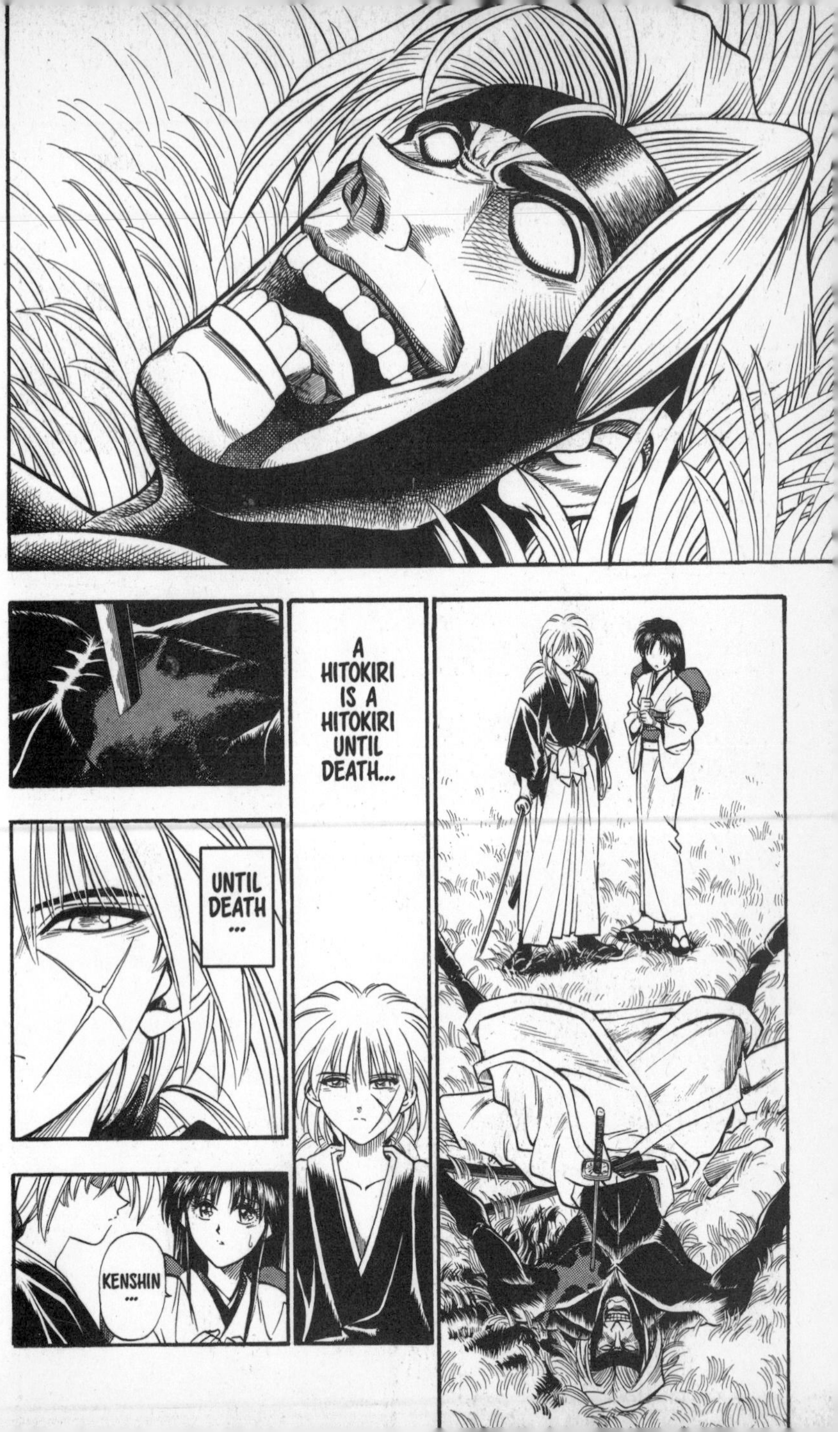
A HITOKIRI IS A HITOKIRI UNTIL DEATH...
UNTIL DEATH ...
KENSHIN ...

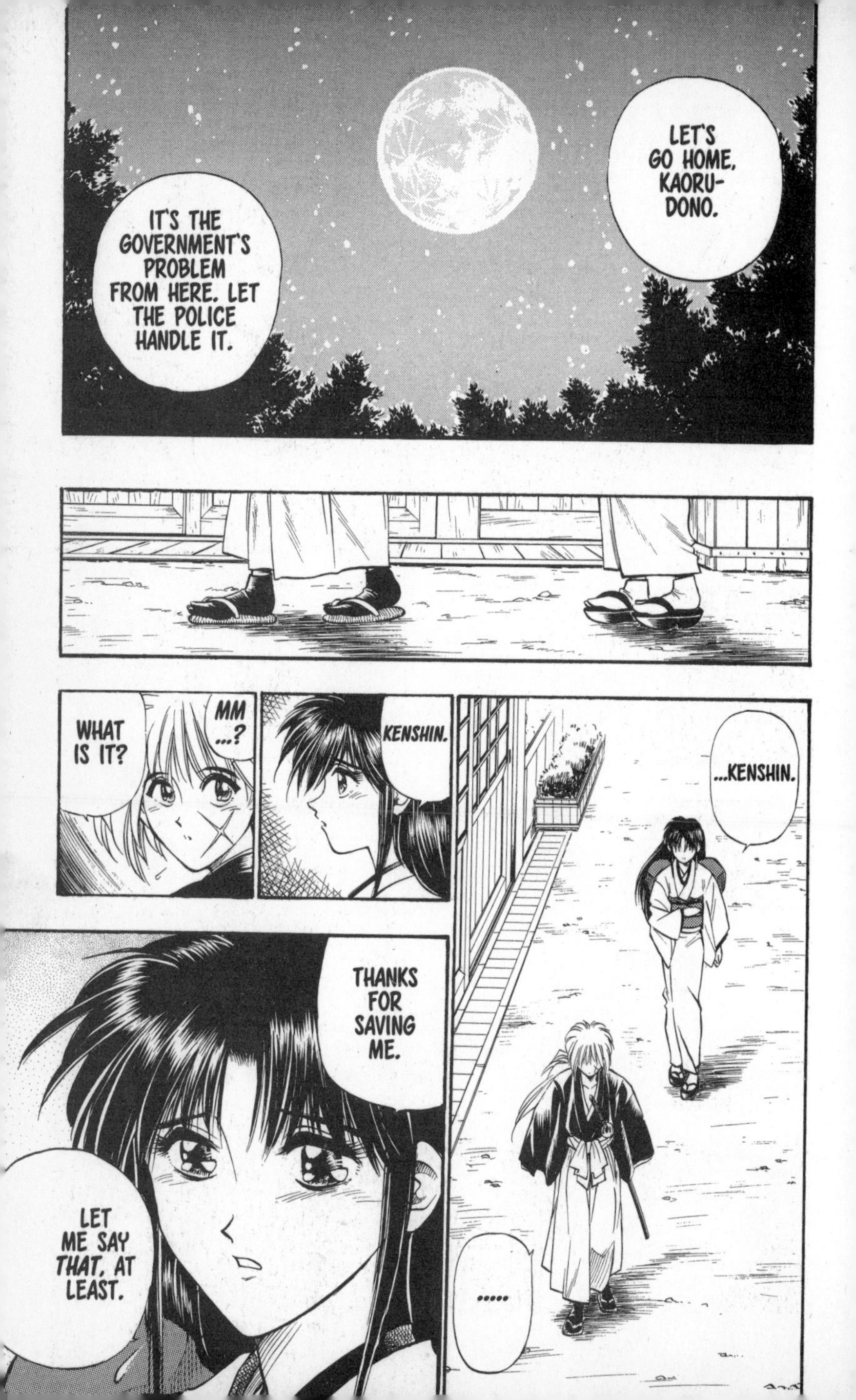
LET'S GO HOME, KAORU-DONO.
IT'S THE GOVERNMENT'S PROBLEM FROM HERE. LET THE POLICE HANDLE IT.
...KENSHIN.
.....
KENSHIN.
MM ...?
WHAT IS IT?
THANKS FOR SAVING ME.
LET ME SAY THAT, AT LEAST.

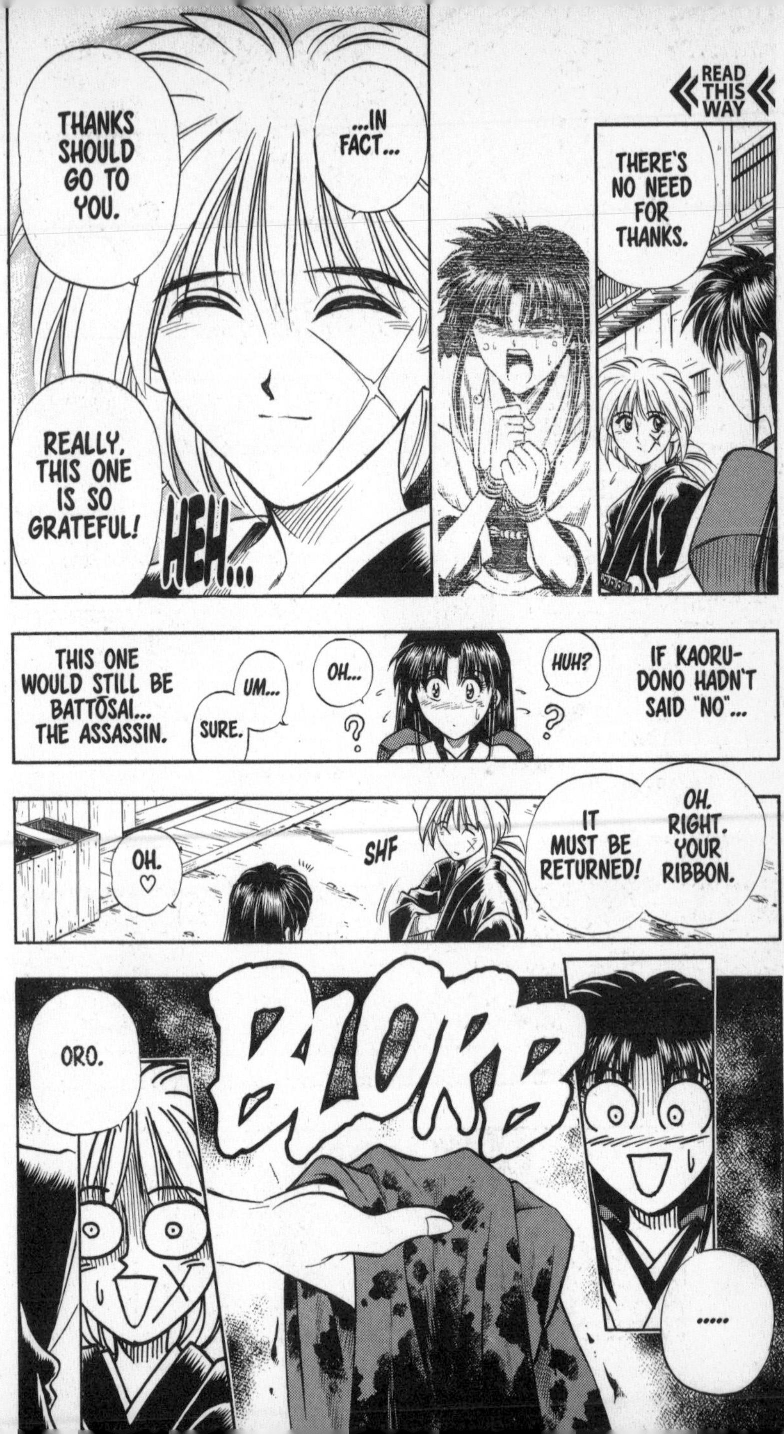
READ THIS WAY
THERE'S NO NEED FOR THANKS.
...IN FACT...
THANKS SHOULD GO TO YOU.
REALLY. THIS ONE IS SO GRATEFUL!
HEH...
IF KAORU-DONO HADN'T SAID "NO"...
HUH?
OH...
UM...
SURE.
THIS ONE WOULD STILL BE BATTŌSAI... THE ASSASSIN.
OH. RIGHT. YOUR RIBBON.
IT MUST BE RETURNED!
SHF
OH. ♡
.....
BLORB
ORO.

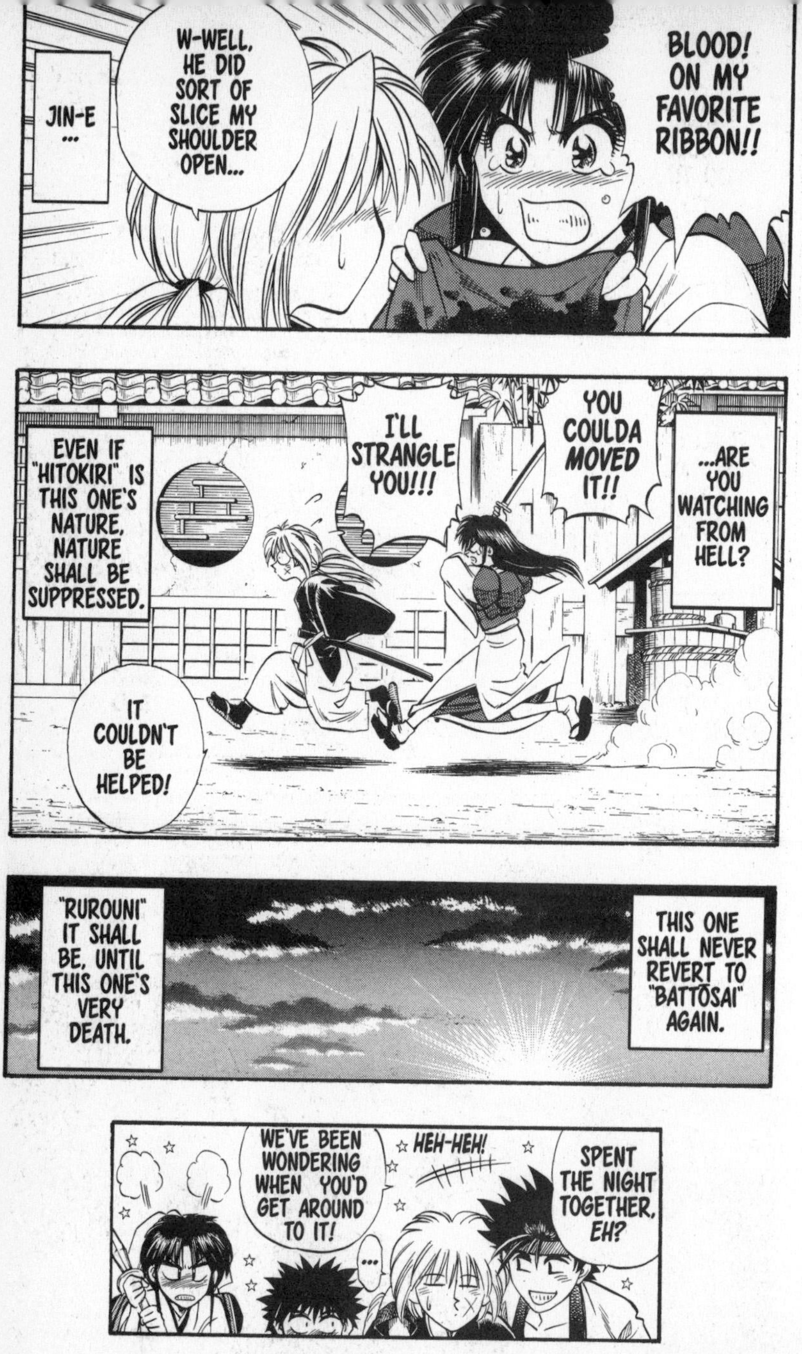
BLOOD! ON MY FAVORITE RIBBON!!
W-WELL, HE DID SORT OF SLICE MY SHOULDER OPEN...
JIN-E ...
...ARE YOU WATCHING FROM HELL?
YOU COULDA MOVED IT!!
I'LL STRANGLE YOU!!!
EVEN IF "HITOKIRI" IS THIS ONE'S NATURE, NATURE SHALL BE SUPPRESSED.
IT COULDN'T BE HELPED!
THIS ONE SHALL NEVER REVERT TO "BATTOSAI" AGAIN.
"RUROUNI" IT SHALL BE, UNTIL THIS ONE'S VERY DEATH.
SPENT THE NIGHT TOGETHER, EH?
HEH-HEH!
WE'VE BEEN WONDERING WHEN YOU'D GET AROUND TO IT!
...

## The Secret Life of Characters (7)

# —Udō Jin-e—

**The motif for this character is the No. 1 hitokiri of the Bakumatsu, *Okada Izō*...or so it was *supposed* to have been, but Udō Jin-e looks even less like his real-life, historical counterpart than Kenshin does. So, Izō fans, no letters with razor-blades in them, please? (I wish I were kidding.)**

**That aside, I designed the character to be a polar opposite of Kenshin, and what I came up with is Jin-e. *Satsujin-ki* or "murderous ogre" that he is, Jin-e is the sort of complicated fellow who's not only crazy-acting, but *crazy*-crazy. It was tough, but both the character and the story proved worth the trouble. Jin-e being the No. 1 fan favorite for bad guys and all, it was also tough deciding how to end it, but ultimately I reasoned that, his "art of *hitokiri*" not otherwise being complete, he would have to commit a tearful suicide. Technically he may not have defeated Battōsai, but in another sense, Jin-e was the only one ever to defeat Kenshin. *That* is Udō Jin-e.**

**His outfit comes from a Shinsengumi manga that came out 14, 15 years ago—from its cool main character, *Serizawa Kamo* (we're talking Hijikata-cool here, kids). If you by chance happen to already have *known* this, then you have passed beyond the realm of mere Shinsengumi otakudom. You, my friend, are a Shinsengumi *master*.**

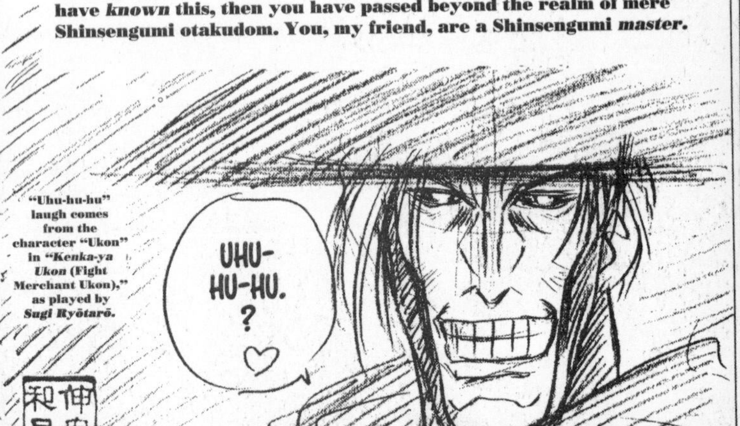
UHU-HU-HU. ?
伸宏和月

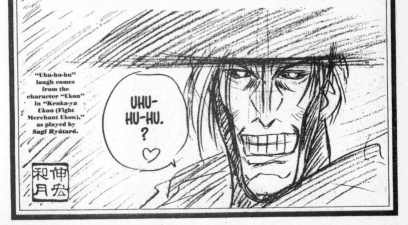

**"Uhu-hu-hu" laugh comes from the character "Ukon" in "*Kenka-ya Ukon* (Fight Merchant Ukon)," as played by *Sugi Ryōtarō*.**

READ THIS WAY

# Act 15
# Beauty on the Run

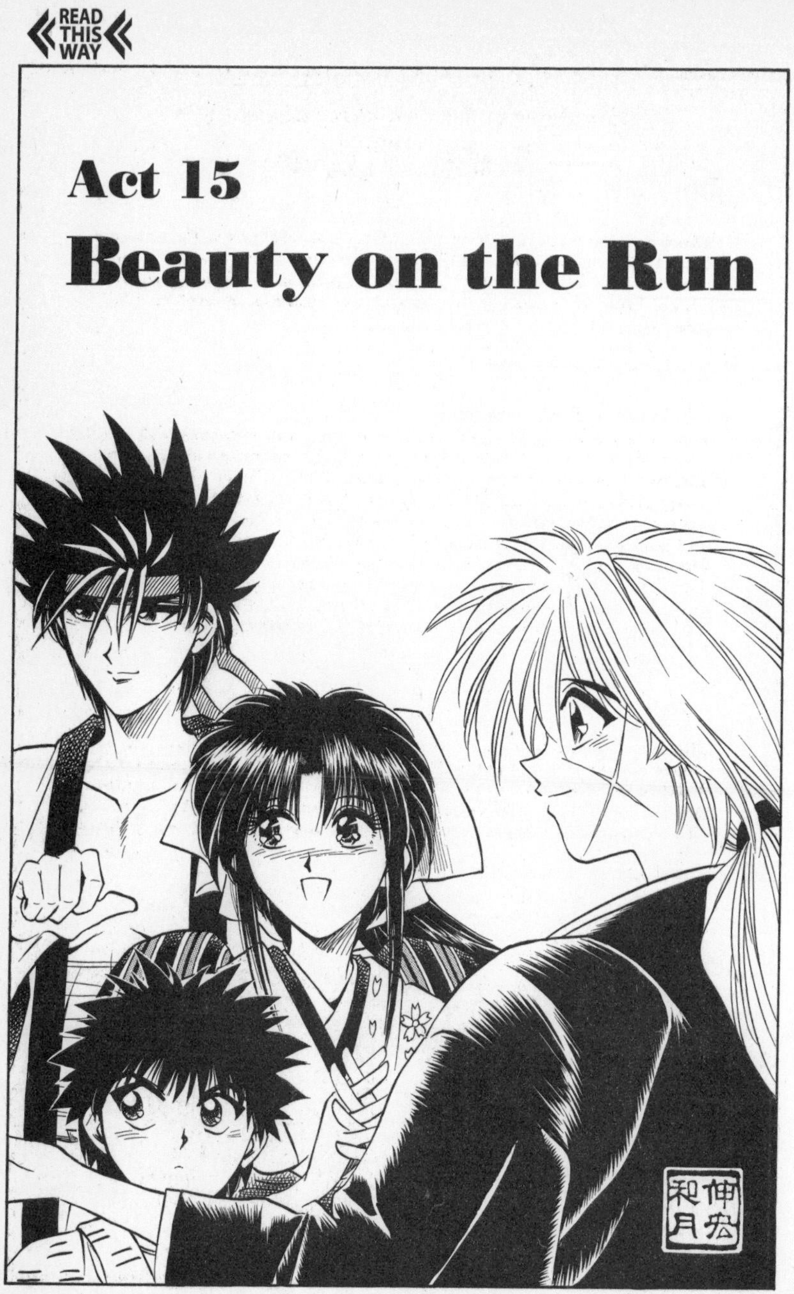

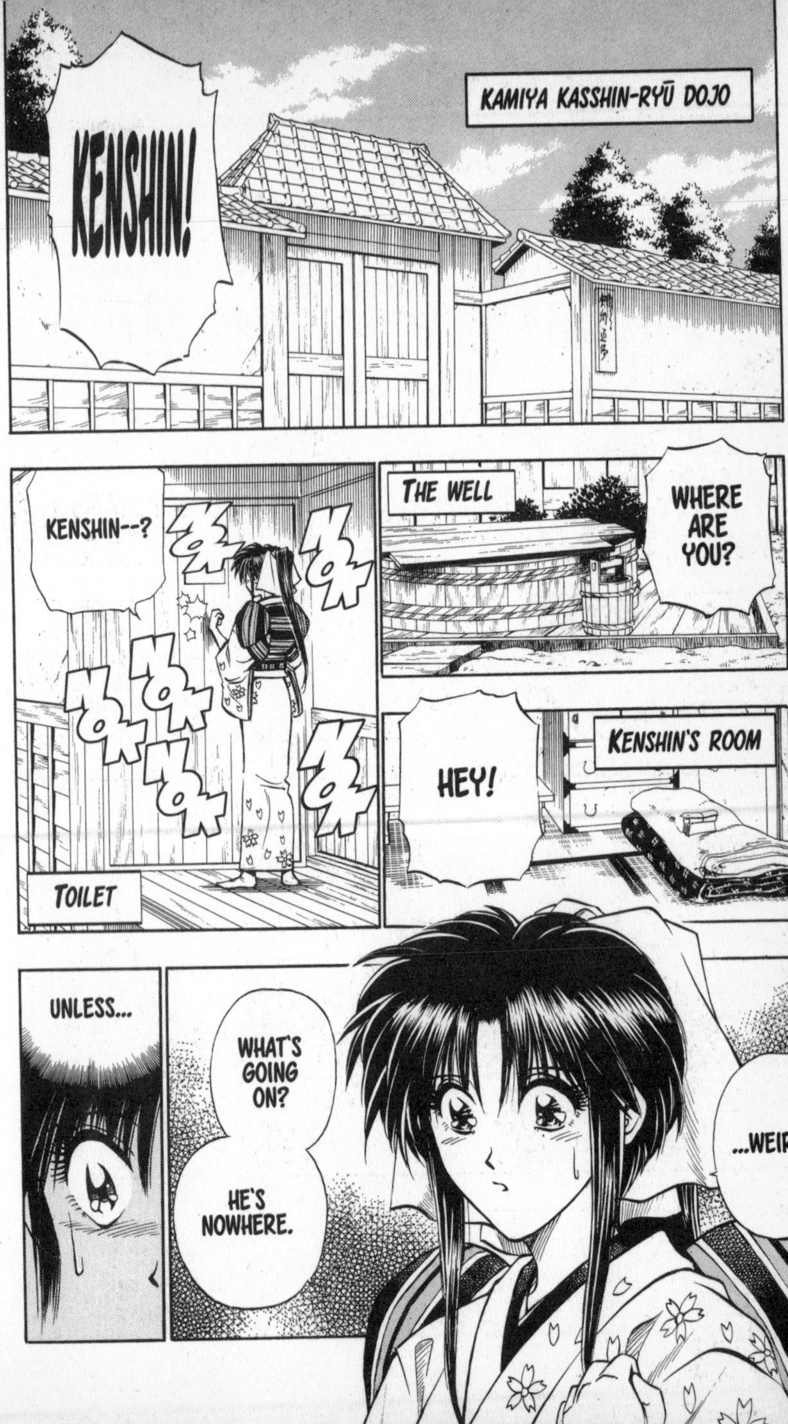
KAMIYA KASSHIN-RYŪ DOJO
KENSHIN!
THE WELL
WHERE ARE YOU?
KENSHIN'S ROOM
HEY!
KENSHIN--?
TOILET
...WEIRD.
WHAT'S GOING ON?
HE'S NOWHERE.
UNLESS...

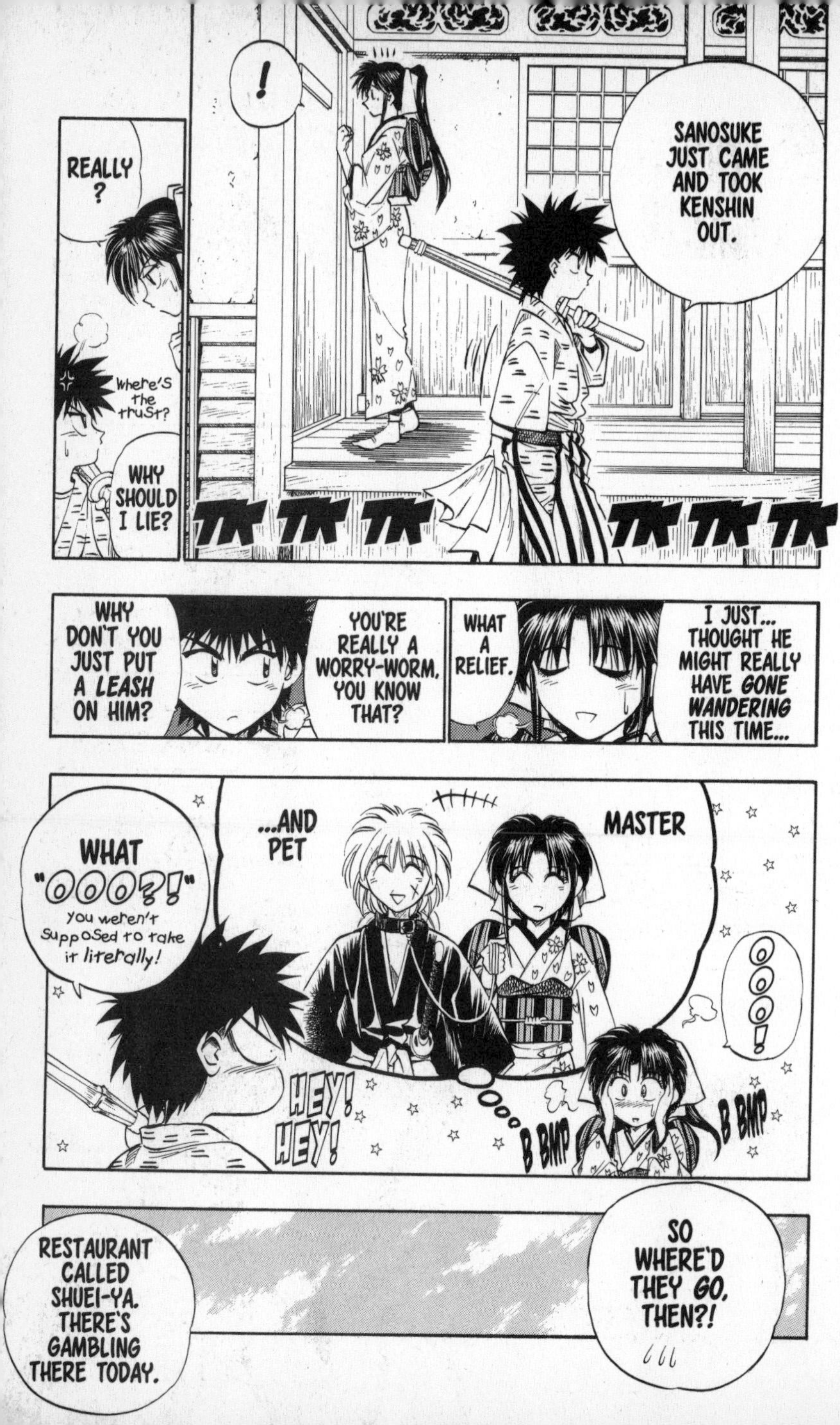
SANOSUKE JUST CAME AND TOOK KENSHIN OUT.
!
TK TK TK TK TK TK
REALLY ?
Where's the trust?
WHY SHOULD I LIE?
I JUST... THOUGHT HE MIGHT REALLY HAVE GONE WANDERING THIS TIME...
WHAT A RELIEF.
YOU'RE REALLY A WORRY-WORM, YOU KNOW THAT?
WHY DON'T YOU JUST PUT A LEASH ON HIM?
MASTER ...AND PET
ooo!
B BMP B BMP
WHAT "ooo?!" you weren't supposed to take it literally!
HEY! HEY!
SO WHERE'D THEY GO, THEN?!
RESTAURANT CALLED SHUEI-YA. THERE'S GAMBLING THERE TODAY.

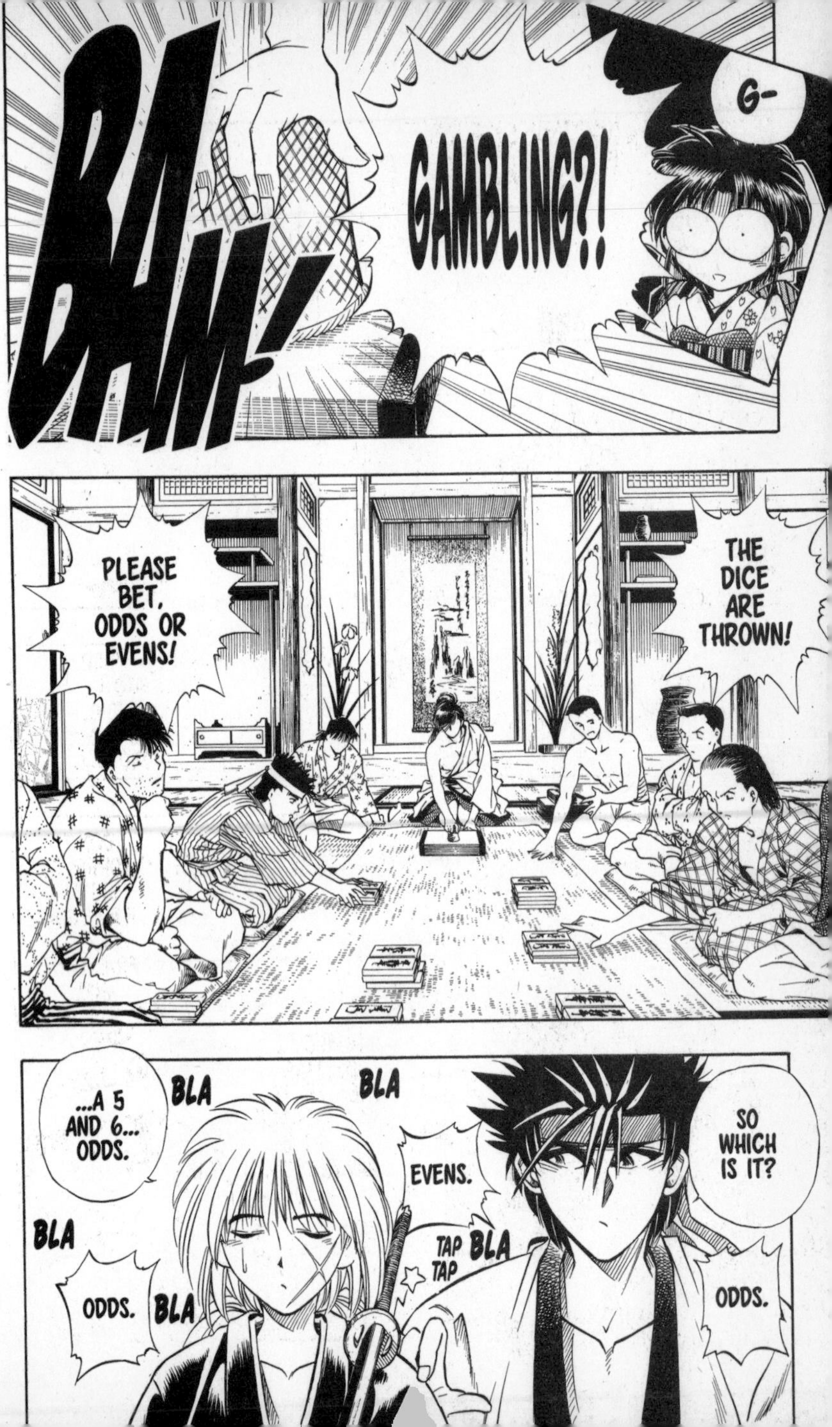
G-
GAMBLING?!
BAM!
THE DICE ARE THROWN!
PLEASE BET, ODDS OR EVENS!
SO WHICH IS IT?
ODDS.
BLA
BLA
EVENS.
TAP TAP
...A 5 AND 6... ODDS.
BLA
BLA
ODDS.
BLA

READ THIS WAY

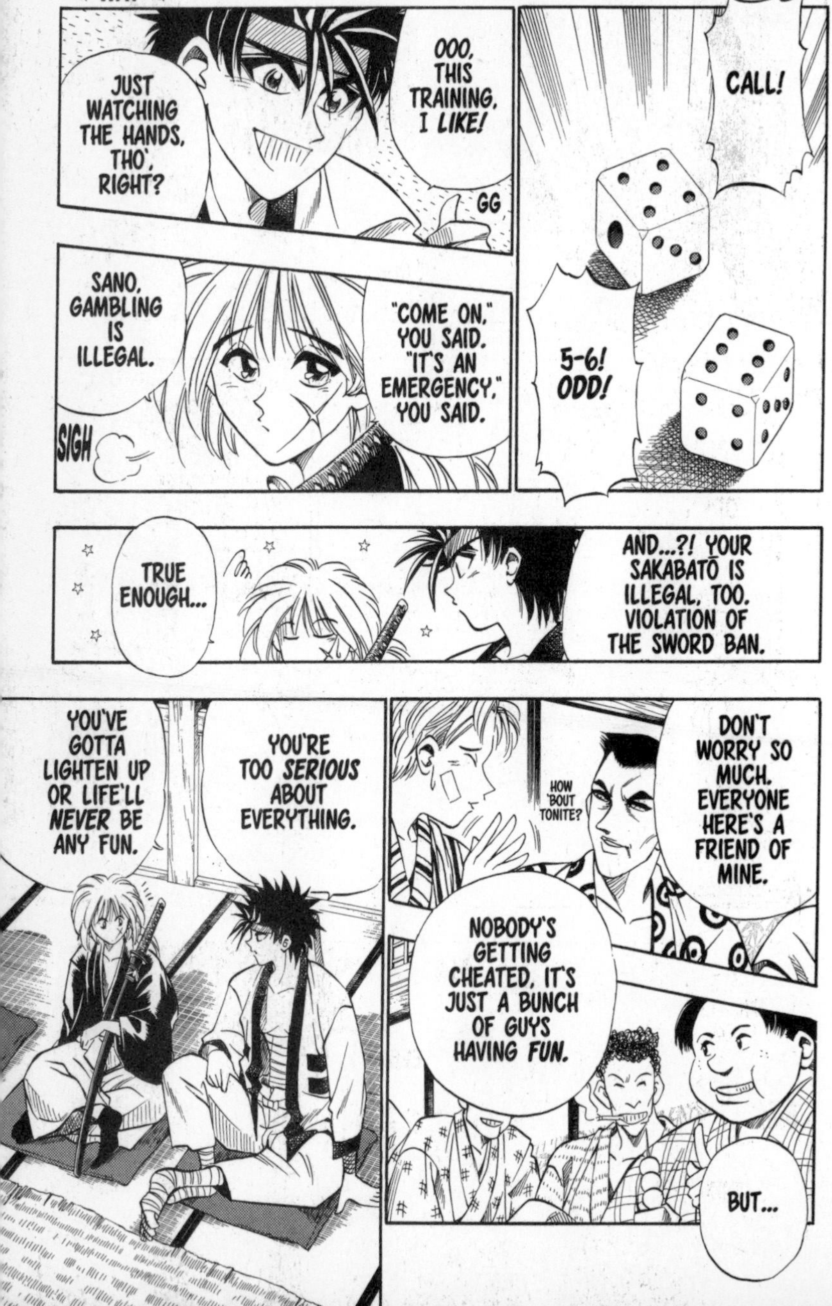
CALL!
5-6! ODD!
OOO, THIS TRAINING, I LIKE!
GG
JUST WATCHING THE HANDS, THO', RIGHT?
"COME ON," YOU SAID. "IT'S AN EMERGENCY," YOU SAID.
SANO, GAMBLING IS ILLEGAL.
SIGH
AND...?! YOUR SAKABATŌ IS ILLEGAL, TOO. VIOLATION OF THE SWORD BAN.
TRUE ENOUGH...
DON'T WORRY SO MUCH. EVERYONE HERE'S A FRIEND OF MINE.
HOW 'BOUT TONITE?
NOBODY'S GETTING CHEATED, IT'S JUST A BUNCH OF GUYS HAVING FUN.
BUT...
YOU'RE TOO SERIOUS ABOUT EVERYTHING.
YOU'VE GOTTA LIGHTEN UP OR LIFE'LL NEVER BE ANY FUN.

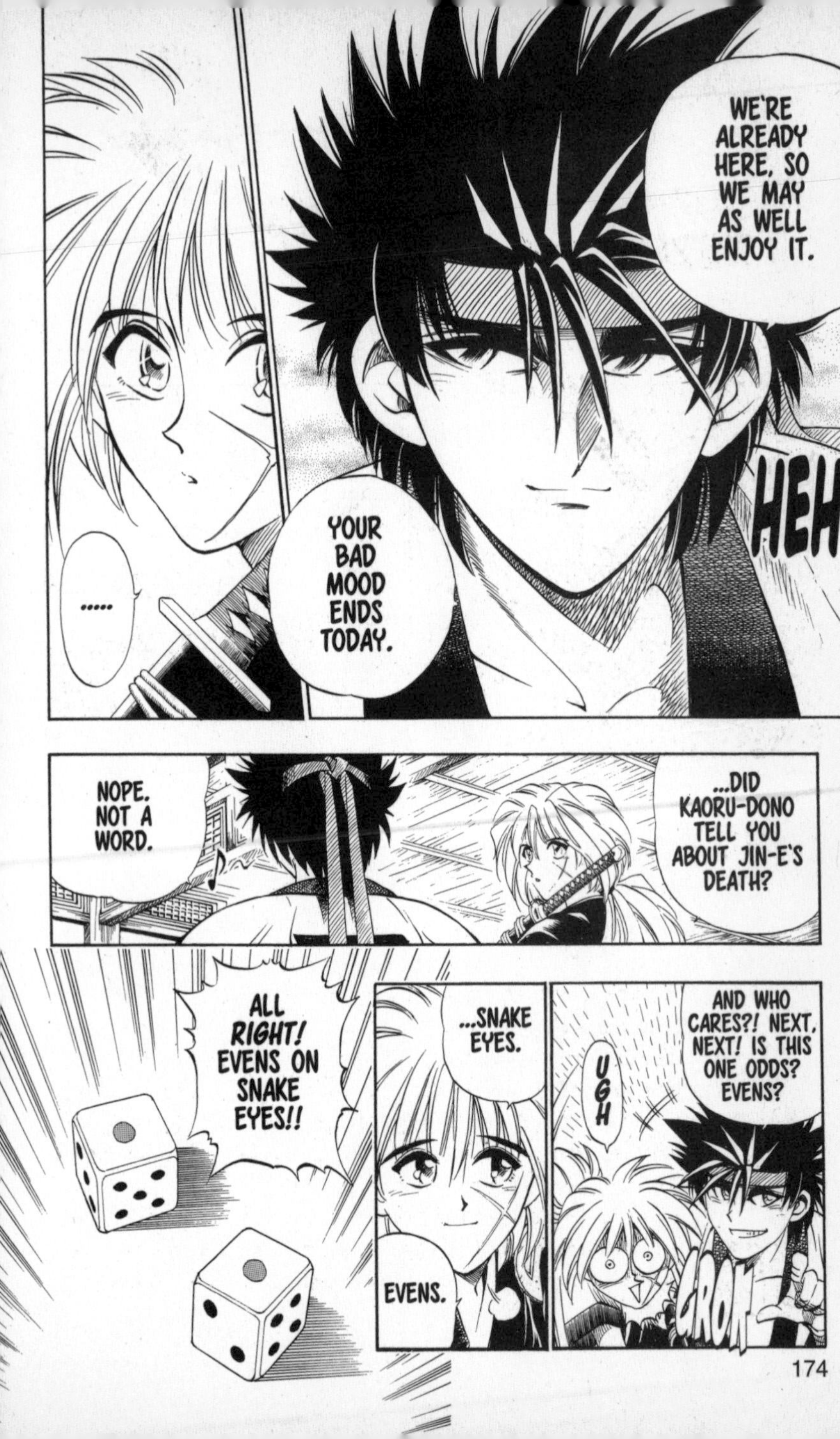
WE'RE ALREADY HERE, SO WE MAY AS WELL ENJOY IT.
HEH
YOUR BAD MOOD ENDS TODAY.
.....
...DID KAORU-DONO TELL YOU ABOUT JIN-E'S DEATH?
NOPE. NOT A WORD.
AND WHO CARES?! NEXT, NEXT! IS THIS ONE ODDS? EVENS?
UGH
...SNAKE EYES.
EVENS.
ALL RIGHT! EVENS ON SNAKE EYES!!

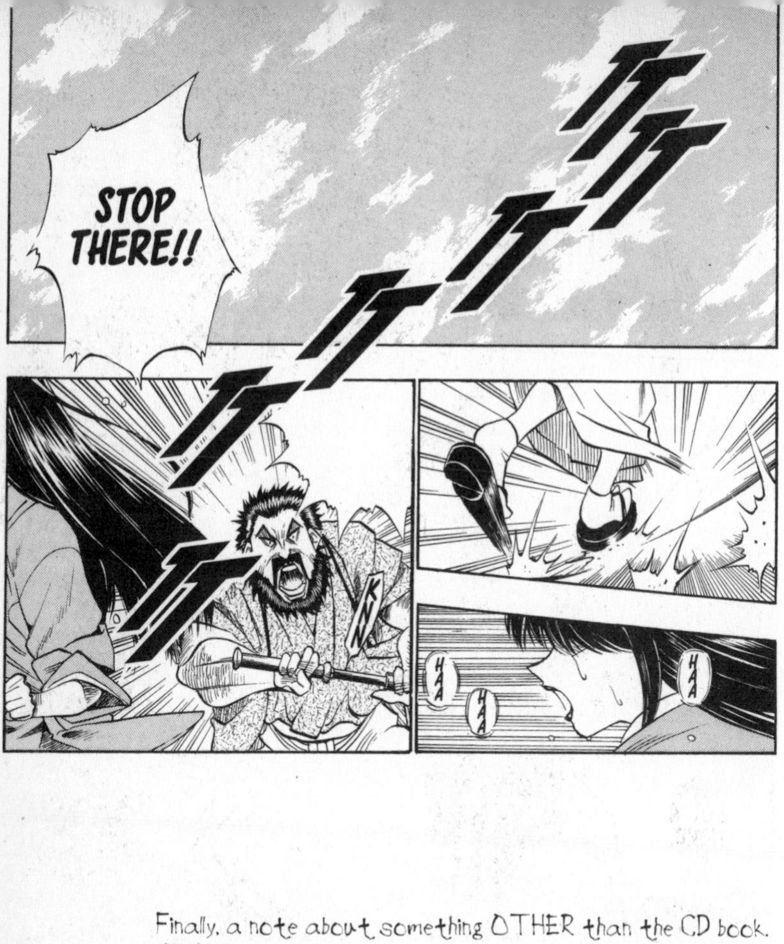
STOP THERE!!
HAA
HAA
HAA
KNN

Finally, a note about something OTHER than the CD book. First, thank you for the fan letters which keep coming in. Recently, even though the male-female readership ratio has changed a bit, it's still running around 2:8, with females in the lead. I'm always wanting to pen replies to your letters, but the amount you guys keep SENDING isn't even funny. Worse, work's been piling up and there's no "days off" in sight...not for another couple weeks, anyway. Forgive me!! Sometimes you write, saying you've made dōjinshi "fanzines" and ask if it's okay to send them. Bring 'em on! I've got like 20 of them here already. As it happens, I'm "pro-dōjinshi" myself, so send them on in without fear. For now, then, see you in Volume 3!

伸宏和月

Watsuki

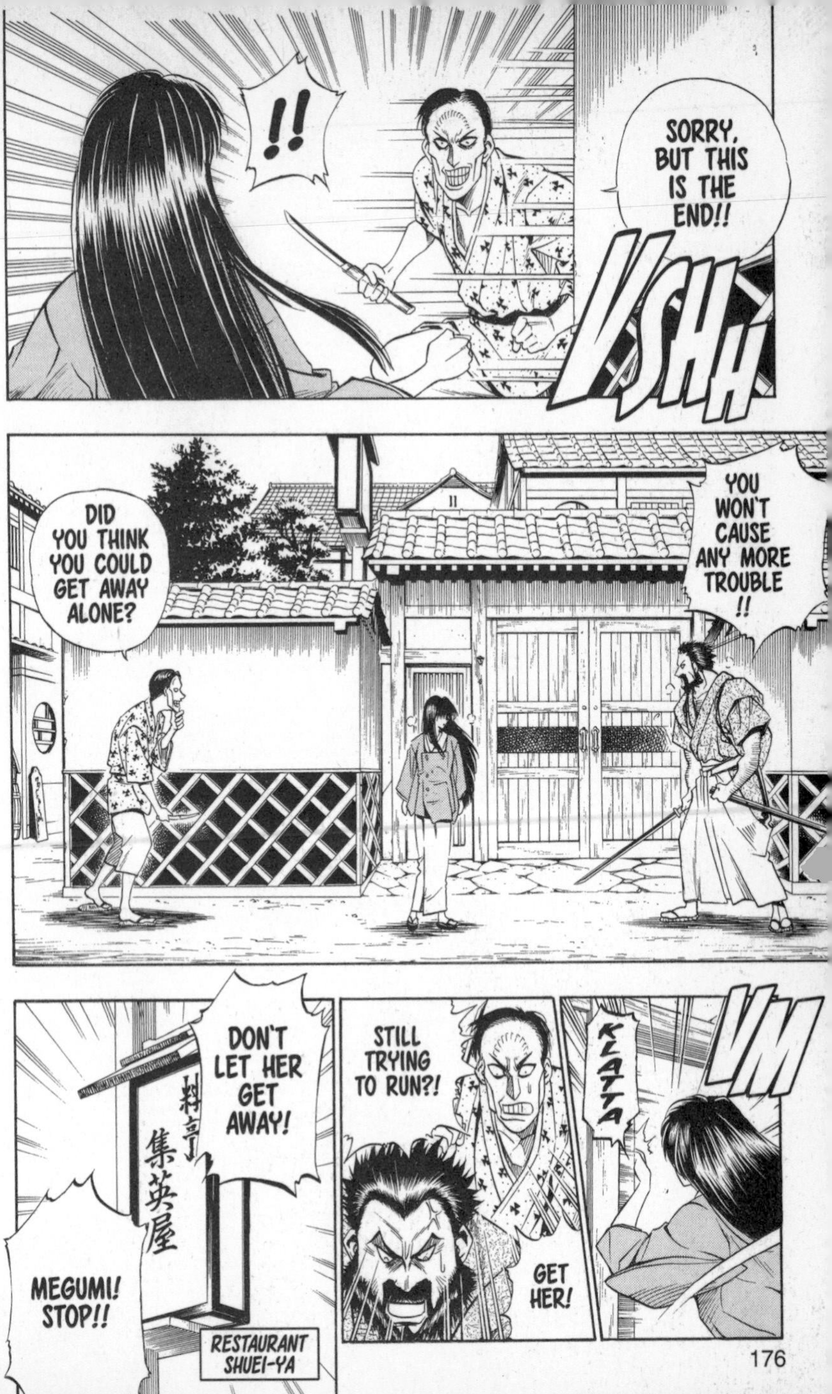
SORRY, BUT THIS IS THE END!!
!!
VSHH
YOU WON'T CAUSE ANY MORE TROUBLE!!
DID YOU THINK YOU COULD GET AWAY ALONE?
VM
KLATTA
STILL TRYING TO RUN?!
GET HER!
DON'T LET HER GET AWAY!
料亭
集英屋
MEGUMI! STOP!!
RESTAURANT SHUEI-YA

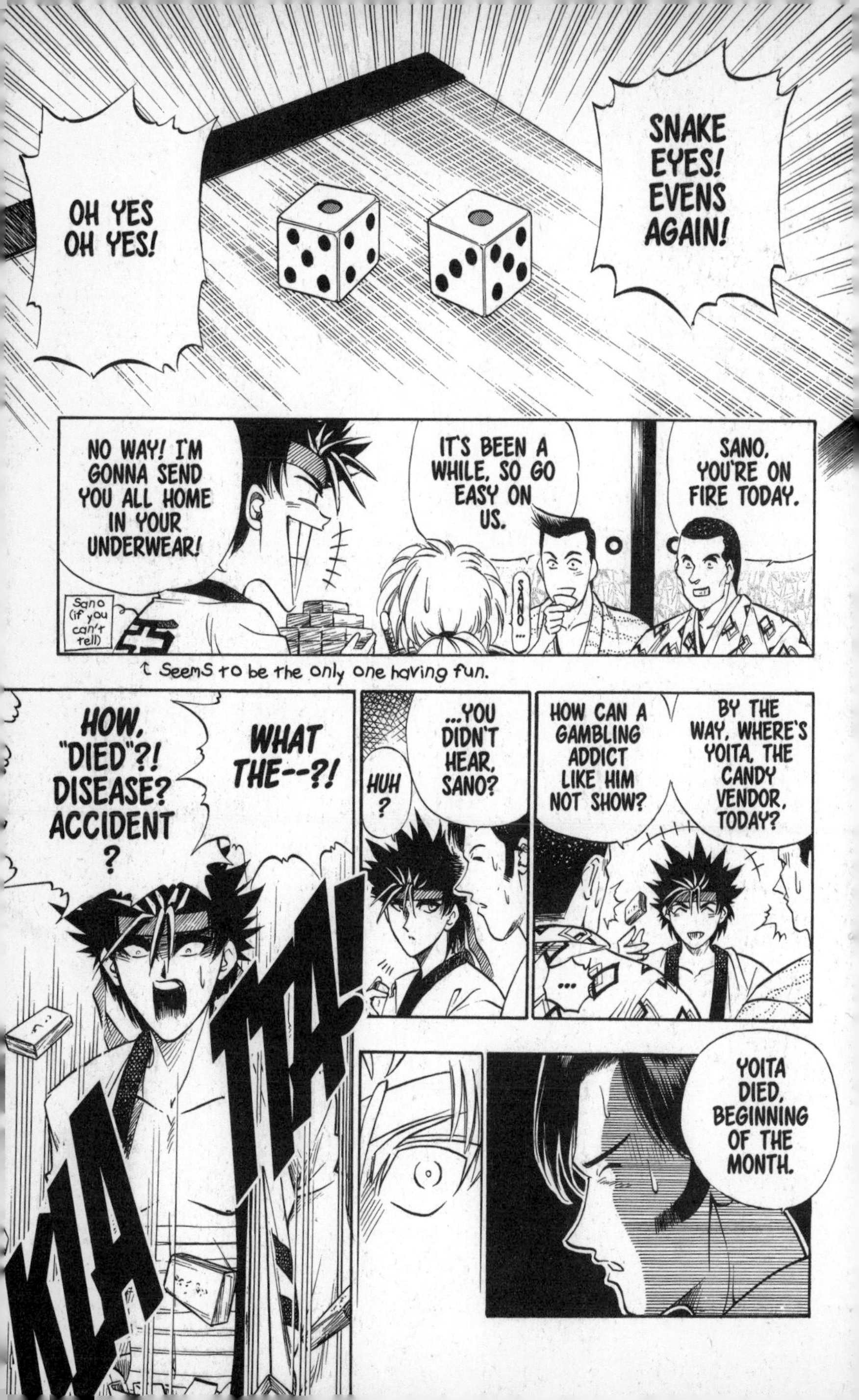
SNAKE EYES! EVENS AGAIN!
OH YES OH YES!
SANO, YOU'RE ON FIRE TODAY.
IT'S BEEN A WHILE, SO GO EASY ON US.
SANO...
NO WAY! I'M GONNA SEND YOU ALL HOME IN YOUR UNDERWEAR!
Sano (if you can't tell)
↑ Seems to be the only one having fun.
BY THE WAY, WHERE'S YOITA, THE CANDY VENDOR, TODAY?
HOW CAN A GAMBLING ADDICT LIKE HIM NOT SHOW?
...
...YOU DIDN'T HEAR, SANO?
HUH?
YOITA DIED, BEGINNING OF THE MONTH.
WHAT THE--?!
HOW, "DIED"?! DISEASE? ACCIDENT?
KA TA!

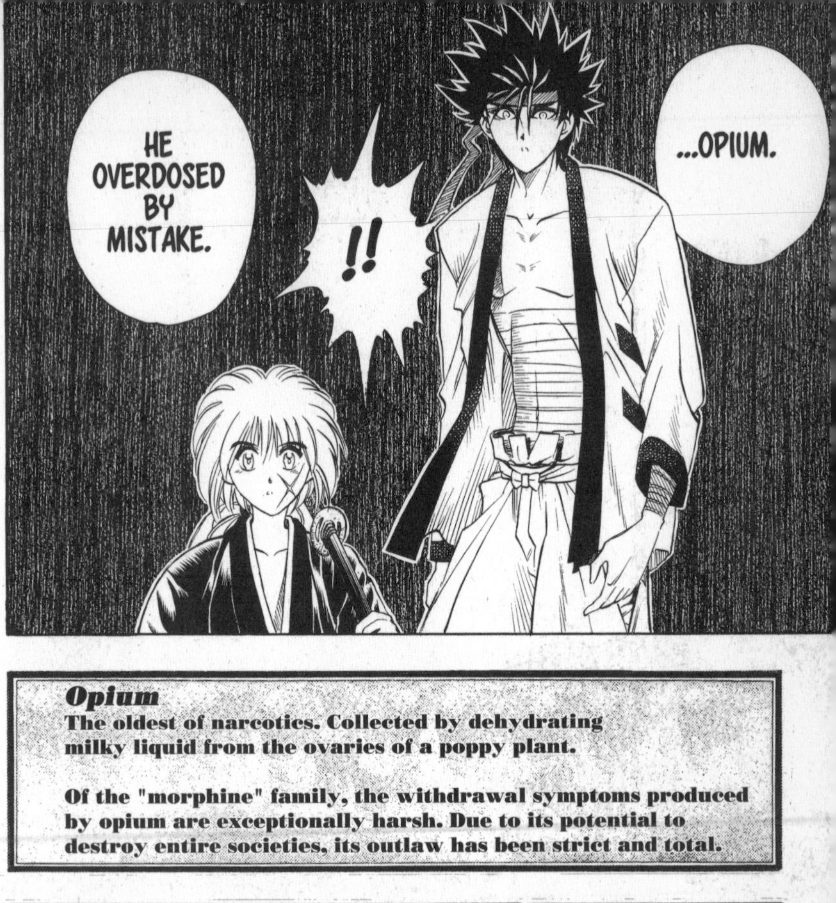
...OPIUM.
HE OVERDOSED BY MISTAKE.
!!

***Opium***

**The oldest of narcotics. Collected by dehydrating milky liquid from the ovaries of a poppy plant.**

**Of the "morphine" family, the withdrawal symptoms produced by opium are exceptionally harsh. Due to its potential to destroy entire societies, its outlaw has been strict and total.**

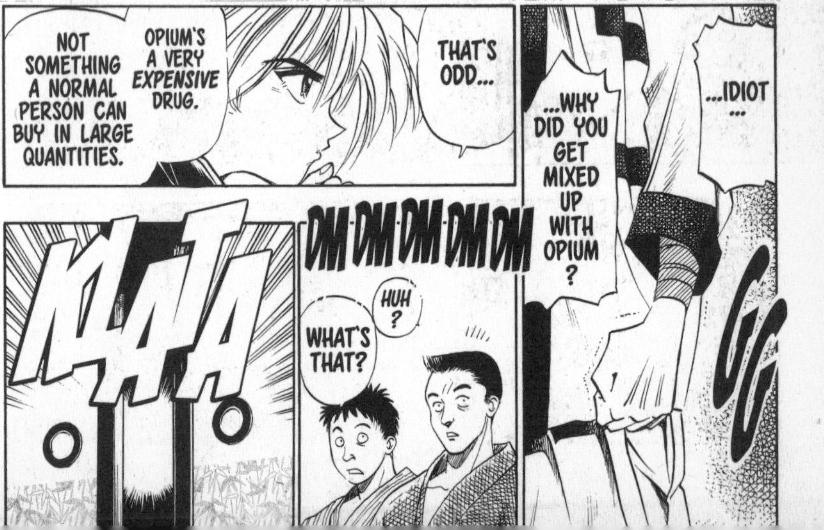
...IDIOT ...
...WHY DID YOU GET MIXED UP WITH OPIUM ?
THAT'S ODD...
OPIUM'S A VERY EXPENSIVE DRUG.
NOT SOMETHING A NORMAL PERSON CAN BUY IN LARGE QUANTITIES.
DM·DM·DM·DM·DM
HUH ?
WHAT'S THAT?

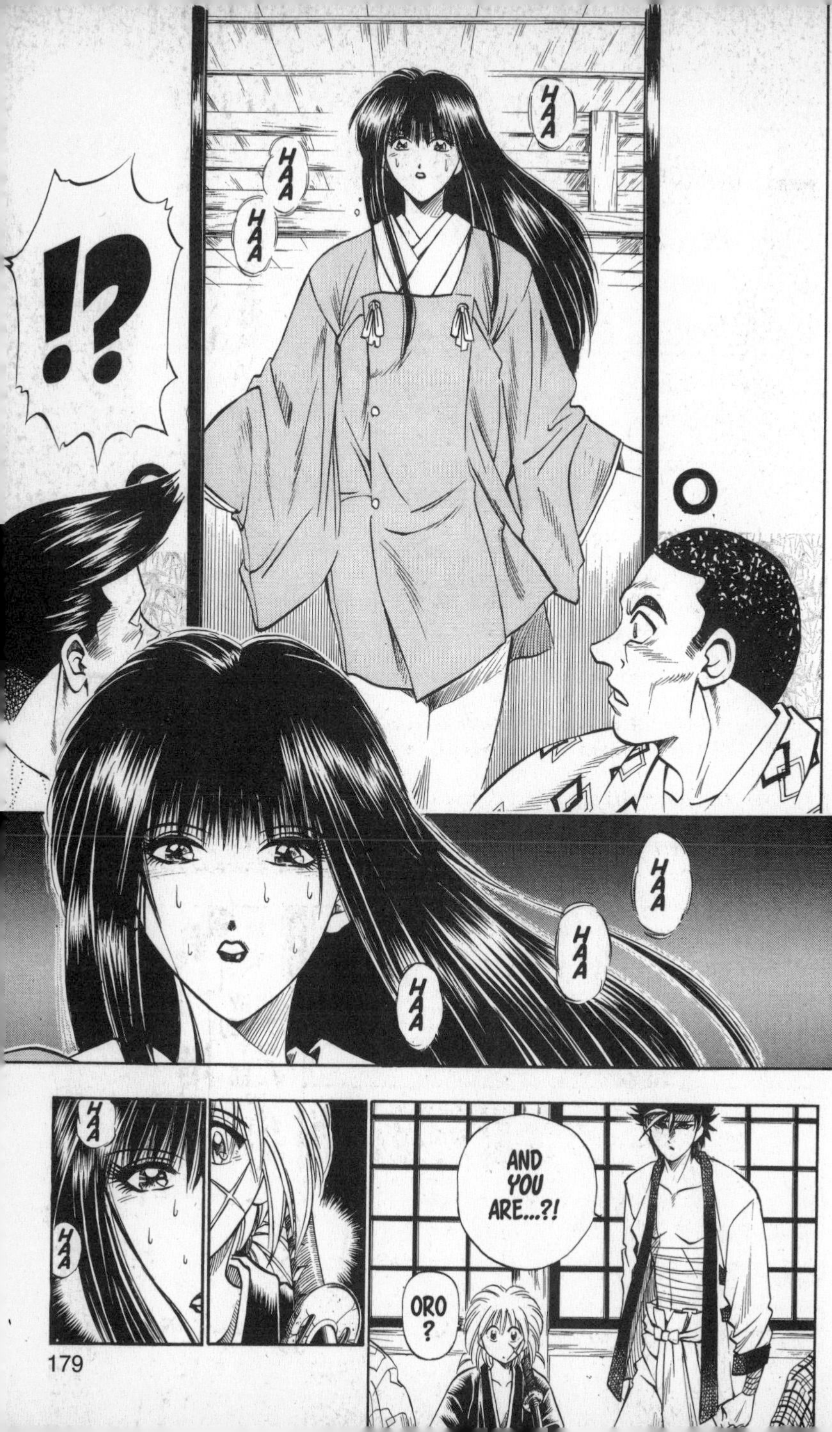
HAA
HAA
HAA
!?
HAA
HAA
HAA
AND YOU ARE...?!
ORO ?
HAA
HAA

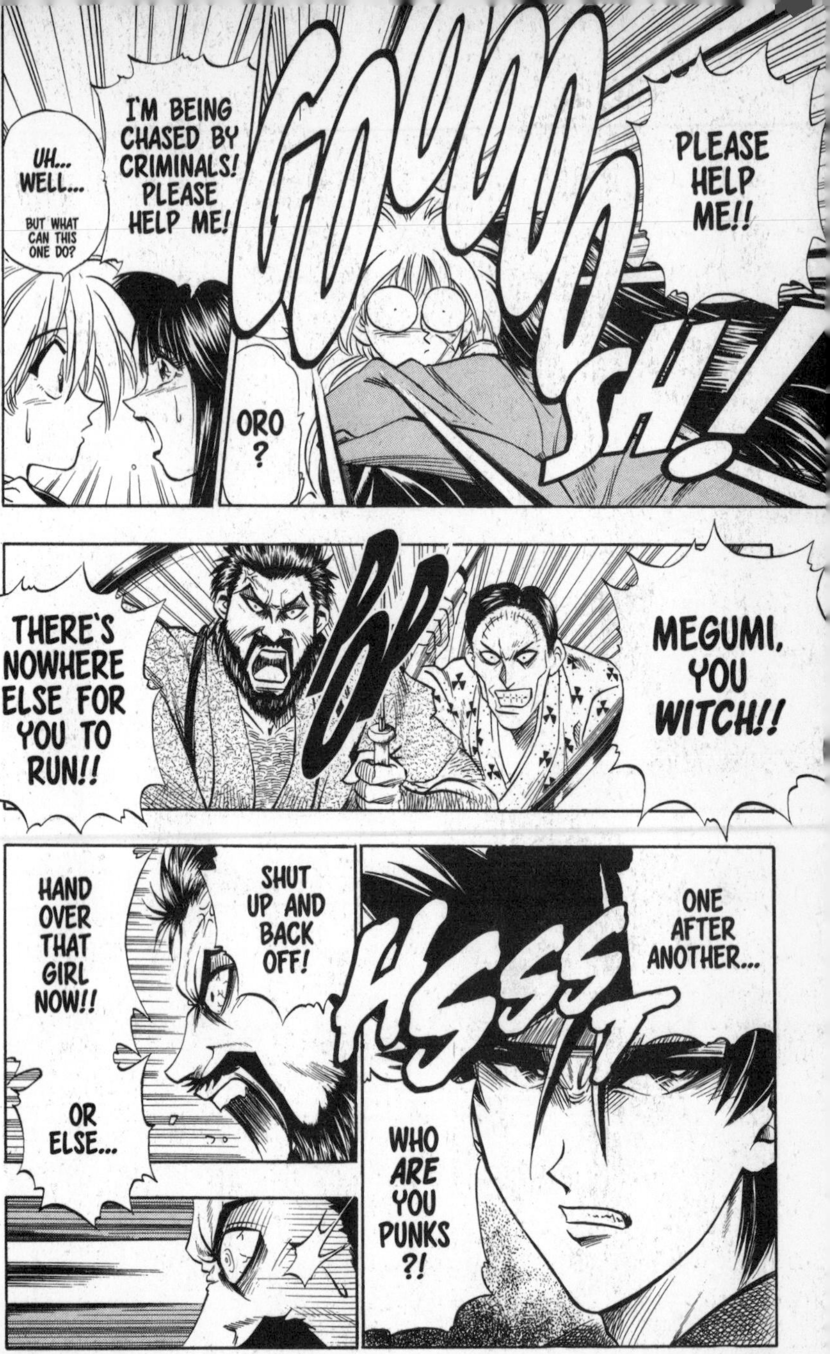
PLEASE HELP ME!!
I'M BEING CHASED BY CRIMINALS! PLEASE HELP ME!
UH... WELL...
BUT WHAT CAN THIS ONE DO?
ORO?
MEGUMI, YOU WITCH!!
THERE'S NOWHERE ELSE FOR YOU TO RUN!!
ONE AFTER ANOTHER...
HSSS
WHO ARE YOU PUNKS?!
SHUT UP AND BACK OFF!
HAND OVER THAT GIRL NOW!!
OR ELSE...

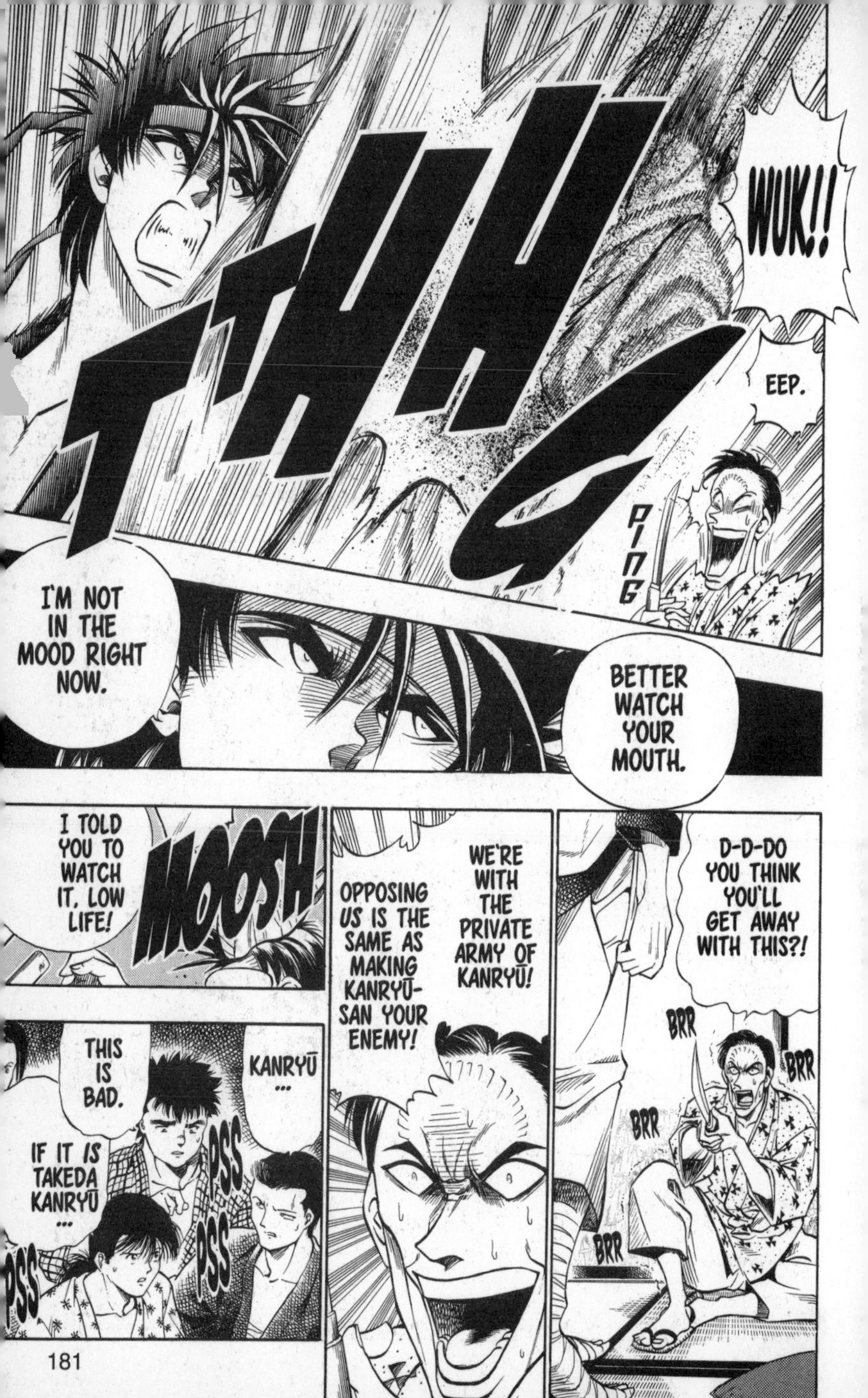

WUK!!
EEP.
PING
BETTER WATCH YOUR MOUTH.
I'M NOT IN THE MOOD RIGHT NOW.
D-D-DO YOU THINK YOU'LL GET AWAY WITH THIS?!
BRR
BRR
BRR
BRR
WE'RE WITH THE PRIVATE ARMY OF KANRYŪ!
OPPOSING US IS THE SAME AS MAKING KANRYŪ-SAN YOUR ENEMY!
I TOLD YOU TO WATCH IT, LOW LIFE!
WOOSH
KANRYŪ ...
THIS IS BAD.
IF IT IS TAKEDA KANRYŪ ...
PSS
PSS
PSS

READ THIS WAY

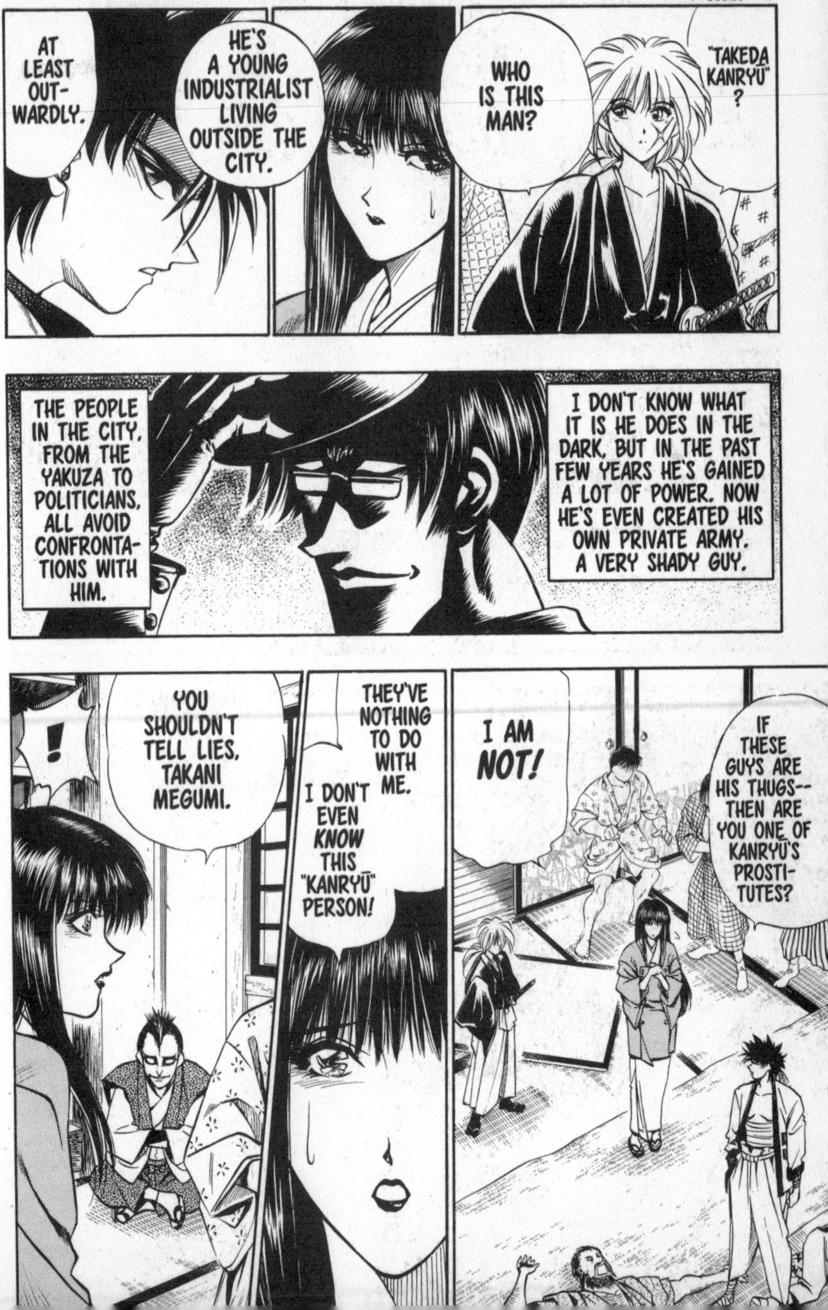
"TAKEDA KANRYŪ"?
WHO IS THIS MAN?
HE'S A YOUNG INDUSTRIALIST LIVING OUTSIDE THE CITY.
AT LEAST OUTWARDLY.
I DON'T KNOW WHAT IT IS HE DOES IN THE DARK, BUT IN THE PAST FEW YEARS HE'S GAINED A LOT OF POWER. NOW HE'S EVEN CREATED HIS OWN PRIVATE ARMY. A VERY SHADY GUY.
THE PEOPLE IN THE CITY, FROM THE YAKUZA TO POLITICIANS, ALL AVOID CONFRONTATIONS WITH HIM.
IF THESE GUYS ARE HIS THUGS--THEN ARE YOU ONE OF KANRYŪ'S PROSTITUTES?
I AM **NOT!**
THEY'VE NOTHING TO DO WITH ME.
I DON'T EVEN *KNOW* THIS "KANRYŪ" PERSON!
YOU SHOULDN'T TELL LIES, TAKANI MEGUMI.
!

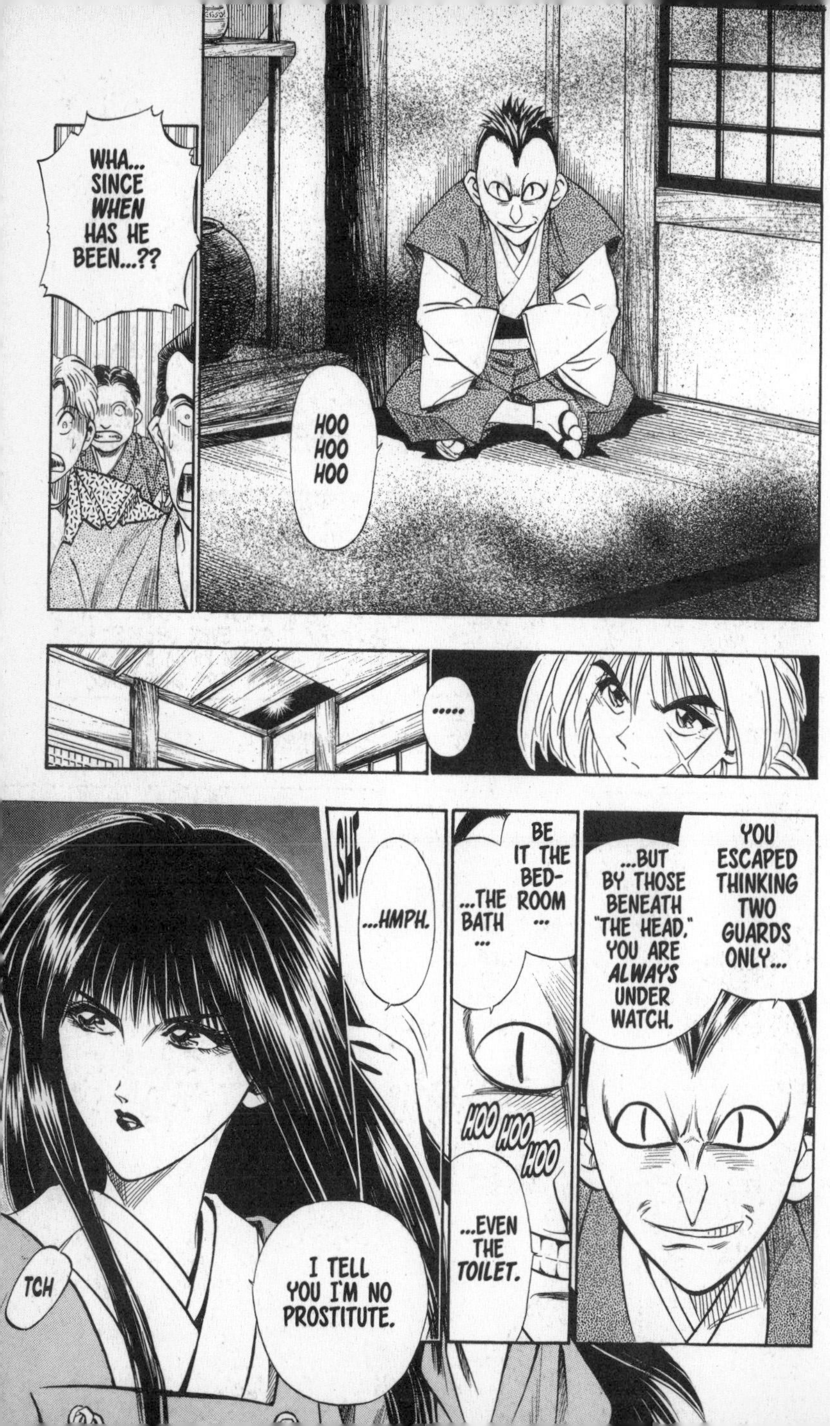
HOO HOO HOO
WHA... SINCE WHEN HAS HE BEEN...??
......
YOU ESCAPED THINKING TWO GUARDS ONLY...
...BUT BY THOSE BENEATH "THE HEAD," YOU ARE ALWAYS UNDER WATCH.
BE IT THE BED-ROOM ...
...THE BATH ...
HOO HOO HOO
...EVEN THE TOILET.
SHF
...HMPH.
I TELL YOU I'M NO PROSTITUTE.
TCH

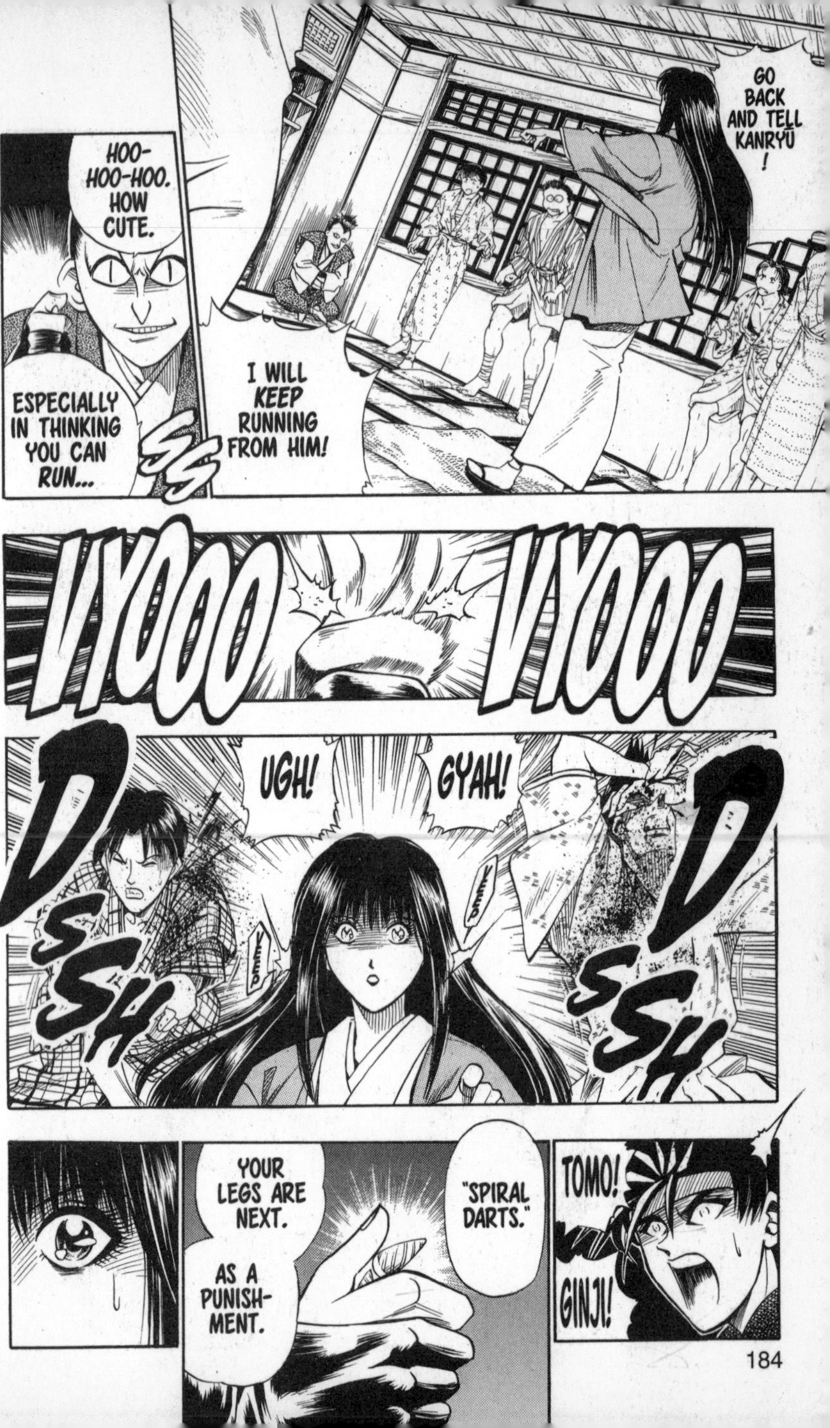
GO BACK AND TELL KANRYŪ!
I WILL KEEP RUNNING FROM HIM!
HOO-HOO-HOO. HOW CUTE.
ESPECIALLY IN THINKING YOU CAN RUN...
SS
VIYOOO
VIYOOO
D
SSH
GYAH!
VEED
UGH!
VEED
D
SSH
TOMO!
GINJI!
"SPIRAL DARTS."
YOUR LEGS ARE NEXT.
AS A PUNISHMENT.

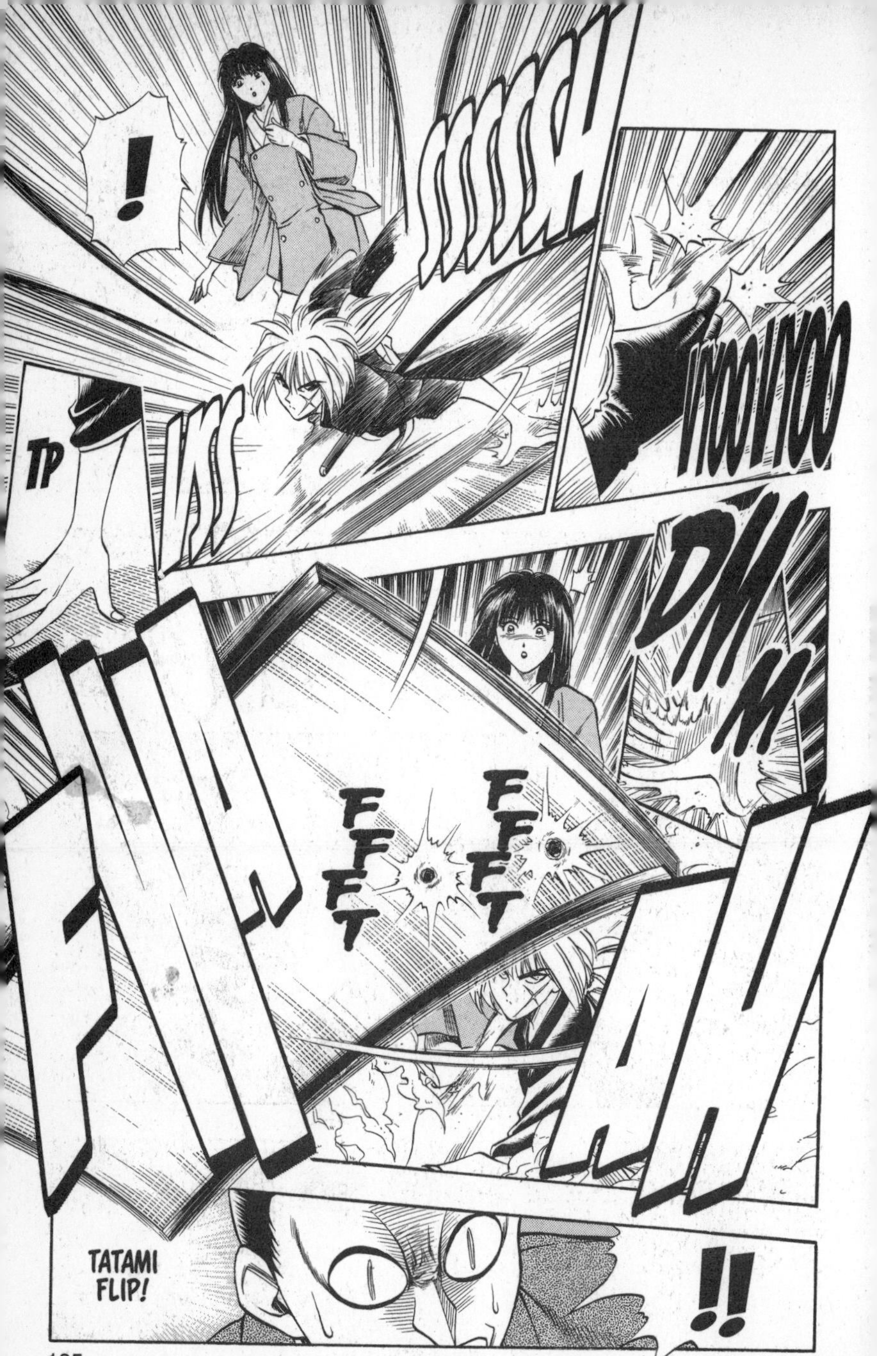
!
SCCCH
VROOVROO
TP
FFFT
FFFT
TATAMI FLIP!
!!

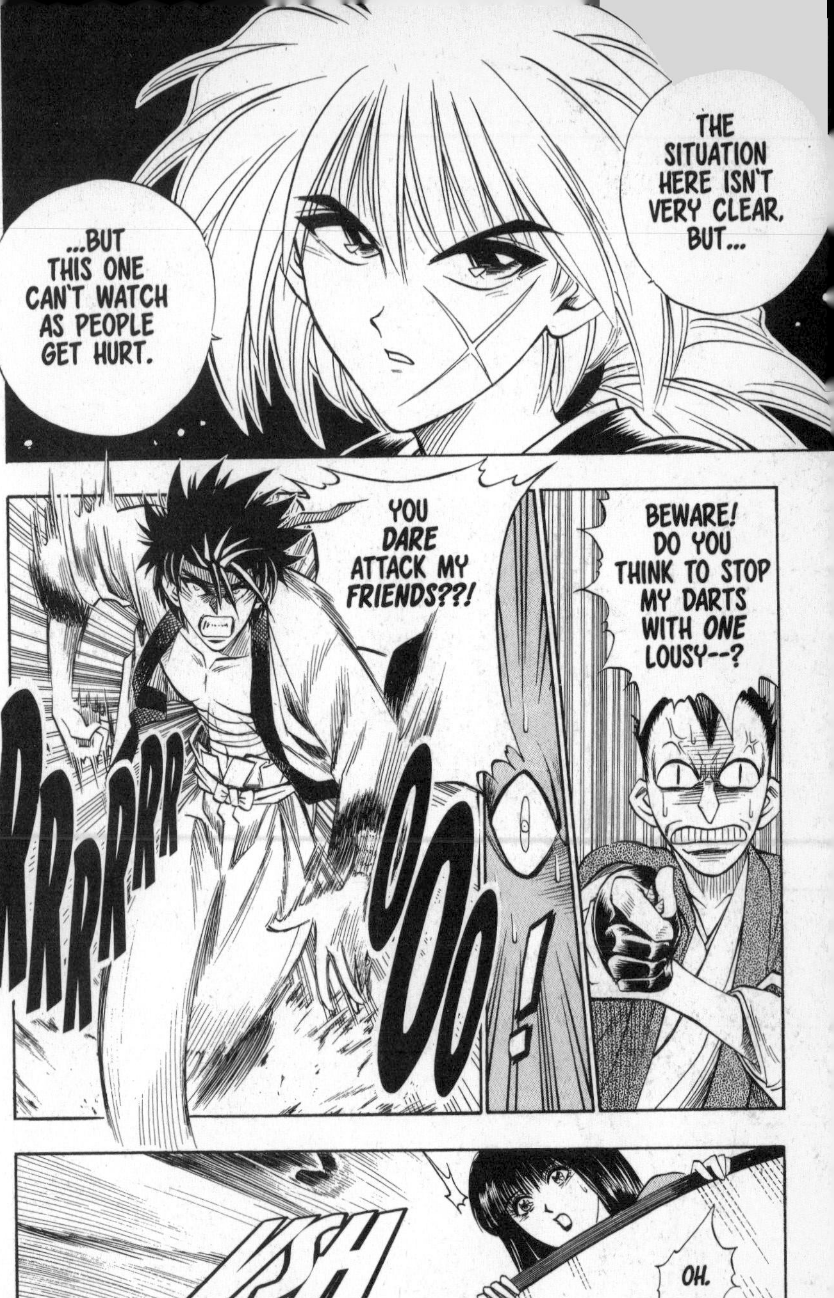
THE SITUATION HERE ISN'T VERY CLEAR, BUT...
...BUT THIS ONE CAN'T WATCH AS PEOPLE GET HURT.
BEWARE! DO YOU THINK TO STOP MY DARTS WITH ONE LOUSY--?
YOU DARE ATTACK MY FRIENDS??!
RRRRRR
OOOO!
VISH
OH.

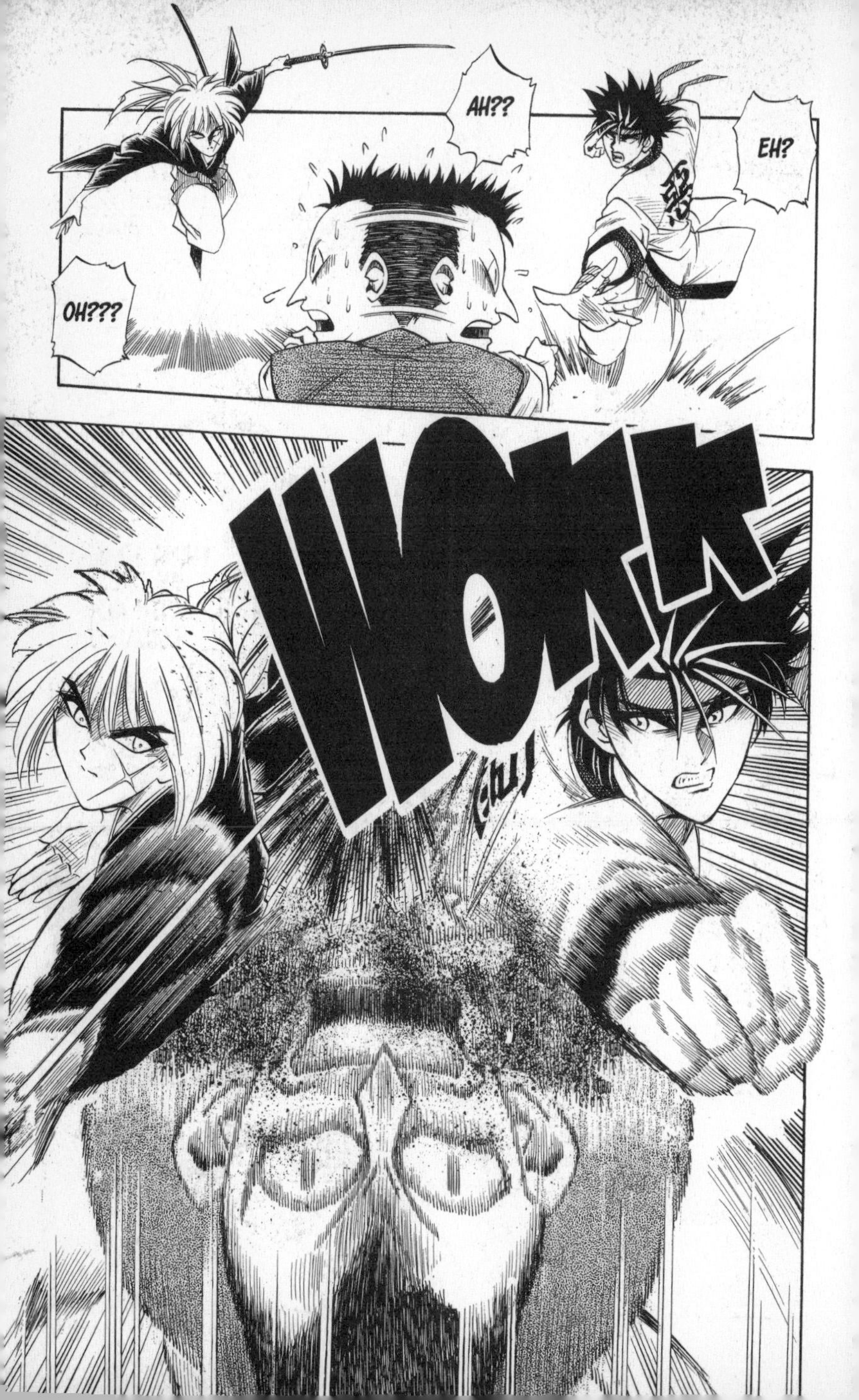
EH?
AH??
OH???

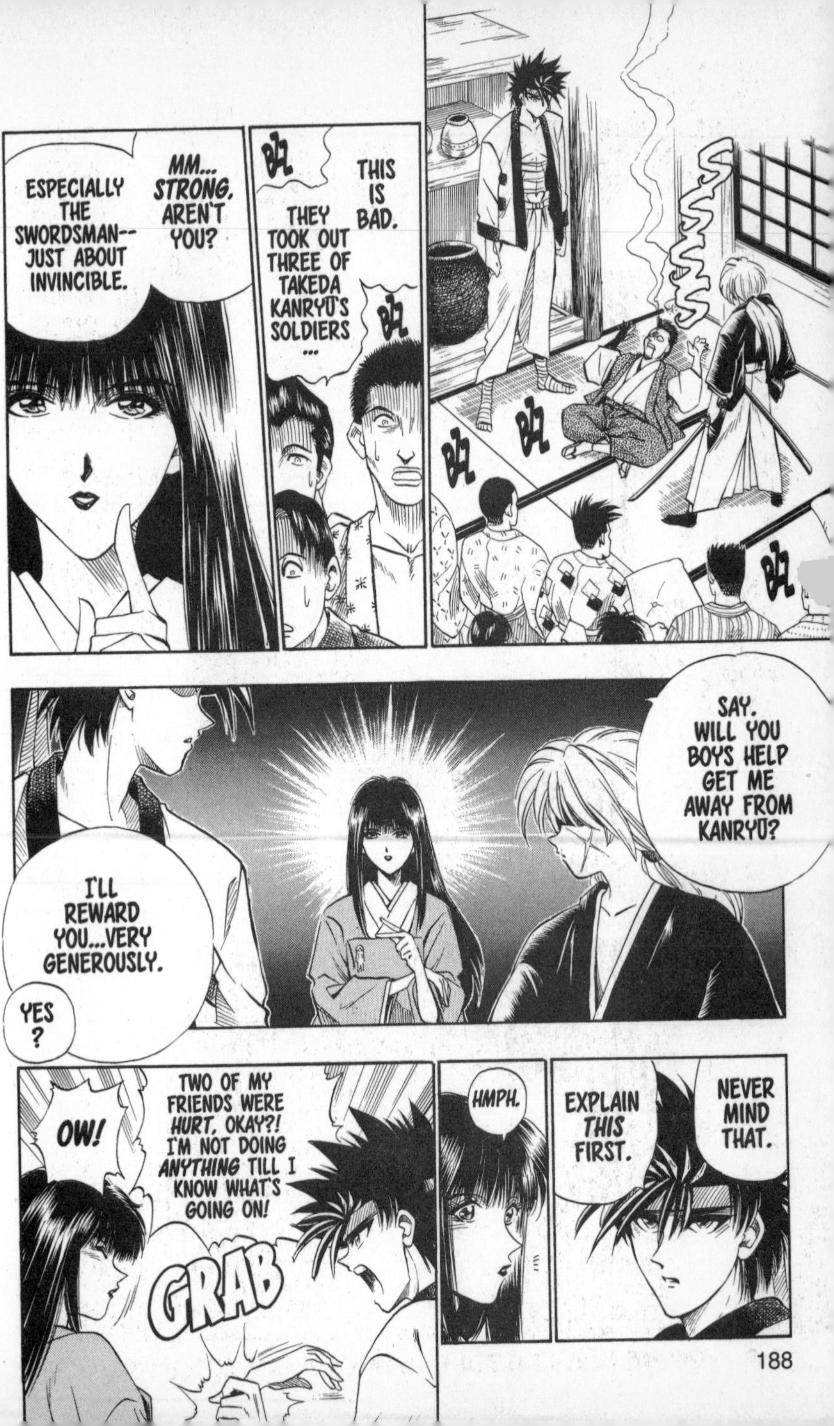
SSSS
BZZ
BZZ
BZZ
BZZ
THIS IS BAD.
THEY TOOK OUT THREE OF TAKEDA KANRYŪ'S SOLDIERS ...
BZZ
BZZ
MM... STRONG, AREN'T YOU?
ESPECIALLY THE SWORDSMAN-- JUST ABOUT INVINCIBLE.
SAY. WILL YOU BOYS HELP GET ME AWAY FROM KANRYŪ?
I'LL REWARD YOU...VERY GENEROUSLY.
YES ?
NEVER MIND THAT.
EXPLAIN THIS FIRST.
HMPH.
TWO OF MY FRIENDS WERE HURT, OKAY?! I'M NOT DOING ANYTHING TILL I KNOW WHAT'S GOING ON!
OW!
GRAB

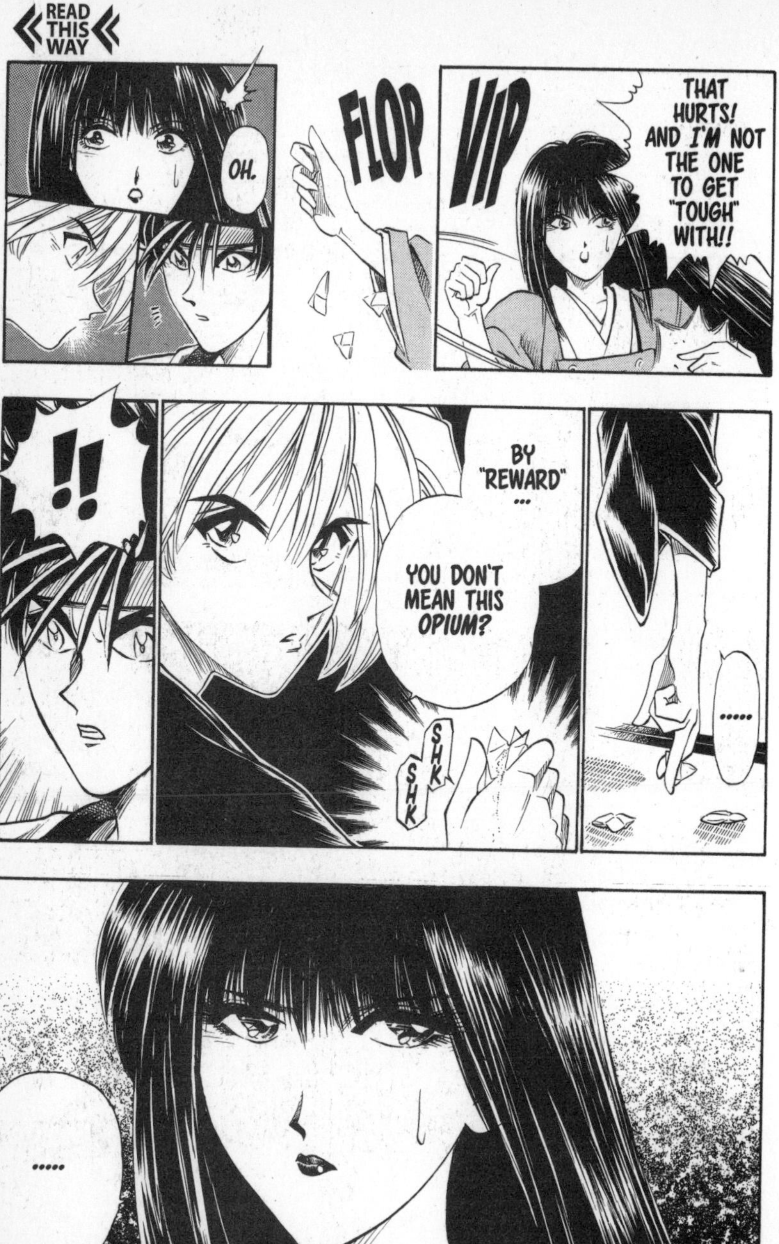
READ THIS WAY
THAT HURTS! AND *I'M* NOT THE ONE TO GET "TOUGH" WITH!!
VIP
FLOP
OH.
......
BY "REWARD"...
YOU DON'T MEAN THIS *OPIUM*?
SHK SHK
!!
......



**TO BE CONTINUED IN VOLUME 3: A REASON TO ACT**

# GLOSSARY of the RESTORATION

*A brief guide to select Japanese terms used in **Rurouni Kenshin**. Note that, both here and within the story itself, all names are Japanese style—i.e., last or "family" name first, with personal or "given" name following. This is both because **Kenshin** is a "period" story, as well as to decrease confusion—were we to take the example of Kenshin's sakabatô and "reverse" the format of the historically established assassin-name "Hitokiri Battôsai," for example, it would make little sense to then call him "Battôsai Himura."*

**Himura Kenshin**
Kenshin's "real" name, revealed to Kaoru only at her urging

**Hiten Mitsurugi-ryû**
Kenshin's sword technique, used more for defense than offense. An "ancient style that pits one against many," it requires exceptional speed and agility to master

**hitokiri**
An assassin. Famous swordsmen of the period were sometimes thus known to adopt "professional" names—**Kawakami Gensai**, for example, was also known as "Hitokiri Gensai"

**Ishin Shishi**
Loyalist or pro-Imperialist **patriots** who fought to restore the Emperor to his ancient seat of power

**Jigen-ryû**
Aggressive swordsmanship style, characterized by one-handed draws/cuts, and the use of turning. Used in this story by Ujiki, a corrupt officer of the Police Sword Corps

**Kamiya Kasshin-ryû**
Sword-arts or **kenjutsu** school established by Kaoru's father, who rejected the ethics of **Satsujin-ken** for **Katsujin-ken**

**Katsujin-ken**
"Swords that give life"; the sword-arts style developed over ten years by Kaoru's father and founding principle of **Kamiya Kasshin-ryû**

**Kawakami Gensai**
Real-life, historical inspiration for the character of **Himura Kenshin**

**kenjutsu**
The art of fencing; sword arts; **kendô**

**Kiheitai**
Fighting force which included men of both the merchant and peasant classes

**Aizu**
Tokugawa-affiliated domain; fourth battle of the **Boshin War**

**aku**
**Kanji** character for "evil," worn by Sanosuke as a remembrance of his beloved, betrayed Captain Sagara and the **Sekihô Army**

**Bakumatsu**
Final, chaotic days of the Tokugawa regime

**Boshin War**
Civil war of 1868-69 between the new government and the **Tokugawa Bakufu**. The anti-*Bakufu*, pro-Imperial side (the Imperial Army) won, easily defeating the Tokugawa supporters

**-chan**
Honorific. Can be used either as a diminutive (e.g., with a small child—"Little Hanako or Kentarô"), or with those who are grown, to indicate affection

**Chôshû**
Anti-Tokugawa (shôgunate) domain; home to many **patriots**

**dojo**
Martial arts training hall

**-dono**
Honorific. Even more respectful than *-san*; the effect in modern-day Japanese conversation would be along the lines of "Milord So-and-So." As used by Kenshin, it indicates both respect and humility

**Edo**
Capital city of the **Tokugawa Bakufu**; renamed **Tokyo** ("Eastern Capital") after the Meiji Restoration

**Hijikata Toshizô**
Vice-commander of the **Shinsengumi**

**Himura Battôsai**
Swordsman of legendary skills and former assassin (*hitokiri*) of the **Ishin Shishi**

**sensei**
    Teacher; master

**Shinsengumi**
    Elite, notorious, government-sanctioned and excep-
    tionally skilled swordsman–supporters of the military
    government (**Bakufu**) which had ruled Japan for
    nearly 250 years, the Shinsengumi ("newly selected
    corps") were established in 1863 to suppress the
    **loyalists** and restore law and order to the blood-
    soaked streets of the imperial capital (see **Kyoto**)

**shôgi**
    Strategic Japanese board game. Often referred to
    as "Japanese chess"

**shôgun**
    Feudal military ruler of Japan

**shôgunate**
    See **Tokugawa Bakufu**

**suntetsu**
    Small, handheld blade, designed for palming and
    concealment

**Tokugawa Bakufu**
    Military feudal government which dominated Japan
    from 1603 to 1867

**Tokugawa Yoshinobu**
    15th and last **shôgun** of Japan. His peaceful abdica-
    tion in 1867 marked the end of the **Bakufu** and
    beginning of **Meiji**

**Tokyo**
    The renaming of "**Edo**" to "**Tokyo**" is a marker of the
    start of the **Meiji Restoration**

**Toba Fushimi, Battle at**
    Battle near **Kyoto** between the forces of the new,
    imperial government and the fallen **shôgunate**.
    Ending with an imperial victory, it was the first battle
    of the **Boshin War**

**Yamagata Aritomo**
    (1838-1922) Soldier and statesman, chief founder of
    the modern Japanese army. A samurai of Chôshû,
    he studied military science in Europe and returned
    to Japan in 1870 to head the war ministry

**zanbatô**
    Sanosuke's huge, oversized sword, destroyed during
    the battle with Kenshin

**-kun**
    Honorific. Used in the modern day among male stu-
    dents, or those who grew up together, but another
    usage—the one you're more likely to find in *Rurouni
    Kenshin*—is the "superior-to-inferior" form, intended
    as a way to emphasize a difference in status or rank,
    as well as to indicate familiarity or affection

**Kyoto**
    Home of the Emperor and imperial court from A.D.
    794 until shortly after the Meiji Restoration in 1868

**loyalists**
    Those who supported the return of the Emperor to
    power; **Ishin Shishi**

**Meiji Restoration**
    1853-1868; culminated in the collapse of the
    **Tokugawa Bakufu** and the restoration of imperial
    rule. So called after Emperor Meiji, whose chosen
    name was written with the characters for "culture
    and enlightenment"

**patriots**
    Another term for **Ishin Shishi**...and when used by
    Sano, not a flattering one

**rurouni**
    Wanderer, vagabond

**sakabatô**
    Reversed-edge sword (the dull edge on the side the
    sharp should be, and vice-versa); carried by Kenshin
    as a symbol of his resolution never to kill again

**-san**
    Honorific. Carries the meaning of "Mr.," "Ms.,"
    "Miss," etc., but used more extensively in Japanese
    than its English equivalent (note that even an enemy
    may be addressed as "-*san*")

**Satsujin-ken**
    "Swords that give death"; a style of swordsmanship
    rejected by Kaoru's father

**Seinan War**
    1877 uprising of the samurai classes against the new
    Meiji government, ending in defeat by the govern-
    ment army. Also known as the "Satsuma Rebellion"

**Sekihô Army**
    Military unit (formed mainly of civilians) who, believ-
    ing in the cause of the Emperor's restoration to
    power, were eventually turned upon by those same
    pro-Imperialist forces and declared traitors

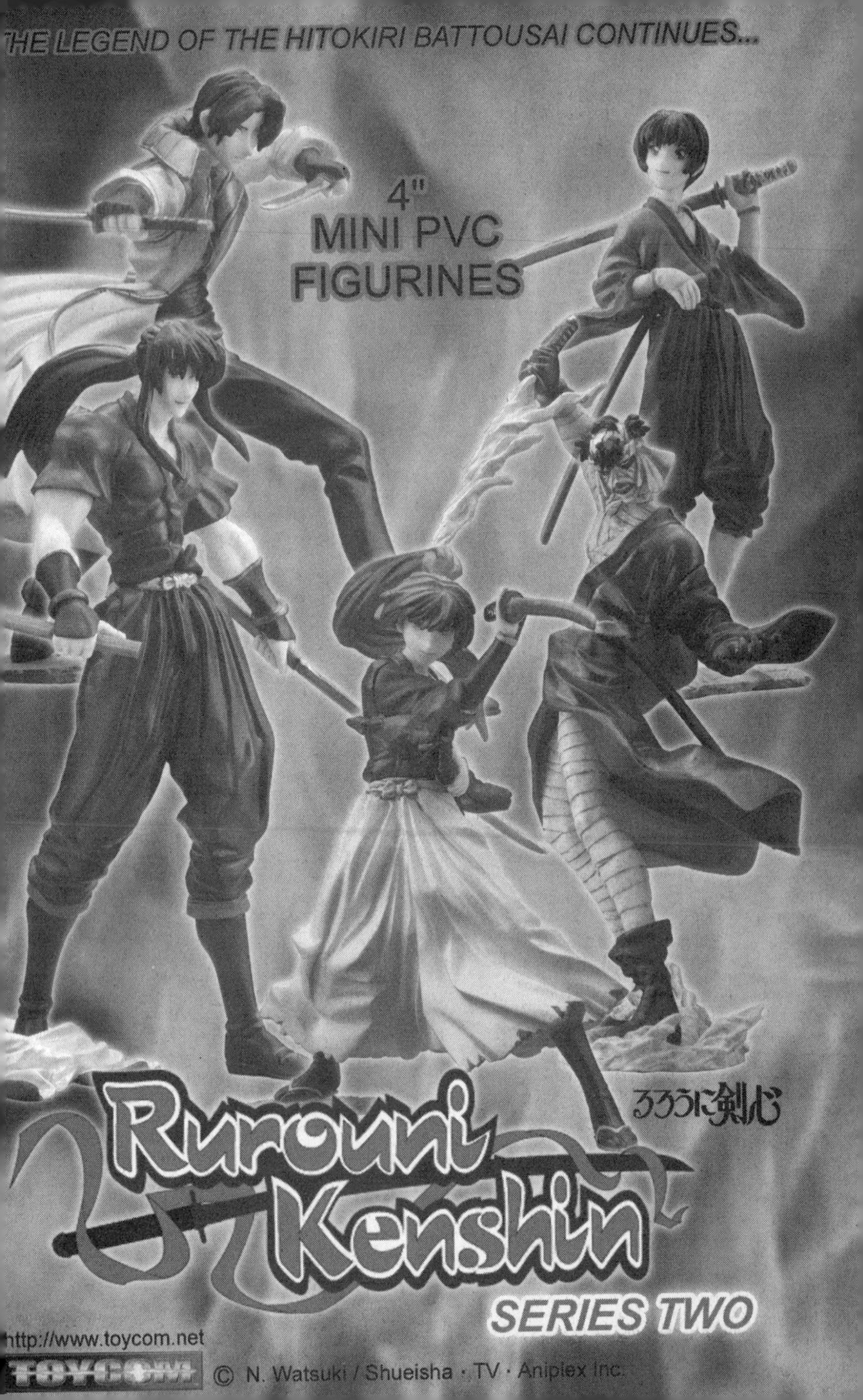
THE LEGEND OF THE HITOKIRI BATTOUSAI CONTINUES...
4" MINI PVC FIGURINES
るろうに剣心
Rurouni Kenshin
SERIES TWO
http://www.toycom.net
TOYCOM
© N. Watsuki / Shueisha · TV · Aniplex Inc.

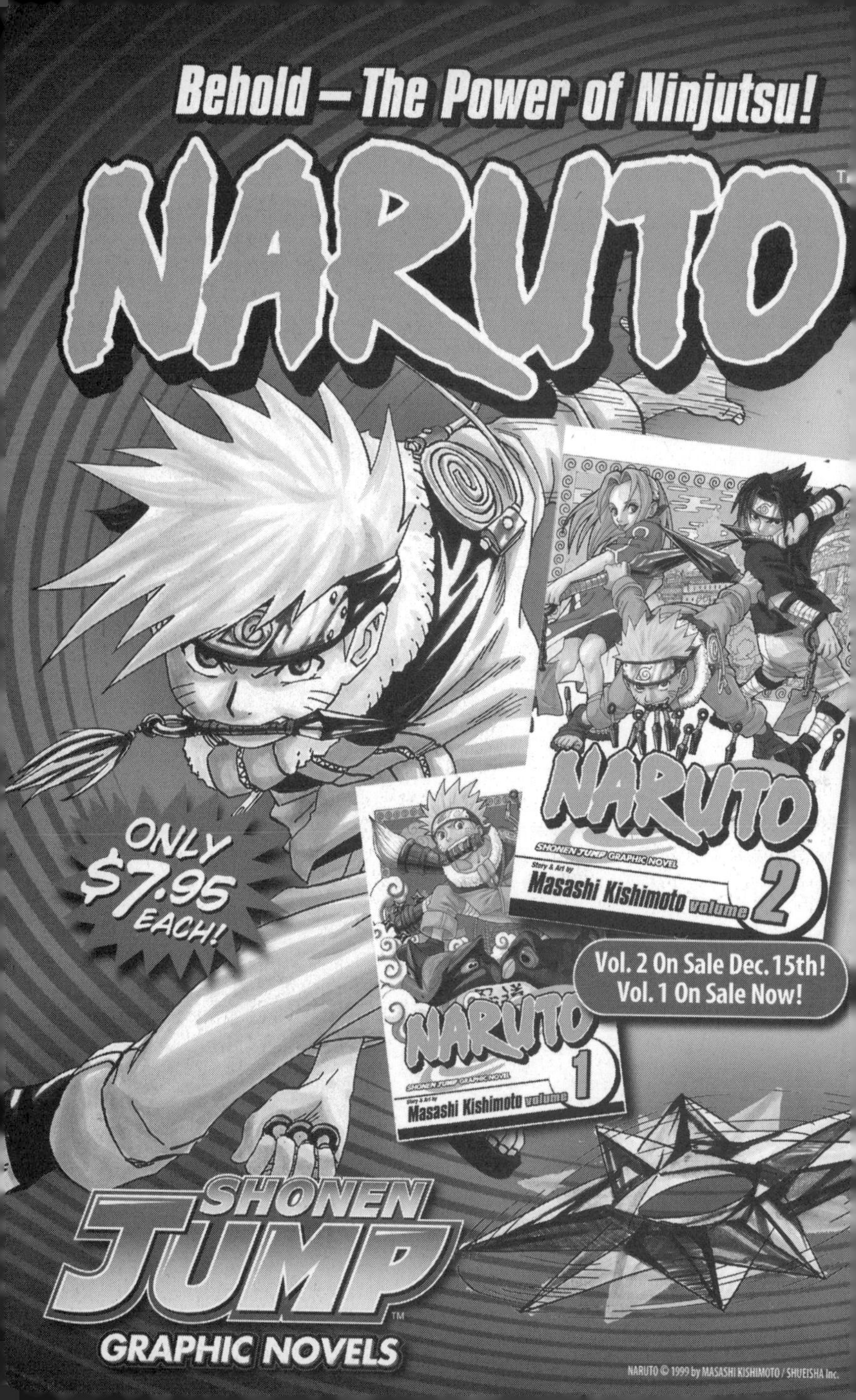

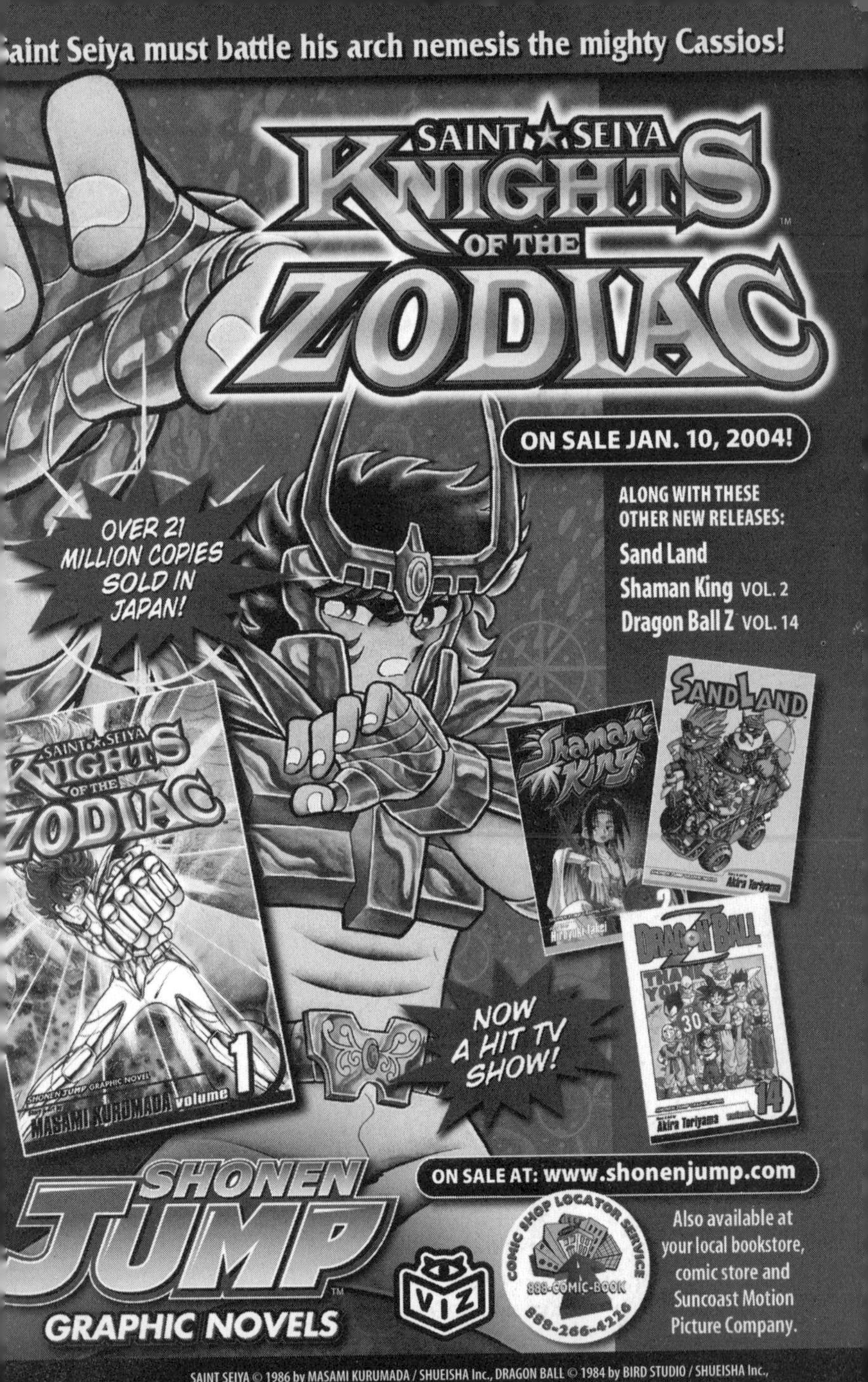
Saint Seiya must battle his arch nemesis the mighty Cassios!
SAINT SEIYA KNIGHTS OF THE ZODIAC™
ON SALE JAN. 10, 2004!
ALONG WITH THESE OTHER NEW RELEASES:
Sand Land
Shaman King VOL. 2
Dragon Ball Z VOL. 14
OVER 21 MILLION COPIES SOLD IN JAPAN!
SAINT SEIYA KNIGHTS OF THE ZODIAC
SHONEN JUMP GRAPHIC NOVEL
MASAMI KURUMADA volume 1
SAND LAND
Akira Toriyama
Shaman King
Hiroyuki Takei
DRAGON BALL Z
14
Akira Toriyama
NOW A HIT TV SHOW!
ON SALE AT: www.shonenjump.com
SHONEN JUMP™ GRAPHIC NOVELS
VIZ
COMIC SHOP LOCATOR SERVICE
888-COMIC-BOOK
888-266-4226
Also available at your local bookstore, comic store and Suncoast Motion Picture Company.

# Save 50% off the newsstand price!

## SHONEN JUMP
### THE WORLD'S MOST POPULAR MANGA

# Subscribe Now to the Magazine!

☑ **YES!** Please enter my one-year (12 issue) subscription to **SHONEN JUMP Magazine** at the **INCREDIBLY LOW SUBSCRIPTION RATE** of just **$29⁹⁵**

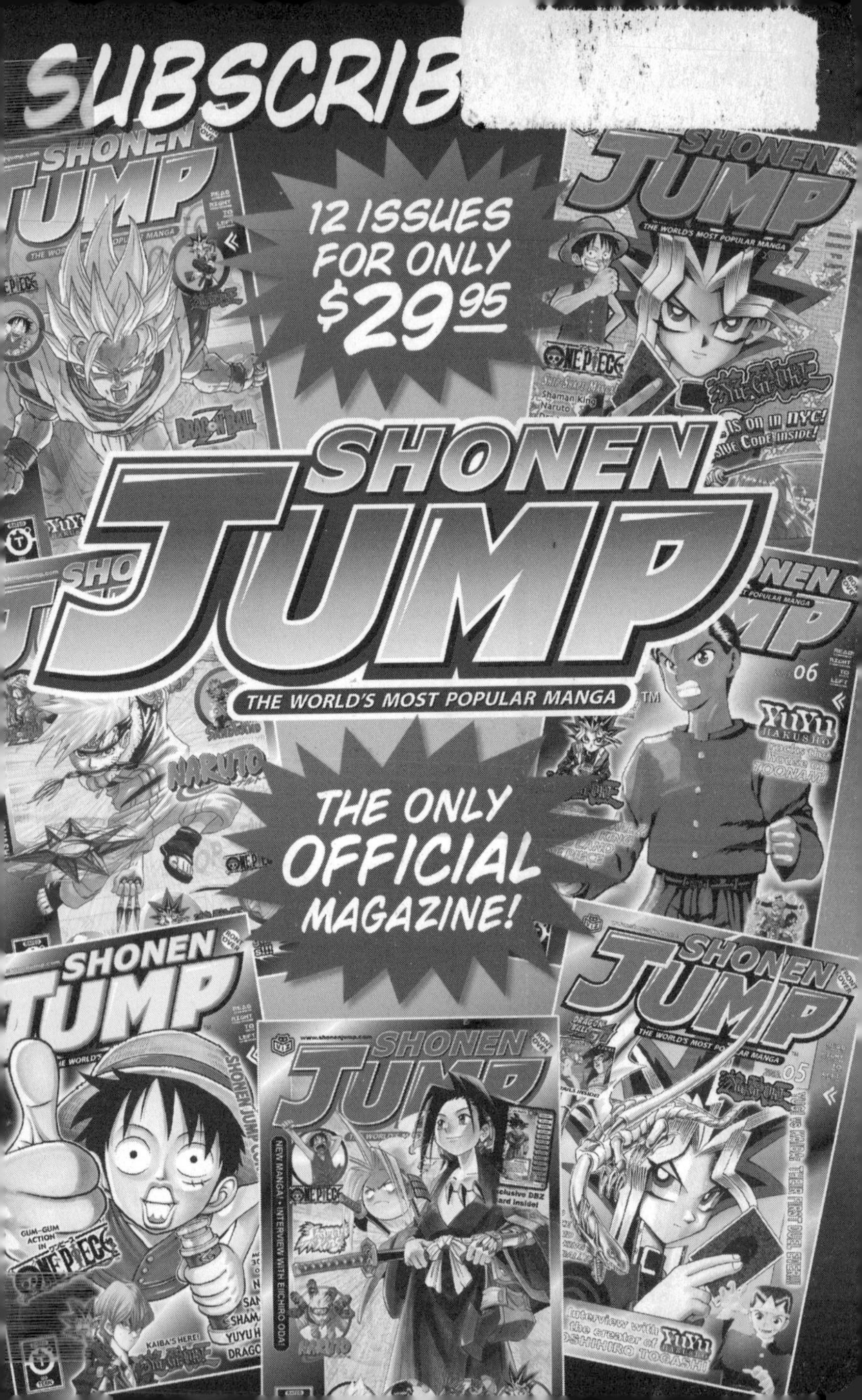
SUBSCRIB
12 ISSUES FOR ONLY $29.95
SHONEN JUMP
THE WORLD'S MOST POPULAR MANGA ™
THE ONLY OFFICIAL MAGAZINE!